ALS. 11 P8

C0-GFM-824

DISCARDED

THE
UNIVERSITY OF WINNIPEG
PORTAGE & BALMORAL
WINNIPEG 2, MAN. CANADA

RUSSELL SAGE FOUNDATION was established in 1907 by Mrs. Russell Sage for the improvement of social and living conditions in the United States. In carrying out its purpose the Foundation conducts research under the direction of members of the staff or in close collaboration with other institutions, and supports programs designed to improve the utilization of social science knowledge. As an integral part of its operations, the Foundation from time to time publishes books or pamphlets resulting from these activities. Publication under the imprint of the Foundation does not necessarily imply agreement by the Foundation, its Trustees, or its staff with the interpretations or conclusions of the authors.

JC
599
.U5O48

ON RECORD:

Files and Dossiers in American Life

Edited by STANTON WHEELER

RUSSELL SAGE FOUNDATION
NEW YORK
1969

© 1969
Russell Sage Foundation
Printed in the United States of America

Library of Congress Catalog Card Number: 73–98421

ACKNOWLEDGMENTS

This volume was made possible by a grant from Russell Sage Foundation. The contributions from the Foundation staff, however, go beyond the mere provision of monetary support. A number of my Foundation colleagues provided helpful suggestions and comments, both in the formulation of the general idea of the volume and in the various stages of preparation. I want particularly to thank Lindsey Churchill, who commented on an earlier draft of the Introduction and on a number of the other chapters.

Carol Levine was responsible for copy-editing and the index, and I am much in her debt. Both she and Betty Davison of the Foundation's publications staff were uncommonly helpful.

Christine Valibus Daillet was responsible for a large share of the typing of the manuscript and for communications with the various authors. She deserves credit for a job well done.

Finally, I wish to express my own appreciation to all the authors for their valuable contributions.

S. W.

THE CONTRIBUTORS

Rodolfo Alvarez
Assistant Professor of Sociology
Yale University

Pierce Barker
Department of Social Relations
Harvard University

Ivar Berg
Professor of Business Administration
Columbia University

Nancy Bordier
Teachers College
Columbia University

David Caplovitz
Bureau of Applied Social Science Research
Columbia University

Burton R. Clark
Chairman, Department of Sociology
Yale University

Kai T. Erikson
Professor of Sociology
Yale University

Daniel E. Gilbertson
Department of Sociology
Yale University

Abraham S. Goldstein
Professor of Law
Yale Law School

David A. Goslin
Sociologist, Russell Sage Foundation

Edwin M. Lemert
Professor of Sociology
University of California, Davis

Roger W. Little
Associate Professor of Sociology
University of Illinois at Chicago Circle

Wilbert E. Moore
Sociologist, Russell Sage Foundation

Jesse Orlansky
Institute for Defense Analysis

H. Laurence Ross
Professor of Law and Sociology
University of Denver, School of Law

James Rule
Nuffield College, Oxford

James Salvate
Graduate School of Business Administration
Columbia University

Joseph Steinberg
Social Security Administration

Stanton Wheeler
Professor of Law and Sociology
Yale Law School

Don H. Zimmerman
Assistant Professor of Sociology
University of California, Santa Barbara

CONTENTS

I *Introduction*

1 *Problems and Issues in Record-Keeping*

STANTON WHEELER

A BIRTH CERTIFICATE DOCUMENTS THE ARRIVAL OF A NEWBORN MEMBER OF our society and a certificate of death his exit. Prior to his birth a doctor will have recorded his prenatal development, and after his death legal files will record the settlement of his affairs.

Between birth and death there will be recorded many significant events of his life as well as qualities and performances that give his life its distinctive character and shape. Beginning at least with his arrival in school, records will accumulate regarding his budding career; his abilities will be measured, his personality assessed, his performance in school recorded, both in and out of the classroom. If his family is on welfare, there will be additional records; should he run afoul of the police and the courts, there will be other files.

When he reaches adolescence, interest in his vocational abilities and choices will be duly recorded, either through schools or employment agencies. And, when he finally leaves the world of schooling (which may not be until he is in his early thirties), his progress marked by more files in more institutions, new records will be initiated regarding his employment history and his financial affairs. At some point, he will have applied for a social security number, which he will have cause to write down again and again during his life.

Also, at some point, he is likely to marry and need a loan, these events often occurring surprisingly close together. The marriage will be recorded, perhaps to become an issue later if the marriage is dissolved. And his need for a loan, or at least for an established checking account, will start another series of records concerning his financial status, his purchasing habits, and particularly his bill-paying habits.

Most of these paper traces of one's existence and career will be developed for any conventional member of the society. But any special interests or activities are likely to initiate another set of files, a set which the individual will share with fewer others, and indeed, which taken as a whole, might describe him uniquely. Should he enter the military, a whole collection of files will be opened, and similarly for entry into "classified" occupations, prisons or mental hospitals, psychiatric clinics or probation offices. If he wishes to leave the country, forms for a passport will be filled out; if he stays within the country but harbors foreign ideas, files may develop in intelligence agencies. And if he joins clubs, buys property, stock, or virtually any other goods or services, further entries will be made. Indeed, by the time he is ready to retire, still further records will be made to justify his receiving retirement benefits; and if he has not done so before, he is likely to have a lawyer draw up a will which will become another part of the record upon his death.

THE SCOPE OF THIS VOLUME

The papers in this volume are designed to shed light on the phenomenon of record-keeping. The chapters describe, for a variety of different organizational settings, the kinds of records that are kept on people and the problems and issues that arise with respect to their use and impact. In all cases the authors are concerned primarily with records on people rather than things. The records themselves may vary from relatively brief and simple cards or files to the more expansive dossier, which Webster defines as "a bundle of papers containing a record or detailed report of a proceeding, or detailed information concerning a person. . . ." In either case they provide a written account or listing of the attributes, qualities, and performances of human beings, the evidence stored by organizations for a variety of purposes relating to their activities.

From one perspective, written records are merely one type of information that may serve as a basis for action. There are obviously other types. We all make direct observations about people as we go about our daily routines, and those observations often provide a basis for our actions. In addition, we learn about people indirectly, either through face-to-face conversation or by means of devices like the telephone. But increasingly in American life, the information upon which we act is drawn neither from direct observation nor informal communication, but from consulting the record about the person in question. And written records have a number of distinctive characteristics that require special attention.

To begin with, a file or dossier is likely to attain a *legitimacy* and *authority* that is lacking in more informal types of communication. Our language itself suggests that this may be so. We talk about the kind of "record" a person develops, typically meaning the sorts of formal evaluations contained in files and dossiers. Or we talk about "verifying" a characteristic of a person by appeal to official documents such as birth certificates, written examinations, and the like. We often confer upon such records, then, a different kind of significance than we attach to less formalized ways of learning about people.

Perhaps one reason for so regarding records is that they have a *permanence* lacking in informal communication. The file is something we can turn back to again and again, whether the individual to whom the record refers is available or not. Like the organizations and institutions that produce them, they have a life far beyond the life-span of given individuals.

A related characteristic of the written record is that it is *transferable;* indeed, it may have a career quite independent from that of the person to whom it refers. Because of its physical properties, it may be copied in whole or in part and sent from one institution to another. We can thus speak of records as literally having a life of their own.

Just as the record may be separated from the person to whom it refers, so may it be separated from those who provided the information in the first place. Unlike direct forms of communication, the written record has the capacity for a *facelessness* that is missing from interpersonal communication.

Finally, since individuals may accumulate records in several different locales, and since the records themselves may be transferred, records from various sources may be *combined* in myriad ways, often without the knowledge of the person whose fate they may be helping to determine. And since each of the pieces of the record may have been compiled with different ends in view, the composite picture provided by the record may bear little resemblance to the person it purports to describe.

The compiling of written records, then, raises problems and issues about the flow of information regarding people that are quite different from those raised by other means of communication. Yet, despite the pervasiveness of record-keeping and its sigificance for individuals and society, relatively little is known about it. There have been no large-scale systematic studies and only a few smaller-scale reports. If the records were stored away, and never used or consulted, they would represent an economic waste with relatively minor social costs. The very development of a system of records is based, however, on the assumption that it will be useful to decision-makers. Because records thus affect both the course of an individual's life and the course of society, they present a problem of social significance.

The most important problem raised by the existence of massive record-keeping systems concerns the appropriate balance between the need for information on individuals as a means to rational decision-making about them, and the often contrasting needs and rights of the individuals themselves. Under what circumstances do individuals have a right to know what information is gathered about them? What types of information are legitimate and what types illegitimate for organizations to gather? Who should have access to the information? These are primary questions of social policy that are raised by the growth of large-scale record-keeping systems.

Our aim here is not to try to resolve these questions directly. Rather it is to provide descriptive accounts of the record-keeping process as it now operates in a variety of different organizations, so that policies can be based on a broad understanding of patterns and pitfalls. In addition, this volume provides the beginnings of an analytical treatment, looking for generalizations about record-keeping and for the different conditions under which it operates, with differing functions and effects. We are thus working in two directions: toward the formulation of responsible social policy regarding the social problem posed by record-keeping systems, and toward a more basic theoretical understanding of the record-keeping process and its effects.

Research of this particular type is referred to as "work in the middle trench" by some of my colleagues at Russell Sage Foundation. This research is short of the front line where actual policy decisions are being made, though it aims to contribute to such decisions by providing a more informed and reasoned background for them. But, by virtue of the kind of problem undertaken for study and the kinds of questions raised about the problem, such work is closer to applied social research than are many academic and scholarly studies produced with a concern for basic or "pure" research. This volume, then, can be seen as one example of a style of work that seems increasingly important as we attempt to bring social science concepts and knowledge to bear on problems of public importance.

In the case of the particular problem being investigated here, this style of work seems doubly important. The problem of record-keeping on persons has come on American society with little advance attention. Until recently, it has been generally taken for granted that organizations will collect information on their members or clients. Little thought has been devoted to the possible social costs. And, as a result, there has been little in the way of developed social thought or public policy with regard to these problems. The extent to which this is true, of course, varies in different organizations; as will be seen, some organizations have been concerned with this problem for a long time and have been constrained by statutes and administrative procedures to gather information about people with due regard for issues of personal privacy and fairness. But in the main, these concerns have been peripheral. The result is that when the concerns were brought to public attention, as they have been recently, there did not exist a body of information about record-keeping that could serve as a basis for considered and rational discussion of the issues.[1]

The same lack of concern is found in the social science literature, even from a theoretical perspective. Indeed, it is surprising that in the vast literature on bureaucratic organizations and rational decision-making, organizational record-keeping itself has not emerged as a problem of distinctive theoretical importance. There has been little effort to spell out the conditions under which different types of records are kept, the social functions performed by record-keeping, and the consequences of record-keeping both for individuals and for organizations.[2]

The absence of an organized body of knowledge about record-keeping, and of a body of experts who have studied the process, means that in planning this book it was not possible to turn to a single individual

[1] The single work that comes closest to addressing the problems raised in this volume is Westin, Alan, *Privacy and Freedom*, Atheneum, New York, 1967. Although Westin is addressing a broader series of concerns, his sections on "Data Surveillance" raise issues similar to those treated in this volume.

[2] Partial exceptions from social science include Wilensky, Harold, *Organizational Intelligence: Knowledge and Policy in Government and Industry*, Basic Books, New York, 1967 and Blau, Peter, *Dynamics of Bureaucracy*, University of Chicago Press, Chicago, 1963. The one area within the social sciences where problems of records have emerged in more than a haphazard way is in studies of the processing of social deviants. See particularly Kitsuse, John, and Aaron Cicourel, "A Note on the Use of Official Statistics," *Social Problems*, vol. 11 (Fall, 1963), pp. 131–139; and Cicourel, Aaron, *The Social Organization of Juvenile Justice*, John Wiley & Sons, New York, 1968.

who was a specialist on record-keeping systems. Russell Sage Foundation thus invited as contributors to this book social scientists who have a thorough knowledge of a particular type of organization and who were thus in the best position to become familiar, in a relatively brief time, with the distinctive features of record-keeping in that organization.

All the authors were asked to respond to some of the following questions: How are dossiers built up? What are the sources of the information that gets into dossiers? How is the information processed? Who uses the information in the dossier? To what extent do "outsiders" have access to the information? What do the individuals to whom the files refer know about the content of the files? What impact does this flow of information have upon the individuals to whom it refers? From the point of view of the organization that maintains the dossiers, what importance do they have? What effects flow from the use of computers with their vast capacity for handling and processing information in various organizational settings? Beyond these questions, the authors were free to proceed in whatever manner they felt would best contribute to our understanding of the significance of record-keeping.

The reports of the various contributors fall naturally into five parts. Part I deals with educational institutions, Part II with economic institutions, Part III with governmental and military organizations, Part IV with institutions of public welfare and social control, and Part V with the legal implications of record-keeping.

Taken together, these reports cover a broad spectrum of record-keeping in a variety of settings. Obviously, however, several more types of record-keeping could have been treated within each institutional sphere. Within the economic sphere, for example, we do not cover banks; among welfare institutions, we do not have a study on record-keeping on adult criminals; among governmental institutions, we do not look at record-keeping by state governments, or at such important agencies as the Internal Revenue Service.

And, of course, other institutional spheres might have been tapped. We do not have a review of record-keeping by religious organizations, by political parties, or by labor unions. Nor do we assess the considerable pressure on record-keeping generated by the growth of the social science enterprise itself. In addition, all the chapters refer primarily to record-keeping in the United States. It is clear that in some institutional spheres, particularly those of welfare and governmental institutions, some countries have engaged in much more extensive record-keeping systems than our own. It would be important to know the consequences of their record-keeping apparatuses. I point out these omissions simply to show that our aim has been to illustrate problems of record-keeping, rather than to provide a thorough descriptive review of the total range of record-keeping systems.

One omission, however, needs further comment. The single most important factor leading to the emergence of concern for record-keeping systems is the computer and the possibilities it presents not only for the extremely rapid and efficient processing of huge amounts of information on people, but for the sharing of information from a variety of different sources. Indeed, in the past two years there have been Congressional hearings with regard to prospects for a federal data bank, articles devoted to the threats to privacy contained in the increased use of computer data-processing systems, and separate studies devoted specifically to computerization of government files.[3] Although we have asked our authors to comment, where appropriate, on the effects of computers in their particular organizational spheres, we have not attempted a separate and independent review of the effects of new technology on record-keeping. In part, this job is being done by the sources just cited. In any event, we have felt that a primary need has been to develop descriptive information with regard to the way in which records are used and processed, and this task is not accomplished by focusing primarily on the computer and its effects.

The remainder of this introduction is designed to highlight some of the special problems posed by the keeping of files and dossiers on individuals and particularly to draw from the chapters in the volume to illustrate both general themes and variations in the ways of handling particular problems.

[3] The primary references are the following: "Computerization of Government Files: What Impact on the Individual?", Los Angeles: *UCLA Law Review*, Vol. 15, No. 5, 1968; U.S. House of Representatives, Committee on Government Operations, Special Subcommittee on Invasion of Privacy. *The Computer and Invasion of Privacy: Hearings before the subcommittee.* Eighty-ninth Congress, Second Session, July 26, 27, and 28, 1966. Washington, D.C.: Government Printing Office, 1966; U.S. Senate, Committee on the Judiciary, Subcommittee on Administrative Practice and Procedure. Computer Privacy: *Hearings before the subcommittee,* Ninetieth Congress, First Session, March 14 and 15, 1967. Washington, D.C.: Government Printing Office, 1967; U.S. Senate, Committee on the Judiciary, Subcommittee on Administrative Practice and Procedure. *Computer Privacy: Hearings before the Subcommittee. Part II.* Ninetieth Congress, Second Session, February 6, 1968, Washington, D.C.: Government Printing Office, 1968; E. S. Dunn, Jr., "The Idea of a National Data Center and the Issue of Personal Privacy," *American Statistician* 21, pp. 21–27, 1967; and Jack Sawyer and Howard Schechter, "Computers, Privacy, and the National Data Center: The Responsibility of Social Scientists," *American Psychologist,* Vol. 23, No. 11, November, 1968.

The Growth of Record-Keeping Systems

What determines the amount of personal information recorded? The primary forces behind the growth of record-keeping systems are the same ones that underlie the general development of large-scale bureaucratic organizations and the growth of rationality as an organizing principle for society. In most of the organizational settings discussed in this volume, there is an indication of the rapid growth of record-keeping on persons. Thus Goslin and Bordier note the growth of record-keeping in public schools since the earliest use of the standardized record form in the early nineteenth century. The most important factor behind the growth of this particular record-keeping system, as well as many others, is the increase in size and scale that led to a demand or a felt need for systematic records. Similarly, Little notes the growth of the military record-keeping systems as an integral feature of the growth and complexity of military organizations. The chapter on consumer credit by Rule, Caplovitz, and Barker also notes these features and in addition the increased mobility of persons as conditions underlying the growth in consumer credit reporting. Alvarez and Moore indicate that in nursing education, in contrast to medical and legal education, the presence of both large organizations and very high rates of turnover generate pressures for extensive record-keeping.

These are only examples of the trend reflected in several other chapters toward the growth of greater and greater amounts of information on people in the files of organizations. However, this trend is not found everywhere: Ross notes that in life insurance, if anything, there is a decline in the amount of record-keeping. This decline is partly a result of the change from individual to group writing of insurance policies, in which less detailed personal information is needed. And Berg and Salvate note that there may be a decline in the amount of information that corporations gather on their employees.

Quite apart from the general trend, the chapters document a wide range in the amount of information currently gathered and suggest a number of factors that may explain the variations. A principal factor appears to be the degree of specificity of the decisions that are made as a result of the information contained in records. In some situations the grounds for decisions are relatively straightforward and simple, and the record-keeping apparatus is likely to be limited to a few essential items. The clearest example is in life insurance, where a small number of crucial bits of information on a person's physical condition and medical history may suffice. At the other extreme are those instances in which an individual's total life history is viewed as potentially relevant. Erikson and Gilbertson found that this circumstance prevails in mental hospitals, where the psychiatric ideology suggests that a whole series of events and conditions from birth to the patient's admission to the mental hospital must be considered. Also at this extreme is the record-keeping on juvenile delinquents where, as Lemert notes, the prevailing rehabilitative ideology suggests the relevance of a person's total personality and social background to an understanding of his present situation.

Another determining factor is the available opportunity to make observations about persons across a wide range of their daily activities. Little sees, for example, that the information in military dossiers is full and detailed in part because soldiers are under nearly constant control and observation of their superiors. The mental hospital, again, illustrates this phenomenon, as do prisons and other settings having the qualities Erving Goffman describes as "total institutions."[4] It is precisely in these institutions that authorities apparently feel they have a legitimate right to gather all kinds of information about persons and where there has been little concern for the invasion of privacy. Different circumstances prevail, for example, within the Bureau of the Census, where, according to Steinberg, there are pressures to limit the amount of information gathered to what is essential for making large-scale social policy decisions, and where the addition of any item to the census schedule requires the approval of a series of groups and agencies.

A related condition results from the development of *cumulative* records. Participants remain in some organizations over a period of years. The longer they remain, the greater is the experience of the organization, and hence the greater the amount of systematic information about them. Thus something like a cumulative record is found in most organizations that process people, the prototype being school records, where the total stay is divided into years, which in turn are subdivided into semesters and often smaller temporal units. Goslin and Bordier note the importance of the cumulative record in school systems and Clark makes a similar observation about colleges and universities.

This preliminary and partial listing is simply suggestive of the kinds of conditions that may relate to the sheer quantity of information that is gathered on persons in different organizations. More systematic studies

[4] Goffman, Erving, *Asylums*, Doubleday, Anchor Books, Garden City, New York, 1961.

across different types of organizations will undoubtedly produce a more complete understanding of the sources of variation.

The Uses of Records

It is one thing to document the general growth of record-keeping systems, but quite another to determine how records are actually used in organizations. As many of these chapters indicate, determination of the way in which records are actually used requires a very subtle type of social investigation, one which was not possible for many of the authors to follow. Even so, some of the *different* ways in which records are used stand out clearly.

Records are sometimes used to make decisions with respect to specific individuals, sometimes used to make decisions with respect to policy making, and in some cases the same records serve both purposes. The records in education, business, and welfare institutions are clearly used in making decisions about individuals: who should be promoted, who should be released, who should go to court or prison. There are differences, however, in how persons draw from the existing information in the files, the selective biases they employ, and the like.

Materials from the Census Bureau, on the other hand, are typically used primarily to get a broad picture of changes in the social aggregate. It is often unnecessary, in these cases, to know which particular individuals have provided the information, for it will be summarized in a statistical form. Even those institutions that typically use the records for individual purposes will often summarize the individual records in a manner that allows us to get some general picture of the organization. Thus, schools, hospitals, prisons, corporations, and others may be able to explain something about the typical characteristics of their students, patients, inmates, or employees.

When the records are used in the latter way, there is a pressure for the use of descriptive items that are easily summarized and quantified, and ones that will be comparable across the various units of observation. Standardized record forms, standardized "face sheet" information, and discrete factual bits of information such as age, marital status, education, and so forth, all lend themselves to quick summarization and counting. The more delicate, subtle, clinically evaluative, and complex bits of information are not so easily bent to these purposes. Indeed, there is often a natural tension and strain in an organization between those who will use the information to draw an aggregate statistical picture, and who therefore need to have easily quantifiable bits of information, and those who wish to assure that the records present a rich and clinically accurate portrait of a person, one that is likely to defy presentation in other than discursive written form.

To say that records are used to make decisions is much too gross a statement. In some instances, to be sure, persons consult the record with an open mind, and use what is in it in addition to whatever else is known to make some critical decision regarding an individual. But, in other cases, the record may be used in order to *justify* a decision already made. Especially in those instances in which a voluminous amount of information may be available, as in the case of the records of probation officers, prisons, and mental hospitals, information may be drawn selectively from the records to show how a particular decision can be justified. This process produces a curious type of feedback on the record-keeping system itself, for the records may be written in such a manner as to point to a particular kind of decision as the most appropriate one. The chapters on welfare institutions give the best indication of this process, but the process is clearly not limited to them. In any event, it seems clear that what is in the record in the first place and what is drawn from the record in decision-making are both determined to an important degree by the values, tastes, ideologies, and biases of those who contribute to and draw from the record system.

A special part of the process of using records to justify decisions is their use for purposes of evidence and proof. Zimmerman's chapter on public assistance gives special attention to this particular use of record-keeping. He describes in detail how particular items of information become certified as authoritative and official facts. Indeed, one of his interesting insights has relevance for dossiers and record-keeping in many other settings. He notes that from the welfare workers' perspective, a "good" client is one who has lived his life in such a way as to provide easy documentation. And we know from other settings that some people, far from attempting to avoid their lives being recorded, find it useful to ensure that they will have official records. A number of persons who apply for consumer credit apparently can afford to pay cash for their purchases, but want to establish a favorable credit rating so that it will be available if they should happen to need it later.

It should not be assumed, however, that information once recorded will be fully used. A number of the chapters suggest that a great deal of the materials that accumulate in organizational files is never referred to, never read, and never acted upon. In some cases, the data would be useful for research purposes, but are seldom used. In other instances, information is apparently retained long after it is likely to be consulted. There is clearly no necessary correspondence between the gathering of the information and its actual use.

Finally, it should be noted that the record forms themselves can serve as useful indicators of social change. The forms contain those matters that the organization in question believes it is important to know about, and therefore changes in the kind of information that is requested reflect changes in the organization itself or its problems. One can study changes in penology, for example, through examining items that have been dropped or added to the basic "face sheets" made out for incoming prisoners. At one point in American history, there would have been room to note in some detail physical attributes and abnormalities of inmates, because it was believed that these had much to do with their becoming criminals. Less space is devoted to such matters now, and relatively more to items reflecting the inmates' social patterns and family life.

Similar kinds of changes can be traced in most of the organizations reported on in this volume. The United States Census Bureau is a particularly relevant case since it generates data about the nation as a whole. In this connection it is interesting to note that the 1970 census, for the first time, will include questions about the ownership of second homes. Such ownership is numerically significant enough in an affluent society to merit explicit counting. In any event, it is apparent that what is asked, as well as answered, may be important data about the organization in question, its ideology, its problems, and its fundamental concerns.

The Social Functions of Record-Keeping

As Goslin and Bordier indicate, when Horace Mann introduced the first systematic school record system into the Massachusetts school system, he noted among it virtues that it "becomes a powerful incentive to good and dissuasive from evil." Mann was clearly sensitive to an important general function of the record—to act as a *social control.* Though it may appear as a passive mirror of events, the existence of the record itself serves as a social constraint: persons are generally motivated to develop a "good" record and not a "bad" one. Hence we find persons who want the record to "show" that they are old enough to receive old-age benefits, that they have the abilities to be admitted to colleges, that their superiors consider them eligible for promotion, and so forth. We also find, as Orlansky's chapter on loyalty and security investigations makes clear, that persons refuse to join some organizations precisely because they are afraid it will become a matter of record.

This indeed is one characteristic that gives records their fundamental importance. It is not important merely that someone is engaged in a particular line of conduct. What is significant is that this line of conduct will become a documented and recorded fact about the person, something that can be used to characterize him. So a powerful form of social control may be wielded by those who have it within their discretion to make an event a "matter of record." Perhaps the best example here is Lemert's chapter on juvenile delinquents, where it becomes clear that to handle a case formally has consequences for the individual in question that go far beyond the consequences when he is handled informally.

The record-keeping system also serves an *identity-giving* function, especially in those situations in which the records about a person are likely to precede his arrival. This function is stated clearly by Clark, who notes that high school records and letters of reference establish expectations about a new college student and may be a basis for making decisions about him prior to his matriculation. The new entrants to the college are type-cast, as it were, on the basis of the information in their files.

To some extent this process undoubtedly occurs elsewhere, and it is matched by a *memory-tracing* function of the record system after an individual has left the setting. That is, the same file that established what the individual might turn out to be can be referred to after he has left to establish what kind of person he was. Our capacity to turn back to the record-keeping system many years after an individual has left the setting in question means that whatever identity he has established there will not be easily overridden by later events. And even in those extreme instances where it is possible to speak of "expunging the record" or "sealing the file" as in the handling of juvenile delinquents, the available experience suggests the sheer impossibility of these tasks. So the record-keeping system, in addition to its social control function, has an identity-giving and identity-maintaining function.

Each of these functions has its organizational counterpart. Just as the organization's record-keeping system serves as a social control on its individual members, the fact that organizations themselves have to report on their activities means that they are subject to similar constraints. This is certainly true of most public bureaucracies, where the enabling legislation is likely to require periodic reports with regard to agency activities. It is also true of both profit-making and nonprofit-making institutions in the private sector. In times of crises or doubt about the legitimacy of a given type of enterprise, there may be clamor for fuller reporting on the nature of that enterprise—reporting designed explicitly as a means of social control. In present-day American society examples include the move to require members of the judiciary to report their outside income and requirements for fuller reporting by foundations on the nature of their grants and programs. Here again, then, it is clear that putting matters on record is a means of making visible, and hence accountable, the activities of organizations and their members.

There is also an organizational counterpart to the identity-building and identity-maintaining function of records. Alvarez and Moore note, for example, that professions in the making, such as nursing, may view their elaborate record-keeping systems as symbolic of their aspirations to recognition as a system of professionals. The police, to choose a group not reported on fully in this volume, establish their identity as an efficient public service by maintaining a high percentage of crimes that are cleared by the arrest of an offender.[5] These are only two examples of the way in which organizational identities, like their individual counterparts, may be affected by the types of records kept about their performance.

The Accuracy, Validity, and Predictability of Records

The possibility of inaccurate or misleading information and the damage such information can do to an individual is a theme found in many chapters. Goldstein's review of the legal status of dossiers outlines the remedies available in law for those who feel they have been wronged by publication of erroneous information, and notes particularly the undeveloped state of both statutes and case law on the subject. The substantive chapters provide further examples of problems in this area. For example, Rule, Caplovitz, and Barker note that credit agencies take no responsibility for verifying facts that they report to potential creditors. Orlansky notes that the demands for completing reports on loyalty and security checks often mean that rumor or gossip cannot be completely and fully investigated; hence the possibility that they may enter the record as fact. And when decisions are made on the basis of such information, with the basis for the decisions not reported to those whose fates they alter, there is little chance of correcting the record. Thus, there is a justifiable concern shown in several chapters for the development of high standards with regard to verification of information.

A related problem concerns one of the characteristics we described as distinctive of dossiers and record-keeping, namely the difficulty of updating and modifying the record as new events take place. Lemert's

[5] Skolnick, Jerome, *Justice Without Trial,* John Wiley & Sons, New York, 1966.

chapter on delinquency indicates that sometimes prior arrest records will be used to characterize a person, even though the arrests may have been dismissed and may not have led to a conviction.[6] Similarly, Rule, Caplovitz, and Barker state that there are no systematic procedures for updating the information in credit files. An individual's refusal to pay a bill because the goods he purchased were defective may simply be reported as nonpayment of bills in a credit investigation, thereby lowering the applicant's credit standing, even though the purchaser may ultimately win a legal case against the seller. Other examples can be given of the same phenomenon—a record once developed is hard to change, even if it is incorrect.

Finally, important questions can be raised with regard to the relationship between the information in the file and the decision-making tasks faced by those who use the files. The agencies and organizations often develop decision-making policies designed to distinguish among candidates for a variety of different positions. Again, according to several of the authors in this volume, there is often little factual validation of the *relevance* of the particular items used for the decisions that are being made. Does it make sense, for example, to rule out of consideration for some jobs all persons who have had a criminal record? How are specific "cutting points" for particular types of decisions established?

Here again there appears to be a good deal of individual variation both within and across the organizations reviewed here. At one extreme are the actuarial life insurance tables, where persons with particular conditions can be located reliably within particular risk categories. But often information is used without any such systematic build-up of experience tables, and decisions made on the basis of myths about what kinds of records predict what kinds of conduct. Of course, this same process operates quite apart from record-keeping itself, but the systematic existence of the recorded information without concurrent efforts to show its predictive value for the decisions being made surely opens up the possibility of wide-spread use of documentary information in a discriminatory way. Berg and Salvate, in their chapter on record-keeping in corporations, note that most employers act as though it is important to have high levels of education for particular jobs, though they often do not have supporting evidence to indicate that more highly educated persons actually do better work on the jobs. In any event, the often unclear relationship between

[6] The potential impact of being mislabeled a criminal is suggested in Schwartz, Richard, and Jerome Skolnick, "Two Studies of Legal Stigma," *Social Problems*, vol. 10 (Fall, 1962), pp. 133–142.

the data and the decisions becomes yet another problem to be investigated. The "self-fulfilling prophecy" is a particularly acute danger and emphasizes the need for independent evidence on the relevance of past experiences for predictions of future conduct.

Access to Files and Dossiers

The records of a particular organization are likely to be stored in that organization, though they may well be stored in different places and therefore be under different persons' control. Inevitably the question arises: Who should have access to the records?

In the case of the official records of public agencies, there is often a legal requirement that the record be available for inspection by any interested party. Indeed, as we see in the chapter on consumer credit, retail credit agencies often begin to establish their files by consulting public documents that list court actions, property exchanges, and the like. At the opposite extreme may be other public agencies whose records are closed by law from access to private individuals or even governmental investigating agencies. This is true, for example, for the Bureau of Census and the Social Security Administration, as Steinberg points out. Goldstein's chapter outlines the legal contours of the problems of access and disclosure for both private and public records, and points to the relatively open texture of the law on these matters.

Within the limits set by law there is a wide range of variation—in the explicitness of policies, in the types of persons who have access, in the information to which they have access, and in the conditions under which they have access. Indeed, the variation appears to be at least as large within organizational types as between them. Almost all the chapters here testify to the differences within organizations of a particular type in the kinds of policies they have developed to handle problems of access. Some schools, for example, make virtually any part of the school record available to teachers, while others rule out from availability materials pertaining to the mental health of the children. Some probation departments are required by law to make their presentence investigation reports available to both the prosecution and defense, while in other jurisdictions they are available to neither. These differences, and many others, require both justification and explanation.

The variations within a given type of organization appear to have several sources. One is the extent to which the persons in charge develop their own idiosyncratic styles with regard to the problem of access. The chapter by Alvarez and Moore in particular, but others as well, suggests some of these individual variations. Other variations also appear to result from the way in which the organization defines its mission vis-à-vis those outside the organization. Clark develops a typology of colleges and universities that is related to the extent to which information is routinely made available to others. Public junior colleges, he points out, are likely to see their role as importantly related to local community institutions, and make available to those institutions, particularly employers, virtually any information they have about their students. Many prestigious private institutions are much less ready to open their files to outsiders, often doing so only after receiving the consent of the students.

Variations in access are also related to the technical nature of the information. Erikson and Gilbertson point out, for example, that psychiatric interpretations and diagnoses of patients in mental hospitals are often not freely available to the lower level staff, it being assumed that they will not have the technical competence to interpret the information and use it appropriately. Little's report on military institutions, on the other hand, indicates that such materials often will be used and interpreted by nonmedical personnel, sometimes for purposes and decisions quite unrelated to the initial reasons for gathering the information.

Particular problems of access arise with respect to two categories of individuals. One category involves official investigative agents or agencies. A number of the authors note that the police are often routinely given access to information in the records, and occasionally either administrative policy or statutes will specifically provide exceptions to a general principle of nonaccess. When the record-keeping system is that of a federal agency, however, it appears that access even for investigative purposes is likely to be severely restricted. Orlansky notes, for example, that those engaged in loyalty and security investigation are specifically restricted from access to the records of the Internal Revenue Service, the Social Security Administration, the Veterans Administration, and the Census Bureau. My discussions with a private investigator who is experienced in such matters confirms that these records are indeed practically impossible to get, whereas it is often possible to gain access (for an appropriate payment) to records of schools, major employers, and the like. He reports that it is surprisingly common for a clerk, a janitor, or even a high official to make a file available for an evening.

The other special category includes those who have a very close relationship to the person and therefore a natural interest in his dossier. The primary example here is parents of school children, who have an obvious interest in everything from ability test scores to disciplinary reports and mental health examinations. As Goslin and Bordier show, there is apparently great variation among school systems in their policies with regard to access of parents to school records.

Problems of access, then, are a crucial part of the dossier problem. To the extent that knowledge is power, access to dossiers confers power on those who attain it, and the function of the "gate-keepers" who control access emerges as more important than their formal status in organizations often implies.

Personal Control Over the Dossier

Of course, the individuals whose interests are most affected by the dossier and who therefore have the greatest stake in the record are those to whom the record specifically refers. To what extent does an individual have either knowledge of or control over the contents of the files that concern him? Here again there is immense variation. In some organizations, records are literally required to be read and understood by the persons to whom they refer. This is true for the evaluations of nursing students by their superiors, and for portions of the military record. If we had a chapter on civil servants, we would find that they too are often asked to sign the evaluation reports provided by their superior.

Precisely the opposite holds in many organizations. Rule, Caplovitz, and Barker note that consumer credit agencies are under no obligation to expose any of their information to the consumer himself; nor are agencies for the processing of deviants, such as courts, prisons, and mental hospitals obligated to allow the deviant to see his cumulative record.

The principles governing access to one's own file are in part similar to those governing access generally. If the information is believed to be technical, or if the person to whom it refers is believed to be incapable of interpreting it meaningfully, as in the case of a school child, he is likely to be denied access. But to an important extent, access is denied for another reason. Much of the material in many dossiers will consist of letters of reference or of evaluations written by persons who know the individual in question and are asked to provide an appraisal. This is particularly true for letters of recommendation for admission to schools or for employment, but is also true of the personal evaluations requested of neighbors on matters of loyalty and security, credit risks, occasionally in insurance, and the like. The whole process of confidential evaluation would break down, it is believed, if individuals had access to their own records.

It is interesting to speculate, however, on the long-term effects of the organizationally induced duplicity that may result from confidential files, and the degree to which they allow the written evaluation of people to diverge from what they are directly told by those who evaluate them. Some persons avoid this problem by sending carbon copies of any evaluative letter to the individual to whom it refers, thereby ensuring that the individual knows what has been said about him and to whom. But this is a relatively rare response and may simply mean that the individual will choose not to write a recommendation at all rather than write a negative one.

The biases here are by no means one-sided, however. Anyone who has been in the position of interpreting written evaluations is aware that styles of letter writing differ markedly. Most administrators could easily write an article entitled "How to Read Letters of Reference and Recommendation." In the academic world, for example, recommendations from some individuals are likely to be discounted because they uniformly preach the virtues and ignore the vices of the applicants. Others will have developed a reputation for harsh judgments, so that minor complaints will be dismissed and favorable comments given extra weight. But these modes of interpretation are not available for those who know little of the person who is writing the evaluation.

The matter of personal control of one's dossier, of course, goes far beyond mere access to it. In some instances, individuals have opportunities to "doctor" their dossiers. The problem of false dossiers is mentioned in the chapter on professional schools and a prospect for doctoring mentioned in the chapter on military institutions, where the individual soldier may often be in the position of hand-carrying his own records. But the more important modes of influencing what is in the dossier lie in controlling what is entered into it in the first place. And here it is apparent that there are systematic differences in the degree of control.

The differences between educational institutions and those for the social control of deviants appear most marked. In the former, as an individual progresses up the educational ladder, he gains increasing control over the contents of his dossier. He is able to suggest who should write letters of recommendation, and at some point may even prepare his personal resumé which will serve as a basic document in the developing file. He can thus present, within limits, the most favorable image of himself that can be drawn from his present and past history. And by being able to select those who will write letters with regard to him, he can screen out potential detractors.

It is quite different in an institution for the control of social deviants, where the problem is often to explain how the person got off the conventional track. As the chapters in this volume indicate, there is likely to be a sizable effort to search out those negative features of the individual's past that may explain why he is currently in trouble. In a mental hospital, say Erikson and Gilbertson, the result may be a social history of a *patient* rather than a *person*. A similar pattern is apparent in the handling of juvenile miscreants: letters of inquiry with regard to their background may be sent routinely to welfare agencies, courts in other jurisdictions, psychiatric facilities where family members may have been treated and, of course, police and FBI files. There is typically not a similar search among those institutions or individuals that might have something favorable to report. As a result, there is a great differential in control over one's dossier, and therefore to some extent over one's fate, which is related to whether one is following a conventional or a deviant path.[7]

The Record, the Person, and Society

Whatever may be said about the nature and character of record-keeping on persons, variations in its form and function in different organizations, or the problems of accuracy, access, and personal control, the most crucial and sensitive issues today concern the effect of the records and record-keeping on individual members of society. There is abundant evidence of the impact of records on individuals. Persons are put into and out of school programs on the basis of the record, accepted or rejected for colleges and professional schools on the basis of the record, given or denied credit, employed or not employed, insured or not insured on the basis of the record. The record keeps some people out of the military and (especially in the case of military discharges for other than honorable reasons) affects the later fates of those who do serve. The record may become a basis for denying employment in sensitive jobs, for granting or denying welfare benefits, or sending a child to reform school rather than returning him to his home, or for deciding when and indeed whether to release a patient from a mental hospital. And of course, similar types of decisions are made in organizations not discussed here.

It might be argued, however, that we are fundamentally wrong in saying that the record accomplishes these tasks and therefore has all these effects. To the extent that the record is merely a passive indicator of a person's performances, the actions are really being determined by his performances, not by records of them. It is as though one were to argue that when a driver is stopped for speeding because an electronic device

[7] Stanton Wheeler, "The Structure of Formally Organized Socialization Settings," in Orville G. Brim and Stanton Wheeler, eds., *Socialization After Childhood*, New York: John Wiley & Sons, 1966.

indicates he was exceeding the speed limit, it is the electronic device rather than the driver's haste that caused the arrest. Shouldn't we simply assume that persons ought to be responsible for their conduct? As long as their conduct is appropriate, how can they be harmed by the record of it? If their conduct merits reward, the record should show it. And if it goes outside appropriate boundaries, the record should show that too. Hence it is not the record of conduct, but the conduct itself, that leads to the various dispositions and decisions that so affect people's lives. From this perspective, we are essentially wasting our time by examining the record-keeping procedures themselves.

This argument overlooks the fact that the making, keeping, and reading of records is itself a form of conduct, and indeed an increasingly important one. We actively decide to record some aspects of an individual's behavior and to ignore others. To an important extent the actions we later take regarding them will depend upon what we have decided to record. The very record-making process itself, then, must be regarded as problematic and we can ask not only for the conditions under which events in a person's life will become a matter of record, but whether it is *legitimate* for them to become a matter of record. Do we not wish to leave some spheres of individual lives free from both observation and recording by others, even if knowing the information would allow us to make more accurate predictions of future conduct and hence more rational decisions regarding the persons in question?

In addition to this problem, there are two types of errors or biases that may creep into a record-keeping system, each of which may have an important effect upon the individuals to whom the records refer. We have already discussed the errors due to inaccuracy in information, incomplete information, and the often-cited lack of predictability from the information to future conduct. But a second type of bias may be more pervasive. Even if the individual facts and items that enter into an individual record are all accurate and true, they still may not give a full and faithful portrait of the individual. We have seen in connection with the personal control over the dossier that if the individual achieves greater control, the dossier is likely to present a more and more favorable image of him, perhaps more favorable than that which a more "objective" evaluation would provide. And the reverse appears clearly to happen as persons lose control over the dossier—as they run afoul of the institutions for the processing of deviants in our society, where, as is especially noted by Erikson and Gilbertson, the pressure may very well be to develop information explaining the deviance rather than explaining the person. Thus even when we set aside the issues concerning the wisdom or appropriateness of some individuals' recording information on others, there remain large questions of the relationship between that information and the person as we might know him by other means.

There is a still larger issue raised by the growing amount of recorded information on people. This issue is reflected indirectly in a number of chapters, but is raised most clearly in Clark's review of college and university dossiers. The point that records are increasingly used as a basis for making important decisions about people has not been overlooked by those to whom their records refer, and he talks of the prospects for an emerging "dossier consciousness" among the population. His observations have a very clear relevance that runs far beyond the colleges and universities. What is the likelihood that we will become a dossier-conscious society? If we do, what will be the long-term impact? Will people develop an increasingly bifurcated personality, one part oriented to their private lives, a second part oriented to matters of record? It is conceivable that the record-keeping process itself could so blur our collective vision that we will become increasingly concerned, not with what we are, but with what the record makes us out to be.

THE POLICY ISSUES

The themes just discussed flow naturally from the substance of the various chapters. Other editors might have raised additional issues and neglected some considered here. And if we had sampled in a different manner from the available array of record-keeping systems, further insights and perspectives would have been apparent. But the task at this stage of our understanding of record-keeping systems is to open up inquiry rather than to provide definitive answers for the various practical and theoretical questions that can be raised about files and dossiers. Indeed, the limitations of time and resources under which the authors worked required such an orientation.

Perhaps it is appropriate, however, to close this introductory chapter by stating as clearly as possible the series of policy questions that arise when we consider the dossier problem. Some authors have resolved these questions in their chapters, some have addressed them but not resolved them, and others have not raised them at all. At a minimum, it would seem that any organization or agency that either feels it necessary to collect data about people or is specifically charged with that task should develop a considered policy, subject to review by parties affected by the results of that policy, with respect to the following problems or issues:

1. What kinds of information on people is it necessary and legitimate to collect? Is the information essential to the organization's functioning and relevant to the decisions that will flow from it?
2. For the information that meets the criteria of necessity and legitimacy, what measures can be developed to ensure that the information is accurate and up to date? If the organization in question has no such procedures or if the procedures are weak and ineffective, does the organization still have a legitimate right to gather the information?
3. Does the organization in question have a developed and considered policy with respect to access to the information, both by members of the organization and outsiders? With respect to specific persons who have access, are there procedures for informing them of the limits to be placed on their use of the information?
4. Has the organization or agency established a set of procedures that will ensure that only those persons who have legitimate right of access to the information are provided access to it?
5. Does the organization have specific procedures for informing the individuals to whom the records refer (a) of the nature and existence of the records and (b) of the use to which they are put? If not, is there a clear, powerful, and legitimate set of reasons for not informing the individuals of the contents of the files and dossiers regarding them?
6. When individual records are challenged as to their accuracy or validity, are there procedures for review such that errors can be corrected?
7. Does the organization have established procedures and mechanisms for continuing appraisal of its record-keeping system with respect to the criteria and policy issues suggested above?

This is not an exhaustive list of policy issues, but it will suffice for a start. It is relevant to note that, with the exception of Steinberg's chapter on the Census Bureau and the Social Security Administration, and Orlansky's chapter on loyalty and security investigations, there is little evidence that most of the organizations reported on have addressed these issues fully. If a reasoned response to these policy issues is forthcoming, it should help to prevent an irrational revolt against record-keeping and to protect the positive functions record-keeping serves for any modern society. It should not be impossible, in a society such as ours, to arrive at a reasoned and appropriate balance between the need for information as a basis for rational decision-making, and the need for controls over the amount and quality of information, as well as the use which is made of it.

II *Educational Institutions*

2 Record-Keeping in Elementary and Secondary Schools

DAVID A. GOSLIN AND NANCY BORDIER

RECORD-KEEPING, IN ONE FORM OR ANOTHER, IS AN INTEGRAL PART OF THE educational process. At the simplest level, an educational record describes changes taking place in individuals that may be attributed, at least in part, to their participation in the teaching-learning experience. Since change (learning) is presumed to be the primary goal of education, the record of such change provides a measure of the effectiveness of the educational process as a whole as well as the performance of each of the participants, principally teachers and students.

From the beginnings of human society teachers have no doubt kept track of the performance of their pupils. Effective teaching, no matter how informal, requires that the teacher have some idea of what his pupil knows and does not know, how quickly he is able to grasp new ideas or acquire new skills, and what kinds of learning are especially easy or difficult for him. Similarly, the student's motivation to continue to engage in the educational process is no doubt related to his perception that he is making progress, a perception that is facilitated by the maintenance of records. Moreover, the record of an individual's performance in learning situations has long been used as an important indicator of his capacity to handle tasks that require the utilization of previously acquired skills or knowledge, or to engage in new (especially similar) learning.

Educational records may be expected to reflect accurately characteristics of the educational process. Simple educational systems, typified at the extreme by a one-to-one teacher-pupil relationship focused on the transmission of a single set of interrelated concepts or skills (for example, a father and his apprentice son), are characterized by highly personalized and informal record-keeping techniques: a diary, collections of work done at various stages in the process, or even individual recollections corroborated by the observations of others. Complex systems, on the other hand, necessitate more complex record-keeping procedures.

This chapter is concerned with record-keeping in what is probably the most highly developed and complex educational system any society has ever created. In addition to describing, in as great detail as is possible and/or practical, current record-keeping practices in American elementary and secondary schools,[1] we would also like to speculate on the relationship between the development of our educational system and record-keeping procedures. This speculation reveals a number of social, ethical, and legal issues which deserve further exploration. These issues are illuminated, we think, by the general points just oulined: namely, the intimate relationship between, on the one hand, what kinds of information about individuals we think it is important to collect and what uses we make of the resulting personal records; and, on the other, how our educational system is organized and what we expect it to do for us.

Record-keeping procedures do not emerge independently of the system in which they exist. They arise as a consequence of pressures within the system and they, in turn, often lead to changes in it. In the following section of this chapter a modest attempt will be made to depict the broad outlines of this interactional process. In succeeding sections we shall examine the historical development of pupil accounting systems in concrete terms; current practices of elementary and secondary schools regarding the maintenance and use of pupil records; current trends and prospects for the future; and, finally, the major issues generated by present procedures as well as likely future developments.

AMERICAN EDUCATION AND EDUCATIONAL RECORDS

A great many changes have taken place in the characteristics of educational institutions in America during the past fifty years. These changes have been the result of (and in turn have contributed to) broad changes

[1] The primary focus of the chapter is on public as opposed to private educational institutions, although much of our commentary has direct implications for record-keeping in private schools.

occurring throughout the society—technological advances; demographic changes, including urbanization and suburbanization; shifts in political and religious attitudes and values; and so on.[2] Although, as one of the authors has suggested elsewhere,[3] these major alterations in the society as a whole have had less of an impact than some observers have claimed on the basic *conduct* of education (that is, what is taught and how it is taught), they have resulted in radical alterations in the *structure* of our educational institutions. The most important of these structural changes are related to increases in the size and complexity of the educational enterprise, both with respect to units within the system and the system as a whole. Put simply, a much larger proportion of a larger population is attending bigger schools that are part of bigger school systems for a longer period of time. Concomitantly, the society's investment in education has increased substantially at all levels; schools and colleges have become more specialized; the range of options open to individuals with respect to the educational experiences available to them has expanded rapidly; and, finally, the conduct of education has become a major focus of concern to many segments of the population that formerly took for granted what went on or did not go on in schools.

In sum, education has become an increasingly important enterprise, both from the point of view of the individual and the society. For the individual, recognition that time and effort invested in acquiring the proper educational credentials (if not the associated skills and knowledge) is likely to pay handsome returns in terms of income, status or prestige has resulted in increased motivation to make the required personal investment. From the standpoint of the society, recognition that maintenance of our current rate of economic and technological development requires an adequate supply of highly trained manpower has made education a matter of national interest and concern.

How are these changes related to the development of school record-keeping systems? As will be noted in the following section, elementary and secondary schools have kept basic records of pupil attendance and performance since the early part of the nineteenth century. As educational institutions (particularly the public schools) have developed in response to changes in the society, pupil record-keeping practices have also

[2] Goslin, David A., *The School in Contemporary Society,* Scott Foresman & Co., Chicago, 1965.

[3] Goslin, David A., "The School in a Changing Society," *American Journal of Orthopsychiatry,* vol. XXXVII, no. 5 (October, 1967); and "Education, Social Mobility and College Culture: The Problems of Adolescence in a Changing Society," paper presented at a Conference on Adaptation to Change sponsored by the Foundations' Fund for Research in Psychiatry, Dorado Beach Hotel, San Juan, Puerto Rico, June 21–27, 1968.

changed. School records have been more systematically maintained; and, at the same time, they have become more elaborate and detailed with respect to the kinds of information recorded. Five specific trends may be noted that have contributed to this development. The first four describe changes that have taken place in the educational system as a whole; the fifth is related to innovations in the technology of record-keeping itself.

First, as the society's investment in educational facilities has expanded and more people have been attending school for longer periods of time, schools and school systems have grown significantly in size. Until the early 1950's the trend was in the direction of increased numbers of both schools and school districts. Since that time strong tendencies toward consolidation and administrative centralization have reduced the number of school systems and increased the enrollment in individual schools (especially secondary schools) within districts.[4] With centralization has come the adoption of an essentially bureaucratic model for the administration of school systems, as well as individual schools. Administrative as well as teaching functions have become increasingly specialized; procedures, including curricula, have been formalized; and more uniform, less personalized, standards for evaluating pupil (as well as teacher) performance have been adopted. At the same time student bodies have become more heterogeneous and curricula have become increasingly diversified, while the basic format of age-graded instruction has persisted except for scattered experimental programs. Keeping track of and evaluating the performance of larger numbers of pupils; making sure that prerequisites for advanced courses are met by potentially qualified individuals; providing teachers with information about their pupils so that wasted effort is minimized; and counseling pupils effectively regarding the increased number of options open to them constitute only a partial listing of the necessary functions served by the maintenance of more systematic and comprehensive pupil records in such systems.

Second, in addition to increased size and specialization within schools, educational institutions themselves have become increasingly diversified. Vocational and trade schools, schools for the academically gifted or retarded, specialized junior colleges, and other post-high-school programs

[4] According to U.S. Office of Education figures, the number of local school districts fell from 40,500 in 1959–1960 to 21,990 in the fall of 1967 (consisting of 20,388 operating districts and 1,602 nonoperating districts), a decrease of nearly 50 per cent in less than ten years. During the same period total enrollment in full-time public elementary and secondary day schools rose from 36,281,294 to 43,886,805. U.S. Department of Health, Education, and Welfare, Office of Education, *Fall 1964, Statistics of Public Schools,* Government Printing Office, Washington, 1965; and U.S. Department of Health, Education, and Welfare, Office of Education, *Fall, 1967, Statistics of Public Elementary and Secondary Day Schools,* Government Printing Office, Washington, 1968.

offer students a wide choice of educational experiences. In practically all of these cases, evaluation of the qualifications of applicants requires an adequate record of past performance. Moreover, this record, of necessity, must contain information that may be meaningfully compared with similar information contained in the records of competing candidates having different educational backgrounds. Thus, pressure is generated by the system for the development of standardized record systems containing information based on measures applied to all pupils, regardless of what school they attend.

Third, the rapid technological and industrial development of the society as a whole has created a constant demand for talented and highly trained individuals that, in turn, has placed a high premium on the ability of educational institutions to identify qualified young people and encourage them to develop their talents to the utmost. At practically every occupational level we are engaged in a massive talent hunt that has had interesting consequences for our schools as well as for the children who are the focus of the search. Among other things, it has resulted in considerable preoccupation with the problem of predicting future performance—in school and beyond. The search for indicators of future performance led in the early 1900's to the development of the concept of IQ, as well as, more recently, to attempts to measure a variety of other personal qualities; including potential for creativity, personal and social adjustment, and the like.[5] Emphasis on maximizing personal growth, whatever one's inherent capacities, has caused schools to pay serious attention to the question of why Johnny does not seem to be learning as much as he should be learning (given his intellectual potential). Thus, there is a quest for more information about Johnny—his family background, possible troubles at home, early inhibiting experiences, personality characteristics, and so on—that might enable the school to unlock his full potential. Modern school records clearly reflect all of these developments.

Fourth, the increasing involvement of state and federal agencies in local educational matters through the funding of a variety of special programs as well as general legislative and fiscal activities has led to a reduction in the historical autonomy and independence of local school systems. State requirements relating to such things as attendance, minimum pupil performance levels, standardized testing programs, and even racial integration have forced local systems to institute many new administrative practices, including new record-keeping and reporting procedures. In addition,

[5] Goslin, *The Search for Ability, op. cit.*, chap. II.

many state education departments have had considerable influence on the adoption of uniform pupil record forms by supporting the design of a model record form and assisting local districts to modify their record-keeping practices in order to incorporate the new form.

Finally, two important technological developments have had a direct impact on school record-keeping practices: standardized tests and the computer. Standardized tests of aptitude and achievement have become, during the past fifty years, an integral part of American education. Virtually every school system in the country gives some standardized tests to pupils.[6] Most school systems make regular use of such tests to measure achievement as well as general intellectual capacity and specific aptitudes. The result of a standardized test is a numerical score that may be converted into a percentile ranking on the basis of standard norms of performance for a school system or the nation as a whole. A great deal of information concerning a pupil's achievements (and potential for subsequent achievement) relative to other pupils in his age grade may therefore be summarized in a relatively precise and spatially economic way. Record-keeping procedures reflect the widespread use of standardized tests by the practically universal incorporation of a section of the permanent pupil record devoted to standardized test scores (including percentile rankings, type of test taken, and the like).

Even more important, mechanical scoring procedures for standardized tests, based in large part on the rapid development of computers, have improved the accuracy of data recorded in pupil records and have speeded up the process by which this information is incorporated into the record. These developments, in turn, have influenced schools to adopt more uniform record forms and record-keeping procedures. Many large school districts, and at least one entire state (Florida), have computerized their record-keeping systems. The technology of record-keeping, therefore, has itself contributed to, and in turn has been influenced by, many of the previously mentioned factors.

THE HISTORICAL DEVELOPMENT OF RECORD-KEEPING PROCEDURES

Among the earliest school records were the school "registers" developed in Massachusetts and Connecticut in the 1820's and 1830's. Their primary purpose was to collect information on school enrollment and attendance

[6] *Ibid.*, chap. IV. See also Goslin, David A., Roberta R. Epstein, and Barbara A. Hallock, *The Use of Standardized Tests in Elementary Schools*, Technical Report No. 2 on the Social Consequences of Testing, Russell Sage Foundation, New York, 1965; and Goslin, David A., *Teachers and Testing*, Russell Sage Foundation, New York, 1967.

which could be used by the state legislatures for planning as well as by the localities interested in curbing absenteeism. In addition to attendance data, the forms typically included entries for recording the names of members of the school examination committee and the dates on which it administered its examinations.[7] Frequently space was provided for a teacher to keep "a daily account of mental progress and moral deportment."[8] Horace Mann, secretary of the State Board of Education in Massachusetts, induced the state legislature to be the first among the states to pass an act (1838) requiring that "a blank form or register be kept by all school districts.[9] His annual reports proclaimed the virtues of the registers:

(1) "Efficient preventive of irregularity in attendance"; (2) More accurate statistical reports; (3) Enables the teacher to note the mental and moral progress of each pupil; (4) Contains the entire school history of the child; (5) Furnishes each pupil a means of self-comparison; (6) Becomes "a powerful incentive to good and dissuasive from evil"; (7) Fastens "the delinquency of absence upon the particular offenders."[10]

The practice of keeping pupil accounting records spread rapidly during the latter half of the nineteenth century. Despite the efforts of prominent educators to press for the adoption of uniform records, different regions developed widely divergent record-keeping practices, a diversity which still persists.[11]

In the 1870's the liberalization of curricula and expansion of college enrollment placed new demands upon secondary school records. Expanded enrollment meant that no longer could all applicants be admitted on the basis of a personal interview; the evaluation of an applicant required a record of secondary school achievement. The trend away from a rigid classical course in both secondary schools and colleges made it necessary for college applicants to submit detailed transcripts of their secondary preparation.[12] The purposes of record-keeping expanded from simply recording attendance and scholastic examinations for accounting and planning needs to reporting particular subject matter preparation for college admission.

Scholastic achievement as recorded by the first accounting devices included teachers' observations of "mental and moral progress" and the

[7] Heck, Arch O., *A Study of Child Accounting Methods,* Ohio State University, Ohio, 1925, chap. III.

[8] *Ibid.*, p. 34.

[9] Heck, Arch O., *Administration of Pupil Personnel,* Ginn & Co., Boston, 1929, p. 184.

[10] Heck, *A Study of Child Accounting Methods, op. cit.*, p. 185.

[11] *Ibid.*, chap. IV.

[12] Stibal, Willard O., *The Historical Development of Student Personnel Records in Colleges and Universities,* Kansas State Teachers College, Emporia, Kansas, 1959, Vol. 8, No. 2, pp. 8–9.

school examiner's evaluation of pupil performance at an oral examination. Toward the end of the nineteenth century oral examinations by boards of visitors were replaced by written examinations required by college admissions practices.[13] Consequently school records were designed to convey information to colleges regarding students' preparation and performance on subject matter examinations. To meet the requirements of the secondary school itself, the outside examinations were replaced by appraisals made by the classroom teacher. Thorndike and Hagen suggest that these appraisals tended to be "highly subjective, depending upon the standards and prejudices of the particular scorer."[14]

By 1900, however, traditional curriculum content and evaluation began to be influenced by developments in experimental psychology and measurement. Until then, basic educational outcomes had been limited largely to the acquisition of information and skills, and the training of mental faculties as based on the theory of formal discipline in education.[15] The design of effective experimental procedures in England and Germany during the last half of the nineteenth century produced statistical techniques and tools which were utilized in the investigation of individual differences, a field of study which developed subsequent to Darwin's work on variation among members of a species. Simultaneously, clinical study of deviates exposed the need to develop measures of intelligence. During the first decade of the twentieth century, continued experimentation with the Binet scale for evaluating intelligence and the beginnings of achievement tests introduced the modern concepts and methods of testing.[16] In the next fifteen years standardized tests were developed for a whole range of school skills. Achievement batteries appeared, and following World War I, group intelligence tests were widely used. After this period of early enthusiasm for standardized tests, Thorndike and Hagen[17] report a period of critical reappraisal in the light of the limited scope of specific tests and their emphasis upon restricted and traditional objectives. This reappraisal was directed at the underlying philosophy of quantification and the use of numbers to express psychological qualities. What followed was a redirection of attention away from merely "measuring" a limited range of academic skills to "evaluating" achievement of the whole range of educational objectives. . . . It was a period in which the holistic,

[13] Thorndike, Robert L., and Elizabeth Hagen, *Measurement and Evaluation in Psychology and Education*, John Wiley & Sons, New York, 1961, p. 2.

[14] *Ibid.*

[15] Stibal, *op. cit.*, p. 22.

[16] Wrightstone, J. Wayne, *et al.*, *Evaluation in Modern Education*, American Book Co., New York, 1956, p. 12; and Goslin, *The Search for Ability*, *op. cit.*

[17] Thorndike and Hagen, *op. cit.*, p. 6.

global projective methods of personality appraisal came to the fore.[18] Wrightstone[19] reports that beginning in the 1940's the emphasis was upon developing methods and techniques for evaluating broad personality changes; for example, in attitudes, interests, powers of thinking, and personal-social adaptability. Schools adopted instruments of evaluation such as personality tests, projective techniques, interest inventories, attitude scales, and anecdotal records. In summary, according to Wrightstone, there occurred a shift away from measurement of "isolated information, skills, and abilities" toward "functional learning outcomes, many of them less tangible and less easily measured than the subject matter, concepts, skills and abilities of previous decades."[20]

At the turn of the century, school records as described above contained primarily attendance and scholarship data. The scientific movement in education, in addition to broadening educational objectives, provided a significant stimulus toward more adequate and uniform school records. According to Yeager,[21] Thorndike's study of "Elimination of Pupils from School" (1907), and Ayres' study "Laggards in Our Schools" (1909) called attention to inadequacies and inaccuracies of school records. He cites as the most obvious deficiencies: the absence of original records, isolated and disconnected practices from which significant facts for the whole system could not be deduced, the lack of cumulative record material, the underdeveloped character of units of measure, and lack of uniformity of standards for comparisons.

In 1925, the National Education Association Committee on Uniform Records and Reports recommended that local systems should be devised so as to permit uniformity and comparability; that extraneous data should be eliminated and that the data recorded should be exact; and that the various records of a school system should be coordinated and unified. It recommended the following types of pupil records: (1) teacher's daily register book; (2) pupil's general cumulative record; (3) pupil's health and physical records; (4) guidance record; (5) pupil's psychological clinic record; (6) principal's office record. These recommendations called attention to several different purposes of keeping school records: (1) compliance with state record-keeping regulations; (2) retention of records necessary for proper reporting of promotion, transfer to college or another school, for comparative purposes, survey needs, etc.; (3) at-

[18] *Ibid.*
[19] Wrightstone, *op. cit.*, p. 12.
[20] *Ibid.*, p. 13.
[21] Yeager, William A., *Administration and the Pupil,* Harper & Bros., New York, 1949, chap. XXI, esp. p. 329.

tendance information; (4) guidance; (5) reporting to the home; (6) recording pupil progress for admission, classification and promotion.[22]

Thus the scientific movement as reflected in the Thorndike and Ayres studies called attention to the shortcomings of record-keeping practices, and set in motion forces that were to change not only forms of school records but, more important, their content. The most immediate effect of the advances in measurement technique and broadened educational objectives was to increase the range and variety of information which could be known and recorded about each child. Interest in child guidance began to grow during the 1920's as a result of these advances, and also as a result of the improvements in child accounting systems. In 1927 the first cumulative record form was devised by a committee of the American Council on Education. It was intended to accommodate the information traditionally collected for accounting, administrative, and transfer purposes, but principally it was intended to provide for the continuous collection, by a variety of persons, of a wide range of data about each student's school career to be used for the purpose of guiding him instructionally, personally, and vocationally.[23] The committee published four cumulative record forms, which included a folder for college students, a folder for secondary school pupils, and a card for elementary school pupils. Although it was hoped that this cumulative record form might lead to the standardization of record forms throughout the country, there is no indication that it had such a widespread effect.

In 1934, the results of the Progressive Education Association's Eight-Year-Study lent support to those advocating the collection of more types of information about students than simply test scores and course work.[24] In 1941, the Smith Committee revised the forms of the American Council on Education. Because Smith had previously been chairman of the PEA Eight-Year-Study Committee, revision of the portion devoted to behavior description closely parallels that developed by the Eight-Year-Committee. Traxler[25] suggests that the forms developed by the Smith Committee placed less emphasis on subjects, credits, and marks, and more emphasis on behavior description and evaluation of personal qualities, than other similar forms. They also gave greater attention to synthesis and evaluation, and provided amply for description of behavior. The current form provides for a six-year record, including grades 7 through 12. Space is pro-

[22] *Ibid.*, pp. 330–331.

[23] Allen, Wendell C., *Cumulative Pupil Records*, Teachers College, New York, 1943, p. 1; and Traxler, Arthur E., *Techniques of Guidance*, Harper & Row, New York, 1966, p. 190.

[24] Stibal, *op. cit.*, pp. 17–18.

[25] Traxler, *op. cit.*, p. 197.

UNIVERSITY OF WINNIPEG
PORTAGE & BALMORAL
WINNIPEG 2, MAN CANADA

vided for the summary of previous school records and for two photographs (some states prohibit inclusion of a photograph on the permanent record form). The card is arranged to permit flexibility in choice of categories of evaluation.

On the front of the form is a record of subjects and academic achievement, with space for the evaluation of work habits, ability to think logically, mastery of technique, oral and written communication, and estimate of achievement. Scores on academic aptitude, reading, achievement, and other tests may be recorded; and provision is made for interpretation of the test record and its relation to other measures of academic achievement. Further spaces provide for entry of information concerning attendance, interests reported by student, experiences in and out of school, work experiences, financial aid, educational and occupational plans, health and physical characteristics, and academic and personal discipline.

The back of the form is devoted to descriptions of the pupil's background and behavior. It requests information on each of the following items: health, decease of either parent, birthplace, citizenship, changes in type of occupation of parents, language spoken, type of community, study conditions or other factors such as "broken home." The categories of behavior include: responsibility, creativeness, influence, adjustability, concern for others, serious purpose, and emotional stability. Each of the behavioral categories includes six qualifying subcategories. For example, under creativeness are the following classifications: general, specific, promising, limited, imitative, and unimaginative. A small box labeled "Post-school follow-up information" provides space for entering information regarding college, other schools, work, marriage, and civic activities.

The original ACE cumulative record forms were not copyrighted, and one of the most widely used adaptations is that of the Educational Record Bureau—the ERB Cumulative Record Card for Independent Schools. As suggested above, the forms differ from the ACE revised forms in that greater emphasis is placed upon subjects, credits, and marks, and less emphasis upon behavioral description and interpretation. It provides a graph of percentile ratings on test results.

In 1958, the National Association of Secondary School Principals devised a cumulative record and transcript form which has been widely accepted by schools and colleges. It is intended to cover the following areas: attendance, health, guidance, academic achievement, test record, personality evaluations, and educational and vocational plans. A transcript form for college or employment was also developed by the NASSP, and revised in 1964 in cooperation with the American Association of Collegiate Registrars and Admissions Officers, in collaboration with the Educational Testing Service. It includes a record of subjects and marks, honors, activities, and test scores; and a summary of teachers' descriptions of the following: "participation in discussion," "involvement in classroom activities," "pursuit of independent study," "evenness of performance," "critical and questioning attitude," "depth of understanding," "personal responsibility," "consideration for others." There is space for further comments and space for entering any health factors ("physical or emotional of which this college should be aware") and space for the school's recommendation.

In 1964, the U.S. Office of Education issued a handbook entitled *Pupil Accounting for Local and State School Systems*[26] as a guide for the items of information to be used in pupil accounting in local and state school systems. The product of four years of cooperation between the Office of Education and ten national educational associations, it was initially compiled from a survey of the pupil information systems of 50 states and more than 200 local school systems. Each of the items of information was discussed by the representatives of the ten cooperating agencies.

The eight major classes of information include: personal identification, family and residence, physical health, standardized tests (behavioral and psychological), enrollment, performance, transportation, tuition and special assistance. A major classification may be broken down into several subcategories, each consecutively numbered. Included in the handbook are definitions and examples of each item of information. Under the category "Standardized Tests; Behavioral and Psychological Information" it states:

> when an examination is made and the findings (including the identification of exceptionality) are recorded under the headings of this section, the individual making the examination or identification should be technically and professionally qualified to do so. . . . Some of the information which might be recorded under the following headings may be of a confidential nature and should be used and transferred with discretion.[27]

Thus far no studies have been designed to discover how extensively the OE handbook has been introduced in schools around the country. Nor is it possible to generalize about what kinds of records of whatever derivation, including those mentioned above, are presently most widely used throughout elementary and secondary schools. In the past, studies have been

[26] U.S. Office of Education, *Pupil Accounting for Local and State School Systems*, U.S. Department of Health, Education and Welfare, Washington, 1964.
[27] *Ibid.*, p. 36.

made only of particular regions and of specific record systems, but no over-all picture has emerged.

In large part, the absence of such data is due both to the historical development of record-keeping, and to the fact that local autonomy of educational authorities leads to broad diversity in the forms on which information about educational goals and achievement is recorded, as well as in administrative practices and procedures for collecting such information. Evaluation experts, hoping to improve local systems, have often urged school people to develop record-keeping systems which reflect their local needs and objectives. Ruth Strang admonishes, for example, "Grow your own records—then you will be sure everyone in the school understands and appreciates them."[28] Thus while the over-all purposes of record-keeping vary little from school to school—since all schools have much the same requirements for accounting (for administration and planning purposes), guidance, transfer, and reporting to parents—the form of their response to these charges may vary considerably. While most cumulative record forms contain roughly the same general categories of information—health, family background, academic marks, standardized tests, behavior and personal qualities, extracurricular activities, interests and special talents—record-keeping policies differ markedly from region to region, and from school district to school district.[29] Heck's study in 1925, for example, revealed that 1,515 different items were included on the record forms of 131 cities; 50.2 per cent occurred only once, while only 11.3 per cent occurred on more than ten forms.[30]

In 1938, an item analysis of the records of 177 school systems was made by the U.S. Office of Education in 37 states which had recently adopted new record-keeping systems.[31] Its general findings were that the junior and senior high schools were more concerned than elementary schools with items of entrance and withdrawal, intelligence test results, extracurricular activities, vocational and educational plans, college or vocation entered after leaving school, special abilities, photographs, and out-of-school employment. The junior high school was found to use more items in its records than either senior or elementary school. The elementary school appeared to be concerned slightly more than junior and senior high schools with attendance, social and character ratings, health and residence

[28] Strang, Ruth, *Reporting to Parents,* Teachers College, Columbia University, New York, 1947, p. 82.

[29] Traxler, *op. cit.*, p. 181; and Segal, David, "Nature and Use of the Cumulative Record," *U.S. Office of Education Bulletin,* 1938, no. 3, chap. II.

[30] Heck, *Administration of Pupil Personnel, op. cit.*, p. 190.

[31] Segal, *op. cit.*, chap. II.

record. Of 94 items mentioned concerning character and social traits, the most frequently included were conduct, courtesy, dependability, effort, honesty, industry, initiative, leadership, personal appearance, reliability, and self-control.

Segal, the author of the study, found little uniformity regarding the description of traits to be rated.[32] Neither was there agreement on the use of any particular set of character or social traits, nor uniform notation for rating, nor any common scale used by different school systems. He emphasized the need for research to establish the validity of the individual items used in the cumulative record, and for continuous reconsideration of choices among items, in order to keep up with advances in measurement techniques and improved understanding of the prognostic value of items of evaluation. He noted, however, that the cumulative nature of pupil records helped to minimize the shortcomings of present evaluation techniques, since so many entries could be made throughout a pupil's academic career by a variety of school personnel. Nonetheless he emphasized that every program of pupil analysis was heavily dependent upon interpretation by teachers and counselors.

Traxler[33] summarizes the basic concepts of the cumulative record system as follows: (1) the child as a developing organism; (2) continuity of education from kindergarten through college; (3) organization according to time sequence; (4) the concept of comparable measurement; (5) graphical presentation of numerical data; and (6) the concept of behavior description (which he contends is one of the outstanding contributions to record-keeping). One of several types of behavioral descriptions discussed by Traxler is anecdotal records, "a specialized form of incidental observation" that attempts to summarize the child's conduct and personality in terms of frequent, brief, concrete observations of the pupil made and recorded by the teacher. Structured observational techniques, another type of behavior description employing previously defined categories of activities in a running account of pupil conduct, is described by Wrightstone.[34] Wrightstone, Traxler, and Strang all call attention to some of the shortcomings of these tools. Traxler observes that behavioral description must not be complicated by the opinion of the observer.[35] Wrightstone emphasizes the need to avoid generalized evaluation of behavior as op-

[32] *Ibid.*, chap. III.
[33] Traxler, *op. cit.*, pp. 219–234.
[34] Wrightstone, *op. cit.*, p. 133.
[35] Traxler, *op. cit.*, p. 231.

posed to description of specific incidents, the tendency to record negative data only, and generalizing before sufficient data are collected.[36] Strang, regarding cumulative records in general, contends that teachers have not yet learned to observe the significant behavior of individual pupils, that records do not always provide headings for recording certain significant items, and that persons lacking a "professional attitude toward confidential personal data may use it to the detriment of the pupil."[37] She urges the cultivation of a professional attitude toward personal data, "such as that characteristic of a social worker, doctor, or psychiatrist."[38]

CURRENT PRACTICES

A great many questions may be posed concerning current record-keeping practices. These include:

- What kinds of pupil record-forms do schools use and how much do they vary from school system to school system?
- What kinds of information are contained in school records?
- How adequate are pupil record-forms for recording information?
- Do schools keep complete records for all pupils? If not, what information is lacking for what pupils?
- How do schools use the information they have?
- Do schools *need* the information they have (and what information do they need that they don't have)?
- How accurate are school records?
- Who has access to school records?
- How much do parents know about what information schools have?

An accurate description of current record-keeping practices in American elementary and secondary schools is not a simple matter, for two reasons. First, as we have pointed out, educational policy is still primarily determined at the local level in this country, despite the increasing interest of the states and the federal government in education. This is particularly true of administrative procedures such as record-keeping. Consequently, record-keeping practices and procedures vary considerably. And second, like many aspects of education, formally stated policies and actual practice often diverge significantly. Moreover, many of the questions one might raise concerning school practices are not easily answered,

[36] Wrightstone, *op. cit.*, p. 134.
[37] Strang, *op. cit.*, p. 77.
[38] *Ibid.*

even by the most conscientious and informed administrator; for example, how much use do teachers actually make of pupil records? Inferences, therefore, from policy statements collected from various school systems, even if the latter were available, as to actual practices and their effect on pupils, parents, teachers, and the like are certain to be risky. The alternative, interviews with superintendents, principals, counselors, and teachers from a sufficient number of school systems to constitute a representative sample, is a major research project in itself.

Although some scattered bits of relevant data already exist from studies of related aspects of educational practice; for example, the Russell Sage Foundation program of research on the social consequences of testing,[39] to the best of our knowledge, a major study of pupil record-keeping practices has never been conducted. Given the dearth of systematic data concerning school policies in this area, we felt that some preliminary effort, short of a major study, should be made to outline empirically the dimensions on which record-keeping practices vary and to estimate roughly the amount of variance. Consequently, we undertook a mailed questionnaire survey of a small number of school systems selected so as to be as representative as possible (given the small sample size) of the various types of school systems in the country. No claim of scientific rigor can be made for the sampling technique (which is described below), and the questions we were able to ask provide only the barest minimum of descriptive data. Nevertheless, the results of this survey provide a better basis for a discussion of school record-keeping practices than any material available thus far.

Characteristics of the Survey

A short questionnaire was mailed to the superintendent of schools in 68 school districts in February, 1968. Completed questionnaires were received from 54 districts in 29 states after one follow-up communication. The school districts chosen were those surveyed in the Russell Sage Foundation study of testing practices in American secondary schools. The quota sampling technique used in the latter study is described in Brim, *et al.*[40] Because of the failure of 14 school systems to respond to the pres-

[39] See, for example, Goslin, *Teachers and Testing, op. cit.*, and Armor, David, *The American School Counselor*, Russell Sage Foundation, New York, 1968.

[40] Brim, Orville G., Jr., David A. Goslin, David C. Glass, and Isadore Goldberg, *The Use of Standardized Ability Tests in American Secondary Schools and Their Impact on Students, Teachers, and Administrators,* Technical Report No. 3 on the Social Consequences of Testing, Russell Sage Foundation, New York, 1965, pp. 17–24.

Table 1 *Background Characteristics of 54 School Systems*

Characteristic	*Number of districts*
Number of elementary schools in the district	
None	2
1–5	30
6–20	19
21 or more	3
Approximate percentage of male graduates attending college or junior college	
Less than 20	7
21–49	22
50	5
51–80	10
81 or more	2
No answer	8
Type of area most pupils in district live in	
Urban	4
Suburban	7
Small towns (under 5,000 pop.)	7
Rural or farm	25
Small towns, rural or farm and unincorporated areas	11
Approximate percentage of Negroes in district	
None or "virtually none"	30
2–10	6
11–50	13
51 or more	4
No answer	1

ent questionnaire, however, findings reported in the following pages must be viewed as tentative. Table 1 provides data on four background characteristics of school systems from which responses were received. It shows that our sample is composed primarily of small districts, located in small town or rural areas, whose pupils are predominantly white and of which approximately 20 to 50 per cent attend college or junior college. Three major urban school systems—Los Angeles, Baltimore, and Memphis—are included in the returns. The characteristics of our sample correspond roughly to the distribution of types of school systems in this country; the bulk of the nation's 20,388 operating school districts[41] being located in small town or rural areas and having less than five elementary schools. Nevertheless, it should be noted that these school systems enroll only a

[41] See footnote 4.

TABLE 2 *Types of Pupil Record Forms*

Type of form	Number of districts: Elementary	Junior High	High School
A. Standard form especially designed for local school system	16	11	14
B. Standard form designed by outside agency (testing company, state education department, etc.) and used in other school districts	28	24	28
C. Standard form designed by outside agency, but modified for use in local system	5	4	6
D. Both A and B	2	1	2
E. No standard form	3	3	2
No answer; no such schools in district, etc.	0	11	2
	54	54	54

small percentage of the school-going population;[42] consequently, administrative practices of the minority of large systems are of special interest.

In order to make the questionnaire as easy to complete as possible, no open-ended items were included and only basically descriptive data were requested. In addition to the questionnaire, however, superintendents were asked to send us blank copies of their current pupil record forms and any related materials. Actual forms were received from 32 school districts.

Record Forms and Files

Of the 54 school systems responding to our questionnaire, roughly a third indicated that they had developed their own standard pupil record form; 15 reported that they used commercially manufactured forms (in practically all cases, different forms); and 19 replied that they made use of state-approved forms. The remaining systems either could not be classified or reported using some combination of the above (see Table 2). Virtually all of the actual forms sent to us were different from one another in format detail although basic similarities were apparent. Included on all of the forms we received were the following kinds of data: (1) scholarship record (grades, etc.); (2) health record; (3) general background information (varying considerably in amount of detail, items included); and (4) subjective comments (by teachers, counselors, etc.) concerning characteristics of the pupil. All but one of the forms received contained spaces for

[42] For example, systems enrolling less than 600 pupils account for 53.7 per cent of all school systems in the country, yet only 4.2 per cent of all public school pupils attend such schools. *Education Directory: Public School Systems,* 1968–69, Part 2, Government Printing Office, Washington, 1968, pp. 5–6.

recording standardized intelligence and/or achievement test scores. In addition, many forms contained spaces for recording personality data (derived either from psychological tests or from ratings by school personnel), extracurricular activities, and outside interests (including reading, hobbies, and the like).

Besides information included on the pupil record *form* itself, other significant data are often contained in the pupil's permanent *file*. Table 3 presents a summary of school system responses to the question: "In addition to information recorded on the permanent pupil record *form*, what other kinds of records are kept about pupils?"

These data indicate that a variety of information may find its way into any individual's permanent file in most school systems. It is, of course, impossible to determine to what extent schools actually *do* maintain such records for any significant number of pupils, especially in cases where "occasionally" is given as the response to the question. An even more interesting question is: For what types of pupils are extensive records likely to be maintained, assuming that some pupils' records are more complete than others? We are unable to answer this question from our data. In most school systems responsibility for recording information in the permanent file is divided between clerks, teachers, counselors, and the school psychologist (if the school has one). Several factors may be assumed to influence the process by which individual pupil records are kept up to date. These include (1) the interest taken in specific pupils by teachers or counselors; (2) the amount of time teachers or counselors have for such activities; (3) the extent to which a pupil may have been absent (for example, on days when standardized tests were administered); (4) degree of parental interest in their children's progress which, in turn, is likely to cause school personnel to maintain more (or less) adequate records; and (5) the adequacy of record forms themselves. Systematic research on the record-keeping process itself is needed before we can estimate the relative importance of each of these variables or their cumulative effect on the completeness of pupil records in different kinds of school systems.

The small sample of actual record forms received from school systems surveyed reveals considerable diversity of practice with respect to the amount and nature of background information maintained. Table 4 shows the percentage of school systems that make provision for recording data on race, nationality of pupil or his parents, parents' occupation, siblings and birth order, and religion. Half of the forms received included a space for a photograph. Although less than half of the total number of forms received contained a place for data on race, it is of some interest to note

TABLE 3 *Information About Pupils Not Included on Permanent Pupil Record Form, but Kept Separately or in Permanent File*

Type of information	*Number of school systems*							
	In permanent file, but not on permanent record form		*Kept separately*					
	Always	*Occasionally*	*Always*	*Occasionally*	*Not kept*	*No response*	*Included on permanent record form*	*Total*
Anecdotal records	8	20	2	5	3	6	10	54
Notes on interviews with parents	9	16	6	5	5	4	9	54
Notes on interviews with pupil	8	17	7	5	6	3	8	54
Correspondence with home	16	9	15	3	6	1	4	54
Reports from teachers	14	10	7	7	1	9	6	54
Records of referrals	19	6	8	2	1	9	9	54
Special health data	21	1	12	0	0	15	5	54
Samples of pupil's work	6	14	4	11	12	0	7	54
Tentative program plans	8	8	10	8	11	1	8	54
Personality ratings	11	5	5	2	13	10	8	54
Diaries and autobiographies	4	9	4	4	16	1	16	54
Delinquency reports—other "high security" data	15	6	16	3	7	3	4	54

TABLE 4 *Pupil Record Forms Containing Spaces for Recording Selected Background Characteristics*

Background characteristic	*Percentage*[a]
Parent's occupation	84
Pupils' rank of birth (number of siblings, order)	53
Photograph	50
Pupil's or parents' nationality	44
Race	38
Religion	34

[a] Total number of forms received = 32.

that all but one of the record forms received from those school systems reporting any Negro enrollment made provision for recording race of pupil.

Uses of Pupil Records

As we have pointed out, data on actual uses of pupil records by teachers, counselors, administrators, and others are practically impossible to obtain. Impressions gathered from a number of educators, school officials, and outside experts, such as testing company representatives, lead us to believe that only rarely are pupil records used by school personnel to the extent that they might be used. Guides to record-keeping procedures specify a wide variety of uses to which pupil records may be put, including counseling pupils regarding future academic and employment opportunities, understanding discrepancies between aptitude and performance and helping pupils to work at maximum capacity, designing curricula and course content so as to meet pupil needs, recognizing the need for special services to individual pupils as well as groups of pupils, and so on.

Few school systems, however, make explicit administrative provision for facilitating the use of pupil records by school personnel, especially teachers. The records are available if teachers or counselors choose to make use of them and no doubt they are referred to frequently in individual cases. Counselors, of course, must consult pupil records regularly in order to assist students in planning their academic program, particularly at the secondary level. Data from a recent study of the social effects of standardized testing[43] indicate that elementary school teachers often receive their pupils' test scores routinely at the beginning of the school year. Other teachers report that they consult pupil records occasionally in order to obtain test scores and other information about pupils (in virtually all

[43] Goslin, Epstein, and Hallock, *The Use of Standardized Tests in Elementary Schools*, *op. cit.*, and Goslin, *Teachers and Testing*, *op. cit.*

school systems teachers have complete access to records of their pupils). In many school systems decisions regarding the assignment of pupils to homogeneous instructional groupings are made on the basis of pupil records, including test scores as well as grades. Parent conferences, whether called at the initiative of the school or the parent, often involve the transmission of information contained in the permanent record. Except in cases of routine counseling and administrative decision-making such as that involved in homogeneous grouping, however, the use of pupil records appears to be largely a matter of individual initiative on the part of school personnel. Thus, pupil records tend to be consulted primarily when special problems arise, either disciplinary or academic. Although many school systems encourage teachers to familiarize themselves with the records of their pupils to facilitate maximum individualization of instruction, time pressures on teachers, not to mention administrative regulations concerning curriculum content, impede this process.

Moreover, increased use of pupil records by teachers and others is itself a matter of some debate in schools. Many teachers feel that they do not want to know too much about their pupils' abilities, past achievements, and the like. They feel that their students should have an opportunity to start fresh at the beginning of each year, without teacher prejudice based on knowledge of earlier performance.[44] Teachers also have a tendency to believe that their judgment about the capabilities of their pupils is best and that earlier judgments (even those made by other teachers) are suspect.

In summary, pupil records are a resource to which school personnel turn when difficulties arise or when administrative procedures require a decision based on past performance, measures of intellectual capacity, or some other datum about pupils. We may assume that a great deal more information about most school children is collected and maintained in their permanent record files than is ever used by their teachers or counselors. The implications of this assumption will be discussed in a subsequent section of this chapter.

The Adequacy and Accuracy of Pupil Records

Figure 1 provides an example of a state-approved permanent pupil record form. Based on a review of actual forms received from 32 school systems, it is representative of a large number of school record forms,

[44] The effect of teacher expectations on performance of elementary school children is explored in Rosenthal, Robert, and Lenore Jacobsen, *Pygmalion in the Classroom: Teacher Expectation and Pupils' Intellectual Development*, Holt, Rinehart & Winston, New York, 1968.

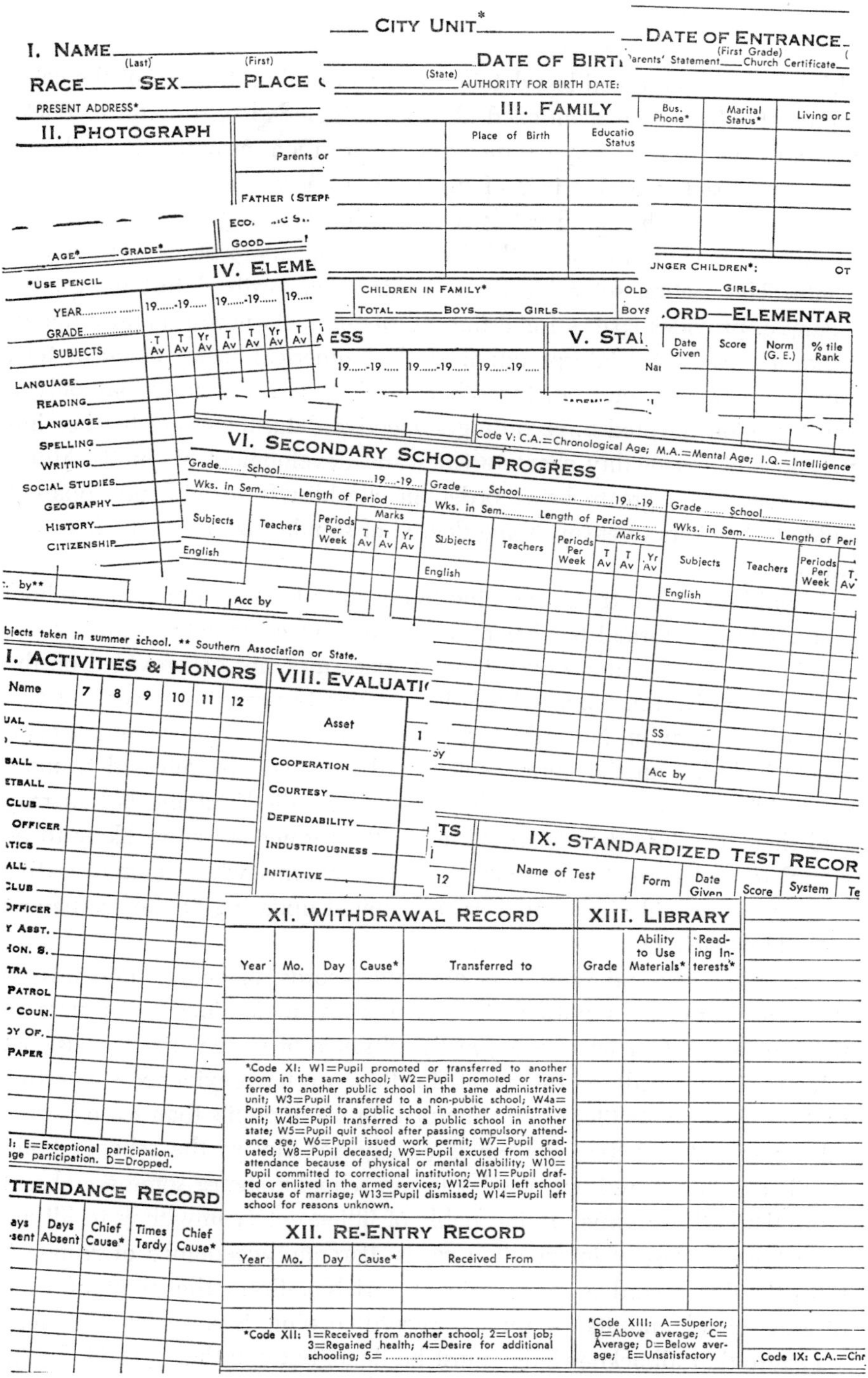

FIG. 1. Portions of North Carolina Cumulative Record–Grades 1–12. Used by permission of North Carolina State Department of Education.

although both more and less detailed files were submitted. All of the categories of information mentioned above are included on this form. Background data are relatively detailed and, in addition, provision is made for recording teacher evaluations of personality characteristics and the like. With regard to the basic categories of information—grades, test scores, health and background data—the form itself appears to be more than adequate. The section set aside for recording standardized test scores, for example, provides spaces for listing all of the facts necessary in order to make a meaningful interpretation of the numerical score; name of test, raw score, norms, etc. On the other hand, the record form has only a small section devoted to recording subjective data, including teacher impressions of personality characteristics and development of pupils. Moreover, these data are to be recorded in checklist form with no apparent guide to teachers to ensure some degree of standardization in their evaluation.

It will be recalled that, according to our questionnaire data, most school systems keep informal teacher observations and comments regarding pupils in the permanent file even though space may not be provided on the official record form. Some schools have separate forms for recording this type of information. Nevertheless, it seems likely that the summary comments included on the permanent record itself will be referred to more often than the occasional more lengthy and detailed statements that may find their way into the file. In addition, the former are more likely to be complete and correct, especially in school systems whose administrative regulations provide for annual or semiannual updating of the permanent record by teachers.

The adequacy and usefulness of pupil records, of course, depends on the conscientiousness with which records are maintained, regardless of the form used. Our impression, in the absence of systematic data, is that schools differ greatly on this point. Further, we have evidence suggesting that more complete files are maintained for some pupils than for others in all systems. The latter problem is clearly not always the school's fault. Pupils transfer in and out of schools and school systems; some are absent more than others; some are incapable of filling out or unwilling to fill out even the simplest of information cards. Parental acceptance of responsibility in this regard is an additional variable. From the point of view of the school and its personnel, record-keeping is a major headache —a chore that all acknowledge must be done, but one that is tackled with little enthusiasm by teachers and counselors alike. Given these facts it is little wonder that the adequacy and completeness of pupil records is less than one might desire in all cases.

The accuracy of records is another matter. Ensuring that pupil records are accurate is primarily a responsibility of the school and school personnel. Once again we find it impossible to judge, on the basis of available data, the extent to which school systems live up to this responsibility in general. The problem is twofold. First, to what extent do clerical and other errors creep into the record-keeping system and go unchecked throughout the pupils' school experience? Second, and more important, how accurate are the measures which are the basis for the data recorded?

Regarding the first question, little can be said except to observe that errors are a normal part of every clerical procedure. School systems are no exception to this rule, but they do have the advantage of working with cumulative records, the responsibility for the maintenance of which is divided among many different individuals as the pupil moves through the system. Early mistakes may be caught and corrected through vigilance on the part of each new recorder. Administrative procedures and guidelines should acknowledge the possibility of prior errors and make provision for rectifying them when discovered. The recent adoption of computerized record-keeping systems by several school districts may make detection of errors somewhat more difficult unless extreme care is taken by school personnel. The more frequently that records are examined by teachers, counselors, parents, and even pupils themselves, the more likely it is that mistakes will be discovered and corrected. The eventual widespread use of computers in schools, therefore, should be accompanied by policies encouraging more frequent access to school records by parents, as well as school personnel.

The accuracy of measures of pupil performance, intellectual capacity, and character development is a much more critical issue. The usefulness, as well as the very legitimacy, of school records depend on how accurately they describe the capacities and progress of individual pupils. Teacher reports of academic achievement are, of course, the core of any individual's record. Because of the cumulative character of this record, the care with which it is maintained, and the fact that it is made up of more or less independent judgments by many different teachers, it generally may be assumed to be an accurate assessment, when taken as a whole. Moreover, this is the part of the record that parents routinely see through grade reports, thereby giving them an opportunity to protest what they perceive to be errors, inaccurate judgments, or inequitable treatment.

However, measures of intellectual *capacity* (for example, standardized intelligence test scores), may be, *in particular cases,* less reliable. Standardized tests, especially measures of intelligence or scholastic aptitude, are administered (in most school systems) with less frequency than that with which teacher evaluations are recorded; scores tend not to be reported to parents or pupils (see following section on Access to Pupil Records); and test results may be very difficult to interpret in individual cases due to special circumstances. The test records of some children may be inaccurate or incomplete for a variety of reasons: absence on the day standardized tests were administered; low motivation to work on the test; inordinantly high anxiety leading to poorer performance than might be evidenced in other situations; special intellectual handicaps, such as reading or language difficulties; health problems such as poor eyesight, and so on; and clerical errors or simple neglect in recording scores.

We should emphasize that all of the evidence regarding the validity of standardized tests supports the view that they are extremely useful indicators of individual capacity and performance. At the same time, it is recognized that they are not perfect measures even of achievement. A growing body of literature on the social effects of testing[45] has raised a number of issues that have direct relevance for the policies of schools regarding test score recording and interpretation. General conclusions that may be drawn from these studies and others include the following: If standardized tests are to be used at all in schools, (1) they should be given frequently enough to permit children to gain experience in taking them and to have an opportunity to erase an unusually poor performance; (2) too much emphasis should not be placed on one or two scores, especially when those scores are derived from tests taken early in the child's educational experience or there is evidence of significant discrepancies between the child's performance on different tests or between test scores and classroom performance; (3) increased access should be given parents to information about their children based on standardized tests; (4) care needs to be taken in recording test scores in a pupil's permanent record to make sure that numbers are supplemented with adequate information concerning the type of test involved, what the numerical score means in comparative terms, the conditions under which it was given, and any

[45] Goslin, David A., "Standardized Ability Tests and Testing," *Science,* no. 23, vol. 159, (February, 1968), pp. 851–855; Goslin, David A., and David C. Glass, "The Social Effects of Standardized Testing in American Elementary and Secondary Schools," *Sociology of Education,* vol. 40 no. 2 (Spring, 1967); Goslin, David A., "The Social Impact of Testing," *Personnel and Guidance Journal,* March, 1967, pp. 676–682; *Teachers and Testing, op. cit.;* and Armor, *op. cit.*

mitigating circumstances that might account for unusually low (or high) performance by an individual child.

Evidence gathered thus far leads us to assert that school systems need to give more attention to this aspect of their record-keeping procedures and practices. Responses to our prior studies, along with questionnaires on record-keeping practices and the actual record forms received, indicate great diversity of practice on the part of schools regarding the extent to which tests are given, how they record test scores, the uses they make of this information, the amount of access pupils and parents have to test results, and the like. Our general impression is that many, if not most, school systems have tended to deal with the recurrent controversy over standardized testing by doing everything possible to avoid calling undue attention to the school testing program. Most parents, of course, especially those who take an active interest in school affairs, know that their children take standardized tests. But most systems still do not regularly provide parents with reports of their children's performance on standardized intelligence tests and give interpretations of the information in their files only when parents explicitly request such information, which few do. School policies in this area clearly need to be made more explicit and open, both for the benefit of the school in making the best use of its records, and for parents and children who should know on what information the school is basing its decisions.

Similar criticisms may be advanced regarding measures of character and personality development that find their way into pupil records. Here, especially, problems of standardization, accuracy and comparability of judgments, and completeness of records abound. There is no easy way of checking the validity of teacher judgments that appear in a child's permanent record. Most record forms do not provide sufficient space for teachers to make detailed evaluations, even if they were capable of making them. Personality tests have been widely criticized as being of too uncertain validity for use as anything other than research devices and some school systems have stopped administering such tests except to individual pupils in clinical settings (see, however, Table 6 below). Nevertheless, school records usually contain an assortment of data concerning nonintellectual characteristics of pupils, the validity of at least some of which may be questioned, in part because of its source and in part because of the lack of adequate standards and techniques of measurement. The solution to this problem lies not only in the development of improved measures, but also, as we have pointed out, in the attitude of schools toward the information they possess.

TABLE 5 *Number of School Districts Reporting that Various Individuals Have Access to Entire Permanent Record, to Part of the Record, or to None of It*

Individuals	*Have access to entire file*	*Denied access to entire file*	*Denied access to part of file*	*Access depends on circumstances*	*No answer*[a]	*Total*
School nurse	31	0	10	4	7	51[b]
Teachers	43	0	3	3	5	54
Parents, guardians, etc.	8	20	14	8	4	54
Prospective employers	9	20	16	5	4	54
Pupils	5	26	13	7	3	54
Juvenile courts (without subpoena)	23	12	7	6	6	54
Local police officials	18	14	9	8	5	54
Health Department officials	21	18	5	5	5	54
CIA, FBI officials	29	12	1	8	4	54

[a] Includes inappropriate responses or conflicting answers.
[b] Three school systems reported "no nurse."

Access to Pupil Records

Explicit and detailed school policies regarding access to pupil records are rare. Expressed general policies vary greatly from district to district, and we have every reason to believe that actual practices often deviate significantly, even from these broad guidelines. According to data gathered in our survey of school superintendents, most school systems give teachers and other school personnel complete access to pupil records, although a few report that they withhold personality data, reports of other teachers, and delinquency reports from teachers. About a fourth of the districts indicate that teacher access to pupil records depends upon the situation. In the case of most other potential users of school records, including parents, pupils themselves, prospective employers, the courts, police, health department officials, and federal investigators (CIA, FBI), policies vary considerably.

Table 5 summarizes the responses of superintendents surveyed to a question regarding access of various individuals to the entire permanent record or parts of it. Some interesting patterns are apparent in this table, although caution should be used in interpreting and generalizing from the findings presented. These data, however, are at least suggestive of the attitudes of school superintendents, if not of actual practices. Most significant of the findings is the fact that parents and pupils are more often *denied access* to school records than any other category of potential users. Nearly half of the superintendents (22 out of 54) reported, for example, that parents in their school systems do *not* have access to any part of the permanent record. Only eight superintendents indicated that parents may have access to the entire file despite legal precedents in at least one state (New York) establishing the right of parents to look at anything in their child's permanent record.[46] On the other hand, more than half of the superintendents reported that juvenile courts or CIA and FBI officials would be given access to pupil records without a subpoena. Where parents and others are denied access to parts of the permanent record, these parts are most frequently test scores, personality data, teacher reports, and other confidential documents such as delinquency reports, according to our questionnaire responses.

Once again, it must be emphasized that the responses to our questionnaire may not accurately reflect actual practice in many school systems. For example, in many school districts whose superintendents indicated that parents were denied access to their children's records, some parents undoubtedly *do* have an opportunity to examine these records. What is particularly significant, however, is the impression that school officials have strong reservations about giving parents very much information (other than routine grade reports and sometimes achievement test scores) about the content of evaluations that are continually being made of their children. The ethical, legal, and social implications of this practice will be discussed in a subsequent section.

TRENDS AND FUTURE PROSPECTS

Schools have increasingly been charged by their constituency with responsibility for making sure that students work up to their capacity, with overcoming deficits created by cultural deprivation during the preschool years, and with helping pupils to choose careers appropriate to their skills and interests. No longer do we conceive of the school simply as an institution offering certain kinds of training and knowledge to those with the interest and energy to learn. The school is expected to take positive action to motivate pupils, to understand their problems, and to remedy their deficiencies, both academic and personal. The school is put in the position of seeking and trying to make use of more information about its pupils. In addition to keeping a record of how much Johnny has learned, the school must also try to find out why Johnny *didn't* learn, how much Johnny *should* learn, and what the school can do to help Johnny learn more, if it is to do what is expected of it.

The result of these changes in the conception of the school's responsi-

[46] Van Allen v. McCleary 27 Misc. 2d 81,211 NYS 2d 501 (Sup. Ct. Nassau Co., 1961).

bility has been an increase in the amount of personality data and qualitative evaluations of performance collected by many school systems. Table 6 shows the responses of our sample of school superintendents to the question: "Can you discern any noticeable trends in your school system during the last five years with regard to the collection of personality data on pupils and qualitative evaluations of pupil performance?" A substantial majority of school systems report an increase in the collection of this type of information, and only one system indicated that there had been a decrease. Therefore, despite public skepticism over the usefulness of personality tests, we appear to be safe in assuming that school records will continue to contain more information concerning personality characteristics of pupils, though not necessarily derived from standardized tests and inventories.

There is considerable evidence that school records have become increasingly detailed and similar in format during the past two decades. State departments of education, through regulatory acts as well as advisory services, have had a great deal to do with this trend. Requirements regarding the reporting of attendance and other data from localities to the state have played a major role in stimulating the development of pupil record-keeping procedures from the beginning of state regulation of local educational systems. As the states, and now the federal government, take a more active role in education, we may expect to see further evidence of this influence on elementary and secondary records. In addition, the development of computerized record-keeping systems may be expected to lead to further standardization (and elaboration) of pupil records, as well as greater reliance on easily codeable measures of pupil performance (such as standardized test scores) and other individual characteristics.

Studies of school testing programs have indicated that there is a discernible trend in the direction of greater openness on the part of school systems, at least as measured by policies regarding the reporting of test scores to parents and pupils on a routine basis. As parental awareness of the kinds of records and other information maintained by schools increases, we may expect greater pressure from parents for access to this information and a corresponding increase in the willingness of schools to make data available to them. Assuming a gradual increase in the sophistication of parents about the meaning of test scores and other indicators of development and adjustment, this trend may be judged to be of potential benefit, not only to parents, but also to the school, since it will provide a necessary check on the accuracy of record-keeping systems.

Another major trend in school record-keeping practices is the increas-

TABLE 6 *Trends in Collection of Personality Data and Qualitative Evaluations*

	Number of school systems reporting							
	Substantial increase	*Slight increase*	*No change*	*Slight decrease*	*Substantial decrease*	*Do not know*	*No answer*	*Total*
Personality data	16	21	9	1	0	1	6	54
Qualitative evaluations	14	22	9	1	0	3	5	54

[a] Responses of 54 school districts to the question: "Can you discern any noticeable trends in your school system during the last five years with regard to the collection of personality data on pupils (personal inventories, psychological reports, etc.) and qualitative evaluations of pupil performance (teacher descriptions, etc.)?"

ing interest in the development of computerized information storage and retrieval systems for school use. Rapidly advancing computer technology has made possible centralized data storage installations that are economically and technically practical for large school systems or for groups of smaller systems. The Cooperative Plan for Guidance and Admission (CPGA) developed by Educational Testing Service,[47] for example, is designed to increase the amount and kinds of information recorded about each student in comparison with conventional records, as well as to provide easier access to such information. Using large-scale computers, it generates comprehensive student reports containing complex analyses of course grades and credits, learning situations experienced, and class rankings. A variety of other types of information may also be stored, including attendance records, home and family data, test record, extracurricular activities, work record, and a summary of descriptive scales concerning personality and behavioral characteristics. A unique advantage of computerized record-keeping systems, in addition to ease of access, is their capacity for analyzing, in combination, a number of items of information about an individual student and presenting results of the analysis in easily understandable form. Wesley Walton[48] suggests, for example, that by the early 1970's it will be possible for individual schools to maintain CPGA type records on magnetic tape. A centralized computer facility could then provide immediately a profile of a student's status at any point in time, including both academic and nonacademic data.

A centralized record-keeping system has already been adopted by the state of Florida. An IBM 1230 Optical Scanner enters identifying data for all pupils in the state into a computer at the ninth grade. Grades, test scores, and activity records are then fed into the computer at the end of each succeeding year. The result is the Florida Student Computer Record containing the following items of information: social security number, name, grade, school, address, type of curriculum, date and place of birth, citizenship, health and physical disabilities, sex, race, religion, marital status, family background, languages spoken at home, academic record, honors, work record, test record, and extracurricular activities. A similar data processing system is currently being designed for the state of Iowa, and other such systems will no doubt be in use within the near future.

As the capacity of computers expands and school systems gain experi-

[47] Walton, Wesley W., "Data Processing as an Administrative Tool in Educational Records," *Innovation and Experiment in Modern Education*, Report of the 29th Educational Conference sponsored by the Educational Records Bureau, American Council on Education, Washington, 1965.

[48] *Ibid.*

ence with automated data processing systems, it seems very likely that the great majority of our schools will adopt some form of computerized record-keeping. While this development will no doubt make it possible for school records to be used in more useful and imaginative ways, it also makes it doubly important that schools take special precautions to ensure the accuracy of the data being recorded. Moreover, it dramatizes the classic issues of privacy and right of access to individual records.

ETHICAL, LEGAL, AND SOCIAL ISSUES

School records typically contain two kinds of information about pupils. The first is the record of their activities and performance in school. It is comprised of the attendance record, teacher observations and evaluations, reports from counselors and other school personnel concerning their behavior outside the classroom, achievement test scores, a listing of extracurricular activities, and so on. The second type of data concerns the pupil's background, characteristics of his family, his out-of-school activities, and basic intellectual and personal qualities, including health, intellectual capacities, and personality dispositions. This distinction is an important one, since many of the ethical, legal, and social issues raised by current record-keeping practices have greater relevance to one or the other of these categories of information. Few persons, for example, would question whether it is legitimate and appropriate for the school to maintain records containing information of the first type. Clearly schools must have a record of the performance and activities of children in order to do their job. Who may see this information, however, and the conditions under which the school permits or does not permit access to it is a more serious question, with which we shall deal presently.

Collection and maintenance of the second type of information, on the other hand, poses the issue of the grounds on which the school may legitimately ask pupils (or their families) to reveal facts about themselves that may or may not be directly related to performance in school. Very important values in American society suggest that it is a basic right of individuals to decide to whom and under what conditions they will make available to others information about themselves. Correlative to this point, however, is the fact that participation in the society carries with it certain obligations and responsibilities. Further, the right of groups to demand information from those who aspire to enjoy the privileges of group membership is clearly understood. Thus, no one is likely to object to being given a driving test before being permitted to operate a motor vehicle. Similarly, few people object to the requirement that they must take an entrance test in order to gain admission to a university or college. In each of these cases, the right of a group, in this case the school, to information that is *relevant* to the stated objectives and goals of the group about members and candidates for membership has been established beyond question. Some important questions remain, however.

First, on what basis do we decide that certain kinds of information are necessary in order for the school to perform its function? As was pointed out above, school officials take the position that in order to do the things expected of them by the society, they must have a great deal of information about pupils. Measurement of intellectual capacity (for example, IQ testing) is defended on the grounds that the school's resources are limited and that pupils with different abilities have different educational needs. Measurement and recording of personality characteristics is justified by pointing out that understanding and compensating for deficiencies in performance, disruptive behavior, or other problems, requires knowledge of the "whole child," not just his intellectual capacity. Similarly, collection of data on family background makes it possible for the school to anticipate educational needs and deficiencies. That schools would cease to function if they did not have access to such information is doubtful. A strong case can be made, however, that in each of the instances information about pupils makes the school's task easier. Whether this is sufficient justification for *requiring* pupils and the families to divulge such information is a matter for continued discussion.

Second, having once established the criteria for assessing relevance (which we do not claim to have done), under what conditions does a group have the right to ask aspiring members for information that is clearly *irrelevant* to the purposes and goals of the group? To answer this question, it is necessary to make a distinction between public and private groups. It seems reasonable to assert that a private group has the right to ask applicants for membership anything it wants to ask them, relevant or irrelevant. In this case, it is up to the applicant to decide whether he wishes to reveal this information. In the case of a group supported by society as a whole, including all of the potential applicants to the group, this is a more difficult question. Would it be legitimate, for example, for the state to ask individuals to reveal information about their sex lives as a requirement for obtaining a driver's license? Most of us would object to such a requirement on the grounds that it represents an invasion of our privacy that is not justified by the service being rendered. Just such objections are being raised to the use of personality tests in schools, and there would appear to be justification for such objections, on the grounds that the questionable validity of many such measures renders them valueless to the school.

We conclude, therefore, that relevance and necessity are absolute prerequisites for the invasion of personal privacy in the case of publicly supported groups and agencies, especially with respect to public schools. In each of the cases presented above, the individual retains a choice as to whether he will submit himself to the test or not. Thus, if an individual does not want to take the College Board SAT, he doesn't have to. Nor does he have to submit to a driver's test. As a result of his decision he may have to give up his chances of attending Harvard or driving an automobile, but the choice in each case is his. But for the most part parents do not have a choice about whether or not they will send their children to school in our society. And once in school, a child does not really have any choice about whether he will fill out the required record forms or take the required standardized tests or not. A parent might move to a community in which the school system did not collect such information (if he could find one), or he might send his children to a private school that did not keep records or administer tests (if he could afford one). For most parents these are not realistic alternatives. Thus, most children or their parents have no choice about the kinds of records that are maintained about them and the information that goes into those records.

Given these circumstances we may make our criteria of relevance and necessity more specific by offering the following hypothetical situation. Suppose children (or their parents) exercised the right to refuse to take any tests given by the school. If a child refused to participate in classroom tests it would, in turn, be legitimate for the school to refuse to promote him to the next higher grade. Few would argue that schools should not have the right to require pupils to demonstrate their *proficiency in school subjects* before according them advanced status. If this happened, however, it would be the child's (or his parents') decision. But, on the other hand, what if the child refused to take an IQ or personality test given by the school, or to fill out the information form describing his family background? Could the school legitimately fail to admit him or promote him in this instance, assuming he was meeting school standards for proficiency in his daily work? Does the school need this information in order to evaluate his performance in school?

It is obvious that we have been straining credulity to make a point; namely, that school personnel have an obligation to consider carefully their reasons for collecting and maintaining certain kinds of information about pupils, especially in light of the access problems. In general, it is our impression that good and sufficient reasons may be advanced to justify the collection of most of the data gathered by schools, although often this information is not used to best advantage by school personnel. At the same time, parents should make a point of learning about record-keeping practices in their school system and exert responsible pressure on the school to require it to defend its need for information.

Once information of either the first or second type (or both) has been collected and entered into school records, the question of access to this information must be faced. Both the rights of certain individuals, such as school personnel, to make use of this information and the rights of the pupil (and his parents) to be protected from indiscriminate use of the information by nonschool personnel are involved. In addition, the right of the pupil or his parents to know what information the school possesses about the pupil must be considered. In the latter case, as we have suggested, at least one court has established the legal right of a parent to look at his child's permanent record, despite the fact that our data show this practice to be contrary to the policies of most school systems. Even assuming that school systems were to accept this judgment at face value, however, the legal definition of the permanent record requires further clarification, especially if school systems were to attempt to avoid revealing certain kinds of information (for example, test scores, clinical evaluations, and the like) to parents by claiming that it was not part of the permanent record. The rights of the pupil in the matter also require clarification. Does the pupil also have the right to know what is in his record? Does he, under any conditions, have the right to prevent his parents from knowing what is in it?

Access of all nonschool personnel and some school personnel (such as teachers not responsible for a pupil, the research staff, and others) to pupil records is a very difficult issue. The major point of contention involves specification of the conditions under which data gathered for one purpose (namely, education) may be used for some other purpose without the consent of the individual (or his parents) from whom the information was collected. It is apparent from our questionnaire responses that schools frequently permit access to pupil records by a variety of outside agencies and individuals, in most cases, we suspect, without obtaining parental permission. Regardless of the strictness of school policy regarding access by outside agencies, all pupil records presently are subpoenable by the courts themselves. Counselors and school psychologists do not as yet enjoy protection from the law accorded lawyers and doctors with respect to immunity from subpoena for privileged communications.

As the amount of information collected and maintained by schools increases, especially that pertaining to the psychological adjustment and family background of pupils, careful consideration of these issues, perhaps culminating in legislation to protect the rights of all interested parties (including school personnel), is clearly indicated. In the meantime, existing school policies should be clarified and publicly stated. It is probably true that the frequency with which current discretionary policies of school systems result in harm to pupils or their families is extremely low. We may decide that the present system is the best one in the long run. Nevertheless, these issues should not be resolved by default.

3 *The Dossier in Colleges and Universities*

BURTON R. CLARK

SEVERAL MAJOR FORCES CONVERGE TO RENDER AMERICAN HIGHER EDUCATION an attractive place in which to build and maintain files. Preparatory agencies must everywhere certify their trainees; and, as Weber long ago emphasized,[1] approval by informal nod gives way in modern society to the written certificate. To certify some, while barring others, the training organization (the university or college) devises measures of performance that, when summed, produce an objective final judgment.

The marks of evaluation can be relatively simple, even kept in the backpockets of students, when, as in Europe of the recent past, external examinations carry the burden of selection. Those admitted constitute a sponsored small minority, and a traditional loose relation of student and professor centers on infrequent examination. Or when colleges are small, as in the early days in the United States, the records may all be kept in one drawer. But the signs, inscriptions, and traces of evaluation gush forth as from a mountain spring and flow down the corridors, requiring offices of

I wish to thank J. Victor Baldridge and Michelle Patterson for fieldwork and analysis that aided the preparation of this paper.

[1] "The 'Rationalization' of Education and Training," in *From Max Weber: Essays in Sociology,* translated and edited by H. H. Gerth and C. Wright Mills, Oxford University Press, New York, 1946, pp. 240–244.

keepers to dam and control, when, as in the United States today, the system is inclusive, the style is repetitive evaluation, and the organization is large.

THE SCOPE OF RECORD-KEEPING

The early move of the United States into mass higher education—from the nineteenth-century origins of the land-grant university to the twentieth-century realities of the public junior college—has made for easy entry, extensive student mobility, and selection by internal measures of performance. The traditional parental responsibilities of the American college have left a legacy of immediate supervision. The modern propensity to develop large campuses, with students numbering first in the thousands and then in the tens of thousands, has helped ensure that the frequent measuring will be objective, universal, and remembered in central files. As a result, nowhere else in the world is academic accounting[2] so highly developed. American universities cannot even dream of offering the degree on the word of a professor or a single examination at the end of four years. Our heritage and structure of higher learning demand semesters and quarters; courses and credit hours; reports about registration and grades; majors, minors, and transfers. Hundreds of markings must go down on paper and be added, subtracted, multiplied, and divided, before the student receives the certificate of approval. As a result, we have a large administrative class whose property is files.

Beyond the massive certification of students lies the requirements of managing a large work force and a costly physical plant. The University of California will reach an operating budget of a billion dollars by the mid-1970's; small universities operate at a level of fifty to one hundred million; even private colleges of 800 students will have a dining-hall budget of a half million, dormitory income and outlay of three hundred thousand, and an over-all scale of operations in which several men may be sent to prison if they cannot publicly and validly account for the annual disappearance of three million dollars. A pencil and the back of an envelope will hardly suffice. Elaborate files come into play to track the allocation of money to departments, residence halls, health facilities, business offices—and, at the large universities, to a host of professional schools, sub-colleges, and research centers. The money is spent primarily on personnel, academic and nonacademic, and each employed person becomes a unit in

[2] Stoke, Harold W., *Viewpoints for the Study of the Administration of Higher Education*, A Publication of the Center for the Advanced Study of Educational Administration, University of Oregon, University of Oregon Press, Eugene, Oregon, 1966, p. 18.

several files that track *him* as applicant, salaried worker, promotion prospect, taxpayer, contributor to Community Chest, and retired employee of thirty years hence. With the nonacademic force of clerks, cooks, janitors, and guards numbering as many as the faculty, a large university keeps multiple books on an employed population the size of a small city.

And then the college or university must keep track of its ever more elaborate dealings with the outside world, refining its records on alumni, federal offices, state executive and legislative officialdom, and oil-well owners. It is no simple matter to extract money from fifty thousand alumni; it requires special offices to order the relations of a campus with the federal agencies; it is foolish to send other than the fact-armed professional to testify before the education and finance committees of the state senate; it is sensible to work up an attractive picture, with some breakdown of costs, of a proposed new science building before invading the lairs of the wealthy.

In case there is some lingering thought that college files are the minuets of clerks, empty of meaning, let us ask: what happens to a student if his records are lost? The answer, with some assurance, is that the college will not graduate him, business corporations and public agencies will not hire him, graduate schools will not admit him, and he cannot even transfer to another program or major on the same campus. To have the college dossier fall behind the radiator is to lose viability, to have one's public self and social position eroded. Until the file is found or rebuilt, others cannot gain a usable social definition. They say, apologetically but directly: you are here in person and you tell us about your courses and grades, your steady virtues and accidental sins, but we must know more about you, from official sources, and we will see what we can do when the records turn up. College files are appreciated when they are missing, for it is then that we gain a full sense of the critical nature of routine papers.

Finally, the central materials kept on all students, personnel, and organizational units, large as they are, are only part of the campus paper domain. Departments and professional schools have their own records; each professor has his. The counseling office, hospital, and psychiatric service file information in line with their own needs and the norms of the involved profession. The security office is busy accumulating the information that will help it police and secure the campus. The American campus, especially a large one, operates many of the offices of a city—health, police, heating and lighting, sanitation. Part bureaucracy, part community, part profession, part polity, the campus is a heterogeneous social organism whose diverse parts pursue their work with the aid of ever larger, more complex sets of records. Then, too, the campuses of the country vary greatly, beginning with basic differences in purpose and form of control and ending with even greater differences in how they manage their affairs.

Because of the great internal differentiation of the single campus and the great variation among campuses, it is important in this chapter to point to dispersion and variety in record-keeping. The first section describes the primary central records that are somewhat uniform among campuses. The second part then takes up the many locations of the files within the campus and the variation in style of record-keeping that may be readily observed. The third section describes the differences in confidence and individual privacy in college record-keeping. The fourth section points to the use of the college record of the student after graduation. The final section enters into the problem of the behavior of students and faculty when they anticipate the files.

THE PRIMARY CENTRAL RECORDS

Students

The bulk of files in people-processing organizations normally focus on participating clients; the massive files of colleges and universities do indeed take the student as subject. Since he must be admitted, there are records on him in offices of entrance; since he must be moved through the organization, with periodic evaluation, there are records in files of passage; and since he must leave, with official certificates, there are records of exit.

The entrance filing is relatively straightforward and standard. The basic document is the transcript of prior academic work that expresses the assessments of high school personnel. The transcript is commonly complemented with a record of scores on national tests of verbal and mathematical ability and with several letters of recommendation. These outside papers typically arrive before the person and are handled independently of him, to help honesty and hinder tampering and personal influence. Then in addition to these submitted papers there accumulate the in-house ratings, numerical scores, and short statements by personnel in the admissions office, alumni representatives, faculty members of admissions committee, or whatever the combination of persons commissioned to review the outside papers and sometimes to interview or receive a visit from the candidate.

Within an evaluation period of a month or two, the individual assessor and the rating group as a whole must sum impressions into a short definition of whether and how the applicant is appropriate or inappropriate. Then we get such definitions of the person as the following: a bright boy

—a sure admit; an average student, son of alumnus—a marginal admit; good student, excellent athlete—maybe admit on athletic scholarship; good female student, strong artistic interests—not sure she will find what she wants here, but admit; only an average student—reject; a bright, neurotic oddball, will add to our diveristy—admit; poor academic record, but strongly motivated and improving—accept as long-shot. The summary definitions in the folders of applicants are the basis for the decision to admit. For those admitted and who choose to come, the summary ratings predict what the person will be like when he arrives, including usually some suggestion of how well he will do and whether he will present special problems. The key role of the records here is that of serving as basis for entry into the system. The secondary role is the establishing of an initial social definition of the student.

Upon arrival of the admitted student, the above documents move to the background and the records of passage begin to record organizational attention. These records center on short-run performance within the system and must absorb a vast amount of information, submitted by various professors, semester by semester, midterm to final examination, in each course. Colleges and universities never break down around this task, however, nor even come under major charges of inefficiency, since a standard operating procedure has long been worked out and firmly legitimated. The records have four notable characteristics: they are heavily quantitative; they are systematically accumulative over time; they offer easily understood profiles and averages, for both short and long periods of evaluation; they lend themselves to frequent reporting.

The key datum is the numerical or letter "grade" that the professor assigns to each student in each class, at the midpoint of the semester or quarter and then at the end of the "grading period." The midpoint grade is temporary, the end grade is permanently inscribed as the organizational judgment for the "course," the basic unit of academic accounting. The end-grades that a student has received for the courses he has taken in a semester, neatly assembled on successive lines of a record of performance, offer a profile of current organizational judgment: A, B, B, A, C; 93, 87, 84, 91, 75. As the student completes each semester, an identical type of recording takes place, and the record accumulates neatly. Each course has its place; it is a permanent line-item. Each semester has its place; it is a permanent set of line-items. Each year of performance and evaluation has its place, and can be seen fairly readily like the semester, as a profile. But since there are a large number of course ratings for the year, and even more for four years, colleges typically also add averages to the record for these longer periods of time. The record then not only clearly shows an evaluation for each course, and profiles of evaluations for sets of courses, but also typically offers: a figure to summarize all the judgments for the freshman year, another one for the sophomore year, another for the junior year, and another for the senior year; a cumulative average, as well, at the end of the second and third years; and the final cumulative average that becomes *the* college judgment. The student is then a 3.81 or excellent student; a 2.75 or good student, a 2.21 or average student; or his "standing" in his graduating class, comparing summary numbers, was fifth among 180, or "257/450."

The early averages and profiles suggest, at the time they are recorded, what the final judgment will be. When the later ones are set down and added in, the final assessment is defined. Thus prediction is systematically possible and increasingly dependable. Behind the semester, in turn, lies the shorter-term evaluation mark of the midterm; and behind that, in many cases, examinations that occur at shorter intervals of a week, or four weeks, in which marks of the same coinage are assembled. All along the time-line, from the Registrar and professor for the semester grades, and from the individual professor for the within-semester grades, the student receives official ratings. Organizational judgments are frequently reported, coming to the student a few days or weeks after the completion of a defined effort. He receives the line-items from the indelible grade record and hence knows "how he did"—was rated—in each course. He can quickly read the profile of ratings for the semester and year. If the average for the year, and the years, is not transmitted to him, he can compute it in a few minutes. Thus the student possesses an up-to-date organizational judgment, profiled and averaged, that is objective, simple, and universal. We shall later consider, in the last section of this chapter, how students anticipate and attempt to manipulate the frequent and increasingly final judgments.

The terminal judgment becomes the most important item in the records of exit. The core document, as the student goes out the door, is the grade sheet (called the official transcript) that lists, as mentioned above, all courses taken, the grades received, the grade-point-average for each year, and the summations for the years of work; and finally shows that a degree was or was not awarded, with distinction or honors if the record was outstanding. The grade sheet also notes any break in service, such as a leave of absence for a year. The records of exit, apart from this core document, may note health or discipline problems. They may include letters of recommendation, especially if the student wishes to build a set of records, normally kept in a "placement office," that may later be used in seeking a job.

Faculty

With so much file work to be done on each student, and with so many of them in the organization at any one time, relative to personnel, it is clear why the great bulk of college and universities files have these transient members as their subjects. Pound for pound, however, the files that count most have other subjects: personnel, primarily the faculty; and organization units, primarily the departments and the professional schools. These files are so important, and usually so sensitive, that they are kept only in high offices and by privileged clerks. It is not easy for outsiders to develop a deep, dependable sense of their intricacies. That they become ever-more important there is little doubt. On large campuses, the organizational memory of the conduct of faculty members must reside in systematic records; the means of allocating resources to departments and checking on their performance move from penciled figures and direct observations of the dean and the president to the systematic budget breakdowns and the surveillance of accounts provided by modern business machines. Here we shall restrict ourselves to the files on faculty that are used in evaluating their performance.

The basic dossiers of faculty members are usually not steadily and evenly assembled. The faculty is not evaluated as frequently as the students nor are they tested all at the same time. Men come up for review every two or three years—sometimes as infrequently as six years—and on an irregular calendar. The individual's file builds in spurts, with little added for several years and then much put together in a few weeks or months. The key administrative need in respect to faculty are documents upon which to decide reappointment, promotion, and tenure. A young man appointed as assistant professor for three years may receive almost no formal attention about his performance for the first two years; but then in a space of a month in the fall of the third year, he will be asked to submit copies of his published and unpublished scholarly work. The assembled papers will be reviewed by the senior faculty of the department or a committee thereof, to decide whether he should be continued as an assistant professor for another two or three years. The basic evaluation file may then again remain quiescent for several years, followed again by a burst of paper-gathering. As the man comes up to the critical decisions of promotion to associate professor and the granting of tenure, his assembled publications, letters of evaluation, and listings of services and honors are scrutinized more carefully and by more parties. If the senior faculty of the department decide in the man's favor, the dossier goes typically, first, to a faculty committee representing a segment of the campus much larger than the department, e.g., the social sciences, or the college of letters and science, or the academic senate, and, second, to central administrative officials.

At the point when the faculty dossier leaves the department, its contents take on heightened meaning. The evaluation of the man passes from those who stand closest to him, and hence are most likely to know him in ways independent of the papers, to those who are more removed and will have little or no basis for judgment, especially on large campuses, aside from the submitted dossier. On some campuses, the department chairman appears personally before the higher committee and can offer verbal comment along with the account of the man offered by the papers. But on other campuses, no such personal representation is permitted: the department head must also put his own assessment down in writing, along with the letters of recommendation that have been elicited from other scholars in and out of the college. The subject himself, the professor undergoing evaluation, never personally appears. The dossier is his lobby, ticking off his accomplishments in a curriculum vitae, praising him in letters of evaluation, and providing the copies of articles and books that are put on the judges' desks as Exhibits A, B, C, and D.

THE VARIETIES OF LOCATION AND STYLE

The volume of files on campuses is largely a derivative of size of organization and the modernity of academic management.[3] As a small college becomes large, it moves from informal to formal storage of information and from partially subjective to almost wholly objective marks of recorded evaluation. The academic widow who served as registrar as well as secretary to the president in the old college of three hundred students, keeping records as best she could in exquisite longhand, gives way first to a Registrar's Office of a half-dozen women and girls busy folding and filing cards and folders, and then subsequently to the males and machines that signify the arrival of business models of efficiency. The friendly grandmother poised behind the grille of the Registrar's Office is rendered inadequate by the requirements of keeping track of two thousand students. At twenty thousand, the handwork of the clerks becomes ludicrous and the

[3] For one type of exception to this rule, see "Community and the Files," pp. 79–80.

options close toward "scientific management." The formalization of academic information is proceeding rapidly.

Authority and the Files

Formalization does not mean complete centralization, however, for in trying to find out where the files are on the American campus we discover that they are everywhere. He who has authority in the modern organization has files. To hold important office is to have important information in the files. Compared to other organizations, such as business firms, government offices, prisons, and hospitals, authority in colleges and universities is diffused.[4] With the diffusion of authority goes a proliferation of the files.

Dossiers are independently invented in many campus locales and are not neatly stitched together. On a large campus, professorial rights and responsibilities alone create a thousand, two thousand, or any number of separate and unique files. Each professor has some files of his own, on students, courses, department matters, university committees and activities, outside correspondence, as well as on research work and good titles for unwritten books.

The departments, in turn, numbering fifty to seventy-five, gather and store much information, so as to order their own affairs and report to central offices. Some department files are based on categories widely used on campus, but others reflect the special tastes of department chairmen and secretaries, past and present. The style of the files varies greatly among the departments. A department chairman in Economics may outdo the central administrative offices in effective storage of information about the department's personnel and finances. A chairman in English on the same campus may, in all truth, never have mastered arithmetic, and will have been heard to say, upon the introduction of computers, "You mean now we will have to use numbers"?

The professional schools keep their own set of records, with differences among them as great as that among the departments. And then a number of "auxiliary services" sit apart from the central staff—the counseling office, the psychiatric service, the security office—and each becomes a separate accumulation of information about some students and faculty.

In brief, the important records of a college are spread around the campus, they vary greatly in how systematically they are kept, and the sets of

[4] Clark, Burton R., "Faculty Organization and Authority," in *The Study of Academic Administration,* Lunsford, Terry F., editor, Western Interstate Commission for Higher Education, Boulder, Colo., 1963, pp. 37–51. Reprinted under title of "Organizational Adaptation to Professionals," in Vollmer, Howard M., and Donald L. Mills, editors, *Professionalization,* Prentice-Hall, Englewood Cliffs, N.J., 1966, pp. 283–291.

records found in the many locales are composed of various combinations of common and unique categories. The first cause for this unusual state of affairs is the unusual diffusion of authority that is characteristic of colleges and universities.

But more is involved. Files do not simply trail behind authority but affect it; the distribution and nature of the files is a question of accrual and loss of authority. We find men at the center of the university, responsible for coordination of the whole, invariably fighting for uniform record-keeping by such subunits as the departments and the professional schools. The dean or budget officer tries to nudge the departments into using standardized forms on student matters, or faculty, or department budgeting. Where successful, the central official then has knowledge about departments, on an item-by-item and comparative basis, that is equal to or greater than the information possessed by the departments themselves. The right to ask for uniform reporting from departments has largely been won. But central coordinators have not prevailed to the same degree when they face the professional schools, especially the old powerhouses of law and medicine. We find the professional schools insisting on their own records, nonuniform with the rest of the university. Where successful, they protect or enhance their autonomy from central administration. The demand for separate and unique records, throughout the university, is always in part, if not fundamentally, a demand for autonomy.

Thus the files are weapons for many parties on campus and are used to enhance power by men in the "field" units, the departments and the professional schools, as well as by men in the central administrative offices. The files always contain hard data and uniform categories, compared with storage by personal memory; but they vary greatly among themselves in hardness and uniformity, and the style of the files can be predicted from the place of the holders in the organization. The decentralized offices store information in relatively soft and nonuniform ways. Closer to the student and faculty member and hence to the "complexities of the case," influenced by scholarly disdain for business procedure, and always much smaller than the whole, the departments and professional schools find ample reason to so order their files that they do not yield readily to the hard uniformity that would play into the hands of the center. The central offices, on the other hand, store information in relatively hard and uniform ways. Further from the individual student or faculty member and committed to equality of treatment throughout the campus, influenced by administrative disdain for sloppy procedure, and concerned with problems of the whole, the Admissions Officer, Registrar, Dean, and Vice-President find ample reason to so order *their* files as to enhance their own authority against that of the many offices scattered around the campus.

The extremes of file style are, thus, on the soft and nonuniform side, the professor who takes hastily scribbled notes from his vestpocket and places them in his file under headings that no one else can understand; and, on the hard and uniform side, the systems analyst, newly arrived with a battery of computers, who takes already quantified information from already-uniform records and places it in the programmed interior of the machines for extensive quantitative analysis and quick recall and summary of mountainous amounts of campus information. The computer center centralizes further the many files of the central offices; it devises new sets of categories for uniform reporting by the many decentralized offices and, after assembling the reports, quickly prints out summaries appropriate for perusal of comparative performance.

There is no doubt that the introduction of modern data-processing equipment on the campus leads to a centralization of records and affects the power structure accordingly.[5] Once the machines are seriously put to work to absorb the files of the campus, the struggle for jurisdiction and influence takes new forms: Who will be allowed to have in his own office, a "monitor," which at the push of a button can pull information out of the central computer? Who will have access to the "printouts" of the machine analyses? This battle for the computer file seems destined to take place largely within the ranks of the central administration, with various second- and third-echelon administrative officers seeking to maintain their traditional prerogatives against the new systems analysts. The central administration as a whole gains power over the departments and professional schools. Certain central officers will regularly receive printouts on all the departments and will be able at a glance to compare costs and performances, while the department chairman will only get a printout on his own department. The Registrar may get a monitor; the department seemingly has little chance of possessing this means of tapping into the condensed files of the campus.

Thus while thousands of men on the large campus will continue to hold information in their own way and in their own location, the computerization of the campus accelerates the trend toward (1) central filing, (2) hard data and system-wide categories and comparison, and (3) central authority. When used effectively, the computer is the master file and the campus computer center becomes the most important of the file locations.

[5] Rourke, Francis E., and Glenn E. Brooks, "Computers and University Administration," *Administrative Science Quarterly*, vol. II, no. 4 (March, 1967), pp. 575–600.

The varieties of file location and style on the American campus will not readily give way, since they are propelled and protected by strong centrifugal forces of professional and departmental specialization. But it is no longer difficult to imagine campuses where computerization establishes a dozen men at the center as the lords of the files.

Trouble and the Files

Routine files are generated by the requirements of ordinary administration. Sensitive and exciting dossiers are set in motion by deviant cases or events. When a student attracts the definition of being "in trouble," his folder raises its head out of the pack, flagged with special colors or set up for attention in special drawers. If he continues as "trouble," he becomes a fat dossier. A persistent "psychiatric problem" will have an active and sometimes bulging file folder in the private office of his main faculty advisor, the front office of the department, the academic dean's office, the dean of students' office, as well as in the records of the counseling-psychiatric services, with the various dossiers thickened by statements about the student's inability to make normal progress, correspondence with a governmental agency or foundation about the discontinuance of a fellowship, and copies of official action taken by the dean.

The more sensitive the information about trouble—observations about defects and deficiencies that stigmatize—the stronger the pressure to split dossiers into frontroom and backroom components. Whether about students, faculty members, or units of the campus, many college files are likely to receive comments that "would not be proper for others to see"—not even one's close colleagues or successors in office. Professors commonly engage in file-splitting, especially when filling some kind of formal departmental role, giving the secretary the relatively "clean" materials that could, upon call or accident, stand to be seen by many other eyes, and keeping for their own drawers the relatively "dirty" notes of personal comment in which a colleague is sharply downgraded, a student is strongly criticized, or a program or course is symbolically destroyed. Deans have an even stronger need to keep a backroom set of records, "personal files" that can be cleaned out or removed during the last nights in office.

The tendency toward a frontroom-backroom division of the files comes from conflicting requirements and demands—honest assessment versus flattery that maintains goodwill, a private smear versus an acceptable public position—and the split-file can often enhance one's capacity to serve two masters. The campus security officer, considered below in greater detail, is a center of tension on large campuses. As the job is currently defined by many incumbents, one gathers information about subversive students and drug-users on campus, among other duties, and shares this information with local, state, and national police organizations. But the incumbent is also typically under heavy pressure from students and professors not to gather, let alone share, such information. He sometimes even comes under direct order from superiors at the university not to keep "subversive" files—commands that violate the norms of the security establishment in order to secure the higher-education norms of academic freedom. The situation invites a host of adjustments in which files face in different directions and in which a front-room set puts on a public face for the other. One can even physically tear up the official frontroom files that excite students and faculty and are forbidden by one's superiors, while at the same time maintaining notes for one's personal enlightenment and transmitting one's noted impressions, by telephone and conversations, to files on the outside. Such adjustments, topped by careful answers, help one not to have to lie when challenged by the student reporter or the provost. The way to tell the truth most of the time, but still get the job done, is to establish a nomenclature and a division of materials that allows one's office and private files to meet the expectations of contrary groups.

Community and the Files

One ironic twist in the generation of dossiers in colleges is the great bulk of elaborate information secured and maintained on students in some small colleges that pride themselves on close personal relations. These colleges come closest to being communities; but much of what remains unwritten and informal in the small town, transmitted as gossip, is, in the most self-conscious of the academic communities, written down and made a part of formal record. This occurs precisely where faculties have tried to escape the coldness and narrowness of the number or letter grade by evaluating the student more fully, in the round, with long statements about his work, his attitudes, his maturity, his progress, his hang-ups. When the teachers of a number of seminars or courses are required to turn in such evaluations, or where a committee of faculty members is made responsible for periodic full assessments of the person, the result is bulky and uneven dossiers stuffed with personal comment about academic, psychological, and physical characteristics. "She is more neurotic than ever this winter, and very tired, and would probably benefit from a lighter load during the Spring Semester and from Ivar's course in psychology."

Thus small size in college organization is no guarantee of minimal record-keeping. Educational doctrine is also relevant. The small college cut from traditional cloth will largely collect simple academic markings from professors. The more complete knowledge about the student that accrues to professors in such places will remain in the disorder of personal memory, scribbled notes, and the gossip that flares for the day but disappears before a new year begins. But progressive small colleges, committed to a fuller interest in the student, especially in his personality development, will collect many assessments, qualitative as well as quantitative, and on "personal" or "nonacademic" characteristics as well as academic performance. These fuller dossiers must be kept from students, since they are replete with personal comment. They are likely, however, to be open to the registrar, the deans, the president, and interested teachers and advisors. The transcripts which go out for purposes of graduate school application or job employment may, in some progressive colleges, include copies of the professors' lengthy evaluations.

THE VARIETIES OF CONFIDENCE

The privacy granted the person in college files varies greatly both within the boundaries of a single campus and across the more than two thousand colleges and universities that constitute American higher education. Let us first consider the single campus, within which three modes of use and privacy can typically be discerned: (1) use controlled by norms of confidence; (2) action based on norms of sharing information; and (3) a situation, midway between the other two, in which the norms are weak and the use of file material is individualistic.

Within the Campus

The Norm of Confidence. Files may be guarded by the norms of a profession. On the American campus, the records of the mental health service are the clearest example. The work of the psychiatrist and clinical psychologist is based on an initial promise of confidence to the client; he attempts to enter into the most intimate and revealing recesses of personality and with some skill and a little luck comes up with, and writes down in the records, information that is socially "dirty" and has enormous potential for damaging career and adult status. Psychiatry and clinical psychology have attempted to develop powerful normative controls against leakage and circulation of such information. On the basis of a professionally developed conception, the therapist typically locks the file in his own office or places it in a secured area of the mental health office, defines his primary responsibility as to the student, and feels comfortable only in sharing the file with professional colleagues within the office. Professors and campus administrators, as well as outsiders, typically find access to the psychiatric files completely blocked.

This is not to say that full confidence is always maintained nor that therapists always uphold the professional definition. Some summary comment about the nature of the client's difficulty may be given to the dean, the academic advisor, and department chairman, as well as to parents. And upon deep provocation, e.g., a sensational murder, a campus therapist may completely throw over the norm of confidence, giving the file to the newspapers, to try to protect himself, or his staff, or the campus administration as a whole against charges of negligence or incompetence. There is some variation among campus mental health services in what information is routinely shared with others on campus; there are the cases of therapist panic that for awhile turn the mental health service into a public relations office.[6] But the professionally derived norms of confidence are powerful regulators of behavior in this sector of the campus.

The Norms of Sharing Information. The contrasting situation is found in offices where action is steered by norms of sharing information. The security officer is the clearest and most dramatic case. Campus security officers are not as universally controlled by the dominant norms of their occupation as the psychiatrists are in their field; there are conspicuous examples, especially among leading private colleges and universities, where the campus administration forces the security officer not to keep certain files and not to reveal to outsiders the information in the files that are kept, against contrary dictates of the occupation. But most security officers follow the occupational norms. They keep files on car registration, parking tickets, minor and major criminal violations.

The security office often has records on political activities of students under such labels as "subversive" and "suspicion of subversion" following nationally used categories based on the FBI standard filing system. Into these files go membership lists of such organizations as, in 1967, Students for a Democratic Society, Student League for Human Rights, and the Students Non-Violent Coordinating Committee, and the lists of student organizations that invite "subversive" speakers. If the membership lists are not available through normal administrative channels, student informers are used to attend meetings and otherwise get around on the campus. Information about political activities of students that comes in by correspondence or telephone, from faculty members, students, local citizens,

[6] For a sharp but overdrawn criticism of the tendency of some campus psychiatrists to share information, see Szasz, Thomas S., "The Psychiatrist as Double Agent," *Trans-action*, vol. 4, no. 10 (October, 1967), pp. 16–24.

and outside police authorities, is also put into the files. Newspaper clippings and photographs are also assembled. Some security offices also keep such files on faculty members and supply information to department heads, deans, and top campus officials.

It is an everyday working assumption of the majority of campus security offices that subversive files will be kept, complete, if at all possible, with photographs taken by plainclothesmen. It is also the normal assumption that the office will work closely with the FBI, including sending them copies of file materials. The security officer also shares his information with the local police, as a matter of course. And, finally, when asked for a character evaluation of a student by a businessman or a government agency, he will, as part of his job, typically supply an evaluation based upon the material in his files. The security officer, in contrast to the psychiatrist, expects to share information. He is part of a network of interorganizational relations devised for information-sharing purposes.

The security offices have also come alive in more recent years around the files headed "Suspected Narcotics." Information about drug use then also enters the information-sharing network. In the security files of the campus, drugs have joined politics as the place where the action is.

The Situation of Normlessness. A large number of dossiers reside in locations where neither norms of confidence nor of information-sharing are in control. The records kept by individual professors, for purposes other than recording test scores and course grades, constitute most of this domain. How private are these files? For any particular type of information, e.g., "psychological difficulties," can we predict whether professors will share such information and with whom? File privacy varies greatly from one professor to another and we cannot predict usage. One professor, a traditionalist by self-definition, will refuse even to recognize a student's psychological problems, let alone comment on them in writing to share with others. His colleague in the next office, somewhat more "modern" in self-definition, will note the problem, commit his impression to paper, but be reluctant to pass it on. Upon inquiry from the department chairman or the dean, he may or may not divulge fully his accumulated notes. A third colleague in the office around the corner, eager to fill the role of lay psychiatrist, will file much prose on a student's neurotic behavior and attempt to have this part of his own records enter into the mainstream of academic affairs.

Thus, when at the end of the year these colleagues evaluate in writing a disturbed graduate student, the first submits only an A or B or C, just as he does for other students; the second will write in a brief comment that "personal problems affected his academic performance"; and the third will append several paragraphs of comment, diagnosing the personal problem, offering a chronicle of its development during the semester or year, and suggesting treatment. In short, there is no agreement about what information should be kept, how it should be evaluated, and how much it should be shared.

Faculty members are able to predict one another's actions in this regard only as they come to know each other's personal styles. Students can only predict what about them, through the eyes of their professors, is becoming a matter of record as they too perceive the personal styles—something difficult for them to do because they are not a party to the meetings and correspondence in which the styles are most clearly revealed. Since students care deeply about evaluations being made, many, in the absence of norms, will be prone to the anxious guessing about faculty perceptions that generates student myths.

The files of department chairmen are more like those of the individual professor than those of the campus psychiatrist or security officer. The parts of their files that are constructed for reporting to central officers will be uniform and predictable; but the files that are used for internal affairs do not follow a manual or a norm and are relatively unpredictable. On a campus where most of the department chairmen would never consider doing such a thing, a physics department chairman, following his own politics or sense of national duty, may, with a loyal secretary, be keeping his own file of deviant political behavior. Most important, departments differ extensively in the information stored for evaluating faculty members, from no file at all (for long periods of time), to files bulging with bibliography, copies of letters offering positions at other places, evaluative statements by senior faculty, copies of published works, and even occasionally a testimony by a student to the man's teaching ability. The autonomy of departments, reflected directly in nonuniformity of files, contributes to nonpredictability in the privacy granted the person in the files.

"Open-Drawer" and "Closed-Drawer" Colleges

The three situations described above—confidence, information-sharing, and normlessness—can be found within almost all campuses. As indicated, the bulk of the scattered files, those of professors and departments, lean heavily toward the individualism of autonomous units. We can move one step further, however, and characterize whole campuses by degree of confidentiality, despite the heterogeneity of use found within campuses. The central administration will commonly have a discernible file style for its own offices, and its inclinations, together with the inclusive intellectual climate of the campus, will push the more scattered files toward or away from confidentiality, especially in regard to outsiders. Campuses have within themselves relatively open and relatively closed offices. The American system of higher education has within it both "open-drawer" and "closed-drawer" colleges.

Whether a college will keep its records open or closed to the outside is determined primarily by its form of control and secondarily by its administrative ideology. Public control encourages open files; private control, private files. An administrative ideology of service pushes toward openness; an ideology of scholarship pushes toward closedness. Since ideology is often adaptive, operating to rationalize and legitimate enforced lines of action, form of control is the fundamental determinant, with administrative doctrine adjusting to perceived necessity.

For purposes of easy typology and quick illustration, we can devise a fourfold classification based on public-private ownership and service-scholarship ideology. Arbitrarily weighing ownership twice as much as ideology, with simple scores of 1 and 2 for ideology, and 2 and 4 for ownership, we obtain the following picture:

		Ideology	
		Service (value = 2)	Scholarship (value = 1)
Ownership	Public (value = 4)	I The open-drawer college (value = 6)	II The modified open-drawer college (value = 5)
	Private (value = 2)	III The modified closed-drawer college (value = 4)	IV The closed-drawer college (value = 3)

Type I: The open-drawer college (e.g., the public junior college)
Type II: The modified open-drawer college (e.g., the public university, the comprehensive state college)
Type III: The modified closed-drawer college (e.g., the private city- or local-oriented college or university)
Type IV: The closed-drawer college (e.g., the leading private university, the high-prestige private college)

The type of college most open with its records is the public junior college, subject usually to local public surveillance, as well as state supervision and accountability, and possessed of a doctrine of "service to the community." Here is where an open-record policy can most often be found.

The college is free with its information and almost anyone can get some information about a student. "We are a public agency," reported a junior college official in an interview, "and we have a trust to the community to be candid about our students to people who inquire." Little protection may be afforded the student who has been in trouble, in or out of the college, in order for the college to be candid with prospective local employers. College officials are quite willing to give out information to businesses, credit associations, the military and other governmental agencies.

At the other extreme, the type of college most closed with its records is the elite private liberal arts college or university, free of accountability to public authorities and valuing ideas of scholarship and maximum autonomy from political pressures. Here there may even be an official publication of rigid rules of access, agreed on by faculty and administrators and approved by the trustees.

One graduate school of a private university will give out the following information: whether the student is or is not enrolled; the year of any former enrollment; on what page the student's name is located in the student directory. The officials will not even directly give out the address of the student, but will forward a letter to him. No other information is to be revealed.

One undergraduate college of a private university in a memorandum to the heads of university offices closely defines access. Access to the records is restricted to authorized university personnel; information will be given to authorized representatives of government agencies; the agents making inquiry must come in person and show their identification card; they may be given the following information:

Full name; names of parents and spouse (if any)
Birthplace and birthdate
Local and home addresses
Preparatory education
Dates of attendance
Degree received
Major field of study
Names of instructors, advisors, or job supervisors
Extracurricular activities on campus
Formal disciplinary actions, but not the reasons therefore

A memorandum of the agent's visit is inserted in the student's dossier—an act which suggests a host of future possibilities by way of counterinformation, files on those who use files, and, with escalation of hostilities, a war of the files.

Moving from the two extremes of open and closed records, the middle types are colleges where the tendency to one extreme or the other is seriously modified by contrary pressures. Large state universities, inclined by public ownership and state control to open the file drawer to the many other agencies of the state, are pulled back toward a policy of guarded disclosure by the strong opposition of many on campus. There are the administrators who believe in the importance of confidentiality of student records and also wish to protect the autonomy of the university; there are many in the faculty who think about the matter primarily from the perspective of "academic freedom" and "community of scholars"; there are the cogent arguments of the students that the outside use of college records affects adversely the educational processes of the campus. The better the faculty and student body, the greater the pressure for restriction on the use of the records. Administrators trying to assemble and keep a first-class faculty are under very heavy pressure from within to ward off the outsiders. Many administrators at the colleges and universities of highest university status will themselves be thoroughly imbued with the same values.

The private colleges and universities that occupy a modified closed-drawer position are usually ones that are dependent on a local, urban constituency and have adopted an ideology of service to that local population. Though private in formal control, the campus has the role of a public college: e.g., Long Island University, Boston University, the University of Pittsburgh of ten years ago, University of San Francisco, University of Portland. The private colleges that provide a local service commonly have relatively little endowment and do not have the leverage for autonomy provided by hallowed traditions and wealthy alumni. Some are run by conservative Catholic orders that are inclined both to provide strong guidance for the young and to cooperate with such conservative governmental agencies as the Federal Bureau of Investigation. There is a wide range of institutional styles among the campuses that fall in this middle category, as in the other middle category just discussed. A few are just a step away from the closedness of a Swarthmore or a Princeton; toward the other end, a much larger number approach the openness of a public college under close control and direct scrutiny of local publics.

USE OF THE FINAL RECORD AFTER COLLEGE

A student is not finished with a college when he graduates, even if he avoids the alumni association and tears up all letters of solicitation and reunion—and even if all the faculty members and administrators who knew him have advanced their careers by leaving the premises. The files still stand for him, and parts of that representation can be revealed five, ten, and even twenty years later to interested outsiders. He can be confident, or unhappy, that the written record remains steady. The professor's remembrance of the past student is likely to blur as later waves of students wash over the mind, and those who seek information expect the personal remembrance to become undependable; but the memory of the dossier fades only very slowly, if at all. The academic grades remain crystal clear; extracurricular activities are accurately recalled; the qualitative impressions of a professor or administrator, signed and dated, come back, with the slight fading appropriate to old pictures and the prose categories of yesteryear.

The substitution of the dossier for individual memory in assessments granted to outsiders is one of the most important effects of record-keeping in colleges and universities. The highest school years in a modern educational system are freighted with bearing on the life chances of the individual, serving as the final testing ground in the selection processes of the preparatory structure and as the now almost-essential door to the higher occupations and statuses. The college records are used heavily by outsiders in the year of graduation. The records of exit, reviewed earlier, go off to graduate or professional schools to which the student has applied, there to become the basic evidence for the decision to admit or reject. The corporation and government recruiters come to campus and go over the records of a number of students as well as arrange interviews with them. The outsiders study the grade record, course by course, semester by semester, year by year, looking not only at the summary terminal scores on over-all performance but also for patterns of improvement or decline, for specific strengths and weaknesses. The record is *the* organization voice, in the final summary judgment, but at the same time speaks with many voices, in the numerous parts to which so many professors have contributed an assessment.

Three or four years after graduation there may still be heavy inquiry for which the files provide the answers, and the answers can become evermore important as the former student, now junior executive, middle-rank government official, young academic, moves further into the tapering funnels of the world of work. As the criteria of selection toughen—can he stand major responsibility, can he really work well with others, does he have an independent mind—the evaluators double-back on the record, scrutinizing more closely for strengths and weaknesses in academic and work performance. ("Read that part again, please, in the letter of recommendation from his professor.") Has he really outgrown the tendency to slump under pressure? Even ten or twenty years later, the recordings of college performance and behavior will be called up. An "underachiever" in college may find this definition following him for many days of his life.

Certain college offices specialize in providing effective organizational memory of students, with the placement office as the significant case. During the last year before the student leaves college for work, a placement office attempts to assemble the grades, scores, and assessments that will be sent to outsiders upon their request or that of the student; to have the file reproduced so that copies may be sent to a number of places at one time; and to get these copies out promptly to assist the student in the job market. Attempts are also often made in the years after graduation to keep the files up-to-date, particularly if a student wishes to reactivate his inactive file. The records are kept available for a long time; they can also be handed on to another placement office if the student goes on to more advanced academic work at another place.

The procedures of one placement office at a private university, for example, include the following:

1. Students are urged to register with the office in the fall previous to the year in which they wish to begin teaching (in colleges and universities as well as secondary schools). This enables instructors to make recommendations as to "scholarship, teaching aptitude, personality and character while still in frequent contact. Even though a student may secure his first position himself, he will find it useful in later years to have established a file containing, along with other materials, six or more letters of recommendation which might be difficult to obtain when applying for future positions."
2. "As soon as the dossier is assembled, copies are made so that they may be sent to a number of institutions at one time."
3. "Once a registrant is employed, his record will be placed in the inactive file until he wishes to reactivate it when seeking a new position. Upon request, preferably in the summer or early fall of the year preceding the year of a desired new appointment, he will be sent instructions for reactivation procedure and forms for submitting new information and reference letters to be added to his file. In this way, a registrant may be assured of an up-to-date dossier which serves as a cumulative record during his entire professional life."
4. "Inactive records are kept on file for twenty years, after which they

will pass under the jurisdiction of the University Librarian of Historical Manuscripts."

5. The supervisor of the placement office points out to faculty members that even though "some of you are able to take the time to write individual letters of recommendation to each university where your students are applying for positions, the value of a permanent and cumulative file in this office should not be overlooked. The advantage to the student lies in the ready availability of his [college] references in later years when he may be seeking a new position and the references from his first positions, for one reason or another, may not present an adequate picture of his qualifications."

The files of the exit offices, then, not only specifically and concretely extend the influence of the college on the student into the years after graduation; they also extend influence vis-à-vis other organizations, e.g., the places where the early positions are held. The dossier collapses time, allowing the college to move from the past to the present in the biography of the student now ten years out of its halls. Without the dossier, later organizations, recording their impressions of performance and promise, will supersede the college. But with the dossier, the college can remain in contention, presenting data and maintaining, upon disagreement, that the later assessments did not present "an adequate picture." College assessments have legitimacy, having been made by independent assessors at a critical age in the training and development of the person and before he is subjected to the vagaries of the settings of work. When these old but creditable estimations greet the hiring executive on Monday morning, 9 A.M. sharp, placed on his desk by a letter of transmittal, they may appear as the fundamental ones. At least they must be considered, weighed in the hiring scales, along with the statements of recent employers.

THE PROBLEM OF ANTICIPATION

Personal anticipation of the dossier will be strong in the senior training institutions, since the accumulative official definitions of the person bear so directly on the early steps of the work career. The official definitions lead to the granting or withholding of the certificate of completion. For those granted a degree, the final record defines its quality, ranking the student as high or low among degree recipients. With such important distinctions being made, to be used after college by outsiders, students must anticipate throughout the college years the permanently recorded results of present behavior. This includes the anticipation that notes on social or political deviancy, and even errors of clerks in filing papers, may unfavorably shape the permanent file.

Beginning in his first semester, the student interacts significantly with the records of passage. He guesses at how well he is doing, anticipating the assessments that are forming and being recorded. The quantitative symbols that express the assessments are communicated to him within a few days after they are made, e.g., after any important examination, after the end of the semester. As the student anticipates and receives the summary definitions of performance, he decides how further to apportion his time and effort—to add more courses or to try to take fewer; to seek more difficult courses or easier ones; to balance three difficult courses next semester with an easy one—a "gut" or "Mickey Mouse"; to turn away from a prospective major or delve more deeply in it; to concentrate effort only on course work or to read interesting books; to get a tutor; to give more time to a sport, to date more frequently; to become more excited or more cool; to move with the system or against it.

As the student reacts to the results of the semester or the academic year, and defines what he should do in the time still left in his passage, he may tune to the impression held of him in the mind of a professor or two, whether verbally conveyed or surmised. The setting permits this and it will happen occasionally. But what the student characteristically reacts to, especially on large campuses, is the accumulating central record, held by the Registrar, that is larger and more powerful than the pictures in the minds of the individual professors. The profiles and averages of that record provide easily assimilated global judgments. The judgments received are not only indelible in themselves and made a matter of publicly accessible record, but increasingly, over time, take on finality. Since the profiled and averaged record of performance is the impression that most defines the student, within the organization and especially after he leaves the system, it is the one that he wants most to manipulate. In an important sense, the professors that he faces are means to this end.

The feedback of recorded official definitions is always of some importance to the participating clients of people-processing organizations, since the self-definition of the person must absorb, fend off, or otherwise handle these important impressions. Am I really that sick—that criminal—that stupid? The organizational feedback leads on to personal feedback, however, primarily to the degree that there are options for action. Those defined as sick in some form, and thereby located in a general or mental hospital, may have little room to maneuver, constrained by debilitating effects of the illness, the sanctioned and respected professional decisions and rights of the doctor, and sometimes the force of legal commitment. Those defined as lawbreakers, and thereby located in a prison, generally have some room in which to maneuver, since "good" or "bad" behavior in the system will usually determine early or late release under the terms of the original assignment. Since incidents that go down as "bad" in the record can prolong the stay in prison, those that want to be released as soon as possible must steer their own behavior and attempt to manipulate the guards and other prison officials to the end of not having adverse judgments inscribed.

Students, even more than inmates, are in a situation that encourages attention to the contents of the dossier. The long-term consequences of the cumulating judgment may not be as poignant as they are for the "criminal," but they are nonetheless real. The student knows that he will come out with a record. The best predictor of what that record will be is the accumulated official definition that is read back to him at frequent intervals —more frequently than the assessment received by the prison inmate. Most important, the student has a wide range of alternatives in acting back upon the record. As noted above, there are a host of simple, approved devices immediately at hand by way of changing one's work load. If such changes do not improve an "unsatisfactory" record, the student can move on to more drastic actions: change one's major, in pursuit of an "easier" field; embrace some forms of cheating, from the normal ones of roving eyes and whispered answers to the highly dangerous acts of stealing copies of the impending test, doctoring the written record, and sending a substitute to take the written examination; and, finally, withdrawing on a leave of absence, or dropping out altogether and transferring to another college that has the promise of more gentle official definitions.

Knowing that the final record affects job placement and adult status, aware of most of the above means of affecting the record, and receiving frequent assessments, the student, among all the actors of people-processing institutions, will have a high degree of dossier consciousness. He *may* care about what a professor thinks of him; but he *must* care about what the dossier says about him. The professor's judgment contributes to the global organizational judgment, but the rating of any one man is submerged in dozens of ratings submitted by others. When bureaucratic means predominate in the making of the terminal judgment of the student, then the accumulating central record will be the end-in-view.

But then the anticipations of students are not all of similar nature. Students like anyone else must divide their file worries into the normal and the problematic, the dependable and the undependable. The academic record is a normal, dependable worry. Good grades are recorded as good grades; bad as bad. The qualitative comments about academic performance that go in letters of evaluation are less dependable than grades; but they can still be predicted, and somewhat controlled, since the student asks for letters from professors with whom he has done the best work, with reasonable hope that they will manage to praise him. The steering of one's behavior to enhance the academic record is a routine anticipation, heavily influential in the allotment of time and energy, often full of anxiety, but all in all done in accordance with age-old traditions and nigh-universal rules of the game. Undergirding all is the wide and deep acceptance of academic evaluation as necessary and proper in academic institutions.

Other records are more problematic and undependable, however, stimulating serious worry. For those who have entered the portals of the mental health service, the psychiatric guarantee of confidence must be weighed against knowledge that the service is part of a bureaucracy in which serious actions are normally reported and transmitted to other offices. The psychiatrist may well maintain full confidence about the interior of the analysis, but a student must still anticipate that something about the type and depth of his difficulty, its cure or persistence, its impact on future academic work and adult adjustment, will move from the mental health service to the dean of students' office, the academic dean's office, the department office—to a parent, to a part-time employer on or off campus. In his "responsibility" to the student-patient as well as to others around the patient, the psychiatrist may feel he needs to spread his knowledge, to help others understand the behavior they see and to anticipate behavior yet unseen. Both postclinic patients, and preclinic potential patients, are likely to find this a tricky domain to anticipate and clarify. The chance that the initial visit to the mental health service may lead to indelible and lasting comments about one's defective personality restrains the clinical traffic that might otherwise approach the figures for total enrollment.

Even if the later use of mental health evaluations is a source of serious worry, however, the men and offices involved still generally labor under the aura of therapeutic service. The psychiatrists and psychologists are among the "good guys" of the campus: their extra-academic intrusions are generally seen as necessary or helpful, and often both. But not so with the campus security office, with its classifications of crime, personal deviance, and political activity. Here is where the "bad guys" sit, in the student and faculty definition of what is proper extra-academic business of the organization and in the students' anticipation of what can most cloud the permanent record. Much of the security work is not granted legitimacy: of all the many types of dossiers on campus, the security files are the most feared. Here is where anticipations steer behavior in ways full of guile and bitterness.

The politically active students of large campuses now commonly "understand" that they are under the surveillance of local, state, and national investigators, some of which is completely covert, hidden within the investigating agency, and some of which is processed through the campus security officer. As indicated earlier, the actual practices of security officers vary greatly, around an occupation norm of gathering and sharing information on deviant political behavior. Whatever the practices of a campus, students attempt to estimate them. But the practices in their very nature are hidden in shadows and are prone to be protected by official silence or verbal defenses that tell only part of the truth. The context is a natural for misinformation and myth, for anxious anticipation that preforms the attitudes and decisions of students in their pursuit of education and their involvement in politics.

Dossier consciousness, routine and problematic, looms ever larger among the problems created by the keeping of systematic records. In the preforming of decision and behavior, through anticipation of the permanent definitions of the files, lies a fundamental impact of modern formal organization upon the individual. Nowhere is this more true than in the college and university.

4 *Information-Flow Within the Professions: Some Selective Comparisons of Law, Medicine, and Nursing*

RODOLFO ALVAREZ AND WILBERT E. MOORE

AN INCREASING AMOUNT OF THE WORK OF MODERN INDUSTRIAL SOCIETY IS performed by highly trained persons known as professionals. As persons with technically specialized skills, professionals differ in various important ways from other persons who occupy official positions in the formal organizations by which modern society performs most of its crucial tasks. One important difference is that the legitimacy of their tenure in these positions may derive as much from the claims to expert knowledge as judged by their fellow professionals as from the adequacy of their incumbency in an hierarchical position as judged by their organizational superiors.

This authority of knowledge is linked with the claim to autonomy of exact procedures in occupational roles. These characteristics set profes-

All of the research for this paper and the preparation of initial drafts were carried out by the first author. The second author cooperated in planning the paper, in the revision of early drafts, and in the preparation of the introduction and conclusions. Edna R. S. Alvarez and Joyce Semradek made helpful criticisms of the manuscript.

sional occupations apart from others, at least in degree. And it is precisely these characteristics that make the records relating to professionals—their dossiers in an extended sense of the term—of unusual importance. Several aspects of professional records may be stated in summary form.

1. The professional's authoritative knowledge rests in the first instance upon formal educational attainments at an advanced educational level. Thus, accumulated records of educational achievements provide formal testimony of merit. Informal modes of training, such as apprenticeship, are increasingly rare, though elements survive in the relationship between formally qualified but junior professionals and their senior associates.
2. Competence is also judged on the basis of actual practice. Here the judgment rests with professional peers. Who else would be able to tell? Some such judgments are oral, but others do yield records, particularly within organizations that select and employ professionals.
3. To avoid practice by charlatans, formal certification of professional standing, sometimes including licensing, is standard. Such certification provides a kind of open or public portion of a professional's dossier. Unauthorized practice, fraudulent claims to professional standing, and concealment of loss of certification provide situations in which a kind of "dossier search" may be provoked.
4. Because of the trust clients must place in professionals (the counterpart of the professional's claim to autonomy), and because all members of a profession are damaged in some degree by the open misconduct of any member, questions of moral standing and integrity are important. This is likely to be the "dossier problem" that creates the most difficulty, for the opportunity to challenge, much less control, alleged derogatory information may be at least as difficult for the professional in dealing with his peers as it is for the citizen in dealing with public or private investigative agencies.

Judgments about the level of competency and honorable conduct of an individual professional may come from a variety of sources. Although some judgments are oral, much of the evaluative communication about professionals is made in a form that can be recorded on a permanent basis. When a professional moves from one organizational jurisdiction to another, some of those recorded judgments either precede or follow him to his new appointment. In some cases the move is based on that information; in others, the information simply serves to justify the move. These permanently recorded judgments are usually collected in organizational files or dossiers. Some of these relate to his competence as a member of the organizational community, others to his competence as a member of the community of experts. One can hardly participate in modern society without knowing that this pervasive record-keeping takes place. Yet surprisingly little is known about it by way of systematic inquiry. This chapter is an attempt to lay the groundwork for further inquiry into record-keeping and its consequences within the professions by mapping out some of the major dimensions of the problem and its organizational context.

Our discussion of record-keeping and information-flow within the professions is limited to law, medicine, and nursing. We cannot claim that the practices here reported cover the entire range of practices in these and other professions, or even that our materials are representative in the technical sense of a probability sample. Rather, the intent is to present systematically some materials that may be illustrative of both problems and practices. Furthermore, the intent throughout is to "generalize beyond the data" in order to explore possible explanations for the consequences of the practices that were found to exist in the three professions. Two kinds of comparative generalizations are made—within and between the professions. In both cases the intent is to highlight similarities and differences.

Since little appears to be known concerning professional dossiers, some first-hand exploration of record-keeping and information-flow was carried out. Within each of the three professions, interviews were conducted with knowledgeable persons operating within each of four types of organizational contexts: governmental manpower agencies, professional associations, practice organizations, and professional schools.[1] For each organization, an attempt was made to interview the chief administrator as well as several of his immediate administrative subordinates. Practice organizations in law include small and large law firms, government services, and house counsel for private corporations; some examples in medicine are private practice, hospital services, and city departments of public health; in nursing, hospitals, doctors' offices, and visiting nurses associations. The professional schools were divided into three categories involving geographical locale and auspices: Northeastern private, Northeastern public, and Rocky Mountain public.

[1] We did not attempt to classify these into the *autonomous* and *heteronomous* categories of professional organizations suggested by Richard Scott in "Reactions to Supervision in a Heteronomous Professional Organization," *Administrative Science Quarterly*, vol. 10 (June, 1965), pp. 65–81. However, our data clearly draw comparisons between information-flow practices among professionals in these two types of organizations. Additionally, in the case of medical school departments and hospital services, we take cognizance of the professional "department" as a separate organizational form; for a systematic comparison of these three organizational types, see Hall, Richard H., "Professionalization and Bureaucratization," *American Sociological Review*, vol. 33 (February, 1968), pp. 92–104.

Four types of persons were interviewed within each of the schools for each profession: deans, assistant deans or departmental chairmen, registrars, and faculty. Several students in each type of school were also interviewed. The usual procedure for arranging the collection of materials was to interview the chief administrator first and subsequently to interview others in the organization. This served as a means of comparing policy and practice as well as a means of comparing alternative responses to the same questions in a continual effort to achieve an informal (i.e., intuitive) sense of verification. Persons interviewed were asked, first, to describe practices in their immediate organization and, second, to compare them as being more or less similar to practices in other similar organizations or to other organizations in which they had worked. In this way we also achieved a sense of generality beyond the specific organizations we studied.

THE PROFESSION OF MEDICINE

Information-keeping systems in the medical profession present a model toward which nursing and law appear to be moving. The contrasts that will be pointed out later in this chapter indicate that nursing presents one polar extreme, law the other, on various information-keeping characteristics. Medicine appears to fall somewhere between these two extremes. Furthermore, it appears that as both nursing and law experience the demands of organizational growth, on the one hand, and the need to control and standardize quality of professional service on the other, they tend to develop in the direction of the model presented by the medical profession.[2] Thus, while later sections of the chapter will discuss the contrasting characteristics of law and nursing, our first concern will be to describe in some detail the four principal information-keeping systems within the medical profession: governmental manpower agencies, professional associations, practice organizations, and schools of medicine. The schools of medicine are the most important, for in large measure, it is through them that information concerning professional persons in medicine is generated, maintained, and passed on. Also, as other medical organizations grow in size, they tend to approximate the organizational pattern of the medical schools. For these reasons principal attention will be devoted to the schools of medicine. However, this discussion will be reserved until a brief

[2] If we treat formalized information-keeping systems as another dimensional indicator of degree of bureaucratization of the organizational setting in which professionals work, then our findings appear consistent with those of Hall, *op. cit.* Nurses were most bureaucratized and least autonomous. Lawyers were least bureaucratized and most autonomous. Doctors fell between on both dimensions. Our intuition leads us to conclude that as lawyers become more bureaucratized and as nurses gain more professional autonomy, they will come closer to the medical model.

description of each of the other major information-keeping systems within the medical profession has been given. These descriptions will discuss purpose, source, content, processing for specific use, and release of records.

Governmental Manpower Agencies

The principal purpose of governmental manpower agencies' information-keeping systems is to compile annotated lists of medical professionals in various locales and to provide reliable, convenient, and comprehensive statistical summaries of trained personnel in the profession. Thus, the systems yield current information but not cumulative files. The source of data for these annotated lists and statistical summaries is the individual medical professional. Questionnaires, which are accompanied by a letter giving the sanction of the professional association, are sent yearly to these professionals.[3] From these questionnaires are compiled listings containing information such as degrees earned, special technical qualifications, membership on various professional boards, geographic location, and other similar information. Information on personal, social, or political characteristics is not collected and therefore is not a part of the contents of these lists. Disciplinary actions or law infractions are not recorded. Although questionnaires solicit information about income, this is not published in the lists of individuals. Information about income is published only in statistical summaries along with such other items as area of specialization, age, and geographic locale. Processing of information by governmental manpower agencies is limited to tabulation, cross-classification, and analysis of the different informational dimensions available. The principal use of this information is to provide data for decisions concerning the allocation of government resources in areas of greatest public need. In addition, these lists and summaries would be useful in a national or local emergency. Release of the information collected by governmental manpower agencies is through professional newsletters and journals, in addition to the agencies' own reports.

Professional Associations

As with governmental manpower agencies, the principal purpose of the medical professional associations' information-keeping systems is to provide annotated lists of medical professionals. These annotated lists are

[3] Whether questionnaires from previous years are destroyed is not known. If not, it is possible for these agencies to conduct trend studies and to compile cumulative data on the careers of specific individuals.

compiled and published under the auspices of three distinct groups; (1) the national medical association which represents the medical profession as a whole; (2) particular medical associations representing specialties within the medical profession; and (3) specialty boards which certify the physicians' competency within a specific specialty. Once again, the source of information for these lists is the individual professional himself.

The American Medical Association Directory is a list of members arranged alphabetically and geographically. The information given is very brief and includes name, present address, birthdate, year and state in which the member received his license, year certified by National Board of Medical Examiners, year certified by American Specialty Boards, specialty, professional organizations and societies to which he belongs, and the year he received professional appointments. Only that information relevant to the particular member listed would be included. The publications by the various individual medical associations representing specialties within the medical profession are again merely membership lists of dues-paying members. The information is similar to that which appears in the American Medical Association Directory. The Directory of Medical Specialists Holding Certification by the American Specialty Boards, published for the Advisory Board of Medical Specialties, Inc., by Marquis Who's Who is a very select list and includes only those individual medical professionals who have been certified by a particular Specialty Board. Certification is the only requirement necessary to be listed. This particular list identifies professionals who have achieved a certain professional status. The work is divided according to specialty and within each specialty, by geographical location. In addition, there is an alphabetical listing. The information given in this Directory of Medical Specialists is more detailed than that given in the membership directories previously discussed, because the emphasis here is on professional credentials. Some of the information included is as follows: name; year certified and in what specialty; date of receipt of M.D.; years of internship, residency, and hospital in which taken; type of practice (private or otherwise); hospitals with which affiliated; past history (where previously practiced and hospitals with which previously affiliated, armed services); and present address.

Processing of the information collected for these three lists is minimal. The information is merely organized for publication according to the prescribed format. No evaluations in terms of quality of training, affiliations, or practice are made. As a general rule, quality evaluations are kept in the minds of the individual medical professionals and not in files. From time to time a special case arises wherein a man's competency is questioned, and a file might be started. However, this would be only on a case-by-case basis if a serious complaint arose, and definitely not a systematic entry for each and every member or certified specialist. Release of information collected by medical professional associations is through the publications described above.

Practice Organizations

Despite persistent talk about the private practice of medicine, the physician in fact works in and through organizations. Thus, hospitals, public health service agencies, private clinics, and even private offices provide the organizational settings for medical practice. Obviously, this wide variety of settings implies a great variety of procedures for keeping records and disseminating information. However, certain generalizations can be made. The principal purpose of the information-keeping systems within practice organizations is to provide information for the organization itself rather than to provide annotated lists or statistical summaries for third parties. The source of information for the practice organization is generally twofold: the individual professional himself and other professionals who know both the person seeking the information and the person about whom the information is sought. In rare instances, for example, when an established man wants to increase his very select practice by bringing in an associate, a private investigation agency may be used as a source of information about the potential associate's personal, social, economic, and political background.

Some practice organizations do not compile dossiers on their professionals. Where records are kept, there is considerable variation in the degree of formality with which they are kept and also in the type of information kept. For instance, formal records may be kept but not all information that is gathered is recorded formally. Records are kept on doctors who work within governmental agencies of various sorts, whether federal, state, or local, which are very much like the records that these agencies keep on all of their employees. Such records are kept at the immediate organizational level. Name, position, and remuneration is normally sent up the hierarchy for payroll and similar purposes, but any correspondence about the professional is kept at the immediate organizational level.

Virtually no records are kept about doctors who work solely in private practice, since they practice individually or in small groups (less than ten) within which all know each other intimately. Consequently, any information that is gathered by one member on another, except for the very basic type of professional biographical data gathered when a new associate is being considered, is kept in the memories of the persons involved. With the advent of large group practices and large private clinics, formal record-keeping within private practice organizations will undoubtedly increase.

Two sorts of records are kept about doctors who work primarily in hospitals, and especially large hospitals. First, the chief of each specialized service in the hospital (the chief is a doctor of medicine) keeps a dossier on each of the physicians on his service. These contain letters of recommendation from other doctors and all correspondence concerning a particular candidate for a position. The chief and his staff make all decisions pertaining to doctor professionals in all respects including appointments. When, for example, the decision is made to hire a particular man, this is communicated to hospital administrators (nondoctors) who formally process forms, but who have no control over the decision. This second kind of record is kept by administrators, who maintain strict respect for professional autonomy. The dossiers that they keep reflect this respect, since they contain only such information as amount of pay and dates of employment. All matters of professional evaluation are kept in dossiers, controlled by the chief of service.

Medical Schools

In all the professions, the institution where the individual professionals receive their training becomes of crucial importance to the profession at large. Since the professional school is the entry point into the occupation, the kinds of students that the school admits will be the major determinant of the composition of the profession in subsequent years. In addition, the professional school provides one of the principal areas for intellectual growth within the profession. That is, in most professions, the major research and consequential development of the body of knowledge upon which the profession is built takes place in the leading centers of professional training.

Student Records. The degree of variation within medical schools, as well as between them, with respect to the sources from which information about potential students is sought, the kind of information that is collected on persons who do become students, and the processing and release of such information is far in excess of any ascertainable patterns. Variety is the rule. Yet some, albeit few, generalizations may be made.

Information-keeping systems within medical schools concerning the individual medical student reflect the three major relationships that the individual has with the medical school: as applicant, as student, and as ex-student. For the applicant, the information will be used as a basis for deciding whether the individual should be admitted as a student. For the student, the information will be used for deciding what action should be taken by the school for honorific or disciplinary courses and for deciding what type of recommendation should be given for the individual who is about to enter the role of ex-student. For the departing student, recommendations are of a twofold nature, namely, recommendations made to the student as to the type of professional practice into which he should consider going and recommendations to potential employers of the student. The information on former students will be used again periodically for deciding what type of recommendation should be given for the individual when requests are made by prospective employers, sometimes long after he has left the school.

The principal sources of information about the individual student as applicant, other than formal records of undergraduate work and achievement on the medical school aptitude exam, are the letters of recommendation sent to the school. Three main groups of people writing letters of recommendation are professors who have worked intensively with the student on the undergraduate level; doctors who have either been the applicant's family doctor or who have been a personal friend of the applicant or his family and thus presumably know him well; and finally, community leaders, both political and otherwise. The principal source of information about the student as student, other than the information already compiled about him in his role as applicant, is the faculty itself. Additional information about the student as ex-student which is formally entered into his medical school file comes principally from the student himself through personal, though professional, letters written to departmental chairmen or school deans. Only seldom and in unsystematic ways are post-school accomplishments entered in a man's file; and then usually only when he has distinguished himself in some way so that his name is mentioned either in the professional or mass media.

With respect to the contents of the information-keeping system within the medical school on the medical student, several items can be noted. In addition to grades and possibly disciplinary action, schools also keep records of students when they were applicants. Such records include letters of recommendation. There is great latitude in the information included in, or excluded from, these letters. Since assurances of confidentiality are always made, the letter writer is relatively free to evaluate the candidate on the basis of criteria of his own choosing. Some letter writers are chary to say more than what the receivers of the letter will surely already know about the prospective candidate—namely, grades and general classroom performance—whereas other writers include personal, social, and political evaluations that range far afield from academic concerns.

One consistent finding is that letter writers tend to accentuate the positive characteristics of prospective medical school students and not to mention negative aspects to the extent that their consciences allow. This is not difficult to do since most of the letter writers, other than doctors, have a very limited knowledge of the persons for whom they write these letters. Furthermore, there appears to be a general reluctance among undergraduate school personnel to include negative evaluations about their own students or about participants in their own programs for fear that this might reflect badly on their own competency in teaching or in selecting quality personnel. In addition, for the undergraduate college, its reputation is, at least in part, established by the proportion of its graduates who achieve entry into the "best" professional schools and who receive the "best" scholarships and assistantships. The "best" professional schools are usually, although certainly not always, private schools unencumbered by statutory requirements to admit people principally on the basis of grades. Thus these institutions give greater weight to letters of recommendation as a means of selecting judiciously among applicants. Thus, also, it is not surprising to find that in those cases where professors mention that disciplinary action was taken vis-à-vis the student on the undergraduate level, strong qualifiers are placed on such action by the letter writer such that the letter reader may not give it undue notice.

The *contents* of files on students are variable with respect to matters other than grades or honors bestowed. Records on each student are normally kept both in the office of the dean and in the offices of departmental chairman. However, the dean's file contains mostly brief objective documentation of dates, etc., and very little, if any, subjective quality evaluation. Detailed narrative evaluations are written by professors about each student's special skills and level of competence as he performs in each separate department during his passage through medical school. These evaluations are kept at the department level and not sent to the central medical school office.

Disciplinary matters are rarely included, and when they are in the student's file they are merely noted and not described in detail. What will be considered severe enough to be included within a student's file lies within the discretion of the particular dean or departmental chairman. When disciplinary matters are severe enough to warrant documentation of the episode and the reaction to it, the records are as a rule kept in files of an assistant dean on a case-by-case basis. Disciplinary cases are very infrequent and severe cases of this kind even more so.

1. VALIDATION. Procedures for validating the authenticity of information flowing into the medical school was found to be almost universally lacking. We have found one exception, and that experience indicates that validation may be more of a problem than general practice reflects. The registrar of one particular medical school has developed several "follow-through" procedures which, while time-consuming, have successfully revealed errors.

The first procedure involved letters of recommendation received concerning potential students. Upon the receipt of a letter of recommendation, the registrar would send a note of appreciation directly to the party who has written the letter. On several occasions this procedure had revealed a false letter—a letter that was not written by the person who was purported to have written it. The applicant involved was immediately removed from consideration as a potential student and his name was immediately sent to the American Medical Association, which publishes a yearly list of such names and distributes it to all medical schools.

The second procedure involved verification of the decision not to matriculate. Whenever a student who has been accepted by the school decides not to matriculate, he is asked for his reasons and subsequent plans. In 1967 this follow-through procedure revealed that a student whose lifelong ambition had been to come to this particular medical school had received a letter of rejection when in fact the school had accepted him. In a state of dejection he was about to go into the armed services. The registrar's letter inquiring about his reasons for not matriculating led to the subsequent exposure of error. Although the party or parties involved were not identified, it was revealed that this case involved, as it turned out, a deliberate misrepresentation (or a cruel joke) and not a clerical error. Whether the problem of deliberate tampering with the flow of information into and out of medical school student records is a general one appears to merit further study.

2. RELEASE OF RECORDS. Information on medical students is released by faculty members of medical schools for two principal purposes: (1) to generate interest on the part of some other institution into which the

outgoing student desires to achieve entry; and (2) to give recommendations for the student once interest has been shown on the part of some other institution.

The initial generating process by the home institution involves the release of very little information, and usually consists of nothing more than the name of the student and some minimal evaluation. Once interest has been generated, a letter of recommendation usually follows. Most chairmen described letters of recommendation as ranging between good, better, and very good. A truly bad letter is very rare. However, this pattern of apparently consistent positive evaluations may be misleading if not seen within the context of two processes that are operating concurrently: (1) differential letter writing by a particular departmental chairman about the same student depending upon the institution to which the chairman is writing; and (2) differential letter interpretation depending upon the reputation of the letter writer.

The process of differential letter writing depending upon the institution to which the letter is being written was disclosed by chairmen of departments in a high-prestige, very selective, private medical school. Chairmen of departments at the public university medical schools did not make such claims. The departmental chairmen of the private school, when pressed about the details of letter writing for their outgoing students, made more or less the following comments. Any student graduating from this particular school is probably better trained than students from most other schools. A student who barely made it through the program would therefore be billed as a very good student if the letter were going to the dean of a second- or third-rate medical school where he was to do postdoctoral work. The same student would be very differently billed if he were applying for postdoctoral work at a very good medical school. Similarly, if he were applying for an internship at a mediocre hospital, he would be described differently than if he were applying to a very distinguished hospital that took only the best students from the best schools as interns. When pressed further, these chairmen indicated that in their opinion their counterparts in the second- or third-rate schools "wouldn't know what to look for when they spoke to these people, they wouldn't know what questions to ask." Such interpretations may be distorted and self-serving, designed to reassert the prestige of the school. Interestingly enough, faculty members in the same medical school were asked the same questions as the chairmen and their response was somewhat more modest. They did not deny that some people might write differential letters, but just about all faculty members said they themselves would write the same evaluation to all inquirers regardless of the presumed quality of the school.

With respect to differential letter interpretation it was found that as a result of the fact that certain groups of medical schools and other medical institutions tend to recruit their personnel from each other, especially within areas of professional specialization, specific individuals learn to interpret each other's letters of recommendation. A given man may become known as a very tough evaluator so that a student whom he describes as average may be viewed by others as very good. Other persons become known as generous evaluators and the appropriate discount is entered by readers of these letters. Similarly, people learn to read for subtleties of meaning and phraseology to decide whether the writer is trying to be nice to the student and still communicate to the receiver relevant information that qualifies the applicant's abilities. Thus in both the writing and receipt of letters of recommendation a process of differential interpretation is manifested.

The release of "information" through letters of recommendation presumably reflects but does not replicate formal records. The release of information from formal records depends upon what the registrar and his staff permits. The following two case studies demonstrate two distinct approaches or orientations to the release of records by registrars.

The first case involved a young, efficient registrar who exercised considerable initiative and appeared to have a very tight rein over the medical school's records. Physical access to the files containing information was limited. The offices of the dean and the assistant dean were next to that of the registrar. If either needed to see a student's records, the registrar could bring these records into their offices through her own private door, essentially without leaving her office. If other faculty members wanted to see a student's record, they would have to make arrangements with the registrar's office in advance. Faculty would not be allowed to remove student records from the filing cabinets nor would they be allowed to take records from the registrar's office. Rather, the records would be brought to them by one of the filing clerks and would be inspected by the faculty member at a table within the registrar's office. Agents of the Federal Bureau of Investigation were not allowed to see any student records. All clerks were drilled in proper procedures for handling requests by such agents for information. Agents were to be sent to the registrar, and in her absence were to be sent to the professors whom the student had had while in school. No questions were to be answered by the clerks. The registrar herself, however, was willing to answer questions such as when the student was enrolled and if he had completed the degree program.

The second case was the antithesis of the first and involved an elderly woman who had the demeanor of a "little clerk." When asked about the release of information, she revealed that students were definitely not allowed to have access to the files, of which she was the lone keeper. However, the physical situation was such that anyone could easily look into the files without attracting attention during one of the registrar's frequent absences from her small office. Although the registrar preferred that the faculty not take files out of the office, they did in fact take files, leaving a note as to what had been taken. When asked whether the university had any explicit policy on the release of information to investigatory agents or outside parties of various categories, the registrar said "it might" and then recalled having received a written memo on the matter which had not been read because she was too busy. Her own reaction was that she would have nothing to say to insurance agents or private investigators, but that she had had no experience with them. Although FBI and other government agents frequently asked for information, no notation was made in a student's file that such a request had been made (university policy explicitly requires such a notation). She was no exception in this regard, since none of the registrars interviewed (in fact no one interviewed) indicated ever making a note in anyone's file concerning the fact that an inquiry about him had been made by investigatory agents. However, she was an exception in that she was very much impressed by FBI agents. She would have long talks with them whenever they came around because, "Well, if the FBI is interested in some matter it must be important." Although she thought it important not to let just anyone see students' files, she would allow the FBI to scrutinize, physically, the contents of particular files because, "Well, with the FBI it's different."

Private investigators, on the other hand, are not tolerated in any way. All persons interviewed indicated either that they had never been approached by a private investigator, but that they would not answer any questions if approached, or that they had been approached and had in fact refused to answer any questions. However, civil service agents and FBI agents were a different matter. Although most medical school departments indicated that they had never been approached by FBI agents for information about students, other departments indicated that such inquiries were made from time to time and still other departments indicated that it was a very frequent occurrence. The differentiating factor appears to be how many people in a given specialty are employed by the federal government. Most persons indicated that the FBI did not ask about students' political beliefs, but rather only whether the respondent knew of anything that might disqualify the prospective candidate from government employment or that might place doubts on his loyalty to the country. These people usually responded to such questions with a blanket, "No!" Their explanation in the interview was generally, "How should I know what a man's politics are?" However, other persons indicated that the FBI did in fact ask specific questions about student's political beliefs and these persons were much more likely to indicate that they answered frankly what they thought those beliefs were, assuming that these were public knowledge anyway and that the agent was probably only testing the respondent's truthfulness. Finally, given the nature of the contents of most student files (with the possible exception of psychiatric and personality assessments which are most common in nursing), it is doubtful whether student records are worth the FBI's bother.

It is not possible to say whether or not there is an information-flow problem involving the release of information to FBI and other investigatory agents who frequently come around the medical school. It does appear that almost anyone could announce that he was an FBI agent and receive information. As a general rule an agent's identity claims are taken at face value. One interviewee did mention he could tell a real FBI agent because he would "flash his badge" even before he started talking; if other persons interviewed were cognizant of this characteristic they did not mention it. There is no follow-through procedure with regard to checking the identity of FBI agents other than the fact that faculty, deans, and registrars come to recognize the usual agents. However, some registrars indicated that on some occasions there were several different FBI or other government agents investigating during the same day and often during the same week or month. Why wouldn't the central office send out one agent to check on all names instead of sending separate agents with separate (small) lists of names to check through the same department on the same day? Since some registrars were more than ready to cooperate with any outside investigator identifying himself as a government agent and especially an FBI agent, and since all indicated that they would not respond to inquiries from private investigators of any kind, it is at least possible to raise the question of whether some of the latter might not take on an identity that will receive cooperation from the professional schools. On the other hand, it might be possible for private investigators to hire off-duty FBI agents to do some checking very much as off-duty uniformed policemen are hired to officiate at various functions. This would ensure that no charge of impersonation could be brought and that no one's suspicions would be raised by the now routine visits of these agents. It was not possible to check whether either of these possibilities ever took place in fact.

Faculty Records. Recorded information concerning prospective, as well as current, faculty at medical schools is even more skimpy, unsystematic, and subject to variation than that concerning medical students. However, the information collected is not necessarily ineffective or useless. Quite to the contrary, the information-gathering procedure takes on an intensely searching character. The ways in which this intense search is manifested depends on the peculiar style of the persons involved. Even so, there appears to be some abstract order to these procedures. It is this general tendency that we shall attempt to capture in the following discussion.

The collection and processing of information from various sources has two general uses in the medical profession: to *make a decision* about a professional and to *justify a decision* already made about a professional. We believe that there are four areas of information process within the profession as indicated by our chart and that, in very general terms, the movement is from the first to the fourth quadrant in numerical order. The major role of the second and third quadrants is in helping to *make a decision,* whereas the first and fourth help to *justify the decision.*

The chart indicates two major dimensions with respect to information processing. One dimension has to do with the *medium* by which the information is conveyed—either by some kind of *formal* recording such as letters, telegrams, publications, and other such documentation, on the one hand, or on the other hand, by some *informal* means such as face-to-face conversation, telephone messages, etc. The other dimension has to do with the nature of the relationship between the giver and the receiver of the information and, also to some lesser extent, the *subject* of the information. The *private* sector of professional information may be thought to be confined by the boundaries established when giver, receiver, and subject agree that specific-purpose information and evaluations are to be made and circulated among a very limited audience. Departures from this condition certainly exist and the subject is often only tenuously in control. (In later discussions it will be shown that nurses, as a rule, have more control than either doctors or lawyers.) The *public* sector of professional information-processing may be epitomized by the mutual agreement of giver, receiver, and subject that the information is to be shared with the entire profession. Of course, once "the profession" is defined as the bound-

Professional Information-Flow Cycle

Medium through which information is conveyed	*Source of Information*	
	PRIVATE SECTOR	PUBLIC SECTOR
FORMAL	4. *Administrative and Professional Justification* a. Application forms filled out by individual. b. Autobiographical materials submitted by individual. c. Forms for periodic formal assessment. d. Letters of recommendation.	1. *Professional Recognition* a. Publications by the individual. b. Formal announcements by practice organizations, professional associations, manpower agencies; examples might be prizes, awards, and other honorific manifestations or listings of achievement such as membership directories. c. Degrees earned.
INFORMAL	3. *Administrative and Professional Evaluation* Generally consists of a specific individual, *A*, assessing another specific individual, *B*, at the request of a third specific individual, *C*. The request is usually for information about specific qualifications for a specific task. The information usually flows from *A* to *C* through face-to-face communication, or telephone, at the time of the specific need.	2. *Professional Reputation* Generally voiced and accepted opinions about a given individual that become part of general knowledge among the community of professionals and that are passed on without regard to the specific source, the destination of the assessment, or to time or task needs.

ary it may be very difficult to confine the information to that social space. Thus, by the term "public" is meant sources of information on an individual which are readily available to all professionals. By the term "private" we mean sources of information on an individual that are the result of specific task-oriented requests for information by a specific individual from another specific individual usually with the assurance of confidentiality. Such "private" information might also be obtained without a specific request, but such unsolicited information is given with the understanding that it is to remain within the sector of private exchange rather than being given with the understanding that it is for public consumption. The remainder of our discussion of faculty records will focus around the four areas designated by the logically possible combination of these two basic dimensions.

Within the public sector the most important formal sources of information concerning prospective and current faculty are the actual publications of the particular professional. This body of information is the most relevant and decisive in terms of justifying hiring and retention decisions. In a sense a man with a lot of publications comes to the attention of an organization as a potentially desirable person to hire *because,* in terms of the ethos of the profession, the decision to hire would be easy to justify. The informal sources of information within the public sector concerning prospective and current faculty are principally other professionals who through personal contact with the individual in question have collected information on his personal, social, political, and professional characteristics and peculiarities. This information becomes a matter of public knowledge within the profession and is communicated throughout the country through interpersonal contacts and friendships. It is generated, sustained, and communicated without regard to any specific position, or specific intent of any kind. This same process is seen within the confines of a particular institution in the hiring of new faculty members from the current crop of postdoctoral students. During their affiliation with the institution as postdoctoral students, these students have worked intensely in a particular medical school department under a given man's direction. They have been closely observed during their period of affiliation. As a result of this close work relationship, the faculty comes to know the postdoctoral student with a certain degree of depth and intimacy and the decision as to whether to invite the individual postdoctoral student to faculty status is therefore based on long-term personal and professional experience with him. Letters of recommendation may very well never be sought or written on the individual. This particular source of information, the postdoctoral experience, although its initial birthplace and use is within the private sector of the particular institution, quickly becomes a part of the public sector of information on the particular faculty member.

Turning now to the private sources of information on prospective and current faculty, three initial generalizations must be made. First, if a prospective or current faculty member fails to qualify in the minds of the initial decision-makers on the basis of information about him that is available within the public sector, the process of information-collecting ends at that point and no attempt is made to collect verifying information within the *private* sector. In fact, the rule of thumb is to check out a man's criteria on an oral and informal basis very, very thoroughly before any formal written communications, which have to be kept as records, are set in motion. Second, in regard to prestigious, nationally known men, there is practically no need to collect any information other than that which is readily available through the public sector. Whatever information is collected in the dossiers of such faculty members, which are usually compiled strictly as a formality for administrative purposes, is merely a written confirmation and repetition of what fellow professionals already know about the individual but without the details of enthusiasm or displeasure that people do not hesitate to disclose orally and that they would prefer not to communicate within any formal records. Third, in regard to men lacking national reputation, and consequently men about whom there is little in the way of information within the public sector, the private sector source of information becomes most relevant and decisive in terms of hiring and retention decisions. Thus, organizations interested in hiring young men or organizations that are unable to attract the older men of national reputation, tend to rely more heavily on the private sector source of information. A corollary of this third proposition was also found to be true, namely, that departmental chairmen (the men most responsible for the decision on whether a particular man will be hired or retained on the faculty) who were less established men in their profession relied more heavily on private sector sources of information as a basis for their decision-making, thus taking a more bureaucratic view of their position and the tasks they performed in it, whereas the more eminent departmental chairmen seemed to rely much more on the public sector sources of information as a basis for their decision-making. It is not clear whether the distinction is based upon a difference of role interpretation and security of position, or whether it is based upon a difference in the accessibility of public sector information, with the more well-established departmental chairman having a great many more interpersonal contacts with other professionals by virtue of his more eminent position.

The three sources of information within the private sector are (1) institutions which, upon request, send formal records of work taken and completed at that institution; (2) professionals who, upon request, write letters of recommendation; and (3) individuals who, usually without being requested, volunteer information. The most interesting finding concerning the contents of information drawn from private sector sources concerns the method by which medical school departmental chairmen handle requests for letters of recommendation about men who, at the time of the request, are serving on the faculty of the letter writer. The process under consideration involves a deliberate "building up" or "bringing down" of the letters being written about particular persons. The "building up" process involved enhancing the characteristics of the particular individual, or at least the accentuation of positive characteristics, and the by-passing of any negative characteristics. The "bringing down" process is just the reverse.

We may identify some of the pressures that result in a departmental chairman writing a "build up" letter for one of his colleagues. When outside parties inquire about the abilities of a particular faculty member and it becomes apparent that the inquiring party is interested in offering the faculty member a position, the departmental chairman is placed in an interesting dilemma. In the first place, if the man in question was hired by the particular chairman, the chairman's own judgment and capacity for hiring "good" people come into question if he indicated that the man is inadequate. Even if the man was not hired by the particular chairman, a poor letter reflects as much upon the reputation of the organization that hired him as upon the individual about whom the letter is being written. Second, even if the faculty member in question is in fact inadequate, and a "bad" letter would more accurately reflect the man's worth and the chairman's true evaluation of his capacities, the chairman is under constraints to write a positive letter, since a negative letter will almost certainly ensure that the man in question will not be hired by the inquiring institution, but, instead, will become a problem to get rid of in the home institution. Third, if the faculty man in question is judged to be very good, a very positive letter may ensure that there will be a greater pressure to "steal him away." A departmental chairman has various alternatives in such a case. He can write a very positive letter. This will ensure that the man will get increasingly attractive offers from other institutions, but if the departmental chairman can match any offer received by the faculty member, there is little danger of losing the man. Given this situation, the fact that the man is attractive to other organizations increases the chairman's standing with the medical school and the university because he has and can keep people of national repute within his department. The prestige of a department and school is enhanced by having men who are in high demand nationally. In addition, morale within the department and respect for the chairman increase with the knowledge that he writes good letters for his men.

However, some departmental chairmen indicated that sometimes they know they cannot match outside offers for a man whom they consider to be very good. In this case they might write a very good letter and add, in the same letter, the request that the man not be "stolen away" either because he is currently indispensable or for some other reason. This request is more likely to be made when the inquiry comes from a personal acquaintance of the chairman. There is reason to believe that such a request is honored. Whether it works to the advantage or disadvantage of the party in question (the man about whom the letter is written) is uncertain. The chairmen who noted that they had made such requests felt that in the long run it worked to the advantage of the man. Despite all of these pressures to write positive letters, especially for good men, some chairmen indicated that if not "bad" at least "not as good" letters are sometimes written about good men in order to keep them from leaving their departments. How frequently this occurs is not possible to say since the chairmen who did mention it refused to elaborate and spoke of it in the most guarded tones. (Three persons in other, academic, departments of one university indicated that they knew of such instances within their own disciplines.) The impression derived is that in most cases under most circumstances the letter writer is under pressure to "build up" his own men and that in some peculiar and infrequent circumstances they may feel it is necessary to "bring down" their evaluation of a particular colleague.

The processing of private sector information concerning medical school faculty is minimal. Departmental chairmen interviewed identified two types of processing, both of which were rarely employed and were considered to be ineffective as well as potentially dangerous. The first type of processing takes place at the collection stage. A chairman can potentially affect the kind of information he presents to an appointments committee by carefully selecting the parties whom he asks to write letters of recommendation for prospective faculty members. However, such procedure is viewed as desperate at best and as ineffective and time-consuming. People presumed to be overwhelmingly positive about a fellow professional sometimes are not and those presumed to be overwhelmingly negative are sometimes very positive in the letters they write. Predictability is minimal. The second type of processing takes place at the point of disclosure. A chairman can simply fail to disclose to the appointments committee a "bad" letter that he has received about a prospective faculty member. However, men who serve on cross-departmental appointments committees do circulate across the country and do pick up information about specific men from respected knowledgeable people. If it should be revealed that such a person wrote a "bad" letter about an individual, and the departmental chairman did not present the document to the appointments committee for review, the chairman would lose whatever respect he enjoyed and in all likelihood his appointment as chairman would soon come to an end.

THE PROFESSIONS OF LAW AND NURSING: GENERAL COMPARISONS TO MEDICINE

This section has two purposes. First we shall present factual material specifically pertinent either to law or nursing within each of the four basic organizational settings which are foci of information-flow. A second major intent is to draw comparative generalizations concerning law, medicine, and nursing. Even though it is safe to say that there is almost as much variation in the way information is handled *within* each of the professions as *between* them, it is still possible to discern some over-all contrasts.

These over-all differences in information-flow between the professions may be due to differences in the size of the organization in which professionals work, the varying rates of occupational and geographic mobility among them, the nature of the work which they perform on their "most important other" (clients, patients, etc.), as well as, perhaps, the maturity of the particular profession.

It may be well to differentiate between law and medicine as "established" professions which enjoy considerable respect from the society at large, on the one hand, and nursing, on the other hand, as a "becoming" profession. The established professions are granted considerable autonomy to perform specialized work and to exercise judgment in areas where precise knowledge may not yet be available, but which may dramatically affect the patients' (clients') life and affairs. The becoming professions consist generally of highly skilled technicians and staff people who do not enjoy the same level of trust and respect as the established professions. In fact, however, the relationship of the nurse to the patient is much more like the relationship of the staff lawyer in a large firm to the client. However, an important difference is that the background staff lawyer can aspire either to partnership status or to setting up his own firm. In either case he can enter a status that puts him "in command" of his practice, with all that this means in terms of autonomy, decision-making, and respect. The nurse, on the other hand, can hardly aspire (though a very small minority who go on to acquire Ph.D.'s in various disciplines think they might) to hold "partnership" with the doctor in terms of treating patients' medical problems. Even nurses who work on "private duty" do so under the medical authority of the patient's doctor. In short, society can and does accept the model of a completely autonomous professional competent by training to make decisions in the best interest of his client or patient in the case of lawyers and doctors. However, the accepted model of even the most professionally accomplished nurse does not include autonomy of decision on behalf of the patient.[4] The degree of professionalization of nurses appears to be more a consequence of the "professionalization of everyone" required in modern, industrialized, formally organized society.[5] To the extent that skilled workers of all types formally organize themselves into mutual benefit associations through which they keep informed of relevant technological innovations and through which they pressure for improvement of working conditions and remuneration they approximate the model of the established professions. It is in this sense that even the modern soldier can be called a professional. This claim to professional status is thus based more on the organizational context (whether the individual's orientation be cosmopolitan or local) than on expert knowledge. Throughout our discussion it will become apparent that law and nursing appear at opposite extremes in our analysis. Nursing is most dependent on its organizational context and law on its claim to expert knowledge. Medicine, on the other hand, appears to hold a position somewhere between these two extremes. This section, then, seeks to contrast nursing and law to medicine, which has already been described in considerable detail. Nursing and law are presented together in this section, not because they are similar, but precisely because they appear to be polar opposites in these comparisons.

Governmental Manpower Agencies

The purpose of governmental manpower agencies' information-keeping systems is the same for nurses and lawyers as for medical professionals. However, two distinctions can be made. First, these agencies collect more information on medical and nursing professionals than on lawyers since information such as how many doctors and nurses, of what ages, and of what specialties are practicing in what geographical areas is more important to the national health and welfare than is similar information on lawyers. Second, nursing professional associations provide more information to the agencies than do medical associations and both do so more than lawyers' associations. It appears that nurses' associations are more prone to undertake self-studies independently than are medical associations and that lawyers' associations are the least prone to do so.

[4] Hall, "Reactions to Supervision," *op. cit.*, p. 99, also finds nurses consistently under the authority of doctors.

[5] Wilensky, Harold L., "The Professionalization of Everyone?" *American Journal of Sociology*, vol. LXX (September, 1964), pp. 137–158.

Professional Associations

Directories, similar to that compiled by the American Medical Association, are compiled on nurses and lawyers under the auspices of the relevant professional associations. All three professions require licensing in the given state where practice is to take place. Licensing presumably ensures a minimal level of competence that all members of the profession have achieved. However, directories of medical professionals are more likely to give an implicit assessment of quality, beyond mere competence for licensing, because of the very difficult national examinations which a doctor has to pass in order to become a member of the College of his particular specialty. Each field of specialization puts out its own directory. Thus, public listings of doctors may be of two kinds: (1) directories of doctors that specialize in the practice of medicine in a particular area, say, cardiology; and (2) directories that list doctors who have passed the very difficult national examinations required for membership in, say, the College of Cardiology. Directories of lawyers and nurses would simply indicate membership in the professional association and would not contain the "quality" assessment implicit in being designated competent by examination in a special area of practice. However, the area of specialization would be indicated by virtue of being listed in the directory of, say, the American College of Trial Lawyers. No examination is required for admission to such organizations.

Within nursing the professional association serves two additional functions. First the association, with the assistance of state licensing agencies, undertakes detailed surveys of the profession aimed at assessing various characteristics of nursing. Although medical, and to some lesser extent, legal associations undertake such surveys, they appear to be less extensive, less intensive, and less systematic than those conducted by nursing associations. This reflects the drive within the nursing profession toward self-study and improvement of their professional standing. The results of these studies are, of course, published as aggregate statistical summaries. However, the fact is that the raw data on individual professionals are compiled and, at least temporarily, available to the staff of the professional associations. It is not possible at this time to determine what safeguards are placed on the use of this information or how long it is stored after the aggregate statistics are compiled.

Second, the American Nurses' Association (ANA), the principal professional association, provides its members with a "credential compilation" service. The function of this service is to compile a professional dossier on the individual nurse, which will be available to prospective employers. The nurse herself requests that such a compilation of her credentials be made and is responsible for having the released information sent to the professional association. This information includes grade transcripts, records of certification, and letters of recommendation. For the nurse who has just completed her training these letters will be from her professors and/or clinical supervisors, writing individually, and/or from an administrator writing in the name of the institution. There is no processing of the information received in the sense that certain items are included and others excluded, but rather all materials received are put in the nurse's file. There is no verification or evaluation of materials received.

These files are released to prospective employers in three ways: (1) upon the request of the nurse; (2) upon the request of a prospective employer to the ANA which then seeks release from the nurse prior to responding to the request; and (3) upon consent of the nurse after having been notified by the ANA employment service that they have a listing for a job for which she qualifies. Since 1965 the nurse has been permitted review of all materials in her dossier, but, once included, none may be removed. Prior to this date the nurse was not allowed to review the contents. When the file is sent to a prospective employer it carries with it a statement to the effect that the information is confidential and should be returned to the professional association when the prospective employer has completed its review of the contents. Most frequently the file is *not* returned, but rather is kept by the prospective employer in the nurse's personnel file.

An additional function of most professional associations is to provide grievance committees (or some less formal mechanism) to which the public may address its complaints about particular professionals. The grievance committee of a local bar association may provide a prototypical example of grievance committees in the professional associations generally. A complaint from either a lawyer or layman will eventually come to the chairman of the committee. A good many complaints are filed by persons who feel they have been overcharged by the lawyer for whatever services he performed. As a rule these irate clients are "cooled out" and nothing ever comes of the matter. No record is made of the complaint if it came by telephone. If it came by letter some note to the effect that the client reconsidered might be made and the matter is dropped.

Another very frequent complaint is what lawyers call the "crackpot complaint." This kind of complaint is made by persons who in some odd way perceive themselves to have been wronged by a lawyer. These complaints usually take more effort to clear up. The chairman of the grievance committee may have to interview a number of persons who are in some way involved in the incident. He may have to spend a good deal of time making additional inquiries before the complaint is revealed to have no real basis in fact. In any given community there may be a number of people who frequently make complaints of this type and who come to be known as "crackpots." Once these people are identified as such their complaints take much less time to check out. Their complaints are usually made against a variety of lawyers who otherwise have had no history of malpractice. In such cases no formal record is made with regard to the lawyer in question.

A third kind of complaint is the "legitimate" case of deviance by a lawyer. Complaints of this kind are the least frequent and can be of two types. First, there is the case where an equivocal answer has to be given to the question of whether an act of deviance actually occurred. If a particular lawyer accumulates many such difficult-to-prove complaints independently from a variety of clients, then the grievance committee may take some formal action to investigate. A second type of case is that where the charge of malpractice seems obviously valid on its face. In this case an investigation is launched immediately. In either case once an investigation is set in motion by the grievance committee all records, statements, etc. are kept permanently in its files. While the rules of evidence are not usually strictly adhered to and the lawyer is ordinarily not encouraged to be accompanied by counsel in the investigation, participants are sworn to tell the truth and a court reporter records all proceedings and in every other way the atmosphere is like a courtroom. The findings and recommendations of the committee are also permanently recorded in the committee's files. If the committee finds for disbarment, the case is sent to the court of appropriate jurisdiction and from that point handled like any other court case. The court is very unlikely not to find in favor of the committee recommendations.

In most bar associations readmission is handled by the State Bar Examining Committee, which operates by its own rules independently of other committees. In general, admission and readmission involve the same procedure. Among the things that an applicant has to do to qualify for admission to the bar is to satisfy the committee that he is a person of "good moral character." This is done predominately in three ways. First, the applicant must usually fill out a questionnaire consisting of questions as to his morals, convictions for law violations, and related matters concerning his character and integrity. Second, one or more members of the bar must certify to the committee in writing that they believe the person is of sound moral character and should be admitted to the bar. Third, the applicant must appear in person before the committee and answer questions about his character, legal training, knowledge of local legal procedures, and so forth.

Admission of a previously disbarred person presents an interesting problem of information-flow. Since disbarment is a judicial act processed through the court of jurisdiction like any other case, it will certainly be brought to the attention of the Bar Examining Committee. This committee decides whether such an infraction justifies preventing a man from entry into the bar. If not, they then circulate the names of all applicants (without distinguishing between new applicants and applicants for readmission) to the members of the bar so that any member who has reason to believe that an applicant should not be admitted may register his objection. This committee does not generally give official notification to the grievance committee, as such, that a disbarred individual is applying for admission. As a consequence, this allows the grievance committee not to take official notice of the fact that a case it processed in the past is now re-entering the bar since it does not have to respond to any notification. On the other hand, like all members of the bar, the separate members of the grievance committee, acting as individual lawyers, may exercise their right to oppose an applicant's entry (in this case re-entry) by addressing the Bar Examining Committee with their personal knowledge and opinions of why the application should not be honored. Thus, the formal and informal as well as the private and public aspects of the community of lawyers become intertwined but at the same time clearly discernible. On the other hand, all of this generally takes place within the profession. Public announcements of who is charged or convicted of malpractice are not made by bar associations.[6] News media may find out and publicize a particular case, but in general the public is not informed. Depending on their own assessment of the case, individual lawyers may refuse to deal with a person who has been charged or convicted of malpractice, even after the person has been readmitted. Lack of referrals may hurt the man, but, in general, the public is not deliberately made aware. Calling attention to

[6] The American Bar Association Board of Governors has approved establishment at the American Bar Center, effective July 1, 1968, of a national discipline data bank as recommended by the Special Committee on Disciplinary Enforcement headed by retired Supreme Court Justice Tom C. Clark. The data bank would provide the first national repository of information on final disciplinary actions taken by the several states. Information would be supplied only to authorized disciplinary agencies of the legal profession.

one man's malpractice may sensitize the public to such potential dangers and lower its confidence in lawyers generally.

Although the procedure for handling professional deviance outlined for law is probably the model toward which the professions are moving, medicine has far more informal procedures. Nursing, on the other hand, is at the opposite extreme since it does not have viable grievance committees comparable to those of the legal profession. Though nurses are in some ways highly professionalized, under most circumstances they act as ancillary staff to doctors. Within the hospital setting they are under the administrative authority of nonmedical administrators and under the professional medical authority of doctors. Conflicts often ensue, and often nurses are taught not to comply with medical prescriptions which they know to be "contra-indicated." In such cases they are to seek higher consultation and direction. Should they carry out medical prescriptions they know to be "contra-indicated" they are legally liable. However, and this is the point, should a patient bring suit for such action it would be against the hospital (possibly naming the nurse as the hospital's agent) or, more likely, against the doctor who ordered the prescription.

Nurses are presumably also liable for actions not prescribed by physicians. For example, a nurse is liable if she fails to put side rails on the bed of a disoriented patient or if she leaves a patient sitting alone without proper support and the patient falls. In practice, however, it is the hospital that is sued, not the nurse. Many nurses carry "malpractice" insurance to cover a situation in which the hospital would not be the principal in the suit. Nevertheless, nurses are seldom involved in such suits. Complaints about a particular nurse usually go to the patient's doctor or to the hospital and not to nursing professional associations, hence no grievance committees. However, any instances of deviance would be recorded in the nurse's dossier after the incident was discussed with her and would be handled in the usual way all information on nurses is treated once in her dossier.

Complaints about a particular nurse are not frequent. Rather, patient complaints about nurses tend to be generalized to dissatisfaction with the nursing *service* and thus would not reach the dossier of any particular nurse. Again grievance committees do not appear to be an applicable mechanism since no *one* nurse is responsible for nursing care of a particular patient in the hospital. It might be interesting to compare private duty and hospital staff nurses in this regard, but we did not do so both for lack of time and because private duty nursing is not as widespread as it once was.

Practice Organizations

Practice organizations within the legal profession rely minimally on written records, other than grades, in the hiring of lawyers, and compile no records on the lawyer once hired. Letters of recommendation are infrequently requested. Evaluative interviews are always important. Reputation in the community is relevant when a man is changing positions within the same area.

In nursing, one must distinguish among three types of practice organizations, namely, private clinics and private offices, hospitals, and public health service agencies. In private offices and clinics there is almost no collecting or compiling of information in written form. Sometimes the applicant will prepare an autobiographical statement for her potential employer. Rarely will the employer in this setting request that the nurse's credentials as compiled by her professional association or school be sent to him. The major basis for the decision to employ are conversations and telephone calls to local professionals who might know her. Interviews with the candidate are the major basis for the decision.

In hospitals more attention is paid to the collection and compilation of information on nurses than in the case of private offices and clinics. There are three principal sources of information—"credentials compiled," letters of recommendation, and the individual applicant through the employment interview. The "credentials compiled" will be of greatest importance in the case of an applicant who has had some nursing experience and will only be of importance for the applicant who has just completed her training in providing evidence of her technical training.

Letters of recommendation fall into two categories—those from individuals and those from institutions. In most cases only those letters written under the auspices of an institution are recognized. Interviews are normally mandatory. The interview is used as an avenue for verifying information already acquired. It also provides an opportunity for the applicant to explain negative evaluations and/or an opportunity for the administrator to discuss these negative evaluations with the applicant. Given the great demand for nurses, an individual receiving a negative evaluation may nonetheless be hired on the condition that the negative characteristic does not become an impediment in her new position.

Information compiled is released to the school and professional association compiling credentials on the individual if requested by the nurse in question. In addition, information is released directly to persons or agencies potentially hiring the nurse. For insurance agents and credit agents, only *confirmation* of information which they already have is permitted. No information may be *released* to them. For example, if the agent indicates his records show certain dates of employment and a certain residential address, these may be confirmed or denied. But if the agent *asks* for these items of information they may not be released. Very few requests for information on nurses are made by FBI agents of hospitals, and when such requests are made they are for very general information such as "Do you have any reason to believe that the appointment of this person (to the Peace Corps) would not be in the national interest?" Such questions are answered in an equally general way: yes or no.

The Visiting Nurses Association (VNA) is another example of a practice organization within the nursing profession. The following case study is of importance not only as an example of a practice organization but also as an example in high relief of certain procedures that are prevalent in all data-collecting institutions involving nurses other than those concerned merely with the compilation of directories and statistical summaries. Generalizations based upon these procedures will be discussed in greater detail at a subsequent point.

The VNA under consideration consisted of approximately fifty-five nurses of which twenty to twenty-five were replaced each year. There were three principal sources of data on the applicant for a VNA position, namely, the "credentials compiled," letters of recommendation requested directly by the VNA from people or institutions whose names are submitted to the VNA by the applicant, and interviews. Interviews were considered to be the most important of the three sources, so much so that only in the rarest of circumstances would an applicant be hired without an interview. In such a case the applicant was required to submit an autobiographical letter. Letters of recommendation were received from three major groups—persons affiliated with the applicant's School of Nursing, persons affiliated with practice organizations where the applicant had been employed, and persons who knew the applicant in a personal rather than a professional capacity. Blatant discrepancies that came up in the records received were resolved through interpersonal contacts—that is, checking with the source itself or someone who would be able to resolve the conflict—and through the interviews.

Once hired by the VNA, extensive and detailed records were kept on each nurse. There were two major steps involved in their record-keeping system. The first can best be described as narrative proficiency reports. An evaluation report is written on each nurse's work by her supervisors after the first three months, six months, and twelve months of her affiliation with the VNA, and once a year every year thereafter. The reports are written on forms supplied by the VNA and consist of major headings dealing with various aspects of the nurse's competency. For each major heading the supervisor is provided with a long list of items which are to be covered in her narrative evaluation under the particular heading. Each nurse is given the opportunity to read the report and to discuss it with her supervisor. She then must sign the report. In addition, there is a space provided where the nurse herself can make comments.

The second step in the VNA's record-keeping system involved abstracting the narrative written by the supervisors into a form that would provide readily available information on which to base future decisions concerning such things as salary increases, promotions, and letters of recommendation for departing or departed VNA nurses. Here again a form was used. Various characteristics which the VNA had found from experience to be of greatest importance to other organizations in their hiring decisions were listed on the form and, for each characteristic, a definition was given. Clerical assistants would insert, opposite each characteristic described, phrases that had been used by the supervisor in her proficiency report of the particular nurse. When letters of recommendation were requested at some future date, these synopses provided a quick source of information.

Release of information concerning any ex-VNA nurse was only permitted to be made through the administrative head of the VNA. In the event that an ex-VNA nurse submits the name of one of her supervisors to a potential employer as a reference, the supervisor is prohibited from responding personally to the request, but, rather, must turn the request over to the administrator who will write a letter in response to the request. This letter will not be based on the last proficiency report, as summarized on the synopsis report, but rather will be based on a composite of all the synopses written during the entire time of the nurse's affiliation with the VNA. The policy for release to agents was identical to that of the hospitals.

Schools of Law and Nursing

The information-keeping systems within the nursing schools and law schools reflect the generalizable principle that records on legal professionals are minimal, whereas records on nurses are extensive.

Most law schools do not require letters of recommendation on student applicants and those that do are principally private schools that are faced with the problem of selecting the entering class from among a large number of highly qualified candidates. Public schools as a rule do not require letters, since entry is generally based on a legally established minimal grade point average in combination with law aptitude test scores. The principal records kept on the law student *qua* student are grades. No narrative records are kept concerning technical or interpersonal skills.

Records on faculty are also minimal. There are fewer positions available in law schools than in medical or nursing schools. The rate of mobility among law school faculty appears to be lower than that among nursing school faculty. The flow of information may therefore also be lower. In the "best" law schools, there is intensive in-breeding with the best students being invited to return in a faculty capacity after several years of practice or clerking. Letters of recommendation are therefore virtually unnecessary for evaluative purposes since the school already knows the candidate's skills and abilities and has kept track of his general legal activities, but letters may be requested for justificatory purposes. In other schools, faculty is recruited principally through private sector information, either formal (letter writing) or informal (word-of-mouth communications between faculty members of different schools or through interviews at meetings of various bar associations). Letters of recommendation, as in the case of medical schools, usually serve to justify the decision to hire a particular man, to show that there is no apparent reason why the man should not be hired. While the man is in the employ of the school, his work record is evaluated from time to time for purposes of salary and promotion; however, this is usually done by word of mouth among his senior colleagues. He may be informed of decisions, but not necessarily of the details they discussed. No written assessment of specific dimensions of technical competence, personality, or interpersonal skills are recorded in writing.

The schools of nursing present quite the opposite orientation toward record-keeping. Very detailed evaluations are made on both students and faculty. These reports are either in narrative form or in grade form, using some standardized numerical grading system. The major concern of these evaluations is with the individual's interpersonal skills. Technical competency as such is evaluated but is not considered to be as important as the individual's capacity to interact appropriately with peers, patients, and (in the case of students) supervisors. Within this general category of interpersonal skills, one of the most important dimensions is the student's submission to authority and directives. Evaluations are made by professors and clinical supervisors. Evaluations of faculty are sometimes made by the individual faculty member herself as well as by her colleagues. Normally, the faculty member being evaluated will be the one to decide which other faculty member or members will evaluate her.

Disclosure of these evaluations to the individual varies. In some schools reports are discussed in detail and signed by the individual. In other schools, no disclosure takes place. In no school (nursing, medicine, or law) may an individual student or faculty member see his own file or the file of another student or faculty member. A person might be given an item of information contained in the file (social security number, etc.) by a secretary or clerk, but may not peruse the file. This is so even in the case of schools of nursing that have a credentials service for their students, that is, a person may not see the letters written about her which are sent to prospective employers. This is in marked contrast to the similar service provided by the American Nurses' Association.

Release of information is either by letters of recommendation or by "credentials compiled" on the student by the school. Letters of recommendation may be written by individuals as such but will usually be written "administratively." These letters are based principally on the detailed evaluation reports that have been made during the individual's affiliation with the school as student or faculty. The letters are taken very seriously by both writer and receiver. They discuss many interpersonal dimensions and do not hesitate to disclose negative characteristics. They do not merely describe the individual as she is at the time the letter is being written, but rather reflect a historical view, describing in detail her development during her entire affiliation with the institution. Reliance on such detailed systematic assessments in letters of recommendation is of much greater importance in the nursing profession at large than in law or medicine.

Release of information by the nursing school to agencies other than other nursing organizations appears to be the same as in medicine or law, namely, that information already obtained from some other source will be confirmed and that a general question by an FBI agent concerning potential threat to national security of a job applicant will be answered. However, in nursing there was a much greater expressed willingness to cooperate with FBI agents should additional information be desired.

GENERAL COMPARISONS AMONG THE PROFESSIONS

In this chapter the discussion of dossiers has been organized around five major foci (purpose, source, content, processing for specific use, and release) as these become manifest in each of the four major organizational contexts within which professionals operate (government manpower agencies, professional associations, practice organizations, and professional schools). Thus, the major emphasis has been on the way in which practices with regard to professional dossiers vary according to the characteristics of particular organizations. This summary, on the other hand, is written so as to draw attention to the differences and similarities in the treatment of the dossier proper in the three professions and to minimize the impact of the organizational contexts. Three overriding dossier issues will therefore be discussed—compilation, control, and consequences. Throughout, the attempt will be made to present comparative generalizations which bring into sharp focus the differences and similarities among nursing, medicine, and law in regard to the treatment of dossiers.

Compilation

Under this heading four of the major concerns of this study will be discussed: purpose, source, content, and processing and verification.

Purpose. The purposes of dossier compilation within the three professions may be divided into administrative purposes and professional purposes. Looking first at the administrative purposes, certain generalizations can be made. Records are a pervasive phenomenon in modern highly bureaucratized society. As an organization grows in size, it becomes more necessary to keep records concerning those within the organization, even if only for administrative purposes. This is true even within professional organizations where the administrator is himself also a professional.

In those organizations that have high mobility of personnel as well as considerable size, the administrative need to keep records is increased as there are more occasions to justify hiring decisions, and, in addition, to write letters of recommendation for departed personnel. Thus, in nursing, where individuals tend to work in large organizations and where personnel turnover is high, more records, as well as more detailed ones, were found to be the rule. In law, where personnel mobility is least prevalent among the three professions, fewest records are compiled. In medicine, where the professional works within organizations which are generally between those of law and nursing in terms of organizational size and personnel mobility, the volume and detail of the records compiled was found to spread over a middle range.

The differences described here exist primarily in the practice settings investigated, although they also exist to a lesser extent within the professional schools. Differences of organizational size and degree of personnel mobility may explain, at least partially, the differences in record-keeping in medicine and law. However, in nursing an additional factor may account for its position in this three-way comparison—its status as a profession. Nurses, collectively, are seeking higher professional status and, among some of the younger leaders, some deliberate challenge to the physicians' authority is made in favor of greater autonomy for the nurse in making decisions about patient-care. In general, however, the fight is far from won and many older leaders caution their younger sisters to go slowly in asserting the capabilities of nursing to operate as an autonomous health profession. Lacking the autonomy and authority that the physicians derive from their high prestige and professional reputation, the nurses have tried to standardize and formalize methods by which to authenticate their professional competence. Voluminous and detailed records of interpersonal judgments about professional competence may become a substitute for reputation and prestige. This factor, added to those of organizational size and personnel mobility, may explain the greater detail and volume of records kept among nurses.

Turning now to professional purposes, as contrasted with administrative purposes, we found that when asked about the purpose of record-keeping systems, most professionals interviewed were at a loss for an answer. However, upon some thought a response emerged beyond that of "records are necessary." These responses may be grouped into four categories: (1) to keep track of and ensure that minimal standards of training and exposure to technical knowledge are met prior to certification; (2) to keep track of who is and who is not certified so that the public may be protected from practice by charlatans; (3) to assess the level of "quality" achieved by various members of the profession beyond the mere quantity exposure that is needed for certification; and (4) to protect the profession itself against the misconduct of any member however technically competent.

Among all three professions, the first and second reasons for compiling dossiers were seen as routine matters that did not seem to pose any problems. The third and fourth categories of purpose were much more likely to raise the "dossier question." Problems arise more with the means by which information is collected in the case of the first and second objectives, while in the case of the third and fourth, problems arise in regard to both the ends themselves as well as with the means. In the legal profession emphasis is placed on the first and second objectives as justifying reasons for keeping dossiers; while in the medical profession the emphasis is placed on the second and third objectives; and in nursing emphasis is on the third and fourth objectives.

This difference in attitudinal approach toward record-keeping is reflected in the number and type of records kept by the three professions and confirms the differences already noted in the number and detail of records.

Operating policy with respect to professional dossiers ordinarily is made with considerable independence at the first supervisory level: departmental chairman, chief of services. Once the decision to compile dossiers has been made, there seems to be no need within any of the professions to seek outside authority either to keep the records in the first instance or, once the record-keeping system has been started, to expand, systematize, or modify it. Most officials, most of the time, and in most places, exercise good judgment and compile records only to the extent made necessary by the administrative and professional demands of the tasks and services they are called upon to provide. Overriding organization-wide policy is generally the result of some incident or external pressure which leads to the setting of general guidelines for compilation and release of information. From time to time an overzealous individual may compile records that exceed the limits generally thought to be necessary or desirable and that may adversely affect morale in a given organization. The decision to compile records of that particular kind may then be reviewed and rescinded by higher organizational authority. Such action would be taken after these records attracted wide attention, and pressures against them were brought to bear on the organization. These then are the major purposes and justificatory arguments for the compilation of records among the three professions.

Sources. In all three professions the two major sources of information were the individual professional himself and other professionals who had some knowledge of the individual in question. In addition, in all three professions there were both public and private sectors of information-giving sources with formal and informal dimensions within each of these sectors. In nursing, reliance is placed most heavily on formal sources of information within both the public and private sectors. In law, reliance is placed most heavily on informal public and private sector information. In medicine, reliance is placed most heavily on formal public and informal private sources of information.

In terms of control of information sources, nurses have the greatest control. Even though detailed evaluative records are kept on nurses, because of their great mobility, they have a multiplicity of sources from which information about them can be gathered. Since it is the nurse herself who requests that letters of recommendation be written to prospective employers or to the central "credential compilation" service, she may pick her source from many alternatives. In contrast, lawyers have the least control of information sources, because information is most often gathered informally and, when gathered formally, because of the absence of mobility, there are few alternative sources available.

Content. Of the three professions, lawyers compile the skimpiest dossiers on each other, nurses compile the most voluminous dossiers, and doctors fall somewhere between nurses and lawyers. When lawyers compile dossiers on fellow professionals, they tend to put into them relatively incontrovertible "facts" such as law aptitude test scores and law school grades. Matters of personal and social conflicts or systematic periodic assessments of the individual's personality and interpersonal skills are rare. Such evaluations are somewhat more frequent among doctors. Among nurses, however, regardless of the size, locale, or type of organization in which they may work, it is very likely that they will have very systematic, periodic assessments based on generally accepted and established detailed criteria of personality and interpersonal skills.

One possible additional explanation for the difference among the three professions in terms of both the number and type of records kept on the individual professional may be found in an examination of the content of records kept by professionals not on other professionals, but, rather, in their daily professional activities on their "most important other," that is, patients in the case of doctors and nurses, clients in the case of lawyers. The lawyer does not have to take copious notes on the client as client, but, rather, on the details of the case as a set of legal questions irrespective of the client's personal and interpersonal style. From incident to incident, the work which the lawyer performs for a particular client, even a long-term client, may take the form of many separate eclectic units, each case presenting potentially separate legal questions completely unrelated to the other. The potential legal solutions to legal questions most often remain the same for all clients with similar questions regardless of whether or not they may have personal or interpersonal pathologies. In short, the lawyer collects detailed information on eclectic legal matters pertaining to the client but not on the client as a personal and social entity.

The doctor's work, on the other hand, revolves around one biological organism. The patient's medical record becomes a unified history of previous states of health, all of which may contribute in considerable measure to the solution of subsequent pathologies that may arise. Some pathologies (not a few) with which the doctor deals may be psychosomatic or social in nature, involving the patient's personal and interpersonal relations and the effects of these upon the social as well as biological functioning of the patient. The doctor records these observations as potential aids to diagnosis in the course of compiling a medical record on the patient.

Finally, the nurse concentrates to a considerable degree on the patient's personal and interpersonal comfort. Her role involves administering drugs and other medication that the doctor has prescribed, but the full force of her role is to "nurse" the patient. This involves trained sensitivity to peculiarities of personality and interpersonal difficulties which may impede physical and mental comfort if not speedy recovery. Nurses routinely record these observations with greater intensity in psychiatric wards to facilitate the work of subsequent shifts.

The pattern that emerges is that in the course of performing their professional duties lawyers take the least cognizance of clients' interpersonal peculiarities, doctors more, and nurses most. This, of course, does not address the question of the quality of the observations. One could argue that doctors' may be qualitatively of a different kind. However, even if this were true, whatever nurses' observations lost in quality they would more than make up in quantity in terms of our general argument. Our point is that there is a "spill over" effect from the type of record that a professional keeps on his "most important other" to the type of record which he keeps upon professional colleagues. In nursing this "spill over" tends to have become formalized into colleaguial relations among nurses. Under the presumption that she can improve her care of patients by having her strengths and weaknesses pointed out to her, the nurse is constantly evaluated by her peers and supervisors on how well she "nurses" the patient, with all that this implies in terms of her interpersonal abilities to please others (presumably patients but in effect other nurses as well), making them happy, comfortable, rested, and able to accept and deal with their illness.

Processing and Verification of Information. As a general rule, information is not collected and then processed for a specific use in the professions. Rather, whatever processing occurs generally takes place in the manner in which information is collected at the time it is collected. The clear exception to this rule is nursing wherein systematic periodic assessments are made, which are then processed and refined further and prepared for release in the form of letters of recommendation, etc.

In both medicine and law the usual situation is that of a single individual having been asked to write a letter of recommendation for another specific individual with the letter writer using his own experience and recollection to write such a letter. Whatever the individual includes or leaves out of the letter he writes is done at his own discretion and thus he, in effect, engages in a degree of information-processing to the extent that he inflates or deflates his judgment of the individual professional in terms of the destination of the letter.

Evaluations of nurses, while undergoing more processing in the sense that more people work on any given evaluation, eventually emerge as relatively fixed assessments that are sent as such to all inquirers. In this sense, the contents of nurses' dossiers tend to have undergone a much higher degree of verification than either those of doctors or lawyers, though doctors' dossiers are once more in an intermediate position. Nurses are more frequently asked to read the evaluations that their supervisors make of their work and to indicate that they have read them by signing their name. In most situations where the nurse is asked to sign she is also given the option to enter a short dissenting statement.

Very minor efforts at actual verification were found and even those few depended not on the particular profession but rather on the particular individuals keeping their records. Verification by comparison of information received and by interviews with the individual professionals were found to exist among all three professions.

Control

The control of dossiers can be divided into three distinct considerations —physical characteristics and physical location of the dossier, access to and release of the dossier per se, and access to and release of information contained in the dossier. In contrast to the discussion of content where great variation between the three professions was found to exist, in the area of control a great deal of similarity was found. In general, differences in control of dossiers seem to depend not so much on the particular profession but rather on the size of the particular organization in question within the given profession.

Turning to the physical aspects of control of dossiers, in all three professions information on the particular professions consists of some sort of written record. In no instance were computers, tape recordings, or similar methods used. Most records consist of file folders containing the information collected. In some instances, the information is transferred from files into books which consist of single pages bound together. Each page consists of a synopsis of the information in a single individual's file.

As for physical location of the dossier, in the larger organizations the dossiers were located in a specific area designated principally for just such purpose, whereas in the smaller organizations, dossiers were usually located in close proximity to the chief administrator. Size may be a determining factor within organizations as well as between organizations. Where the size of the population about which records are being kept is proportionately high relative to the total population of the organization, separate areas with special personnel were again found to exist. An example of this is the professional school, where student records are kept, as a general rule, in a specially designated and distinct area, whereas faculty records are, again as a general rule, kept in or in close proximity to the chief administrator's office. In all cases use and physical location of records coincided in the sense that where there existed a separate staff in charge of record-keeping a separate and distinct physical area existed for the location of the records so kept.

Access to the release of the dossier per se appears to vary not on the basis of the profession involved but rather on the basis of the size of the record-keeping system. In those instances where the record-keeping system was a distinct unit, with its own staff, within a larger organization, direct access to the release of the dossier per se was found to be almost nonexistent. The person seeking the information would neither ask for the entire dossier nor would he be given the entire dossier, but, rather, a person in charge of record-keeping would relay the specific information requested to the inquirer. In smaller organizational units, access to and release of the dossier per se was much more direct. This is probably because of the limited surveillance possible due to the sheer number of persons who can be around the records at any given time.

Dossiers on either students or full-fledged professionals are from time to time placed on archival status. Within universities they are usually transferred to the university library and placed under that administrative authority, most often when records long unused begin to crowd the space available. Ordinarily it is not a matter of every year getting rid of one more year's worth of obsolete records, but rather the removal of a large volume of records from time to time when the space available becomes filled. This type of release of records usually does not pose a problem of any kind, except possibly for historians.

With respect to release of information contained within the dossier, rather than release of the dossier itself, three aspects will be considered —release to the individual himself of information contained within his dossier, release of information to other professionals within the particular organization, and release to agents of various sorts. It was almost universally stated that no information would be released to the individual professional himself except for information known to him at one time but presently forgotten (such as date he began working for the organization) or information available elsewhere but more conveniently available in the dossier (such as his social security number).

However, in two cases, namely, practice organizations and schools with respect to faculty records, this no-access rule was qualified to the extent that if the individual professional in question presented a compelling reason for the release, he might be given the information he requested. Additionally, although access to information by the individual professional himself is equally limited among the three professions, in nursing the individual has more control of and knowledge about what is put into her dossier in the first instance, as previously noted. As for release to other professionals within the particular organization, it was generally stated that information in the dossiers of other professionals within the organization would not be available to a colleague of equivalent or lower organizational level, but, for appropriate reasons, would be released to a professional of higher rank.

The kind of question that can potentially raise a good many problems is that of release of records to investigation agents of various kinds. Throughout the professions, the Federal Bureau of Investigation receives the broadest unquestioned cooperation among all the agencies which routinely ask for information. Ordinarily FBI agents do not ask to see anyone's records. Rather, they may ask the keepers of the records for confirmation of dates during which the individual was associated with the particular organization, or they ask people who have worked with the individual in question whether they know of anything that would make the individual a threat to the security of the nation. Ordinarily they do not ask more than such general questions. People usually give similarly general responses, such as, "No, I do not." On the other hand, it is left up to the person responding to decide what it is that he considers to be a threat to the country. If he says, "Yes," undoubtedly further questioning would ensue. The restraint in release of information seemed in general to come from the fact that FBI agents did *not* press for information beyond these general questions. There was general impressionistic evidence that people were much more willing to cooperate with the FBI than with any other form of investigatory agency.

None of the people interviewed indicated that he would release any kind of information at any time under any circumstances to private investigators. On the other hand, most said they would verify information already possessed by insurance and credit investigators since they "obviously" had received such information from the party in question in the first place. Although all people interviewed indicated that they would not allow a dossier to be carried away by any investigator, it seems clear that some would allow FBI agents (and perhaps other persons) to peruse the contents of a dossier in special cases. For example, in four cases of particular dossiers discussed during one interview, the interviewer was allowed to handle the contents and ask specific questions about what was observed therein. On the other hand, some persons interviewed simply viewed the contents of dossiers to refresh their memories of incidents they related to the interviewer and did not make any overt move to allow the interviewer actually to see or handle the contents. Both of these responses occurred in the case of lawyers and nurses, while only the latter occurred in the case of doctors. The most frequent response in all cases was what appeared to be a candid response to questions, and, where the interviewee could think of a particular illustrative case, he (or she) would pull out the file in question and refresh his memory and then answer the questions, perhaps holding up a letter, at such a distance that the contents of it could certainly not be determined, and say something to the effect that here was a letter from the man's chief or department head, relating his point of view on the incident. The interviewer would then ask relevant questions about the nature of the content which the interviewee would answer in ways that would address the question without violating the privacy of the dossier. In short, the interviewer was generally impressed with the behavioral discretion which most interviewees used in handling the dossiers in their charge.

Consequences

The intensity of information-flow between information-keeping systems in the professions appears to be in response to developmental pressures in the profession in question, not the other way around. The greater the volume of professionals who are being trained at a particular school, the greater the need to expand record-keeping facilities and the greater the need to hire clerks to maintain the system. The same is true of other organizations where full-fledged professionals work and in the professional associations. The greater occupational mobility (along a horizontal if not vertical dimension), the greater the need for systematic procedures for the transfer of information from one organizational jurisdiction to another. The more subjective the evaluations necessary for the selection of competent personnel for a specific task, the more the opportunities for dissatisfaction and, thus, the greater the need to give these evaluations at least the aura of objectivity. Thus, it seems that nurses reported a greater number of instances in which a nurse was displeased with the evaluations her supervisors made of her than was the case with either doctors or lawyers. In the case of lawyers it may be important how well he gets along with others, but, in the final analysis, it is how effective he is as a lawyer that counts. Even in large firms, lawyers tend to work as single individuals on particular legal tasks. Their efforts may have to be coordinated with those of others, but, at any given time on any particular task it is much more likely that the lawyer will be left alone to do his task. Doctors, on the other hand, more frequently have to work with other doctors simultaneously, and especially so in larger organizations, and, consequently, getting along with others becomes a more important matter though not as important as for nurses where interpersonal abilities seem to be a *sina qua non* of becoming a successful professional.

The content of dossiers and the information that is transferred from one organizational jurisdiction to another reflect these pressures. Detailed multidimensional assessments of "getting along with others" have become highly systematized and institutionalized in the field of nursing. The administrator of one of the practice organizations related that in her eleven years tenure in the organization no one had been dismissed because of lack of technical competence. Many times, however, a nurse had been asked to look for employment elsewhere because of problems which in one way or another could be placed under the rubric of "getting along with others." In another work setting, a large hospital, the administrator of nurses said that a very large proportion of the problems they experienced were "psychological or psychiatric." He added that he didn't know whether people with this type of problem sought out nursing as a profession or whether because they were nurses they were more sensitive to problems because they saw and reported them more frequently. Nevertheless, it appears that, upon further exploration, the usual problems could all be classified under the heading of "getting along with people." It may be that the pressures that a large and therefore highly bureaucratized hospital places on nurses, who as a professional group have an ethos of direct personal aid to others, may generate interpersonal staff conflicts which are labeled as "psychological." In any event, these instances eventually are recorded in relatively "objective" fashion along fairly standardized dimensions and eventually flow from one organizational jurisdiction to another as they follow the nurse's changes in employment.

What is the impact which information flow has on modern highly organized society? Presumably one characteristic of a "community" is that its members are incorporated into it as "whole persons" rather than in terms of some narrowly defined special task-relevant characteristic as may be the ideal-typical member of a bureaucracy. If this is so, then information-flow may tend to make a "community" out of the professions. When a professional moves from one organization to another, he might come as a total stranger to the new organization offering only a narrow part of himself for hire: his technical knowledge. However, the letters of recommendation and other evaluative materials that precede him and upon which the decision to hire him is sometimes based allow the people who meet him at his new place of employment to know him more fully even before he arrives. The dossier shows a man's professional (as well as a good part of his personal) history. From a few minutes of perusing a man's dossier can be learned details of his life that might have otherwise taken a very long interpersonal experience to accumulate. Decisions to hire are usually committee decisions so that a good many people may be exposed to the dossier. If the man is not interviewed or not hired and therefore, possibly, never met, the people who reviewed his dossier still know a good deal about him. People who because of their position review a good many dossiers tend to accumulate a good deal of knowledge about a good many persons over a period of time. If they should meet such a person at some other time they have this knowledge to rely on in building interpersonal relationships. This fact, coupled with the fact that some professionals tend to move around a good deal and, therefore, generate an extended network of interpersonal relations also builds a sense of "community." Thus, since nurses tend to move around the country a good deal and tend to have extensive and detailed dossiers compiled on them, it is not uncommon for them to have a multiplicity of close interpersonal relationships with nurses in many parts of the country. One of the consequences of this "community," as well as the fact that evaluations are often shared with the person evaluated, is that "practically everybody" knows how "practically everybody" thinks of "practically everybody else" in the profession. On a national level, this type of experience is perhaps not as common among doctors and probably much less so among lawyers.

SUMMARY

In summary, the following generalizations can be made about dossiers within the professions of law, medicine, and nursing. First, it was consistently found that nurses in all types of organizational settings kept more records in terms of both quantity and detail and, additionally, that these records frequently emphasized skills in the area of interpersonal relations. Lawyers were found to keep the least records and, for the most part, their records were based on incontrovertible objective "facts." Doctors fell somewhere between nurses and lawyers both in the number of records kept and the inclusion of subjective as well as objective considerations.

Second, two possible explanations for these differences were presented:

namely, that pressures of size and mobility within a profession lead to greater need for record-keeping within that profession; and, additionally, that the differences reflected a "spill-over" of attitudes toward record-keeping by the professional on his clients to his attitude toward record-keeping on fellow professionals. Thus, nurses who keep the most records on their "most important other" and who additionally have the greatest pressures of size and mobility, kept the most records. The second interpretation is clouded by the circumstance that physicians in private practice are likely to keep the most extensive *cumulative* records.

Third, the consequences of record-keeping were most apparent within nursing where there is a much greater flow of information between professionals on each other and where the information that is flowing includes many subjective aspects of the individual nurse. Thus, on a national level, there appears within nursing to be a somewhat greater sense of community than is the case in medicine and, especially, in law. It should be noted, however, that this somewhat "mechanistic" interpretation is not the sole, and may not be the primary, source of occupational identification among nurses. Nurses collectively seek higher professional status, and most particularly full autonomy in practice. Failing that, nurses through professional associations have sought to standardize methods of authentication of competence, to verify by formal and centralized dossiers the kind of standing that more securely situated professionals handle by supplementing formal certification with the informal judgments of peers. Records become a substitute for reputation. The patient's trust rests, however improperly, with the physician, and not with the nurse. The nurse accumulates a record of competence, other professionals a reputation that needs documentary authentication only if his formal qualifications or his professional conduct are challenged.

The trust that inheres in the claim to autonomy in practice by fully qualified professionals implies that clients have only limited access to dossiers, and even more limited control over their contents. Professionals, and occasionally lay administrators, determine what records will be assembled and how they will be used on behalf of the client. We cannot state unequivocally that all things work for the best that way, but we can state that that is the way things work.

III Economic Institutions

5 *The Dossier in Consumer Credit*

JAMES RULE, DAVID CAPLOVITZ, AND PIERCE BARKER

ALTHOUGH CREDIT BUREAUS MAINTAIN RECORDS ON VERY MANY AMERICANS, perhaps one hundred million of them, public understanding of these practices appears quite superficial.[1] Most Americans seem aware—often rather uncomfortably so—that they have such a thing as a "credit rating," but few seem to have more than a sketchy understanding of what credit bureaus are and how they maintain and use records on consumers. And yet, given the extensive dependence of our economy on consumer credit, the activities of credit bureaus affect most Americans at one time or another in their lives.

Whenever an American consumer applies to make a purchase "on time," whenever he seeks a personal or mortgage loan, the chances are that the merchant or lender, before completing the transaction, obtains and re-

In preparing this study, we have relied heavily on the generous cooperation of many people connected with the consumer credit reporting industry. We are in debt to so many for such help that it is impossible to mention them all here by name. Instead of trying to do so, let us express our thanks to the organizations with which our informants have been affiliated: The Associated Credit Bureaus, Credit Data Corporation, American Bankers Association and numerous individual credit bureaus, large and small, including the Credit Bureau of Gainesville, Georgia, the Credit Bureau of Greater Boston, and the Credit Bureau of Cook County, Illinois. Pierce Barker has also drawn from his experience as owner and manager of the Credit Bureau of Winder and Monroe, Georgia.

[1] There are no systematically compiled figures for the total numbers of credit files existing in this country. One hundred million is the best approximation we can make, in light of the numbers of reports issued per year, the number of bureaus throughout the country, and the numbers of files maintained by individual bureaus that we have encountered.

views a credit report on the applicant.[2] Credit bureaus, the source of these reports, now issue more than one hundred million of them annually.[3] The contents of the reports vary according to the amount of information available on the individual in question. But virtually all reports list the name of the applicant, his address, marital status, the name of his employer, and his salary. In addition, the report will list his outstanding debts and other financial obligations with accompanying information about his promptness in meeting these. Still other information, depending both on the thoroughness of the issuing bureau and the nature of the individual's credit history, will include records of past debts and the promptness of their payment. The sale of such reports to interested parties such as retailers, lenders, and sometimes landlords and employers is the main, and usually the only, source of income to the local bureau. Yet the existence of the bureau remains a matter of which most individuals are only vaguely aware.

Credit bureaus are organizations which specialize in gathering, storing, and transmitting information relating to the desirability of individual consumers as credit risks. It is important to distinguish credit bureaus, in this exact sense, from organizations like Retail Credit Company and Hooper-Holmes, which also maintain dossiers and issue reports on individuals, but mainly for purposes of insurance rather than for consumer credit.[4] The Associated Credit Bureaus (ACB), the national trade association, lists 2,100 members in the United States and Canada, and there are probably not more than two hundred unaffiliated bureaus.[5] These bureaus range in size from tiny one-man offices to enormous businesses employing more than five hundred.

The role of the dossier in this industry is bound to differ from the corresponding role in other organizational settings in one basic respect: for

[2] There are some transactions where the retailer or lender does not draw a credit report, e.g., cases where the customer is already well known to the firm. Some firms, too, do their own checking on applicants, thus assuming the functions of the credit bureau. In our opinion, however, credit reports are used in the majority of credit transactions across the country.

[3] The Associated Credit Bureaus (ACB), the national credit bureau trade association, reports that its members made more than 97,100,000 reports during 1967. This figure excludes the reports issued by the computerized reporting system of Credit Data Corporation, which must have numbered at least several million in that year.

[4] These two firms are often falsely identified as credit bureaus. Both of them do maintain dossiers on individuals—Retail Credit is said to have 45 million such dossiers—but their reporting is primarily to insurance companies and employers. Credit reporting represents a distinct minority of their business, and an even tinier minority of the total consumer credit reporting done in the United States. Remarks in the following pages concerning credit bureaus are not intended to apply to these two firms. [Also see Chapter 7 on life insurance in this volume.]

[5] Because of their very lack of ties, the unaffiliated bureaus are difficult to number. In our studies we have encountered very few, and, with the exception of Credit Data Corporation, these have mainly been engaged in specialized lines of reporting such as mortgage reporting.

the credit bureau, maintenance and use of the dossier is not an *adjunct* to the function of the organization so much as its *raison d'etre*. For this reason, we are concerned in this chapter as much with the social organization of the industry as with the credit file itself. Since the creation and use of the credit file represent the purpose of the credit reporting industry, understanding the industry's social structure and functioning will help illuminate the workings of the credit file.

HOW CREDIT REPORTING WORKS

History and Social Structure of the Industry

Both the organization and development of the credit bureau industry depend on the unparalleled use of consumer credit in America. Nowhere outside North America is the use of consumer credit nearly so extensive.[6] Nor is the credit institution an old one; neither consumer loans nor extended payments on merchandise were widespread before the turn of the century. At that time, consumer credit consisted mainly of informal arrangements between some merchants and certain specific customers, and of personal loans made by banks to fairly solvent depositors. Personal debt had a moral tinge ranging from suspect to downright disreputable.[7] Since then, this disapprobation has reversed itself; the steady trend has been to make consumer credit more routine and formal, more widely available, and to extend its use to consumers further and further down the scale of socioeconomic status. The dramatic increase in consumer debt since World War II is evident in the following figures.

Increase in Consumer Debt, 1945–1968[a]

Year	*Outstanding debt in billions of dollars*
1945	$ 5.6
1955	39.0
1965	84.0
1968 (August)	103.7

[a] Including both instalment and noninstalment debt, but excluding mortgage debt.
SOURCE: Various issues of *Federal Reserve Bulletin*.

Not the least important impetus for these trends are the substantial profits realized both from consumer lending and the extension of credit on the purchase of goods and services. Since World War II, competition

[6] According to estimates from ACB spokesmen, there are not more than a few dozen credit bureaus outside North America.

[7] For fuller discussion of this point, see Caplovitz, David, "Some Sociological Aspects of Consumer Credit," paper presented at the 62nd Annual Meeting of the American Sociological Association, August 29, 1967.

for credit business has become particularly intense, with significant results for the credit reporting industry. Consumer credit, which began as a means of increasing profits on merchandise sold by retailers, has become a source of enormous profits in its own right; some major retailers are said to realize more profits from extension of credit on their merchandise than from sale of the merchandise itself, though we have not been able to substantiate this. The extension of credit both in lending and retail business to lower and lower income groups has been one result of the intense competition for the profits realized from such transactions.[8]

Growth of Credit Bureaus. But we are anticipating the main issue—the growth of credit bureaus themselves. The extension of credit is profitable only when the percentage of bad debts is small, and it was not long before the first retailers to feature charge accounts, around the turn of the century, had to come to terms with this fact. The first credit bureaus began as simple lists, maintained jointly by credit-granting retailers, of customers whose accounts had gone bad. By referring to these lists, the retailers aimed to prevent such people from repeating their performance. While the bias toward derogatory information has continued, credit bureaus have expanded their functions over the years to meet the needs of other kinds of customers; these changes included the filing of information on good accounts as well as bad. During the 1920's and 1930's, credit bureaus spread from the largest cities to medium-sized and even small towns. According to figures published by the national trade association, 46 per cent of its member bureaus are now located in towns smaller than two thousand, and 94 per cent in towns and cities smaller than one hundred thousand.[9] Following World War II, and throughout the 1950's, the number of bureaus increased rapidly, finally leveling off during the present decade.[10]

As the industry has grown, the nature of its operations has changed; no modern credit bureau is as simple as the original bad-debt listing systems of the turn of the century. Files now contain information from court records, newspapers, and listings of paid-up as well as unpaid accounts, although "bad" accounts continue to be the most sought-after information for credit files. Yet the underlying principle remains fairly constant; bureaus continue to gather information on the financial status of local resi-

[8] Another interesting result has been the advertising campaigns aimed at encouraging people to borrow or buy on credit—a sharp departure from the earlier view of consumer credit as an ignominious last resort for the desperate family.

[9] From the Annual Report of the Associated Credit Bureaus of America in March, 1967.

[10] No exact figures exist to document this trend; it was described to us by an industry spokesman with considerable first-hand experience in such matters.

dents, especially in regard to their debt-paying habits, and to sell such information to their clientele, most of whom are grantors of credit. This pattern helps to explain an interesting quality of localism which, to a lessening extent, has characterized the industry from the beginning. The "product"—reports on individuals' willingness and ability to pay their debts—is manufactured from primarily local sources and sold mainly to local users. Until the advent of computerization, it was however, grossly impractical to contemplate a more centralized organization of credit reporting, since the expense involved in bringing the "raw materials" together in a single place, processing them, and then sending most of them back where they came from would be unjustified. More recently, though, computer technology has been eroding this localism by making transmission of information easier.

Conspiring with the appeal of electronic data-processing to bring about a trend toward centralization has been the increased mobility of the American populace. The fact that the typical consumer patronizes stores over a much larger area than before, and changes his place of residence more often, makes it more difficult for a bureau with a very small area of operation to maintain an over-all description of that consumer. Credit reporting for a small locality, carried on from a credit bureau within that locality, is viable only so long as most residents of the place do their buying and litigation there. When the same small town becomes a suburb of a large urban concentration, the single local bureau often must give way to larger operation whose intake of information coincides with the larger life-space of the residents. Still another kind of centralization is resulting from the need of national credit card grantors, especially oil companies, to buy reports on applicants from all over the country. Receiving all credit card applications at a single national office, these immense firms often find it laborious to make contact with a local credit bureau for each one. Instead, they submit the applications to Credit Bureau Reports, a national agency which funnels them to the appropriate local bureaus, collects the resulting reports, and, for a fee, turns them over to the original companies. Like the growth of very large, big-city credit bureaus, this form of centralization has its roots in other broad changes in American social structure.

Ownership of Credit Bureaus. The largest bureaus—those in major urban centers—are also the oldest, generally having been founded by groups of major retailers as described above. These bureaus, numbering about fifteen, have nearly all remained in the ownership of the original groups of merchants, representatives of whom now comprise their boards of directors.[11] One interesting result of this form of control is that profitability is not of the highest priority for these bureaus. Rather, the controlling merchants often tend to put greatest emphasis on maintaining low prices, since they are in effect selling to themselves. Private ownership becomes common as the size of the bureau decreases, though some smaller bureaus are also under the formal control of local business interests. To speak of the size of a bureau, incidentally, is almost the same as citing the size of the community; the two are almost perfectly correlated.[12]

Regardless of the size of the community in which they are located, bureaus sell their reports to a predictable range of users. According to figures published for 1965 by the ACB, retailers accounted for 40.7 per cent of the business among association members. Also accounting for major shares of bureau business are finance companies, with 18.3 per cent, and banks, with 8.6 per cent. Other credit bureaus, through fees charged for interbureau reporting, generate 8.6 per cent of the typical member bureau's revenue, while a variety of miscellaneous users account for very small percentages, e.g., advertising, with 0.1 per cent, medical and related health services, with 2.5 per cent, and insurance, with 0.8 per cent. In addition to other tiny percentages of business deriving from various categories of customers, it should be noted that this breakdown includes 13.9 per cent of revenue from "other sources." The latter include, among other things, reports sold to employers and other noncredit grantors like landlords. Along with reports made to law-enforcement agencies, which account for 0.3 per cent of revenue, these noncredit uses of bureau information, though not numerous in comparison to sales credit grantors, are matters of concern to critics of the industry.[13]

Nearly all credit bureaus organize their services on a membership basis. For most bureaus a small minority of the total customers account for the greater proportion of business. The main clientele of a bureau become members, which entails paying a yearly or monthly fee and receiving in return reduced prices for reports. Membership fees generally run from $25 to $150 per year, and the reduction in price per report is around 50 per cent.[14] Members also agree to supply the bureau with information

[11] Again, an exact tabulation is unavailable on this subject. The information came from a knowledgeable industry representative.

[12] In fact, the ACB levies dues according to the size of the community in which the member bureau is located.

[13] The advent of the bank credit card in the past few years has greatly increased the proportion of reports issued to banks.

[14] These figures represent our estimate, based on experience with a number of bureaus. Bureaus which provide their members with certain extraordinary services, e.g., a "credit guide" listing the credit standing of all members of the community, may charge much more.

on their own customers, though nonmembers also may supply such information on request from the bureau. To become a member, or to purchase reports as a nonmember, a customer must identify himself to the bureau as having a "legitimate" interest in the use of the reports, and must promise to use them confidentially. It is important to remember that the members of the bureau are not the same as its owners. Where a group of major retailers owns a bureau, they will usually also be members, but members as such represent the clientele rather than the directorship of the bureau.

Localism and Lack of Capital. No understanding of the social organization of the credit reporting industry is complete without some reference to factors more subtle than the size distribution of bureaus and the nature of their ownership and membership. Behind such basic realities there remain two facts essential to an understanding of the industry—the relative absence of centralized control and the lack of capital. The fact that until recently credit reports could only be "manufactured" locally has apparently worked toward creating an industry in which no single interest owns more than a few local installations.[15] For whatever reasons, it remains true that most of the more than twelve hundred local bureaus are subservient to purely local interests. Whether the orientation of the local bureau is toward making profits for its owner or toward providing inexpensive service to controlling local business interests, it is unlikely to be subject to influence from other members of the industry. Such dispersion obviously is not auspicious for creating a pool of funds for investment in new, industry-wide ventures. This fact helps explain why the credit bureau industry has been slow to computerize its operations—for such a conversion requires very large investments. In recent years however, some of the largest credit bureaus have undertaken to computerize with the backing of the national trade association.

Another force contributing to the slowness of the industry to undertake new ventures has been the traditional weakness of competition within the industry. In most medium-sized and small communities, there is only one credit bureau. In the largest cities there are apt to be a number of bureaus, but, besides one very large, dominant operation, the others usually restrict themselves to specific suburban reporting areas or a specialized line of reporting, like mortgage reports. With the significant exception of cities served by Credit Data Corporation, an insurgent computerized credit re-

[15] We have encountered three "chains" of credit bureaus in the course of our study, apart from Credit Data Corporation. One of the three chains is owned by Retail Credit Company, but is operated independently.

porting system, we have been able to establish the existence of two large bureaus in direct competition with one another in only one major city.[16] One can understand this situation when one realizes that the most valuable asset of any bureau is its files, and that bureaus have traditionally been able to accumulate a backlog of files only over years of operation. Once established, the pool of filed information represents a major competitive advantage that discourages would-be competitors from trying to break into the market. The ways in which Credit Data Corporation has been able to make a sharp departure from this pattern are discussed below.

One force working to countervail against the tendencies toward autonomy and dispersion of control is the national trade association, the Associated Credit Bureaus, whose headquarters are in Houston. As mentioned above, its member bureaus numbered over 2,100 as of 1967.[17] Members pay dues graduated according to the size of their businesses. Like other trade associations, the ACB acts as a lobbying organization working against state and federal attempts to regulate the industry. In addition, it carries on other activities that one might associate with a national trade association, including public relations, research, and the presentation of seminars and other educational services for its members.

Perhaps the most important ACB activity in terms of the social organization of the industry is the institutional mechanism which it has created for transmission of credit information from one member bureau to another. According to ACB statistics, member bureaus in 1965 realized 8.6 per cent of their total income from other credit bureaus.[18] This is the result of "foreign" reporting, or reports purchased by one bureau from another—something which is necessary whenever a bureau requires information on an individual not resident in its area of coverage. The ACB maintains a list of all of its members, along with references to which communities they serve; the Houston office issues this directory in loose-leaf form to its members every year and updates it frequently. A bureau needing a report from outside its own area of coverage simply consults the directory and makes its request directly to the appropriate local bureau. Payment, according to the kind of report requested, is made in the form of coupons also supplied by the national association. Members purchase these coupons, then redeem those that they receive as payment from other bureaus. As a result of a federal antitrust action in 1933, member

[16] This city is Savannah, Georgia.

[17] According to the ACB, the total membership in its Credit Reporting Division was 2,046 at last count.

[18] According to figures published by the ACB in March, 1967.

bureaus are constrained against refusing to supply credit information to the small minority of bureaus who are not members of the ACB; this means, at least in theory, that any bureau may obtain information from any other, though nonmembers pay higher prices than do members when purchasing reports from ACB bureaus.

The Houston office also acts as referee in disputes among member bureaus. Such conflicts most commonly center on the provision of reports by one bureau to another, something which is necessary whenever a bureau must prepare a report on an individual outside its area of coverage. If such reports are slow to arrive or are inferior in quality, the delinquent bureau can, at least in theory, be expelled from the national association. Actually, though, the powers of the ACB are quite limited, and no major bureau has been permanently expelled. Because competition is weak within the industry, users of reports have little choice but to buy from the local bureau or to do without the information. Given this situation, the national body cannot do very much to deprive a local bureau of its business.

Computerized Credit Reporting. The above might represent a balanced picture of the history and structure of the industry if we were writing in 1965 instead of 1969. But in 1965 Credit Data Corporation was established in California as the first computerized credit reporting system and has since grown to represent a major contrast to the noncompetitive, decentralized, capital-poor, "traditional" credit bureau industry described above. Operating independently of the ACB, to which nearly all other bureaus belong, Credit Data has amassed and invested a great deal of capital to create a credit reporting service whose "files" are maintained in computer storage and which serves areas much larger than any conventional bureau. One computerized file, with access in San Francisco and Los Angeles, now maintains information on consumers over most of California; a second file in New York City covers not only that metropolitan area, but also large areas of New Jersey and Connecticut. Representatives of CDC claim that these two repositories already contain information on from fifteen to eighteen million individuals, with additional files coming into existence at the rate of fifty thousand per week. Another installation is expected to open shortly in Detroit.

Besides bringing together files on more individuals than conventional credit bureaus have done, CDC is attempting to bring about another kind of centralization within the industry. In many areas of the country, banks and loan companies have traditionally been dissatisfied with the services provided by credit bureaus, and have consequently established their own "exchanges" of credit information. These exchanges are simply listings of individuals holding loans, to which lending institutions can refer in evaluating a loan application to determine whether a given applicant may already be overcommitted. Credit Data claims to be able to assume the functions of these exchanges, and apparently has so persuaded many lending institutions. As the banks and finance companies tend to abandon their own exchanges in favor of CDC, information from their files is combined with retailers' information, creating an ever more centralized data pool.

To say that the advent of Credit Data Corporation has jolted the credit reporting industry would put the matter mildly. Several ACB bureaus have now computerized their operations or will soon do so, evidently in response to the threat of encroachment by CDC.[19] The question now preoccupying the people close to the industry is to what extent computerization will become the norm for all bureau operations, and whether CDC will be the prime beneficiary of such changes. To the outside observer, though, the most pressing question is what changes will ultimately come about in the structure of the industry as a whole, and what will be the effects upon individuals.

Whether the agent of change is CDC or some innovative element of the rest of the industry, it is not difficult to envision a handful of highly centralized, computerized operations serving most of the country. Indeed, a single pool of computerized credit information for the entire country, technically feasible already, could become practically justified within the foreseeable future—say, twenty years hence. Just as the growth of single computerized systems for large urban concentrations will probably put an end to the autonomous existence of smaller suburban bureaus, regional systems may take over from city-wide ones. Credit Data, in its California and New York operations, is already building such regional systems. Outside observers almost invariably quail at the prospect of monolithic, unitary repositories of information, and it is not difficult to sympathize with such reactions. But we do not believe that such concentrations of information are *necessarily* more pernicious than the systems that now prevail. Since credit reporting has always tended to be an industry where local bureaus dominate their own local markets, what we are viewing now appears more a movement from a congeries of local monopolies to much

[19] We have just learned of a recently concluded agreement between ACB and the International Telephone and Telegraph Co. in which the latter will make available a computer time-sharing service to ACB members. This development will no doubt hasten the growth of computerized credit reporting among these "conventional" credit bureaus.

smaller numbers of large monopolies, rather than the growth of monopolies from a field of competitive firms. A new development, too, is the advent of competition between CDC and the ACB bureaus over control of the giant new systems. It is not impossible that the more highly centralized credit reporting industry of the future will prove more amenable to the public interest than the traditional one.

The Operations of Credit Bureaus

At almost any credit agency, the visitor will find roughly the same spatial arrangement of work. Whether the business is large or small, activities will focus around a single large room lined with file-drawers. In these drawers are the individual credit files which represent the bureau's stock-in-trade, arranged one to an individual, usually in alphabetical order by surname. In the center of the room the visitor sees a series of desks or tables, perhaps a single very large table, with telephones to receive calls from customers. Plying the phones and files is a staff, almost always female, much of whose work consists of pulling files from the drawers and reporting the contents by phone to waiting customers. Nearby, but to the side, will be other desks with typewriters where the staff prepare the lengthier written reports. The visitor will see evidence of a good deal of correspondence, consisting both of incoming requests for reports from other agencies and outgoing reports both to agencies and other customers. In all but the smallest bureaus, the manager and other supervisory or specialized staff will occupy separate offices around the periphery of the main room.

Information in the Files. The files, in the form of index cards, letter-sized folders, or envelopes with records stored inside, list first the basic information mentioned above as appearing in most credit reports. The full name of the subject and his spouse, their occupations and places of employment, how long the subject has held his present job, address, his salary and number of dependents. Depending on how long a file has been in existence, it will contain corresponding information for previous years, as well; files are cumulative, and bureaus generally never discard any information until the individual dies.

The basic entries just mentioned, interestingly enough, are not "credit records" in one narrow sense; that is, they are not reports of the individual's debt-paying behavior. Contrary to popular expectation, both bureaus and their customers often place as much importance on information like length of job tenure as they do on records of past credit accounts. Other facts not directly referring to credit, yet often included in bureau files, are the individual's criminal record, if any, marriage and divorce notices, lawsuits involving the individual and, less often, note of his major assets such as real estate holdings.

Records of past credit transactions, of course, are also listed. The quantity and quality of this information vary greatly from the files of one individual to another and from one bureau to another, depending both on the nature of the individual's credit history and the filing practices of the bureau. The most common entries will be records of retail accounts, i.e., charge accounts, time-payment arrangements and the like with department stores, furniture dealers, etc. Home and auto financing will figure importantly in the files as well. In nearly every case the bureau will list the promptness with which the individual has met such obligations. If payments have been in arrears, the bureau will want to record whether the individual succeeded in clearing the debt at length; if the account passed to a collection agency, this fact will also be likely to appear in the record. Personal loans from banks or finance companies will be treated in the same ways. Bankruptcies, a cause for panic on the part of present or prospective creditors, will be listed. The manner in which the bureau records these data will vary in formality and exactitude. Necessarily, the bureau will want to condense the information to fit in the limited space of the files; other than that, practices range from modified prose to a code recently developed by the national trade association. Indeed, variability from bureau to bureau is probably even greater in terms of what information finds its way into the files. Beside differences in thoroughness, there may be simple differences in judgment as to what information is pertinent to desirability as a credit risk. In the absence of any legal strictures in the matter, bureaus are free to file any information of their choice.

Sources of Information. How do bureaus compile these records? For past and current credit accounts, the membership of the bureau will be the main source of filed information. Part of the relationship between the member retailer or lending agency and the bureau is an agreement that records of the member's accounts will be turned over to the bureau for inclusion in bureau files. Often the member is supposed to report all such accounts automatically; in practice, however, this is not common. Most frequently, members regularly report only bad debts, and "good accounts" are listed in response to requests from the bureau for information on a specific consumer. These requests typically come when the bureau is writing a report for which it requires current information. Bureaus also sometimes contact nonmembers for the same information, if they have reason to believe that the individual has had credit at the establishment.

The second major source of information in credit files is the so-called "public record" material. These are facts gathered not from credit-grantors, who have a special relationship to the bureau, but from sources theoretically available to anyone. Many of these data are available from court records—including lawsuits, criminal and civil actions, bankruptcies, and divorce notices. If a bureau is thorough in its operations, a major expenditure of time and money will be allocated to sending staff members to local courthouses to cull such information. But such excursions are not necessary for the collection of all such information. Many bureaus rely heavily on local newspapers, clipping and filing marriage and divorce notices, records of criminal cases, and the like. In some localities special publications list pertinent information such as bankruptcies, births and deaths, mortgages and other loans contracted, etc. Bureaus clip and file such information directly.

We noted above that bureaus most frequently take more pains to collect word of "bad" accounts from their members than to record the good accounts. Most bureaus place a distinct premium on unfavorable or "derogatory" information in all phases of their operations. The reasons for this are easy to understand, if not to admire. Most people's credit records, after all, are fairly sound, and even the minority who are manifestly unwilling or unable to pay will still have some "good" items somewhere in their credit histories. For this reason, it is more efficient for the bureau to gear itself to identifying poor risks than the good ones. Bureaus therefore often solicit lists of debts written off for tax purposes, or lists of accounts turned over to collection agencies.

It is very common to find credit bureaus operated in conjunction with collection agencies, thus facilitating the collection of derogatory information for bureau files. Conversely, the association with the credit bureau makes it easier for the collection operation to achieve its ends, since collectors purposely emphasize the link to the credit bureau to persuade reluctant debtors that failure to pay will result in loss of all credit. One bureau *cum* collection agency that we encountered in the course of our study advertised itself with a large lighted sign above its premises, showing the name of the firm superimposed on a sinister silhouetted figure apparently clad in a trench coat and carrying a briefcase. Many credit bureaus also supply their customers with dunning forms under the bureau's letterhead; it is claimed that receipt of a notice on such stationery, with appropriate wording, greatly increases the debtor's desire to pay.

We have already noted that the activities of the Retail Credit Company and the Hooper-Holmes Bureau are outside the main purview of this study, since consumer credit reporting does not represent a major proportion of their business. Nevertheless, they do issue credit reports in addition to their more numerous reports to employers and insurance companies. Their operations differ from those of most consumer credit bureaus in that they maintain staffs of outside investigators who gather information on individuals from their friends, neighbors, relatives, co-workers, and others. These interviews, generally conducted without the knowledge of the individual under investigation, aim to elicit information on the individual's drinking habits, family life, marital stability, "morality," and other sensitive matters. Like consumer credit bureaus, these two firms place a premium on derogatory information; Hooper-Holmes, for example, maintains a file of more than ten million items of exclusively derogatory material. In many cases, the interviewers for these firms work under a quota system for derogatory information. Needless to say, such pressures upon investigators dealing with sources of questionable accuracy is bound to increase the likelihood of entering erroneous but nonetheless damaging information in individuals' files.

Reporting Procedures. How do bureaus convert their filed information into reports for sale to their customers? To answer this question, we should first point out that bureaus issue a number of different *kinds* of reports; the ACB itself issues different reporting forms for the use of its members, and some bureaus may even do some form of reporting which they regard as not corresponding to any of these forms. Reports vary both quantitatively and qualitatively. Qualitatively, of course, most deal with the willingness and ability of an individual to meet credit obligations. Some focus on special details of credit standing, however; for example, some reports, called "collection aid reports," list the individual's assets to help a collector in recovering bad debts. Other reports, though, refer to individuals' desirability as employees, rather than as credit risks. These are a minority, though a significant one. Most reports aim at helping a firm evaluate an individual as a credit risk, and they range in complexity from very sketchy to very detailed, in relation to the size of the contemplated credit transaction.

For most bureaus, a very large proportion of the total volume of business involves reports at the simplest end of this continuum of complexity. These are the "in-file" reports, or reports made up only of information already contained in the bureau's files. Most of these reports are issued by phone; the customer, typically a representative of a department store or other retail merchant, phones the bureau, and a clerk immediately pulls the file of the individual and reads the contents back to the customer. Sometimes the firm will put this report in writing, but the requirements of most buyers currently run much more to immediate reporting. The urgent desire of retailers to extend credit on-the-spot, before the potential customer leaves the store, is responsible for the prevalence of this service. The charge for an oral in-file report is fifty cents to a dollar for a member, perhaps twice as much for a nonmember of the bureau.

More complex reports, required for larger credit sales and loans, involve research by the bureau to obtain information more extensive and more recent than that contained in bureau files. In some cases such additional work will involve no more than phone calls to a few firms listed by the individual in his application to the organization requesting the report. These reports are usually in writing, and most bureaus attempt to produce them within one working day of receipt. The cost is from one to two dollars for bureau members, and again twice as much for nonmembers. The most carefully researched credit reports are those drawn in connection with mortgage applications. Here the bureau will check a great many sources besides its own files, and the results will cover about two typed pages; unlike other kinds of reports, these are not broken down into code or abbreviated English. Prices for these reports run from four dollars to much more, presumably depending on the amount of research involved.

Though the specialized, noncredit reports do not make up a major percentage of most bureaus' business, they have aroused widespread indignation and controversy. This angry response is scarcely surprising. In preparing a report for a prospective landlord or employer, bureaus investigate not only an individual's credit standing, but also question his previous employers, friends, neighbors, and others in regard to his personal habits, home life, and morals. The results are then written up for the buyer of the report, and usually without the knowledge of the individual reported upon. It is very difficult to generalize concerning bureaus' policies regarding these reports. Some bureaus decline to issue such reports at all, while others take special pains to promote this kind of business. Hooper-Holmes and Retail Credit Company make this kind of reporting a particular specialty, and their activities probably account for a large proportion of all such reports issued. Fees for this kind of reporting range from approximately five dollars up, according to the amount of research involved; twenty-five dollars might be a median, but this figure represents only educated conjecture, since fees for this kind of report are not fixed. That these reports represent a minority of most bureaus' business, however, should not distract attention from the seriousness of their implications. Their use can result in denial of a job or a place to live; yet, as with other credit reports, the issuing bureau assumes no responsibility for their accuracy.

In closing this brief review of the kinds of credit reports that bureaus issue, we should mention one issue that virtually haunts spokesmen for the industry—the misunderstandings over the evaluative quality of credit reports. Our informants within the industry have unanimously emphasized that credit bureaus do not evaluate an applicant's desirability as a credit risk, but merely report "facts" about him. This is basically correct. Bureaus generally do not attempt to make credit decisions for their customers. Because policies on whether to grant credit differ greatly according to the granting firm and the size of the transaction, it would be impossible for any bureau to make a single decision about any one person for use by all buyers of reports. One wonders how this erroneous view of credit bureau functions began. It appears that "credit rating" may be the one term from credit reporting to enter the vocabulary of the general public. In any case, credit bureaus maintain not "credit ratings," but discrete items of information about individuals.

Operations of CDC Bureaus. The operations of the computerized Credit Data installations differ enough from those of conventional bureaus to deserve special treatment. The physical arrangement of work, of course, is bound to be strikingly different, since the bureau searches its files not manually but electronically. As in conventional bureaus, a large, all-female staff receives requests by phone, but there the similarity ends; the CDC operator, without leaving her seat, then prepares an IBM punch card and feeds it by a high-speed conveyor to the computer, which returns a report from its files within two minutes. CDC returns information to the caller either by phone immediately or, if the caller prefers, in writing. These two kinds of "in-file" reports are the only ones that CDC issues. It does not issue reports to employers or landlords, for example, nor does it engage in other specialized forms of reporting like mortgage reporting. CDC sells its reports only to members, who pay no membership fee but who must qualify as *bona fide* credit grantors.

We mentioned above that the difficulty of accumulating files has traditionally represented an obstacle to creation of a competitive bureau, once there is an established bureau operating in a given locality. CDC attempts to meet this problem by incorporating its members' back credit records in their entirety into its own files. Since virtually no conventional bureau assimilates all of its members' records into the credit files, this practice on the part of CDC represents a shortcut to the creation of a substantial backlog of information. It is an expensive shortcut, though, since a great deal of time and effort must go into collecting such information and feeding it into the computer files. Like conventional bureaus, Credit Data also files public record information from courts and other sources.

A crucial question concerning the expanding reporting areas of Credit Data Corporation's operations is its thoroughness of coverage. It is not clear whether CDC, with its appetite for total ingestion of its members' back records, develops a more complete picture of an individual's credit standing than a conventional bureau, which may collect less information from its members but at the same time maintains contact with more different sources of information. A large area of coverage is hardly meaningful in itself, without reference to how much relevant information from that area the bureau collects. This matter of completeness of coverage may figure importantly in the competitive struggle between Credit Data Corporation and the ACB bureaus. We do not mean to imply, however, that either side necessarily has an advantage in this field as of now; conventional bureaus are extremely uneven in thoroughness, and the issue is very difficult to judge.

Quality of Reports. We ought not to close this discussion of the mechanics of credit reporting without some mention of the quality gradient of service among various credit bureaus. An outsider might naturally assume that all credit bureaus' files and reports contain the same quantities and quality of information, but this is not the case. There are, after all, no effective strictures, either in the law or elsewhere, which dictate how assiduously a bureau must collect information for its files, or how far it must go in researching its reports. Moreover, building a truly complete file of information takes both time and considerable money. The amount of scouring through court records which a bureau can do will alone cost thousands of dollars in wages, and, even when the money is available, such information cannot be accumulated overnight.

Then, too, most bureaus have at least until recently been virtually immune from competitive encroachment on their markets. The user of credit reports usually often has only the choice of buying or not buying. And even then, it is not always easy for the user of the report to determine how good or poor it really is; the crucial question is not so much the validity of reported information as whether there exists additional information about the individual which the bureau has failed to list. This the user is often in no position to know. The temptation, consequently, is for the bureau to do as little research as possible and submit large numbers of relatively favorable reports—which do satisfy buyers at least in the short run, for they do not encourage them to refuse potential customers. Taken together, all these factors result in enormous variation among bureaus in the thoroughness of their reports.

HOW SHOULD CREDIT REPORTING WORK?

Having described how credit bureaus work, we now turn to the more critical topic of how the industry serves or fails to serve the public interest. As we shall show, many practices in the creation and use of credit files so seriously disserve the individual consumer's interests that apparently only general public ignorance has permitted their continuation.

People do not realize, for example, that their own credit files are accessible to virtually anyone who understands the workings of credit bureaus and has a few dollars to spend on a report. People are generally not aware that credit reports can result in the refusal of a job or the refusal of a landlord to rent an apartment. It is not widely known that law enforcement agencies, including both local police and the FBI, regularly purchase credit reports. Nor does the typical consumer, if indeed he is aware that he has a credit file, realize that information added to the file is subject to systematic biases which can be extremely prejudicial to the accuracy of credit reports. Finally, people do not generally appreciate the fact that although these reports affect their lives in many ways, the credit bureau assumes no responsibility for their accuracy. For although credit bureaus make money by selling information on individual consumers, the nature of bureau operations is such that the consumer usually remains unaware of them. Credit bureaus are run by business for business—and generally run *as* businesses in their own right. While individual consumers in effect pay to be investigated through credit bureaus, the nature of credit transactions is such that the kind of unawareness described above is unaffected. This lack of understanding on the part of the public has its unfortunate counterpart in the absence of legal codes pertaining to the operation of credit bureaus. As Alan Westin cogently pointed out in a statement before the House Subcommittee on

Invasion of Privacy, there is virtually no state or federal legislation regulating the operation of credit bureaus.[20]

Can anyone seriously defend this lack of representation of the public interest in consumer credit reporting? There are, after all, some who still insist that those outside the credit bureau industry and its immediate clientele have no legitimate interest in the workings of bureaus. The argument is that, since bureaus "only report the facts," and since "the truth never hurt anybody," credit bureaus deserve as much latitude in their operations as if their product were steel ingots instead of confidential information about people. The weakness of this argument scarcely requires exposition. "Mere facts" are never neutral in a setting like consumer credit, but entail considerable interest and competitive advantage to whoever has access to them. Of course, nearly everybody desires privacy concerning certain kinds of facts about himself purely for its own sake. But besides being inherently desirable, privacy carries with it very tangible practical advantage in all sorts of competitive and contractual relationships. The general who can obtain "mere facts" on his opponent's position and capabilities will never regard such facts as neutral. Likewise, the businessman or employer who purchases a credit report commands a wide array of information about the subject of the report, who may have no comparable inside information on the integrity of the firm with which he is dealing or the quality of the merchandise he is to purchase. Indeed, the bitter opposition of business interests to the recent "truth in lending" and "truth in packaging" legislation demonstrates that no one on that side of the economic fence really believes that "mere facts" are neutral.

Mistakes in Credit Files

Having entered these criticisms of the ways in which consumer credit reporting affects people, we must not delay in justifying our critique. We might best begin by citing what we would consider a typical case of the effects of a credit file upon the individual. Probably it would run as follows. Sometime in early adulthood, the average American, without knowing it, has a credit file opened in his name. The file will most likely come into existence when he first applies for a credit account to buy a car or some other consumer item. As mentioned above, the file will soon come to include the individual's residential address, date of birth, occupation, salary, and some notation of the size and nature of his credit accounts.

[20] Westin, Alan F., Statement Before the Subcommittee on Invasion of Privacy of the House Government Operations Committee, March 12, 1968.

These data will usually enter the files as an outgrowth of the bureau's investigation for the first account. Or the file may begin with an announcement of the individual's marriage, clipped by the bureau staff from local papers. In any case, the bureau will open the file from time to time as the years pass, most likely for the preparation of reports required for the opening of new accounts. The more credit accounts the consumer pays faithfully, the easier he finds it to open additional accounts, and in fact the typical individual does pay fairly regularly. Given a normal progression through life and the typical sound paying habits, most Americans probably never realize the existence of their own files, let alone take time to contemplate their effects on their lives. The credit file may be an indispensable condition to enjoyment of the basic material trappings of life, including one's house, automobile, home furnishings, and entertainment; yet if things function smoothly, as they most often do, the existence of the file remains completely hidden.

We take this "typical" case as a starting point for analysis of the effects of credit files on individuals for two reasons. First, it should help to show how and why the uses of credit files can remain outside the attention of the public, at least in the most common situations. Second, it should emphasize that the more dramatic and flagrant misuses of such information —significant though they are—do not represent the norm. In the overwhelming majority of cases, consumer credit files are opened only for the routine credit reports which make up the bulk of most bureaus' business. But this fact should yield no grounds for complacency. Even where there is no use of credit files for purposes other than credit, the possibility of erroneous information or other "mistakes" raises serious ethical issues. Spokesmen for the industry insist that the proportion of mistakes in credit reports must be small, and in some sense this is probably correct. But if we assume the existence of, say, one hundred million credit files throughout the country, a mistake ratio of even 1 per cent would imply that a very large number of individuals are subject to unjust adverse effects. This figure is especially disturbing when one realizes that such mistakes could readily be corrected if credit bureaus operated more openly.

One major source of misleading credit reports is erroneous information in credit bureau files. Often these result from problems as common as several people's sharing the same or similar names. Bureaus generally try to file all information under the subject's full name, including a middle initial. But in any large city there are bound to be many people sharing with others the same name, even including the middle initial. Against this contingency, bureaus generally attempt to list residence, place of work, and certain other basic information in each file. Still, the system is not fully effective. A file may come into existence, after all, with very minor scraps of information, such as a marriage notice clipped from a local newspaper, providing only very sketchy means of distinguishing the subject from others with similar names. Subsequent information, e.g., notice of the filing of a lawsuit against someone else with the same first and last name, may then be added to the file. The buyer of the report on either of the two parties—or on some third person who also happens to share the first and last name—may receive a mixture of facts pertaining to the two. Sorting out the identities of parties with similar names, given elliptical information from various sources, is an exacting job under the best of circumstances. And the bureau workers who actually do the job are usually modestly paid, semiskilled operatives working under the pressure of dealing with large amounts of material as rapidly as possible.

Probably there are many mistakes resulting from misidentification that are completely indifferent in their effects upon the individual. But notice of past bankruptcy or of certain kinds of lawsuits will often result in the flat refusal of credit, even if the rest of the applicant's record is very sound. What aggravates the situation is the fact that the individual, once refused credit, often has not the slightest idea why. Many merchants apparently try to conceal from customers their use of credit reports, and the ACB report forms used for most reporting include a provision that "this information . . . must not be revealed to the subject reported on." And if the individual should make his way to the credit bureau and persuade its staff to show him his record, he will find that the bureau is under no obligation to change the incorrect information, though most would probably do so once it reached their attention.

A second major source of mistakes is the mishandling of information on a single individual during the course of its being gathered, filed, and reported. From the origin of credit information among the credit accounts of retailers, through its processing by the bureau and subsequent transmission back to the buyers of reports, it passes almost exclusively through the hands of low-level clerical workers. Some potential for distortion is present at every point. The ACB has recently moved to eliminate some of these hazards by introducing what it calls its "New Language for Consumer Credit." This is a series of simple codes for the communication of credit information, to be used in the writing of credit reports and in the collection of credit information for filing. By reducing discursive prose to a simple series of letters and numbers, this innovation may help eliminate some errors in reporting. Still, it is worth noting that credit bureaus disclaim legal responsibility for the accuracy of the information that they report; in part of the same statement quoted above, the ACB report forms read, "This information has been obtained from sources deemed reliable, the accuracy of which this organization does not guarantee." To date, the law supports this disclaimer.

Still another source of misleading credit information is the failure or inability of bureaus to take account of extenuating circumstances affecting the payment of credit accounts. Illness, for example, may force an individual to delay making credit payments, but credit records, as they are usually maintained, fail to take such matters into account. Or there may be a dispute between merchant and consumer as to whether a bill is valid; the merchant is nevertheless free to "punish" the customer by reporting nonpayment of the debt to the local credit bureau, if he so desires. Here again, it takes a rare consumer to be shrewd enough and persistent enough to bring these matters to the attention of the credit bureau before the inaccuracy can be disseminated in further credit reports.

Similar dangers, and probably more serious ones, inhere in the filing of so-called "public record" information, consisting of material culled from sources like newspapers and court records. As we have said, the systematic collection of information from such sources is an expensive and time-consuming part of any credit bureau's routine. When a bureau lists a series of arraignments for criminal charges in its files, or records the institution of a series of lawsuits, the temptation is strong not to go to the added expense and trouble of noting the ultimate outcome of the actions. The *Wall Street Journal* recently quoted the head of the major New York City credit bureau as saying, "It's impossible to get the disposition of a suit. . . . It would be extremely expensive."[21] Thus the initiation of such actions is much more likely to be included in the file than their outcome—a state of affairs which invariably works to the disadvantage of the individual.

Public record information is particularly volatile when entered in credit files, since lawsuits, bankruptcies, and criminal actions reflect very unfavorably on a man's credit standing, at least in the eyes of most users of credit reports. Imagine, then, the hypothetical case of a homeowner, say, who contracts with a dishonest firm for repairs on his house. The promised repairs prove unsatisfactory, and the homeowner refuses to pay. The firm, in an effort to frighten the homeowner, institutes a lawsuit with no real hope of collecting. In time, the suit is dropped or thrown out of court, but the local credit bureau nevertheless files record of its institution. The

[21] *Wall Street Journal*, vol. 171, no. 25 (February 5, 1968), p. 1.

individual may suffer no direct loss from his brush with the dishonest firm, yet may find all sorts of further credit denied him.

We mentioned above that the industry places a definite premium upon collecting derogatory information. It is more efficient for bureaus to identify the minority of "bad" risks with derogatory items than to identify the great majority of "good" risks by long, unbroken histories of regular payment and the like. It should not be necessary to point out that this procedure maximizes the damage caused by mistakes in individuals' files. The inclusion of a lawsuit, for example, will very often result in flat refusal of credit. When, as in the case of Retail Credit Company, Hooper-Holmes, and some other firms, the information concerns not only credit transactions but also extremely sensitive material on one's family life, morals, and so on, the matter becomes especially serious.

Mistakes do happen, then—not just at random, but at predictable points in the creation, maintenance, and transmission of credit information. These mistakes are particularly pernicious in that the individual is very likely to remain unaware of them, even though they may cause him harm. It is true that such mistakes affect only a minority of all credit reports. But this minority may add up to very substantial figures in the absolute sense, given that American credit bureaus issue some one hundred million reports per year. As we have said, the general public's ignorance of credit bureaus' activities seems to be the only explanation for the continuation of these practices without some legislative regulation. The prospects of such legislation are under close discussion at this writing, however. We hope very much that those concerned will consider the points raised above: Who can file information, especially derogatory information, with credit bureaus? What kinds of information should and should not be subject to filing? Should the subject of the information not have some means of knowing when information is filed under his name, and what has been filed? And should the bureaus concerned not be legally responsible for the accuracy of the often potent contents of their files?

This last point deserves special emphasis. The law actually supports credit bureaus' routine disclaimer of responsibility for the effects of the information that they supply. Professor Alan Westin noted in his testimony before the Subcommittee on Invasion of Privacy of the House Governmental Operations Committee, "The leading cases hold that credit bureaus can circulate information to participating credit grantors and that they are privileged in this reporting against suits for libel or defamation if the reports were furnished in good faith to someone having a legitimate interest in it. Suits for invasion of privacy have been rejected by the courts on the ground that individuals had compiled their own credit record by their commercial dealings."[22] Thus, no matter how flagrantly negligent a bureau is in compiling and issuing its reports, the individual reported upon can not successfully sue for damages caused by such reports. It should be clear that such damages can be substantial, both to one's financial standing and to other areas of one's life such as one's job. One wonders how many other industries are legally absolved from responsibility for the quality of their products, or from responsibility for the damages caused by faulty products.

Access and Accountability

All of these issues would be much less troublesome if consumers had ready access to their own files. Mistakes would then be subject to easy correction, at least if the bureau were willing to cooperate. We have noted that public ignorance and the secretiveness of merchants and bureaus conspire to keep the use of credit files outside general scrutiny, and this lack of understanding is certainly responsible for the relatively slight demand for access. Credit and employment applications do usually contain a statement authorizing the prospective creditor or employer to investigate the information supplied by the applicant, sometimes "by any means." But applicants usually do not realize that this investigation may involve opening a specific file about themselves, located in an organization which specializes in maintaining these files. When a store refuses credit, it may decline to explain the perhaps crucial role that the credit report has played in the decision. Credit bureaus, after all, make no money from talking to the individuals who do turn up on their doorsteps with grievances, so they may form tacit agreements with their members to conceal the effects of credit reports on the individual. And, once a disgruntled consumer does present himself to the local bureau, the bureau remains under no legal constraint to discuss the record with him. Many bureaus, of course, do so regularly; some of the largest operations have staff members who devote themselves full-time to meeting with such troubled consumers.[23] But no bureau, to our knowledge, will go so far as to sell an individual a report on himself, as they would to any regular customer of their business.

[22] Westin, Alan F., Statement Before the Subcommittee on Invasion of Privacy of the House Government Operations Committee, March 12, 1968.

[23] Still, the large bureaus are acutely aware of the expense involved in meeting with customers. The Credit Bureau of Cook County, Illinois, charges $5 for a consultation with an individual concerning his file. The purpose of the fee is not to make profits for the firm but to discourage such consultations.

In light of these formidable obstacles to access to credit files for the ordinary uninformed consumer, it is all the more ironic that there is virtually nothing to prevent anyone who really understands the workings of credit bureaus from ordering a report on anyone else. According to policies observed throughout the industry, bureaus sell reports to anyone whom they deem to have a "legitimate" interest in obtaining them. In practice, this means that reports are available both to businesses and to landlords, law enforcement agencies, employers and some others. Whether they purchase their reports as members of the bureau or as nonmembers, the buyers must establish to the satisfaction of the bureau management that their purposes are "legitimate." How careful the bureaus are in checking out the buyer of a report before making the sale no doubt varies greatly from one bureau to the next, but we do not believe that any bureau's practices in this regard could withstand a determined effort at deception.[24] All that need be established, after all, is that the would-be purchaser is in fact the representative of a business, an employer or renter of real estate. A convincing story and a bogus letterhead would probably do the trick in most cases; at most, it might be necessary to set up some kind of simple "front" operation. Or, if an "illegitimate" seeker of a credit report lacked the inclination to approach a bureau directly, he may prefer to find someone who *is* a member of the bureau who will purchase a report on his behalf. Finally, since both the transmission of reports from the bureau and their receipt by businesses are typically in the hands of low-paid clerical workers, these individuals may also represent a source of reports destined for other than "legitimate" uses.

The point is not that credit bureaus encourage the use of their reports for purposes other than those that they would consider legitimate, for there is no reason to believe that this is so. Our assertion is rather that the safeguards against such use are virtually meaningless against a determined seeker of information who understands how to go about procuring a report. As they now operate, bureaus can not possibly check in detail the background of everyone who purchases reports from them, and they certainly cannot check how their members use each report that they buy. And the system of intercommunication among bureaus is such that literally any credit file in the country is available to any customer of any one credit bureau. Despite the stated aim of credit bureaus to maintain confidentiality in their reporting, then, the system is actually extremely vul-

[24] Credit Data Corporation appears to check applicants much more carefully than do conventional bureaus, before granting membership status; and CDC sells reports only to members. It is very difficult to see, however, any means by which CDC could identify an "illegitimate" request submitted by one of its members.

nerable to use by any knowledgeable person. Nor does the individual whose file may be involved in such "illegitimate" reporting have any way of knowing who has purchased information, or, for that matter, that a report has been drawn.

Throughout this discussion, we have been using the term *legitimate* in quotation marks, for we are reluctant to accept the concept of legitimacy as the credit bureau industry seems to interpret it. Interpretation of what represents a "legitimate" use of credit reports generally rests with the managers of local credit bureaus, anyway, except in the rare instance where a dispute concerning the uses of a report comes to involve the ACB. But even in areas where the industry as a whole agrees on the legitimacy of a use of reports, we find reasons for concern. For example, we question very strongly whether *any* credit information should be available without the consent of the individual to whom it pertains. Is it right that landlords, say, or employers should be able to draw on a file of "confidential" information about an applicant, especially when the applicant is unaware that the reporting is taking place? Should the applicant not be able to decide in his own right whether to supply such information? Similar arguments would hold in the case of law-enforcement agencies, which are also major customers of credit bureaus. Given that such information is available upon subpoena to police and the FBI, should the individual not be able to withhold such information in the absence of subpoena?

Access to credit files, then, both by the subject of the information and others, is another area that deserves full and critical appraisal in the light of the public interest. Like the issue of the accuracy of filed information discussed above, the matter of access has been prominent among the discussions of the several legislative committees which at this writing are studying consumer credit problems. We hope that these committees will consider some of the issues raised above. Specifically, we hope that all those concerned with consumer credit will question whether information should be available without the express consent of the individual to whom it applies, whether some kind of release from the consumer should not be necessary for the issuance of any report. Should not individuals be able to obtain reports on themselves at least as readily as regular members of credit bureaus? And should people not have available to them a record of those who have purchased information from their files?

Various remedies have come under discussion. Some have suggested legislation which would require bureaus to send duplicates of all written reports to the individuals reported on; this would represent only a partial solution, since the majority of all reports are made orally. Another suggestion has been that a release from the individual reported on should be necessary for the issuance of any credit report; considerable study would be necessary to determine how to implement such a requirement, to be consistent with the on-the-spot, immediate credit which many consumers seem to desire. In any case, the readiness of legislators and others to entertain such suggestions appears an optimistic sign, providing hope that strong, sound legislation will ultimately result.

Toward Justice in Credit Reporting

Our criticisms of credit bureau practices should hardly be taken to minimize the role of the industry in contributing to the remarkably high standard of living now enjoyed in America. As we have said, credit buying has become so important to most American families that their ways of life would be almost unrecognizable without it. And though only a small proportion of American consumers are basically unwilling or unable to pay the debts that they contract, the losses suffered if all individuals enjoyed unrestricted access to consumer credit would be substantial enough to place the whole system in jeopardy. The credit bureau industry, then, deserves recognition as a necessary condition to the material prosperity enjoyed by most American families, for its function of identifying sources of potential disruption to the system before damage is done is vital.

The overwhelming majority of paying customers, then, share an interest in maintaining some kind of credit reporting system. But this is scarcely to say that the specific practices of contemporary credit bureaus incorporate the most desirable ways of serving such functions. The job can be done, after all, within a wide range of advantage and disadvantage to the various parties concerned. The ideal goal, it would seem to us, would be a system equally responsive to the interests of both sides of the credit transaction, that is, both user and subject of the report. Such a system of parity would represent quite a contrast to what we see as the domination of present-day credit reporting by the interests of the credit bureaus and the buyers of reports.

This "parity of control" principle, however, is much easier to admire in the abstract than to apply to specific, workable suggestions. The principle would be consistent with a stipulation that no reports be available except at the desire of both buyer and subject; that is simple enough. But matters become much more complicated when one tries to apply the principle, say, to the filing of derogatory information. Most people would agree, for example, that there should be some restrictions against filing biased, erroneous, or otherwise misleading derogatory information; and there are some instances where almost everyone would agree that bias exists, e.g., notice of a lawsuit filed without regard to its ultimate disposition. But, on the other hand, any credit reporting system must make it possible to record *some* derogatory information, for not to do so would make a credit bureau about as viable as a bank from which everyone makes unlimited withdrawals. This would imply that individuals could never have a complete veto on what information bureaus file in their name. But who, then, is to decide when an item of derogatory information is biased, when it is unrepresentative of an individual's total credit reliability—when, in fact, it should or should not enter into the record?

This is simply to say that the serious ethical problems to which we have tried to point do not all admit of easy solutions—even in the ideal situation where all concerned would strive for solutions. Spokesmen for the credit bureau industry have complained bitterly, as spokesmen for industries are apt to do, about what they consider the "uniformed" attempts to regulate the business. They may mean by this *all* attempts at regulation, but the fact remains that some proposals put forth recently have been grossly impractical. One report, which we have been unable to substantiate, described a bill introduced in a state legislature which would require all credit bureaus to send a copy of in-file information yearly to everyone whose names appeared in the bureaus' files. Despite its superficial appeal, this proposal is clearly unfeasible, since most bureaus have more names in file than the number of yearly reports that they issue. The yearly costs of such a policy would be far greater than any bureau could sustain, and the benefits to consumers would be limited, since a very large proportion of most bureaus' files are inactive anyway.

The "parity of control" principle, then, cannot by itself lead to solutions of all the ethical problems entailed in consumer credit reporting. Such solutions obviously must also be practical in the light of the need for some means of identifying patently poor credit risks. And, we feel, there must also be some code which will define and limit the ways in which various parties can use consumer credit information in their dealings with one another—some kind of "due process" principle for consumer credit. In many areas of social life where opposing parties regularly contend with one another, after all, the law establishes in great detail what resources and options are available to each side. In criminal cases, for example, it is quite explicit what information should be made available by each party to the other, and there are categories of information, such as confessions made under duress, which can never enter the proceedings, no matter how "true" they may be. This is only one of many areas in which society creates "rules of the game" through which conflicting interests can play out their conflicts in relatively defined ways. In consumer credit, this kind of "due process" idea would add something to what we described above as a principle of equal control. It would suggest, for example, that certain kinds of information should *never* be part of consumer credit records, on the grounds that they are inherently unsuitable for inclusion.

It is not clear, for example, that the filing of all kinds of criminal record information is justified. Should a past conviction for assault and battery be allowed to bear on whether an individual has access to credit? Or, to put the case more strongly, we might ask whether credit bureaus should have the right to file, for instance, marriage counselors' affidavits concerning the stability of a consumer's marriage. Credit bureaus do not usually have access to these kinds of information, but if available, it would clearly bear on the desirability of an applicant as a credit risk, since divorce and separation are in fact associated with bad paying habits. And as things stand now, there are no restrictions on the kinds of information which bureaus may file, if they are willing and able to file it. Most people would probably agree that information from a marriage counselor is in some sense "too personal" for inclusion in credit files, no matter how pertinent to an individual's willingness and ability to pay debts. But if one admits that there are *some* kinds of information which should be invariably "off limits" for credit reporting, one must also recognize that we have not yet developed specific standards of "due process" in this area, let alone put them into effect.

In practice, we should note, these possibilities for adverse effects to the individual are often mitigated by the superficial reporting of most credit bureaus. Most credit bureaus are nowhere near the point of seeking out information from sources such as marriage counselors; they are, in fact, much more likely to be cutting corners in their collection of routine information such as past credit accounts. This superficiality can also harm the individual, for it leads to the emphasis on derogatory information and the failure to check dispositions of court actions that we mentioned above. But overall, most credit bureaus probably make more mistakes in the direction of failing to identify the extent of consumers' obligations than in the direction of creating an erroneous impression that he is unable or unwilling to pay.

One form of inaction by bureaus which does *not* favor the interests of the consumer is the retention of outdated information in bureau files. Except for computerized reporting services, systematic purging of bureau files is extremely expensive, and most conventional bureaus maintain all filed information indefinitely. Thus a very old bad debt can still create obstacles for a consumer desiring credit, even if his recent paying habits are sound. A concept of "due process," we feel, would suggest some kind of "statute of limitations" for derogatory information in credit reporting, just as the law limits the time available to the state to prosecute a crime.

FUTURE TRENDS AND ISSUES

Like many other institutions, the credit bureau industry is now changing more rapidly than at any time in its history. In the controversy which has recently developed concerning the uses and abuses of credit information, as much attention seems to pertain to the implications of the growing new credit reporting systems as to the workings of those already extant. Should we be concerned about these developments? Does the movement toward larger and larger repositories of credit information, potentially containing more and more comprehensive descriptions of people's lives, and more quickly accessible to users, represent a threat of totalitarianism? Or will the drift of change, along with increased public and governmental concern, help to bring credit reporting more within the control of the individuals reported upon?

First, the "monopolization" issue. In light of the ascendance of Credit Data Corporation and the response of the rest of the credit reporting industry with its own computerization program, there seems little doubt that more and more records are finding their ways into fewer and fewer repositories. As noted above, there is some question whether it is helpful to characterize this trend as monopolization, since competition within the industry has traditionally been weak, and the advent of CDC has actually made the situation more competitive in some ways. Regardless of the labels used, these changes will tend to make a complete picture of the individual available from fewer and fewer central storage points. Information on single individuals will be less likely to be dispersed among several bureaus, but there is some reason to believe that such dispersion is not too common even today.

We find no grounds to assume that a handful of very large credit information centers, or even a single national file, is inherently more objectionable than the more dispersed system which has prevailed to date. Indeed, assuming increasing concern about credit reporting activities on the part of the government, a few large systems may be easier to regulate and monitor than the more than one thousand that we have now.[25] From our point of view, the compelling ethical questions—accuracy of filed information, control over filed information, and access to files—will continue to be central as the new systems grow.

What about the accuracy problem? Will computerized systems be more or less prone to report mistaken information to buyers of credit reports? Proponents of the computerized operations unsurprisingly proclaim their systems superior in this respect. By eliminating extensive manual processing of information, they assert, the computerized system reduces chances of mistakes. Spokesmen for the conventional bureaus respond by pointing out that manual processing allows for correction of obvious mistakes by bureau personnel, instead of perpetuating such mistakes blindly in computer storage. It is very difficult to say at this point which claims have greater merit. Certainly anyone who has had to contend with erroneous bills sent by computerized accounting systems will be skeptical about the infallibility of the machines. Moreover, in assimilating the enormous amounts of members' records which Credit Data Corporation stores in its files, the firm clearly runs the risk of misinterpreting such records and filing erroneous information, since the records are maintained in forms unfamiliar to Credit Data personnel. But, on the other hand, the CDC practice of filing *all* of members' back accounts may mark a significant departure from the unfortunate bias, virtually universal among conventional bureaus, toward recording derogatory information.

In terms of access to and control over filed information, we likewise see no reason to believe that the new, centralized systems must necessarily prove more dangerous than their predecessors. It is not true, for example, that computers are unable to "forget" facts fed to them. Indeed, purging information is much easier in computerized systems than in conventional ones, and Credit Data Corporation claims to delete outdated facts automatically. Concerning access to credit files, Dr. Harry Jordan of CDC caused some concern when he testified before a Congressional Committee that computerized files could readily be "tapped" without consent of the firm owning the computers.[26] Still, it is hard to see how any system could be more open to penetration by knowledgeable outsiders than the conventional ones; Credit Data, at least, appears to maintain more stringent membership requirements than conventional bureaus. It is safe to say that

[25] Some observers have suggested that the industry should become a public utility, thus subject to explicit strictures to conform to the public interest. Further centralization of the industry is likely to increase the currency of such demands.

[26] Jordan, Harry C., in testimony before the Subcommittee on Invasion of Privacy of the House Government Operations Committee, March 13, 1968.

unauthorized access to credit files is now and will continue to be a major problem. Perhaps compiling more information in fewer places will facilitate illicit use of files, or perhaps it will make it easier to enforce safeguards against such use. Again, it is too early to tell.

Perhaps the most important problem implicated by the rapid changes in the credit reporting industry stems not from the technology or social organization of the industry as such, but from the growing importance of credit information to more and more areas of individuals' lives. As people depend upon credit for more and more of their purchases, as credit information is used more and more widely, all of the ethical issues presented above grow more important. The more the contents of a man's credit file affect his life, the more compelling the importance of accuracy and justice in the maintenance of that file. Much more important than the form of the industry, we feel, are the "rules of the game" which society must create to regulate the play of interests inevitably surrounding any resource as potent as credit files.

In a paper calling attention to the public's interest in various forms of governmental largesse, from subsidies and franchises to licenses and welfare, Charles Reich has coined the phrase "the new property" to refer to the fact that citizens have a kind of property right in such governmental largesse and should not be deprived of their access to it without due process of the law.[27] Much the same argument can be developed for a man's stake in his credit rating. Since more and more of the individual's life-chances are affected by whether he is defined as a good or bad credit risk, his credit rating is very much a form of property that should be protected by the concept of "due process" of the law.

We note with satisfaction that one recent trend has been toward a reversal of public ignorance about credit reporting and of legislative inaction in the matter. At this writing, Congress is entertaining several bills related to credit bureau activities and hearings on the subject have been held by several congressional committees.[28]

[27] Reich, Charles A., "The New Property," *Yale Law Journal*, vol. 73, no. 5 (April, 1964), pp. 733–787.

[28] Congressmen Wright Patman and Clement Zablocki have introduced bills in the House concerning the regulation of credit bureaus, and Representative Cornelius J. Gallagher's Special House Committee on Invasion of Privacy held hearings on the possible invasion of privacy by credit bureaus. In the Senate, Senators William Proxmire and Philip Hart have spearheaded proposed legislation relating to the regulation of credit bureaus. In the face of this congressional activity, the ACB has rushed to set up committees to draft codes of ethics that presumably would make governmental regulation unnecessary. The tentative proposals that the ACB has evolved cover such topics as consumer access to the files, the rendering of reports to noncredit granting agencies, and the updating of files. Thus the proposals before the members of the ACB would give the consumer free access to his file (some credit bureaus now charge a fee in order to discourage this practice) providing that

Despite the significance of legislative attention *as such,* we would like to close with the observation that it will take not just legislation, but perceptive, well-informed legislation to meet these problems. The fact that some credit bureau practices have been and remain outrageous does not mean that sledgehammer regulation will suffice to set the industry right. Many of the issues involved, e.g., what kinds of information should be admissible to credit files, are ethically quite subtle. We hope that those concerned with changing industry practices will approach the task with an appreciation of such subtleties and with sophistication concerning the workings of the industry.

---

he makes the request in person. They also call for restrictions upon information given to noncredit-granting agencies. Records of suits, arrests, and indictments would be filed only if the disposition of such cases is systematically recorded, and a definite file-life, seven years for most kinds of information, would be instituted. These proposals touch upon many of the egregious practices of credit bureaus, but whether such a code of ethics will be accepted by the member bureaus and if so, will be enforced, remains to be seen. It would seem that these belated efforts by the industry to clean house will not ward off some kind of governmental regulation. Such regulation is especially likely as a result of the trend toward centralization in the industry.

6 Record-Keeping and Corporate Employees

IVAR BERG AND JAMES SALVATE

OBSERVERS OF AMERICAN BUSINESS FIRMS DIFFER CONSIDERABLY IN THEIR evaluations of corporate behavior, but they tend to agree that firms respond, more or less sensitively, to information. Some theorists, in analyzing *some* economic problems, see the firm as only a theoretical construct, a "uni-brain," a "decision-unit," a "postulate in a web of logical connections" that adjusts to changes in data.[1] Others consider that a firm's success, or lack of it, is determined by ". . . the judgments of flesh-and-blood businessmen, guided by knowledge imperfect though it may be. . . ."[2] Both approaches give considerable analytical weight in managerial decision-making to the role of information about markets and market-related factors.

Seen in this perspective, the collection of information on clients, customers, competitors, employees, critics, and on the friends, associates, and even the wives of these individuals, is part of the corporation's general

[1] Machlup, Fritz, "Theories of the Firm: Marginalist, Behavioral, Managerial," *The American Economic Review*, vol. LVII, no. 1 (March, 1967), p. 10.

[2] See the discussion of the "relative role of markets and managers" in determining corporate behavior in Chamberlain, Neil, *The Firm: Micro-economic Planning and Action*, McGraw-Hill, New York, 1962, pp. 1–6.

efforts to gather data. As the corporation's environment becomes more complicated, it needs more data on more people. Managers, meanwhile, are well aware that their search for information will generate criticism among those who are concerned with the protection of individual rights in a democratic society. But they also know that they are open to criticism if they act without the benefit of pertinent information about relevant individuals.

For example, one top-ranking corporate executive reminded the authors that he saves his company time and money by investigating employees whose backgrounds might jeopardize its prospects for winning desirable contracts. And the Chrysler Motors Corporation might have saved itself considerable notoriety and a costly stockholder suit not long ago if its files on a number of its highest executives had revealed that several of them had substantial (and conflicting) interests in some of Chrysler's supplier companies.[3]

The more closely captains of industry approximate the rational decision-makers assumed in economic theory, the more complete and systematic will be their quest for such information. The closer the manager conforms to the textbook script, the more likely it is that the corporation's legal mask—its *persona ficta*—will obscure the sharp eyes that peer into private lives. At the same time, however, the inefficiencies and ineptitudes of corporations that do not act on the fullest information will not be long hidden from assiduous corporate critics or protected forever from the harsh light generated by heated competition.

It is by no means clear, given the entirely legal status of corporations in American society, how best to balance the rights of individuals to privacy with the rights of the corporation to collect information pertinent to its legitimate interests and actions. As in other areas of American life, values and principles come into irreconcilable conflict and the priorities of individual and corporate rights will ultimately be assigned in accordance with still other values and principles.

The list of corporate concerns that cause executives to maintain abundant files on various individuals is long indeed. Some firms, because of the "classified" nature of the work they may do for government agencies, engage in cooperative screening activities designed to safeguard military and technical information from other interested but unwelcome parties.

[3] For a description of the details of this most complex matter see Kuhn, James W., and Ivar Berg, *Values in a Business Society: Issues and Analyses*, Harcourt Brace & World, New York, 1968, pp. 246–248.

Efforts are accordingly made to collect data that allegedly bear upon the security risks in respect to employees, visitors, customers, vendors, suppliers, and even those with whom particular employees may have personal contacts that are not apparently of a "business nature."

Other firms collect substantially similar data to reduce entrepreneurial risks they perceive to be related to the backgrounds and experiences of relevant individuals. Thus companies have more than a marginal interest in protecting their trade secrets, their technical formulae, their market plans, their files on competitors, their future plans for production, growth, acquisitions, and diversification, their reputations, the skeletons in their organizational closets, and a host of other clusters of information that bear upon corporate well-being.

Indeed, the types of information on various types of people kept in corporate files are very nearly unlimited. The use of "private eyes" to monitor the activities and to scout the backgrounds of their critics, in particular, has been highly developed. It is sometimes part of a corporate strategy of intimidation, comparable to the "rough shadowing" of suspected criminals, simply to be visibly engaged in the accumulation of personal data. A celebrated example is the case of Ralph Nader, consumer crusader, and the General Motors Corporation.[4] Unfortunately for present purposes, there is no way of testing the hypothesis that one of the lesser sociological functions of dossiers in private enterprise is to produce anxiety among certain "objects" of corporate scrutiny, the better to predict and control their behavior. Nor is it possible to consider, in this exploratory effort, the entire range of types of corporate dossiers, though according to at least one troubled Senator, such an effort would have significant implications for American freedoms.[5]

In keeping with the editor's mandate, a preliminary exploration has been conducted into some specific aspects of corporate dossiers, in particular those involving employees. While only limited data are available on even this single segment of corporate record-keeping, they do provide some evidence on (1) the sources of information on managers; (2) records on nonmanagerial personnel; (3) the disclosure of information on employees; and (4) the implications and issues in the use of corporate dossiers.

[4] See Engberg, Edward, *The Spy in the Corporate Structure*, The World Publishing Co., New York, 1967, p. 16.

[5] See the very general and brief discussion of corporate dossiers by Senator Edward V. Long in *The Intruders: The Invasion of Privacy by Government and Industry*, Frederick A. Praeger, New York, 1966, pp. 49–52.

Corporate Recruiters

The initial source of information on an employee is typically his application for a job, though it is not uncommon for corporate recruiters to start files on people whose names have been brought to the attention of a corporate official. Thus campus recruiters will solicit nominations and recommendations from faculty and other contacts at the nation's colleges and universities in order to facilitate the selection and placement of graduates-to-be. This information is routinely entered in folders on "promising prospects" by some of the better organized recruiting teams and, according to one long-time practitioner who represents a heavy electrical equipment manufacturer, it helps him formulate his approach to the candidate.

The chief recruiter for one of the main medical suppliers in America reported to the authors that he never wittingly loses an opportunity to open a file on a person before he bothers to conduct an interview. He is particularly alert to the observations of proprietors of stores that cater to undergraduate male customers. When traveling, he tries to sit near young male companions and engage them in conversation about themselves. He makes mental notes, upon which follow-up "checks" are conducted, before contacting them again. This recruiter attributed his self-proclaimed success to his careful efforts and disparaged his competitors for their more formalized procedures. The authors' experience, in informal discussions with hundreds of corporate recruiters, suggests that this particular recruiter's mode of operation is somewhat unusual; however, most recruiters do collect some information on some candidates before the candidates themselves are approached.

Executive Search Agencies

Though the practice of identifying and scouting upper-level executive talent prior to direct solicitations with candidates is apparently not uncommon, even crude data on the matter are hard to find. The use of outside consultant-appraisers by firms engaged in negotiations with a promising executive is similarly widespread and supplements an employer's own efforts to collect information on such candidates. The dossiers that result from such third-party investigations include clinical-professional judgments as well as personal data. Thus, in a lengthy description of a young plant manager's job search, it was reported that a top-level executive of Cresap, McCormick and Paget ". . . had received a detailed report from [a] consulting psychologist, Dr. Charles McDermid. McDermid's analysis had gone considerably beyond suggestive impressions; he had checked references and had even found out how much equity McGhee had in his home."[6]

Many executives leave their résumés with executive talent hunters, who in some instances supplement this voluntary information with that collected themselves in order to facilitate the operation of a "talent market." When firms operate as employment agencies they are required, in most cities, to be licensed, a fact that may protect corporate and individual clients from a variety of potential abuses of personal privacy by unscrupulous agencies. The problems in this area appear most often to focus on the tendency of "counseling" agencies to charge for undelivered placement services; there has been no conspicuous problem with respect to the information and files of these proliferating agencies.[7]

These talent hunters act as brokers between executives, who are more or less in the market for better jobs, and employers who are pleased to reduce their talent search, if a bad joke be forgiven, to manageable proportions. According to comments of a personnel executive in a large New York firm, the dossiers collected by these search agencies include all manner of data, depending on the talent hunter's individualized styles. The data range from personality profiles scored by consulting psychologists to the notations of "skilled" interviewers who use a variety of techniques, including "stress interviews" and handwriting analysis, in order to give a full picture of the individual executive.

Routine checks with credit-checking agencies, to whose services the talent hunting agency may subscribe, are supplemented by a variety of data collected from references and other sources deemed valuable by the broker agency. No systematic report may be made, however, on the limits set by the agencies, their client firms or the individual himself, regarding what information is collected, how it will be collected, or what portions of it are distributed with and without subjects' knowledge.

RECORDS ON NONMANAGERIAL PERSONNEL

Although information on executive dossiers is mainly anecdotal, somewhat more systematic materials on "non-exempt" employees have been collected by the National Industrial Conference Board (NICB).[8] The

[6] Shelton, William, "How Andy McGhee Got a Better Job," *Fortune*, January, 1967, p. 192.

[7] See "Executive Job Hunters Get a Guide," *Business Week*, January 15, 1966, pp. 45–48; and "Job Counselors Under Fire," *Business Week*, September 21, 1968, p. 92.

[8] Most of the actual data discussed in the remainder of this chapter are abstracted from those collected in a series of studies undertaken by the National Industrial Conference Board. These studies will be cited where appropriate.

Fair Labor Standards Act of 1938 put certain salaried workers on the same basis as hourly-paid workers with respect to overtime pay. Executives and selected categories of supervisors, who are ordinarily paid on a salary basis, are exempted from prescriptions in this Act. "Non-exempt" workers are thus employees in nonsupervisory, nonexecutive positions. This characterization avoids those once-useful distinctions between "wage" and "salary" workers that were made obsolete for certain purposes by the Act.

The data processed by the Conference Board's researchers are based on the responses of thousands of firms, employing more than 10 per cent of the American labor force. Because of the very large number of personnel practices covered in its several surveys, the Board has submitted different segments of lengthy survey instruments to each of several subsamples of cooperating firms. Therefore it is somewhat risky to draw generalizations, although each subsample contains the same distributions of firms-by-industry. Since the studies were in some instances replicated (with different firms) over time, and since the data on the firms are in some instances broken down by industry, by size, and by whether the responses apply to white-collar, to blue-collar, or to both types of workers, we may occasionally consider trends and variations that may be of interest to students of organization and of "class" experiences in America. Since the discussion is based on published cross-tabulations, it has not been possible to make additional breakdowns.

Despite these limitations, the data from surveys done by the National Industrial Conference Board remain the only hard "facts" in this field. One of the basic breakdowns in their data is between manufacturing and nonmanufacturing firms, the principal categories of the latter being insurance, banking, utilities, and retail and wholesale trade. The manufacturing-nonmanufacturing breakdown is interesting, for it permits speculation on the possible effect of unions (since relatively few nonmanufacturing workers in the "private" sector are organized), and on the perceptions managers have of the two different worker groups, the work they do, and their organizational roles. Size breakdowns will be of interest to students of bureaucracy, for whom record-keeping has long been a crude analytical indicator, and for whom the "rationality" of decision-making is often identified with the use of information. Finally, the breakdowns may help illuminate issues that grow out of the fact that there are substantial differences among corporate employees in respect to their contacts with the clients of an organization. One might accordingly postulate that white-collar personnel are more carefully screened by employers than blue-collar personnel, and that white-collar dossiers are more fully developed and utilized than those on blue-collar workers.

Screening of Applicants and Employees

The bulk of all nonmanufacturing firms, regardless of size, undertake centralized screening of job applicants for non-exempt jobs, though this practice is more widespread in some industries than others. Thus in a recent study of 529 of these "service sector" companies, it is reported that whereas between 85 and 90 per cent of banking and insurance companies screen on a centralized basis, the figure is 60 to 78 per cent in wholesale and retail trade.[9] It is by no means clear why there should be such patterned differences, but the fact that centralized screening takes place in a firm has some implications, as we shall see later, for the use to which data in personnel dossiers may be put.

One may speculate, meantime, that the fiduciary responsibilities of banks and insurance companies and the bonding requirements that are operative in these business areas may contribute directly to screening practices; "field" units are simply not organized, in either of these two industries, to conduct any significant volume of administrative work of any kind, including personnel functions.[10]

Test Data. It will surprise no one that corporations collect "test" data on personnel in relatively large numbers, though it may surprise some, in the wake of publicity on psychological "brain watching," that the bulk of corporate testing is of aptitudes, interests, intelligence, and clerical or mechanical abilities rather than of "personality." In general, tests (of all types) are somewhat more commonly administered to manufacturing employees than to nonmanufacturing workers.[11] Employees in both types of organizations are tested on "nonpersonality" traits (intelligence, etc.) in about two-thirds of the cases, but on personality traits in fewer than 40 per cent.

Whatever the type of recorded test data, the scores or profiles apparently become significant to the organizational careers of employees. In 384 manufacturing companies tests are used only on white-collar personnel in 22 per cent of the cases, and on both white- and blue-collar personnel about 40 per cent of the time, in connection with employee counsel-

[9] NICB, *Office Personnel Practices:* Non-manufacturing, Personnel Policy Study No. 197, New York, 1965, pp. 7, 45, 82, 119, 157. Henceforth referred to as Study No. 197.

[10] This speculation does not gain full support in the discussion by H. Laurence Ross on insurance companies, although he acknowledges that practices vary. See pp. 218–219.

[11] NICB, *Personnel Practices in Factory and Office: Manufacturing,* Personnel Policy Study No. 194, New York, 1964, p. 11. Henceforth referred to as Study No. 194.

ing and for promotion purposes. It is by no means clear why white-collar workers' test scores apparently matter so much more frequently in manufacturing than in nonmanufacturing companies. It would be a reasonable guess that the relationships between managers and workers in the manufacturing companies are more "bureaucratic" than in nonmanufacturing companies; some might then expect that managers in the latter setting are less dependent upon impersonal information in reaching judgments about people.

The question of bureaucracy quite aside, there is undoubtedly a difference here, reflecting the unionized versus the unorganized (nonunion) character of these two classes of industries. Champions of privacy, who see dossiers as a threat to cherished values, may take some heart from what appears to be managerial preference for personal contact rather than impersonal records. It must be emphasized, however, that the data reported here are at best *consistent* with such an interpretation; they by no means prove the point. Even the judgment that more bureaucratic forms of organization prevail in manufacturing than in nonmanufacturing firms is a matter of some disagreement among students of economic organization.

The interest of manufacturers in the use of test information for promotion purposes may have declined in the decade 1954–1964. Whereas in 1954, in a sample of 515 manufacturing firms, fully 68 per cent used test data specifically for this purpose on blue-collar workers and 52 per cent on white-collar workers, in 1964 fewer than one-fifth of 384 manufacturing firms used such data for this purpose whether for white- or blue-collar workers.[12] At the same time it is worth noting that, in 1954, there were only small variations in the frequency with which firms of different size used these tests. The hypothesis that increasing size breeds increasing "bureaucratic rationality"—of which such "rationalized" personnel procedures as tests would be an indicator—gains only trifling support in data from 1954; later data do show that test scores and profiles "stay with" an employee in a dossier containing materials used by more than a third of the firms at successive points in an individual's organizational career. In this respect the individual's experience in these organizations is continuous with those in most schools in which IQ and aptitude data have enduring significance.

Thus, in the 1964 survey fewer than one-fifth of nearly 400 manufacturing firms that administer tests retain complete, centralized control over

[12] Study No. 194, p. 14; and Study No. 197, pp. 8, 46, 83, 120, and 158.

the results. *General* results on blue-collar workers are made available to line managers in nearly one-third of the cases—fully 42 per cent in the largest firms. Another quarter of these firms provide line managers with *detailed* test information on their blue-collar subordinates. White-collar workers, meantime, are less than half as likely to suffer (or benefit) from early "typecasting" by their bosses, as a consequence of their bosses receiving prior information on test performance. Students of supervisory practices and of organizational careers may ponder the consequences for the behavior of first-level supervisory personnel and for the organizational mobility experience of workers of making test profiles available in dossiers that accompany new employees from central personnel offices. If the evidence from the education sector is any guide, relatively large numbers of people in industry are permanently marked by these test results.[13]

Most of the intelligence, aptitude, and other tests that are used by respondents to NICB surveys are from commercial sources. This is especially true in larger companies. In addition, from one-quarter to one-third of the firms develop their own tests, personality and otherwise, whether or not they use commercial tests. Since, as we shall see later, dossier contents of former employers are sometimes shared by employers with outsiders, it might make a difference to a worker what specific tests were used. To the extent that test scores can function as a kind of currency in the labor market, particularly in the preliminary phases of job hunting, the matter of standardized versus unstandardized test scores *does* become significant. That test scores may become such a currency is probably only true at the executive level and in management-consulting circles. The statement to a personnel administrator of one firm by a plant manager in another firm, who has read a worker's dossier, that the worker "had an average IQ on his tests" could have immediate economic consequences for a job applicant though the meaning of such a dossier detail would be even more obscure if based on an unstandardized than on a well-known standardized testing device.

About one-quarter of all manufacturing companies, and about twice that number of nonmanufacturing firms, use test results in decisions about the long-run careers of their employees.[14] The difference undoubtedly reflects the fact that in the more unionized manufacturing firms promotions are typically influenced by collectively-bargained rules, including

[13] NICB, *Personnel Practices in Factory and Office*, Studies in Personnel Policy No. 145, New York, 1954, pp. 12, 69. Hereafter referred to as Study No. 145.
[14] Study No. 194, p. 15.

seniority rules, that give less play to psychological devices. The use of tests, especially IQ tests, in white-collar settings may help reduce employee anxiety over the risk that extraneous employer criteria will govern promotion opportunities. In any event, the test data, with the rest of employee dossiers, do "take on a life of their own," though it is not possible to gauge with any precision the effects of these data from the bare statistics on the uses to which they are put.

In the authors' experience the weight assigned to test data by firms is rarely fixed in advance. In those companies in which such data are considered in respect to an individual's promotion opportunity, they are given greater or lesser weight depending on the particular promotion involved, the particular job content at stake, or the particular person using them. In one large New York City utility company scores and profiles required for advancement are modified in accordance with changes in the labor market; when there are many vacancies, men are promoted with lower scores than they would need when vacancies are few. And the more intimately the candidate is known, the less dependence there apparently is upon test data for promotion decisions.

Checking References. In addition to the application form and test results, employers obtain information on their employees from schools, outside persons (including previous employers), and credit bureaus. Table 1, derived from the two most recent Conference Board studies, clearly shows the significance of references. The overwhelming majority of firms turn most frequently to an employee's former employer for information, less frequently to personal or school references (although 80 per cent of the banks check school references), and least of all to credit bureaus.

However, the use that is made of this information is difficult to interpret

TABLE 1 *Types of References on New Employees Checked by Various Firms*

Type of reference	*Manufacturing*	*Insurance*	*Banking*	*Utilities*	*Retail trade*	*Wholesale trade*
			(*percentages*)			
Work	99	94	96	95	99	98
Personal	65	40	77	67	63	44
School	66	59	80	66	51	44
Credit bureau	36	43	54	46	37	18
Number of firms	*473*	*129*	*158*	*92*	*99*	*50*

SOURCE: Manufacturing data are derived from NICB Study No. 194, pp. 12–13; data on other industries are derived from Study No. 197, pp. 7, 45, 82, 119, 157.

because the manner in which it is acquired is itself not easily interpretable. The lower half of Table 2, for example, which compares the percentages of work references checked in writing and orally, does not complement the upper half. The table does not support the assumption that all those references which are not checked in writing are checked orally. The respondents may simply be telling the Conference Board that their practices are conditioned by the fact that they are considering all kinds of applicants for all types and levels of jobs. The fact that practices are so diversified suggests that these firms do not follow a rigid "line" in checking references.

TABLE 2 *Work References Checked in Writing and Orally*

Percentage of employees whose work references are checked in writing	*Manufacturing*	*Insurance*	*Banking*	*Utilities*	*Retail trade*	*Wholesale trade*
Less than half	58	70	30	57	17	70
Half or more	42	30	70	43	83	30
Percentage of employees whose work references are checked orally						
Less than half	69	28	44	32	56	14
Half or more	31	72	56	71	44	86
Number of firms	*420*	*121*	*151*	*87*	*88*	*49*

SOURCE: See Table 1.

Regardless of the particular practices in respect to references, however, it is clear that most companies consider oral checks to be more reliable than written follow-ups on work references, as Table 3 shows.

There is a consistent tendency for these firms to check references on white-collar workers more often than on blue-collar workers,[15] and to use the telephone (in preference to letters) in conducting such checks on white-collar workers more often than on blue-collar workers. These differences, according to four personnel administrators with whom the data were discussed, reflect the fact that it is far easier to locate a white-collar worker's former superior than the former foremen and superintendents under whom blue-collar workers have served and whose work activities complicate the communication process.

[15] This is the reverse of the practices in 1954. Study No. 194, p. 13; and Study No. 145, pp. 10 and 66.

TABLE 3 *Method of Checking References Considered Most Reliable*

Method	*Manufacturing*	*Insurance*	*Banking*	*Utilities*	*Retail trade*	*Whole-sale trade*
			(*percentages*)			
Orally	71	84	71	85	55	84
In writing	13	16	29	15	45	16
Both	16	—	—	—	—	—
Number of firms	*420*	*121*	*151*	*87*	*88*	*49*

SOURCE: See Table 1.

All of these practitioners also pointed out that oral checks are preferred for other reasons. Thus it is obviously quicker to call than to write to a job applicant's former employer, a fact that takes an additional importance as a given labor market "tightens" and forces rapid hiring procedures.

It is not possible to determine how often employees are made aware of these checks; it is doubtful that many workers are aware that credit agencies are used at all, though banking and sales employees may come to recognize this fact as a consequence of later work experience in industries that regularly use such information sources in decisions regarding clients. It is a good guess that as credit agencies, discussed elsewhere in this volume, increasingly solicit subscribers who seek information on prospective employees as well as clients, these agencies will use their field personnel to gather data that go beyond the narrowest information on peoples' handling of their financial obligations.

It is also reasonable to speculate about the growing dependence on telephone conversations in reference checking. One of the formal virtues of written communication, as Chester Barnard pointed out in his studies of status systems in complex organizations, is that it is easier to determine whether such a communication is authoritative.[16] Thus letterheads may reassure recipients of the essential legitimacy of the correspondence they receive. The frequent use of oral communications in discussions about individuals, however, opens the way for almost anyone to call an employer, or ex-employer, for personal information on their subordinates or former workers.

[16] Barnard, Chester, "Functions of Status Systems in Formal Organizations" in Whyte, W. F., editor, *Industry and Society*, McGraw-Hill, New York, 1946, pp. 46–70.

Other Sources of Information. Information gathered within the organization may, of course, also find its way into employee records. In most large firms periodic evaluations that not infrequently contain elliptical references to an employee's manner, habits, or attitudes routinely go to central files and become available for promotion and other organizational decisions. In ten firms visited in connection with other research activities, these files (on non-exempt personnel) were generally incomplete and were consulted unsystematically for promotion purposes by top management. They were regularly consulted by lower-level personnel administrators, however, who consolidated relevant information for decision-makers responsible for processing employee bids for jobs in which vacancies occurred. In two utility companies, meantime, the dossiers were voluminous, and were used with great care in respect to job assignments.

Morale surveys are apparently not often undertaken; less than a quarter of the nonmanufacturing firms, to which reference has already been made, conduct such studies. Thus the feelings of employees about their worlds of work are probably not recorded in their records except to the extent that these feelings are reported directly to employers by individuals whose observations are cited in appraisals and evaluations that are transmitted to central files. Big firms are more likely than small firms to collect such data, but it is doubtful whether the attitudes surveyed can be linked to any particular respondent in a company study, given a general tendency to provide respondents with an opportunity to remain anonymous.

"Exit interviews" are conducted in most firms, and the results are generally preserved in corporate files. These interviews are typically conducted on the initiative of personnel administrators in order to gain a picture of company practices as seen by departing employees whatever the reasons for their separations. Of some interest is the information these departing employees give about *their* former supervisors and co-workers. It is a good guess that the type of information offered, or elicited, depends upon such factors as the departing employee's need for references in the future.

In one organization, a bank, an effort is made to gain information useful in sizing up the performance of managers and others under whom the employee worked. Such comments are more or less selectively recorded by personnel administrators who are, in this company, left to their own devices in the use that is made of the comments. In a one-year period during which irregular observations could be made, the interview was used by headquarters personnel administrators to determine whether company personnel policies were being implemented in field offices.

In contrast with the use made of employee records for decisions that bear upon *particular* workers is the apparently low level of utilization of these records for systematic research on manpower, so to speak, in the aggregate. Job applicants are sometimes assured that the firm's interest in self-study underlies the request for information—such as data on applicants' parents—on corporate forms. The fact is, however, that such data have only rarely been consolidated and used for personnel research purposes.

In preparation of a study on the utilization of educated manpower in America,[17] one of the authors contacted about a dozen firms. Very few of them did any systematic research on manpower that involved data in personnel folders. The exceptions were projects on turnover among college graduates; in these investigations attention was paid to all the information in a junior executive's folder with the purpose of rationalizing selection procedures to reduce turnover. Blank expressions greeted inquiries, for example, about the use of personal information from files for the construction of models useful in explaining individual or group productivity rates.

Since such matters are often a subject of "nonbureaucratic" negotiations with work groups, it is perhaps not surprising that data collected with such great care upon an employee's application for work are largely overlooked in efforts to understand the operation of a business firm and its quest for efficiency. It is ironic that the equanimity with which businessmen often view efficiency and rationalization probably contributes to an employee's privacy. We may recognize, however, in the light of data presented above on the use of tests, including psychological tests, that there is at least a claim that some elements in persons' dossiers are regularly scanned in connection with assignments and promotions.

Unsolicited Information from Consumer Credit Agencies

The extraordinary levels of consumer credit in America have multiplied the prospects that occupational life will become entangled with a citizen's private affairs. Creditors, for example, who seek to put pressures on their "delinquent accounts," provide information to employers simply by contacting them. From 70 to 90 per cent of a sample of 529 nonmanufacturing companies contacted by the Conference Board in 1964 facilitate creditors' efforts through discussions (warnings, advice, and offers of as-

[17] Berg, Ivar, to be published in 1969 by the Center for Urban Education; a brief summary appears in *Transaction*, vol. 6, no. 3 (March, 1969), pp. 45–51.

sistance) with employees.[18] The published data do not show whether the employer provides information of any kind to the creditor during such contacts.

The implications of these contacts by creditors to employers are not irrelevant to employee careers in their organizations. Among these 529 nonmanufacturing companies employees may be discharged by from one quarter to one half of the employers. Employers in the manufacturing sector are somewhat less likely to take such decisive action with their blue- and white-collar workers.[19] Short of discharging people, employers may simply discuss the employee's problems with him. The effect of this additional intelligence about his subordinates' financial affairs can presumably influence a manager's judgment about them with consequences that are unlikely to be helpful to their careers.[20] The authors have come upon five instances in which employers received such derogatory information on employees who, as it turned out, were not derelict in the management of their debt obligations. The creditor himself had made errors in registering payments.

There are apparently great ambiguities in practices in this area, since debtors are not always given an opportunity to check their personal accounts before their alleged misconduct is brought to their employer's attention. Nor do they have any guarantee that corrections will be made in their "records" with the creditor, or that uncorrected information will not be given again and again. It is not easy to identify proper preventive remedies that would protect the "innocent" from inevitable errors and delays in the processing of paper in large, complex creditor organizations.

DISCLOSURE OF INFORMATION ON EMPLOYEES

There are few items more significant to an individual in a democracy than his work opportunities; it is by now clear that there is no real freedom in any society in which people are merely "equally free to sleep on the park bench." While patriots there will always be whose political freedoms take top priorities, one would probably not wish to depend upon them to defend democratic institutions; for most people reasonable economic security, and hence the opportunity to earn such security, is a

[18] Study No. 194, pp. 14, 52, 89, 126, 163.
[19] Study No. 197, p. 38.
[20] It is interesting to note that banks, who claim that laws enabling them to garnish the wages of delinquent debtors help to keep down the cost of credit, are among the firms *most* likely to discharge workers whose wages have been attached or "garnished." Nevertheless they assure state legislators that the garnishment practice has only desirable effects.

prerequisite to a high degree of respect for law, order, and related social values.

On another side, and more concretely, it is equally obvious that employers will not provide work for people who conceal relevant information—though what is relevant may be a legitimate subject for some dispute. Nor will employers wish to hire employees upon whom there is no information that bears upon work performance. Thus employers will ask for, and often obtain, the names of a job applicant's previous employers in order to contact them in search of information. The nature and content of exchanges among employers may therefore have serious implications for individuals since they may weigh heavily in the balance of their work opportunities and hence their well-being as citizens.

The high proportion of employers who check work references, already discussed, makes the interorganizational exchange of information on people particularly significant. What little information there is available on the subject does make one somewhat restive about personal rights, even if one grants that the needs of employers are rational and legitimate. The fact that the subject may not be able to "defend" himself against derogatory information, or, indeed, even determine whether the information given about him *is* derogatory (or even accurate), makes the issue of work references an important one. "Economic capital punishment," without due process or recourse, is not more easily or lightly experienced than conventional punishment for being outside the pale of law.

Work References and Personal Data

Employers in 426 manufacturing companies generally provide work references upon request. Thus almost all of these firms will disclose the titles, lengths of service, and the "reasons for leaving," to outsiders—presumably, but not necessarily exclusively, to new employers. There is no variability by size of firm among these companies, nor do these practices vary in respect to whether the subjects are white- or blue-collar workers. Neither is there any difference over time in the period 1954–1964.[21]

In 1964 a smaller number—from half to nearly three-quarters—provided information on subjects' approximate salaries, a fact that may be significant to creditors as well as prospective employers engaged in negotiations with a subject. The figures for 1954 were approximately the same and in both time periods the largest firms gave out this information less frequently.[22]

[21] Study No. 194, p. 18; and Study No. 145, pp. 70–71.
[22] *Ibid.*

Between one-third and three-quarters of these companies will disclose a subject's home address, while more than three-quarters will report on the quality of a former employee's work; the largest companies give these types of information least often. On this issue, once again, there have been no significant changes in practices over time. The considerable variations in the proportions of firms who provide these different types of information follow no interpretable pattern. There can be no doubt, however, that the consistency of practices *within* industries, suggested by the lack of variation by the size of firms and the lack of differentiation with respect to types of employees, reflects the impact of industry and trade associations.

The privacy of an individual's past record with an employer, or of the data an employer has collected in personnel portfolios is thus not clearly an outgrowth of an employer's economic experience or of market pressures, or of imperatives that dictate policies that will assure higher orders of efficiency. Rather, the degree of employee privacy is a reflection of employers' norms as they develop within an industry as a consequence of interactions among administrative practitioners in that industry. The stability in these practices over time, meanwhile, reflects the longitudinal effect of continuous information-sharing rather than any drive toward efficiency.

Only about one-half of these companies "generally" restrict the information given to prospective employers to items on which information is requested, i.e., to confirming data offered by subjects to prospective employers, with no significant variation in respect to blue- or white-collar employees or by size of firm.

Data for 1954 are broken down in respect to whether information is given to prospective employers or to credit agencies. Employers gave out information on length of service and employment titles about as often to credit agencies as to prospective employers. Employers were *much* less likely to give out information on home addresses, "reasons for leaving," approximate salary and "quality of work" to credit agencies than to prospective employers. (See Table 4.) The motives in giving out information accordingly appear to be infused by some desire to encroach directly only upon the occupational dimensions of an individual's life rather than upon other dimensions.

Political Loyalty

It may be a sign of the times that in the 1964 survey the Conference Board asked no questions about the disclosure, by firms to outsiders, re-

TABLE 4 *Disclosure of Information to Credit Agencies and Prospective Employers*

	Credit agencies				*Prospective employers*			
	Hourly workers		*Salaried workers*		*Hourly workers*		*Salaried workers*	
Type of information	*No.*	*Per cent*	*No.*	*Per cent*	*No.*	*Per cent*	*No.*	*Per cent*
Length of service with company	456	91	480	93.2	510	99	497	99.2
Job title or type of work	446	89	463	89.9	511	99.2	496	99
Home address	347	69.3	381	74	451	86.7	413	82.4
Reason for leaving	276	55.1	318	61.7	490	95.1	469	93.6
Approximate salary	233	46.5	268	52	346	67.2	301	60.1
Quality of work	227	45.3	215	41.7	472	91.7	453	90.4
$N =$	501		515		501		515	

SOURCE: Derived from NICB Study No. 145, 1954, pp. 15, 70, 71.

garding employees' "loyalty to the United States Government." In 1954, however, which was the last year of the late Senator McCarthy's campaign against domestic communism, the question was raised with the results shown in Table 5.

It is a tenable hypothesis that the differences between the percentages of firms whose administrators provide this information to employers and to credit agencies reflects the role of government contracts in the American economy. It is obviously of no small moment to corporations doing business with the government whether the people they hire have more or less conspicuously problematical characteristics. Even allowing that loyalty is an issue in more than two-thirds of a large, representative sample of employers in firms of diverse sizes, it is not by any means clear what kinds of information, in this politically sensitive area, are transmitted. Employees are generally at the mercy of employers who give out any information; they may be even more vulnerable when such information is likely to touch upon their political inclinations in a culture in which one man's disloyalty may so easily be another man's constructive criticisms.

The Conference Board does not suggest why its 1964 and 1965 surveys did not elicit further information on this matter, though for the politically-minded student of American institutions the issue may be of continuing concern. The fact that only about 10 per cent of the companies in later studies require the permission of subjects before giving out information

TABLE 5 *Disclosure of Information on Political Loyalty*

	Firms that will provide information on "Loyalty to U.S. Government"			
	Hourly workers		*Salaried workers*	
Size of firms providing "loyalty" information to credit agencies	*No.*	*Per cent*	*No.*	*Per cent*
Under 250	47	45	47	41
250–999	84	38	104	49
1,000–4,999	52	34	59	44
5,000 and over	14	35	10	24
Total	*197*	*38.3*	*220*	*43.9*
Total firms	*501*		*501*	
Size of firm supplying "loyalty" information to prospective employers				
Under 250	74	70	75	66
250–999	156	71	159	74
1,000–4,999	101	67	88	66
5,000 and over	24	60	16	39
Total	*355*	*68.9*	*338*	*67.5*
Total firms	*515*		*515*	

SOURCE: See Table 4.

about them to prospective employers[23] is not exactly heartening to civil libertarians. Nor is it likely to be heartening that so many employers disclose reasons for termination, or that so many willingly gave judgments, at least in 1954, on employees' loyalty. Since the ex-employee is not likely to be aware of the gross, much less the detailed, nature of the information given, the veracity of those making observations and interpretations, or the organizational status and values of those receiving the information, he may find himself with restricted opportunities without the vaguest idea of the reasons for his difficulty.

IMPLICATIONS AND ISSUES IN THE USE OF CORPORATE DOSSIERS

It is perhaps in this specific area that the "dossiers" on a person may have the most serious implications. Employees may or may not be able to defend themselves, for example, against the "suspicions" of a former employer, or against malicious remarks by employers angered by a subject's resignation. The prospective employer need simply state that "the position in question has been filled," leaving the subject totally in the dark about events that shape his options and prospects.

[23] Study No. 194, p. 19.

Privacy

In larger organizations employees undoubtedly gain some protection from the fact that personnel administrators identify their work with that of other "professionals" who have access to personal information and who strive to be objective in their response to reasonable questions. Few big firms are without reasonably well-trained and even well-indoctrinated applied social scientists who subscribe, at least nominally, to norms of fair play. The probability that such norms are operative among other members of a firm is not estimable. The care with which firms contacted in connection with an investigation mentioned earlier safeguard employee records from nonpersonnel administrators suggests that there is considerable concern about employee privacy. Personal contacts over the past decade with hundreds of executives representing an equally large number of corporations in the Executive Program in Business Administration, conducted by the Columbia University Graduate School of Business, lead to the same general conclusion.

Access to and Ownership of Data

In the face of the data and impression presented so far one could, it seems, be justifiably concerned about the parameters of privacy in America, listening devices, tape recorders and electrified martini olives quite aside. It does not seem to be very difficult to obtain information from employers, to obtain it anonymously by telephone, to obtain information without a subject's knowledge (let alone permission), or to obtain information on matters that go well beyond the simple confirmation of facts that might voluntarily be proffered by a given individual.

It is, moreover, fairly clear that the information given and received on individuals in corporations is quantitatively great enough to suggest that it must necessarily be handled and processed by more than one responsible person. As a result, many Americans are probably unaware of who knows what about them, a fact that might make the process of "presenting" oneself more than a casual matter. One's bargaining position on a host of issues is thus more or less vulnerable, and one's vulnerabilities greater or fewer depending on the policies of organizations whose procedures need not conform to any special, or even general, code. While it is impossible to determine what baseless charges (or "illegitimately" favorable statements) may be entered in a dossier, it is probably true that there are something like norms operating to protect the employee in his labor market travels and negotiations. The sanctions that help maintain such norms are not conspicuous, apart from the bad reputations firms may earn by vicious distortions of available data, nor are they routinely "published" in any way that would reassure nervous employees. Court cases in this area, however, give testimony to the fact that these norms, whatever they are, do not always satisfy Americans. In one case, reported by a colleague, a merchant marine captain sued a former employer for giving a prospective employer derogatory information.

A number of companies open up their files to researchers, an additional population of outsiders which then has access to personnel data. It may reasonably be assumed that such researchers are sufficiently well known to managers that there are few risks involved. With or without risk, however, it is interesting to note that the authors have been unable to find any agreement between managers and employees confirming managers' or corporations' proprietary ownership of personal data "given" by employees. The idea has simply developed out of common law principles that employers have an implicit property right to regulate accesses to their files and they presumably enjoy these rights in unfettered fashion as long as the results—published reports, etc.—do not offend employees who challenge the organization's rights, or do not come to their attention.

Retention and Retrieval of Records

In the face of evidence that business corporations are willing to supply a variety of types of information to a variety of people one inevitably wonders how long personnel information is retained by employers and thus available to those who answer requests, whether orally or otherwise.

There can be no doubt that considerable personal information on executive personnel is retained by corporations. Interviews conducted by the authors in a major steel corporation, three rubber companies, a large metropolitan bank, a packaging corporation, an insurance company, and a diversified textile firm leave one in doubt, however, whether these dossiers are more than the filed accumulations of the discrete pieces of executive careers. None of the company spokesmen could recall that the records were of research significance to the firm; all of them were extremely chary of making the records available to the authors for research purposes and would have had to "clear" such availability with top management. The records on executive performance—sales records, for example—were more typically referred to (for promotion and salary purposes) than the folders on executive backgrounds. One diversified manufacturing company collected considerable quantities of data on executives in a series of ring binders. However, the two highest ranking personnel officers (the only executives below the president who have access to this data) did not even agree on the size of the populations whose records they shared in contiguous offices. One said there were records on 300 and the other on 800 executives!

While there is no current information on this issue, the Conference Board did ask its 1954 respondents "How long before destroying them does a company retain personnel records for employees who are no longer with the company?" The large majority of these 515 firms, according to their own testimony, retain information "permanently," indefinitely, or for between ten and twenty years.

The advent of the computer will undoubtedly help employers rationalize this process considerably. Even as long ago as 1966 the number of firms which were punching personal characteristics on IBM cards or recording them on magnetic tape quickened the interest of *Business Week;* they saw prospects in this development for a "revolution in personnel practices." At that time the firms so engaged were recording relatively little information—400 to 800 characters, each of which represents a letter or number—considering the *very* large size of dossiers that not infrequently contain one hundred or more separate pages. The prospect, judging from recent research experience, is that this new look will facilitate manpower research—the missing aggregations referred to earlier—far more than it will violate privacy. The extraordinary "underutilization" of data may well give way to heightened organizational planning and far more informed patterns of recruiting and job assignment.

Uses and Abuses of Data

On the subject of the uses of these dossiers one may add that most firms conduct individual performance evaluations, and use merit ratings in the determination of wages, salaries, and assignments.[24] Dossiers accordingly do have relevance to people in private employment. Data in their records clearly help to determine not only short-run income, but long-run opportunities, assignments, layoffs, and even discharges. These conclusions do make one wonder about privately collected, privately owned, and privately utilized dossiers in a society in which the public interest is so substantially affected by the "decentralized" acts of large numbers of private decision-makers. The constraints against abuse are largely normative, though court battles may be fought against abuses that are flagrant and, for that reason, observable. The *essential* protection

[24] *Ibid.*, p. 17.

against abuses borrows heavily from whatever influence more general norms of fair play have in a democratic society. Such protection will be judged adequate or inadequate depending on the standards applied.

From one point of view there is some protection, too, from the objectivity, reliability, and validity of the information that is collected as well as from the integrity and fairness of the people whose accesses to dossiers could make them powerful indeed. Community norms probably do reinforce a businessman's desire to be judicious in the use of these dossiers, and to be objective in his efforts to compile their contents. But the latter urge can be more than a little troublesome.

Consider that in their efforts to protect themselves—especially against employee thefts—businessmen are increasingly using "lie detectors," i.e., polygraph tests, on their employees. According to a comparatively recent McGraw-Hill estimate, about 80 per cent of the polygraph operators' income in this country comes from business corporations.[25] These operators ask diverse questions, according to the AFL-CIO, pertaining to "personal activities, physical condition, police records, drinking habits, marital life, political beliefs and many other 'irrelevant' subjects."[26] Though corporations undoubtedly have an interest in cutting the alleged \$4 million daily losses from employee thefts, and can presumably *deter* workers from stealing or embezzling by periodic polygraph tests, one can hardly view the prospect that "broad" data obtained in this fashion would become part of a worker's permanent record; the polygraph, after all, is *far* from an infallible device for measuring truth.

The fact that the Council of Polygraph Examiners, a trade association, is seeking state laws setting licensing standards is not altogether reassuring. Thus it is troublesome that some job seekers who are otherwise qualified may be denied employment if they refuse to take the test. Others, according to *Business Week*'s informants, are required to "sign pledges to take a lie detector test at any time the company may so request."[27] Unless restrictive legislation went beyond the testing standards to include specifications about the uses of information so gained, this issue will remain a vexing one.

CONCLUSIONS

The limited data on employee dossiers leave room for much speculation on a variety of issues that attend the matter of personal information

[25] "Unions Act on Threats to Privacy," *Business Week*, March 13, 1965, p. 87.
[26] *Ibid.*, pp. 87–88.
[27] *Ibid.*, p. 88.

in corporate files. The great variabilities in practices among corporations in different industries suggest that entrepreneurial concerns with profit maximization, which would conceivably generate somewhat greater uniformities in these practices, are less relevant than noneconomic factors that lead corporate managers to their specific policies regarding the collection and distribution of information. It is probably more fruitful to attack the problem, in future research, from a perspective in which the firm is conceived to be a social system rather than an economic apparatus whose practices are inspired by the calculated quest for rationality and efficiency.

It is also intriguing that corporations seem increasingly preoccupied with personal rather than more "bureaucratic" contacts, in their efforts to secure information on their employees. The additional fact that consolidated information is so rarely used for research purposes may underscore the likelihood that corporations are collecting massive quantities of information about people that are put to essentially little use. From the data available, dossiers do not appear to be as purposeful as the investment in them would imply.

At the same time, however, these records do appear to have a cumulative effect on their subjects' organizational careers, even though their contents may contain greater or lesser quantities of materials that are of questionable validity and of doubtful reliability. Since employers prefer oral to written contacts with their job applicants' previous employers, one may conclude that the contents of dossiers do not necessarily influence people's careers directly during a search for new employment. That these files may affect careers indirectly depends upon the former employer's familiarity with and recollection of an individual dossier. The more critical "functions" of these dossiers, however, would appear to be on "intraorganizational" experiences than on the "interorganizational" experiences of American workers and managers.

To view the present-day extraorganizational uses to which corporate dossiers are put with a certain degree of equanimity should not be interpreted to mean that the experiences in gathering these materials have left the authors sanguine about the future. We may remind ourselves that a wealth of data about millions of Americans and their backgrounds are indeed "on record" in corporate offices. These millions are dependent, in both the short and long runs, for the safekeeping of their privacy on the propriety and probity of those in whose care these data are entrusted.

It is, of course, possible that all of these people govern themselves according to the principles of *noblesse oblige,* and that they can carefully balance the interests of naive subjects against, say, the interests of what General Eisenhower darkly disclosed as "the military-industrial complex." But who can assure that opportunity, reputation, and personal rights will be routinely safeguarded by the unilateral decisions and the self-searching judgments of those in corporations who reply, for example, to the requests of well-intentioned (or other) government servants in investigatory agencies? The data, by themselves, provide no answer to this important problem: *quis custodiet ipsos custodes?*

7 *Personal Information in Insurance Files*

H. LAURENCE ROSS

INSURANCE IS AN INSTITUTION THAT TOUCHES THE LIVES OF NEARLY ALL American families, as well as virtually all business enterprises. Five out of six families are protected by life insurance.[1] More than 85 per cent of the automobiles on the road are covered by liability insurance, and more than 90 per cent of our homes are protected by fire insurance and related coverages.[2] Apart from the very poorest strata of society, the involvement of Americans with insurance is virtually total.

The insurance industry depends upon procedures for the selection of risks and the payment of claims which require the gathering of personal information. Information about families and individuals is needed by underwriters to determine whether to accept or reject an application for insurance, and what rate to charge to match the premium as closely as possible to the risks involved in the unique situation of the applicant. The claimsman requires personal information to help judge the validity of claims presented, although such information is less important here than is infor-

I gratefully acknowledge the help of Mr. Robert Friedman, student at the University of Denver College of Law.

[1] *Life Insurance Fact Book* 1967, Institute of Life Insurance, New York, 1967, p. 7.

[2] Estimates supplied by the Insurance Information Institute.

mation concerning the circumstances surrounding the claim. Various additional phases of insurance may require some degree of personal information, for instance, in determining whether to accept an application for a mortgage.

In gathering information, insurance companies have access to the services of the information-producing industry, exemplified by organizations such as the Retail Credit Company and Dun & Bradstreet, as well as to their own staffs of examiners and investigators. Moreover, the typical insurance company is provided with impressive and up-to-date facilities for machine processing of data. In the light of the information needs and data-processing abilities of the insurance industry, one might expect that the files of this industry are a source of detailed personal information concerning large numbers of individuals and families. This expectation, however, is not fulfilled.

The personal information contained in the files of insurance companies is extremely limited. It appears in greatest abundance in the files of life insurance underwriting departments, where it is most needed, and it is on these files that this chapter will focus. Even here, the amount of information in the files is not as great as might be expected, and, according to many insurance men, the ability to retrieve what information is present is quite poor. Output of information generated in the underwriting process is quite scant, as much between departments of a single company as well as among various companies or between insurance and other institutions. Moreover, the amount of personal information being gathered by the insurance industry seems to be declining, counteracting the effect of increasing ability to retrieve and process whatever is gathered. For both the present and the foreseeable future, the role of insurance in the total accumulation of personal data in our society appears minimal.

These conclusions, and the supporting evidence in this chapter, are based on a variety of sources of information. Interviews were granted by sixteen head office executives of three important insurance companies. One of the companies is a mutual life insurance company, and the other two are multiline stock companies. In addition, interviews were obtained from officers of four industry-wide associations. All forms used by the companies in connection with underwriting life, fire and casualty policies were examined, as were various claims forms. Several field agents writing insurance for various companies were interviewed. A search was made of the major trade journals, although it proved unproductive; little has been written concerning files of personal information. Finally, I draw on two years' experience studying the handling of claims by insurance personnel, involving about one hundred formal interviews with adjusters and attorneys, and many days of field observation.

LIFE INSURANCE UNDERWRITING

The principal storehouse of personal information in the insurance industry is the files of life underwriting departments. These files are built of information from four different primary sources: the application, the medical investigation, the inspection, and intercompany information exchanges or indexes, primarily the Medical Information Bureau (MIB). The following sections will describe the information typically gathered through each source.

Applications

Applications are obtained in connection with all individual insurance policies, but not usually in connection with group policies. The group policy generally requires an individual application only when a member refuses insurance on joining the group, and requests it at a later time.

The heart of the application is a set of declarations by the prospective insured in response to form questions. The questions are usually read to the prospect by the agent or salesman, and answers are filled in by the latter, but the applicant signs the application and represents the answers as truthful. An initial series of declarations—name, address, employer, etc.—identifies and locates the applicant. In addition to identifying the specific subject of the policy, in the event of whose death payment will be made, this information is used to activate the inspections and searches of indexes that verify the declarations of the application and provide additional information. Another set of declarations concerns age, occupation, travel plans, avocations, and the like. These items allow a more definitive identification of the applicant, but their main function is to provide information concerning the nature of the risk. The underwriter's principal concern is with age, which is the standard predictor of life expectancy and hence of premium. Various occupations (e.g., coal miner), avocations (e.g., automotive sports), and other factors (e.g., planned residence in foreign countries) which may significantly affect life expectancy must be taken into account in underwriting. A third set of declarations concerns insurance history. The applicant is generally required to disclose his existing insurance, and to indicate whether he has been refused a standard policy at any time. Three underwriting purposes are served by this information: (1) prior refusals alert the underwriter to the likelihood of peculiar risk; (2) the fact of existing insurance will indicate that any adverse information discovered previously may be available through index procedures; and (3) the amount of existing insurance will be compared with common understandings concerning the amounts and types reasonably to be owned by individuals in various circumstances. A fourth set of declarations specifies the nature and amount of insurance applied for—exact coverages, value, method of premium payment, etc.

The application may also contain information to be supplied by the agent in his own right, based on the assumption that the agent may have some knowledge of the applicant in private life. In the main, the agent is asked to confirm the statements given by the insured and to indicate his relationship to the insured, i.e., how the business was solicited. Little information in the files appears to justify the assertion of one executive that "the principal source of our information is the agent."

Medical Investigation

Some kind of medical information is required concerning all applicants for individual life insurance, but the companies studied waive formal physical examinations in the case of applications for smaller amounts of insurance at younger ages. (Procedure in these cases will be described later.) Applicants for substantial amounts of insurance are required to submit to a medical examination before a local physician retained as a consultant by the insurance company. The companies studied have panels of several thousand physicians, who are paid on a fee basis for each examination. This examination has two parts, a medical history reported by the applicant and a general physical examination. In cases where the amount of the contemplated policy is large, or where knowledge or suspicion of a mortality-relevant ailment develops, a more intensive examination by a specialist may be required. The applicant is also required to sign a medical authorization releasing to the insurance company any relevant information in the possession of "physicians and practitioners, hospitals and other institutions" with which he has had contact. This authorization is used in exceptional situations, most underwriting being based on the medical history provided by the applicant and on the standard physical examination.

The medical history consists of a long series of questions in which various ailments are named and the applicant states whether he has had them or been treated for them. Where the answer is positive, the applicant is asked to provide details, including the date, duration, treatment and result, and the names and addresses of doctors and hospitals. A brief inquiry concerns the health of father, mother, brothers, and sisters. This medical history allows the examining physician to perform or to recommend special examinations related to the various ailments named. Moreover, false responses to these questions may result in the policy's being voided by the company if particular ailments produce death within the period in which it is contestable (in most states two years following the issuance of the policy).

The second part of the medical examination is a general physical examination. Particular attention is paid to build, pulse, blood pressure, and heart functioning. A urinalysis is generally included, sometimes performed at the company's head office laboratory. As noted above, a more detailed examination by specialists, possibly including electrocardiograms, chest X-rays, and serology will be required in cases of large policies and where defects are known or suspected.

Inspection

Except where very small policies are at issue, applicants for life insurance are routinely "inspected" for personal information. Most companies employ the services of independent companies like the Retail Credit and Hooper-Holmes agencies, which have a variety of special investigation procedures and reports available for insurance purposes. A minority of companies perform inspections with their own investigatory personnel.

The information for a routine inspection is derived from interviews with the applicant and his neighbors. Four general areas of information appear in the reports. The first is corroboration of the statements on the application. Name, address, marital status, occupation, source and amount of income, and vocational and avocational risks are to be indicated. A second area of information corroborates the medical examination. However, limitations posed by the abilities of the inspectors and the adequacy of their sources of information minimize the amount of medical information that can be obtained reliably; gross matters such as blindness and amputations are the principal items concerning which reports can be made. A third area of information concerns "habits," specifically the use of alcohol and drugs. This area seems to be the raison d'être of inspection. Underwriters believe that various drinking patterns relate in different ways to the risk of death, and they request considerable detail in this matter—how often one drinks, how much, what beverage, and so on. The fourth area of information supplied by inspectors concerns "environment" and "reputation." This is a catch-all category concerning which inspectors have considerable discretion in the answer to such queries as, "Anything adverse about living conditions or neighborhood?" or "Anything unfavorable regarding general reputation, family background, environment, associates, morals, etc.?" The inspection reports reviewed and the attitudes of underwriters suggest that the typical inspection is in these matters perfunctory and shallow, and that it plays little part in underwriting.

Intercompany Indexes

Life underwriting is the only area of insurance in which detailed personal information passes from company to company. It does so principally through the Medical Information Bureau. Impairments known or suspected in the course of processing applications for life insurance are reported to the MIB, and this information is relayed to other insurance companies when the individual makes subsequent application for insurance. The unique import of the MIB in disseminating personal information merits an extended description of its operation.[3]

The advantages of an exchange of information concerning the health of life insurance applicants were apparent many years ago. An organization to perform this function was formed in 1890 by a group of medical directors of American life insurance companies. Called the Rejection Exchange, it transmitted the underwriting decisions of the companies as well as the medical reasons for these decisions. The Rejection Exchange is reported to have functioned poorly because some companies failed to report fully, and companies specializing in substandard policies (issued to poorer risks at higher rates) not only were failing to report, but were using the names in the Exchange as a prospect list. In 1902 the Rejection Exchange was superseded by a new Exchange based on reporting impairments only, without the underwriting decision or even the reporting company being identified in the files. These principles are retained in the present Medical Information Bureau, which was established in 1947. Membership in the MIB is open to all life insurance companies, with certain qualifications concerning capitalization, good standing, medical personnel, and pledges concerning the handling of MIB information. Nearly all important life insurance companies participate. Bureau member companies currently write more than 90 per cent of life insurance issued in the United States and Canada, and have more than 90 per cent of the life insurance assets in these countries.

Member companies report impairments in code form as soon as they

[3] Information concerning the MIB is documented in Wilberding, J. C., "The Medical Information Bureau," *Journal of the American Society of Chartered Life Underwriters*, vol. XX, no. 2 (Spring, 1966), pp. 176–181; and Ginsberg, Harvey N., "Report on Examination of the Medical Information Bureau by the New York State Insurance Department," Albany, N.Y., 1965.

reach a decision on an application. They are bound by rule to report any of the 223 medical impairments on the Bureau's list, as well as 12 "supplemental" nonmedical impairments when these are considered significant. The reports are mailed to the Bureau's servicing agent, a private organization under contract to handle the processing routines. Reports are entered on cards containing the applicant's name, region of residence, date of birth, place of birth, and occupation, along with codes representing impairments, and a notation of the date the impairments were reported. Employees of the servicing agent are kept ignorant of the meaning of the codes, which are explained in manuals restricted in circulation to underwriters and actuaries.

A master file of MIB cards is retained in the office of the servicing agent in Boston. Copies are distributed to 13 large member companies that maintain their own card libraries, as well as to four regional checking offices and card libraries serving groups of companies in New York and Toronto. A company with its own card library will check incoming applications directly against its own MIB card files. The more numerous companies without their own files may have their new applications checked at the regional offices or in one of the card libraries. Though more than ten million cards are currently on file, handling procedures are presently manual. (Plans have been made for computerization.) MIB records are destroyed after seven years, by which time the underwriting usefulness of the data has considerably diminished.

Codes used by the MIB are subsumed under ten classifications, as follows:

General (Medical)
Brain and Nervous
Circulatory
Respiratory
Digestive
Kidneys and Genito-Urinary
Family History (Medical)
Miscellaneous (Medical)
Glands of Internal Secretion and Metabolism
Supplementary

The last category is of most interest in the context of this volume. It contains twelve specific codes:

Nonconformity
Insurance hazard

Finances or speculation
Reckless driving well substantiated by official records
Age
Environment
Foreign resident or travel
Aviation—Regular crew members
Aviation—Persons other than regular crew members with duties aboard aircraft
Participation in hazardous sports
Occupation
Other information

"Nonconformity" refers principally to drinking. "Insurance hazard" may include such matters as sexual deviation, in addition to records of criminal or dishonest behavior. "Environment" refers to the condition of the home and the status of the neighborhood. "Occupation" is reported only when it is hazardous and when its statement on the application is not indicative of the hazard. My informants have not been able to explain "Other information," and state that they have rarely seen this code used.

These "Supplementary" codes may appear somewhat sinister insofar as provisions for restricting MIB information may be inadequate. This danger is particularly strong for those categories such as "Insurance hazard" and "Environment" that depend on the discretion of inspectors, which is the weakest link in the chain of underwriting information. In partial mitigation is the fact that these codes rarely appear. A spot check was made, for this inquiry, of 105 MIB reports received by one company for a ten-day period in 1967. During this period 908 names had been submitted to the Bureau by the company, and no impairments were reported for the other 803. Among the reports received were found six cases of Nonconformity, four of Insurance hazard, one each of Finances or speculation and Environment, and nine of Aviation crew. Insofar as the sample may be representative, it is seen that "Supplementary" reports excluding Aviation constitute only a small fraction of total unfavorable reports.

MIB reports are circumscribed by a set of rules designed to limit their circulation and use to legitimate underwriting purposes. An important rule requires that no underwriting decision may be made on the basis of Bureau information alone. The information must be verified through current medical examinations and inspections. This rule is designed to prevent the Bureau's being perceived and used as a blacklist. The Bureau is intended, rather, to provide a "red-flag list," providing its members with warnings but requiring that they obtain proofs on their own.[4] Although no definitive information is available, several considerations suggest that the rule is followed in practice. First, the Bureau can apply various direct sanctions, including the threat of expulsion, when rule-violation is brought to the attention of its officials. Another consideration is that underwriting is to some degree competitive, under pressure from the agent as well as management, and there is no benefit in rejecting potentially profitable business without proof of hazard. Most important in the opinion of MIB personnel is that the rules are enforced by medical professionals who are pledged to their enforcement. The company's examination will, of course, be informed by the knowledge obtained from the MIB, and a more negative investigative "set" and larger numbers of declinations and rated policies can be expected for applicants with impairments listed with the Bureau than for similar applicants without reported impairments. If this situation seems discriminatory, it can hardly be avoided.

Another rule, previously noted, restricts MIB information to the head office underwriting and actuarial staff of member companies. Despite this rule, official reports of the Bureau note occasional information leaks. Typically, an agent or broker is alleged to have discovered the contents of MIB cards concerning a potential applicant, thus being able to forewarn and forearm the applicant.

It should be noted that more detailed information can be obtained about an applicant when required, by submitting a request to the Bureau, which will forward the request to the reporting company. This procedure is used not only to obtain more detailed medical information, but for identification purposes: to verify that the person on whom the report was made is in fact the applicant now being considered. The number of such requests is limited by Bureau rules, and due to competition the information may not be forthcoming. One underwriter stated: "If I want to write the business myself I may send them nothing; or I may send them everything, painting it as black as possible."

In addition to the Medical Information Bureau procedures, life insurance companies exchange information by means of the Recording Bureau, which reports to its members the identification of applicants for large

[4] From the legal point of view, information obtained by an insurance company from the MIB may be a double-edged sword, as courts have held that the company is on notice concerning disabilities thus indicated. Through various theories of waiver, estoppel, or lack of fraud, companies have been prevented from rescinding or cancelling policies in which false affirmations on the application are contradicted by information in the MIB. See, for example, John Hancock Life Insurance Company v. Brennan, 324 S.W. 2d, 610 (Tex. Civ. App., 1959); Dossett v. Franklin Life Insurance Company, 276 S.W., 1097 (Tex. Comm. App., 1925); Columbian National Life Insurance Company of Boston, Mass. v. Rodgers, 116 F.2d, 705 (10th Cir., 1940).

policies. The Recording Bureau originated in the early 1930's in response to two problems. First, buyers of large amounts of insurance were discovered to be evading the intensive medical examinations required for very large policies by dividing their total insurance coverage into several smaller policies, each written with a different company. A second problem was the purchase of very high amounts of insurance in this manner by prospective suicides. The Recording Bureau tried to meet these problems through providing a source of information whereby simultaneous applications for insurance would be made known on short notice. Members inform the servicing agent (the same one servicing the MIB) when applications are received for policies in excess of $100,000. The notification includes the identifying information of name, birthdate, and place of birth, along with the amount of insurance applied for, the amount declared by the applicant to be in force, and the amount stated to have been applied for with other companies. Information in the Bureau files, and any information concerning the applicant received within the next three months, is sent to the reporting member.

Membership in the Recording Bureau is much smaller than that in the MIB, fluctuating over time from about 35 to about 55 companies. The small membership obviously compromises the efficiency of the bureau. Lack of widespread participation is explained by the fact that many underwriters find the information of little use. The control provided by the Bureau can be evaded if the applicant knows about it and restricts his applications to policies under $100,000. Moreover, the problems that loomed large in the 1930's when the Bureau was formed seem less important today. On the other hand, the Recording Bureau is an inexpensive operation and it gathers enough support to allow its continuation on a marginal basis.

Possibilities of Error

In comparison with other repositories of personal information, underwriting files seem based on more reliable information, and error would appear to be a less pressing problem. The most frequent source of error in these files is probably inspection, which is relatively perfunctory and is performed by personnel who are regarded as being of poor quality. One highly placed informant who believed the problem of error to be insignificant nonetheless stated that the inspection force with which he is acquainted "lacks discrimination" and that their reports are affected by their "conformist views of how to live." However, the weaknesses of inspection are generally recognized, and underwriters probably discount inspection reports that are not confirmed by other file inputs. For example, one observer of hundreds of claims meetings stated that there had never been any reference to conflicts between the word of the insured and that of inspectors. Rather, the discussion nearly always hinged on the information turned up by the medical investigation.

A potential source of more serious error is the MIB, which is cloaked with a presumption of accuracy because of its basis in the medical examination. In fact, confidence in the anonymous MIB report often exceeds that in the company's own physician, who may be suspected of being in collusion with the applicant when he finds no disability. Errors can arise in the MIB through misinterpretations in the original examination, through clerical and mechanical mistakes in coding and printing of the data, and through mistaken identification. Insurance personnel believe that errors in the physical examination are few; the standard examination is unlikely to strain the competence of the average physician, and information prejudicial enough to result in a severe rating or denial is likely to be checked independently in order to meet the anticipated protests of the applicant and his agent. A certain number of errors can be expected in the coding and printing of MIB cards, particularly since the servicing staff is kept ignorant of the meaning of the codes. The most likely kind of error here would substitute one kind of impairment code for another. Although this can be misleading, it is not as serious an error as that of false identification, which can label a perfectly healthy applicant as impaired. In the large companies studied this problem was said to be commonplace. In the words of one executive, "It is utterly amazing how many individuals bearing the same name are born on the same day!" He estimated that his company confronts several such cases every week.

Medical Information Bureau procedures include several designed to minimize any error that does occur. A reporting company discovering its own error may change or withdraw its report by the use of a special form. If the apparently erroneous report was submitted by another company, the member cannot cancel it directly, but is required to call the situation to the attention of the Executive Secretary of the MIB, who takes up the matter with the reporting company. Twenty to thirty such cases occur per year, and when the report is found to be erroneous it is cancelled. If a current examination shows no evidence of a disability previously reported, the favorable information is to be reported with the symbol "Q." The original unfavorable report is retained along with the new favorable information, and both are reported when the individual's file is called for. A sample study undertaken by the Bureau indicated that approximately 2 per cent of MIB reports are "Q" reports.

The ability of the individual to counteract unfavorable erroneous information appears to be somewhat better in insurance than elsewhere where records are kept. One reason is the policy of the companies to provide explanations of ratings and rejections for medical reasons, either directly to the individual, or at least to his physician. No details are provided where rejection is on the grounds of habits or morals, but the general nature of the reason is made known. Not only is the individual given more information here than elsewhere, but he has access to an agent of the company who has an interest in an accurate and favorable image of the applicant in the files. In the case of a whole life policy, the agent or salesman typically receives a first-year commission of 55 per cent of the premium, along with nine annual 5 per cent commissions thereafter. None of this commission will be paid in the event of the application's being denied, or the company's offer being rejected because of a high, rated premium. Moreover, agents of a multiple-line company will find their whole portfolio of business with an individual jeopardized by denials in one line. On the other side, agents are able to communicate with underwriters through informal as well as formal channels, obtaining information and exerting limited influence depending on their volume of business beyond what can be done on the official level. If the agent's ability to overcome unfavorable medical information is limited, he can suggest a supplementary medical examination based on the applicant's denial of a disability, and he will receive sympathetic consideration from the underwriting department. Furthermore, his personal acquaintance with the applicant is a basis for counteracting instances of gossip and mistaken identity in the files. It would seem a reasonable conclusion that denial of life insurance based on erroneous information in the underwriting files is a rare event.[5]

Uses of Information

The information about applications compiled in the underwriting files is used in one of several ways. The most common method assigns weight to the medical data according to life expectancy calculations based on the

[5] In Mayer v. Northern Life Insurance Company, 119 F. Supp., 536 (1954), the circulation of false but not malicious information by the MIB was held nonactionable, under the doctrine of conditional privilege. The holding in this case was based on a California statute, which appears to be a codification of common law doctrine applicable to mercantile agencies generally. The doctrine of privilege rests on the notion that the defendant is acting in furtherance of some interest of social importance which is entitled to protection as a matter of public policy. In regard to privilege generally, "the rule is that defamatory statements made upon an occasion *absolutely* privileged, though falsely, knowingly and with express malice, impose no legal liability, while such statements made upon an occasion only *conditionally* privileged will impose liability if spoken with malice." (2 DePaul Law Review, 69). The conditional privilege doctrine with respect to mercantile agencies is accepted in nearly all American jurisdictions.

company's own experience or the studies of the Society of Actuaries. Various traits predict higher than normal mortality, and others (e.g., sedentary occupation, slight underweight at certain ages) predict lower than normal mortality. If the mortality prediction is close to normal for the applicant's age group, he is issued a standard policy. Excessive likelihood of mortality will require a higher premium or "rated" policy, and above a certain level the application will be declined and no policy will be issued. Occupation, drinking habits, and similar matters can be treated in the same way as the medical data. Other items, such as a criminal record, may result in a flat denial, sometimes without a firm actuarial basis. Although it seems reasonable to the outside observer for an underwriter to deny life insurance to a motorcycle racer, it is not clear that, for example, a man with a prison record is necessarily a bad actuarial risk, yet he may be denied a policy. The President of the Institute of Life Insurance has written in a personal communication: "As far as we can ascertain, and we have reviewed quite thoroughly the actuarial literature and other sources, there is no published inter-company data relating exposure and experience in moral risks."

The vast bulk of serious applications for life insurance are accepted at standard rates. Of ordinary life applications in the United States in 1962, 84 per cent resulted in policies issued and paid for at standard rates. An additional 5 per cent were issued and paid for at extra premium.[6] (The reasons for the extra premium, based on a sample study, were: heart disease, 30 per cent; weight problems, 20 per cent; other physical impairments, 24 per cent; hazardous occupations, 18 per cent; other reasons, 8 per cent.) Only 3 per cent of the applications were declined by the company. The remaining 8 per cent resulted in offers not taken by applicants. It should be noted that an unknown percentage of prospective applicants may have been advised by agents that they probably could not obtain insurance, so one cannot conclude that the above percentages would apply to the general population. However, even making a substantial allowance for this bias, it appears that denial of life insurance is an uncommon event, and denial on nonmedical grounds is quite rare.

The principal output of life insurance underwriting files is to the files of other companies, through the MIB. A disability reported to the Bureau is made known to all companies that have inquired about the individual for the two previous years (corresponding to the period of contestability in most states). On occasions, misrepresentation of previously existing con-

[6] *Life Insurance Fact Book* 1967, *op. cit.*, p. 90.

ditions not caught at the time of the policy issue will be caught when another application is made for more or different life insurance later on. If this is within the contestability period, the policy may be voided on the grounds of fraud. However, in order to void the policy, the company must prove that the disability existed at the time of the issuance of the first policy, which is not always possible. Apart from these circumstances, disabilities discovered in an underwriting examination will be made known to other companies during seven successive years, and the 13 companies that keep their own files of MIB cards may retain them even longer.

Another output of the insurance investigation may occur when an outside agency contracts to do the inspection. The Retail Credit Company, for example, will include in its report information concerning any previous reports on the same individual that it may have been requested to do for the same or another company. Furthermore, they may make a "voluntary report" if asked to report on the same individual for another company within the contestability period. This service is available only to clients of the same inspecting organization, and the diffusion of information is on a much smaller scale and of less significance than that performed by the MIB.

Surprisingly, there is very little output from life underwriting files to other files within the same company. Not only does significant information (e.g., drinking habits) fail to find its way to unrelated lines, such as automobile liability, but generally even the related lines of accident and health insurance do not benefit by information in the life files of the same insurance company. Simultaneous applications by one person for two or more types of insurance may result in large amounts of duplicated effort, including duplicate inspections, and potentially in conflicting information and conflicting decisions on the various applications. MIB information is restricted by Bureau rules to life underwriting only, and may not legitimately be used elsewhere, but the same situation de facto applies to virtually the entire contents of the life insurance underwriting files.

Life insurance files are virtually unused outside the insurance companies. The main exception is that files stripped of identification form the basis for the intercompany actuarial research of the Society of Actuaries, in which 26 companies have been participating. The files in the companies studied are not made available to any person or organization on a routine basis, and there have been very few demands for them on an exceptional basis, although they would be available to law-enforcement agencies and similar bodies upon request.

Decreasing Need for Personal Information

In the light of the fairly costly and extensive investigation involved in insurance underwriting, why is the file so thin, and the output so limited? Three factors are relevant: (1) the specificity of the underwriting decision; (2) the cost of handling information; and (3) the rise of new bases for calculating insurance risk which by-pass the need for personal information.

The principal information required by life insurance underwriting concerns the health of the individual. Most of this information can be obtained by a quasi-scientific procedure, the medical examination, which is most likely in practice to be accurate and error-free. Moreover, as the principal causes of death decline in number, the number of bodily factors to be investigated likewise declines. A very large part of the total information needed to underwrite a life policy is contained in data concerning build and blood pressure. These items are generally easy to measure, both validly and reliably, at a given time. The value of stored and transferred information is thus far less in this field than in, say, evaluating prospective academic performances or payment of debts.

Investigations are expensive, particularly those involving scarce medical talent, long hours of surveillance, or the contacting of numerous informants. They will be undertaken only when the resulting information is worth the cost. Insurance companies have large resources and are willing to invest large sums in investigations where much is at stake. For instance, the suspicion of fraud in an automobile bodily injury claim will warrant the hire of a private detective with camera and tape recorder for extended periods of surveillance. False claims have been frustrated when motion pictures showed the supposedly disabled claimant fixing his roof or even riding horseback. In underwriting, however, even suspected fraud can better be handled simply by denying a policy. The cost involved is merely the lost premium and perhaps an occasional deserving applicant who cannot obtain insurance. Fraud apart, extensive examinations and trading of information would have to be warranted by the prevention of sufficient excess mortality to warrant the cost. The lack of enthusiasm in the industry with regard to the Recording Bureau illustrates that even minor expenses may be resisted if they are felt to yield insufficient savings. Life insurance companies have been discovering that even the standard medical examination may prove an unwarranted expense in groups with low total mortality or where adverse selection on mortality grounds is unlikely to occur.

As a result, there has been a rise in "nonmedical" insurance, that is, an ordinary life policy issued without a physical examination.[7] Early in the history of life insurance, policies were issued without examinations; prospective insureds presented themselves before the boards of directors of the "friendly societies" and were admitted or denied on the basis of their testimony. With the progress of both medicine and actuarial science in the nineteenth century, physical examinations became a universal requirement. Modern nonmedical insurance originated in Canada after World War I, as a consequence of a shortage of doctors and pressures to raise medical examiners' fees. To reduce costs, some companies started to waive physical examinations for small policies issued to younger people. The applicant was still required to answer questions concerning his health, but a physical examination was not routinely required. This experiment was successful, in that increased mortality among insureds cost less in the form of claims than was saved by omission of the physical examination.

Nonmedical insurance has now been widely adopted in the United States. A typical set of limits, used by one of the companies studied, is $25,000 to age 30, $15,000 from ages 31 to 35, and $5,000 from ages 36 to 40. Today, over half of all underwriting decisions are made without physical examinations. Since these decisions involve smaller policies, the bulk of premium dollars is still paid on policies subject to traditional underwriting. However, nonmedical insurance still shows growth, and many companies are raising the limits of policies written nonmedically to as high as $40,000.

The lack of adverse selection is one of the factors responsible for the growth of group insurance, which currently accounts for more than a third of all life insurance in force with legal reserve life companies. Nearly all group insurance is nonmedical, examinations being required only for exceptional groups buying high-limit policies, and for members who do not enroll during specified periods.

The third reason for a lack of personal information in the files of the insurance industry is the availability of new bases for calculating risks and premiums, which do not depend on knowledge of personal factors. An excellent example of such a change comes from a different area of insurance, fidelity bonding. Fidelity bonds insure employers against the dishonesty of their own employees, and at first glance it would seem that here if anywhere detailed personal information would be useful to the insurer. In fact, the original fidelity bonds written in the late nineteenth century did take the form of single bonds on given individuals, and an

[7] Dingman, Harry W., *Risk Appraisal*, The National Underwriter Company, Cincinnati, Ohio, 1957, pp. 680–690.

extensive investigation was undertaken before a bond was issued. In the first quarter of the twentieth century the form of fidelity bonds changed, first to a Name Schedule Bond, listing all persons to be covered, then to a Position Schedule Bond, listing all positions to be covered, and finally to a Blanket Bond, applying to all employees regardless of name and position. As these changes took place, insurance companies still obtained the names of individuals and made investigations, but the costs of investigations mounted as the scope of the bonds increased. Moreover, the companies found that most of their losses in the fidelity business were attributable to employees whose records gave no hint of potential dishonesty. The costs of investigation began to look larger than the rewards. Today, although industry practices vary, many companies make no investigations at all in connection with fidelity bonding, or make only a cursory investigation of new employees in selected positions.

Similar considerations apply to group writing in life and other fields of insurance. The determining underwriting factors are the characteristics of the group and eventually its claims experience, not the characteristics of individuals. The insurer in these circumstances has no interest in individual information, and does not gather any. The files of personal information disappear.

The savings in costs of acquisition along with savings in investigation have made group insurance a cheap and attractive form of coverage, which forms a larger and larger proportion of new insurance and of the total amount owned. Industry executives now speak of and move toward such novel schemes as providing total insurance portfolios for employees on a work-group basis. It is quite probable that payroll deductions will in the not too distant future provide for all personal lines of insurance, including auto and home as well as today's retirement, accident, and life coverages.

Insurance companies are becoming increasingly sophisticated users of their banks of powerful computers. It would seem reasonable that among the uses to which these computers will be put is sharing available and relevant personal information concerning insureds within and between departments of individual companies, as well as among companies.[8] However, as the available information thus becomes more usable, it is likely that less information will be gathered because of continued increase in the costs of investigations, and to increasing utilization of group as op-

[8] Greenig, Robert M., "Electronic Data Processing and Its Implications to Field Forces," *Journal of the American Society of Chartered Life Underwriters,* vol. XIV, no. 4 (Fall, 1960), pp. 369–381.

posed to individual bases of underwriting. If the future of our society is to include growing accumulations of personal information, insurance files are likely to be an exception to the general trend. The files of the insurance industry will be more efficiently used, but will contain less personal information.

PERSONAL INFORMATION IN OTHER TYPES OF INSURANCE

Personal information is collected to some extent in various branches of insurance other than life. The greatest amount after life is found in the automobile liability line, where individual driving records are of central importance. Indicative of the information found useful in this area is the report by the Maryland Insurance Commissioner concerning the reasons given by carriers for canceling or denying renewal of insurance: "The main reasons offered which appear to justify a company's action include: excessive use of alcohol, including conviction for drunken driving by the insured or a member of the family having access to the vehicle; excessive fault accidents; excessive moving violations, particularly by teenage drivers; and physical impairments which cannot be corrected by medical or mechanical means. . . ."[9]

The principal sources of this information are the application and inspection. The latter is usually performed by a commercial contractor, and invariably involves a search of Motor Vehicle Department records of accidents and convictions. The inspection also verifies such rating information as make and model of car, average mileage, use in business or pleasure, location of garage, and ages of drivers. Unlike the life contract, the auto liability contract is of short duration and is renewable (and in effect contestable) or a yearly or other short-term basis. The companies continue their surveillance over time, generally requesting a review by inspection every several years depending on the nature of the risk. (Families with marginal driving records, and those with children just below driving age, are likely to receive more frequent re-evaluations.) Claims are also noted in the underwriting files, and generally affect the rates charged.

Unlike most life companies, which underwrite and maintain their records in the head offices, most casualty insurers underwrite and store their records in local field offices. Since information concerning insureds can be used detrimentally in claims (e.g., by revealing the amount of the policy to a plaintiff's attorney), there is great incentive to keep the file confidential. The nature of derogatory filed information can be learned by the insured, if this leads to cancellation or nonrenewal, where state laws have

[9] *Insurance Advocate,* September 23, 1967, p. 4.

been enacted requiring the company to justify this action and releasing it from liability for false statements. This does give the insured a chance to defend his record which is not formally present in life underwriting, but these laws are not yet general, and the agent is less directly interested in a particular application in this area, where commissions run about 20 per cent, than in life insurance. It should be noted that there is no industry-wide organization in the auto lines comparable to the MIB, but the function of sharing relevant information is performed by public records of accidents and convictions.

The other "personal lines" of insurance—fire, liability, homeowners, etc. —gather less personal information, as underwriting attention focuses on the characteristics of the property insured more than on its owner. However, inspections are routinely made in the personal lines, and unusual personal situations will be entered in the underwriting files. (An interesting illustration of the lesser importance of personal matters is the comment by one underwriter that a prostitute—who would probably be denied life insurance—would be an excellent risk for liability insurance; few prospective plaintiffs would care to admit their association with her.)

Claims departments in the personal lines also gather minimal personal information, largely to identify repeating claimants, who may reasonably be suspected of fraud. Detrimental personal information may also be used by adjusters in negotiation of a lower settlement. In this regard, one of the most successful intercompany exchanges of information is the Claims Index System in automobile liability. The Index System accumulates reports of claims made against its 829 subscribers, and sends minimal records of previous claims apparently attributable to the same individuals to the reporting companies. Unlike the MIB, the Index System identifies the source of each report, and further information can be requested by the claims department of the inquiring company directly from the claims department of the reporting company. As claims departments, unlike underwriting departments, are rarely competitive, intercompany cooperation in supplying details is good. Index System files are kept separately by region, and reports and searches are confined to the region of the latest reported claim, unless a wider search is specifically requested. Information about each reported claim is entered on a small card, which is stored mechanically and is destroyed after an unspecified number of years.

Finally, a certain amount of personal information accumulates in underwriting files in the commercial lines. The information is generally sparse and unsystematic, although in some highly specialized lines, such as the bonding of contractors, considerable information may accumulate over the years. The information formally concerns the corporation, but particularly where the corporation is small this information reflects on the character of the owners and officers.

As previously suggested, the trend to group underwriting is affecting nearly all lines of insurance, thus diminishing the modicum of personal information maintained in underwriting files of lines other than life. Claims, of course, are not grouped, but existing and proposed legal changes, such as the formulas of workmen's compensation, have the effect of lessening the relevance of individual differences and obviating the necessity for gathering personal information. The prediction that the personal information content of insurance files will decrease seems applicable to all insurance functions.

IV *Governmental Institutions*

8 Government Records: The Census Bureau and the Social Security Administration

JOSEPH STEINBERG

THERE ARE TWO BASIC PURPOSES FOR WHICH DATA ARE OBTAINED BY THE federal government.[1] The first purpose is to provide general-purpose statistics for use by the government and the public for analyzing economic and social factors affecting the nation. The other purpose is to aid in carrying out administrative missions. In addition to the federal government, states and other governmental entities obtain data with similar purposes. This chapter concerns only federal data collection. The wide variety of data collected from and about individuals is only part of the total data-collection process. In this respect, this chapter restricts attention to data concerning people in their various categories.

This chapter was written by the author in his private capacity. No official support or endorsement by the Social Security Administration is intended or should be inferred.

[1] Subcommittee on Census and Government Statistics of the Committee on Post Office and Civil Service, House of Representatives, Eighty-eighth Congress, Second Session, Hearings: The Federal Paperwork Jungle, May 1–June 24, 1964; Bureau of the Budget, Office of Statistical Standards, "Statistical Services of the United States Government," Washington, 1968.

General-purpose statistics are collected essentially by four agencies. Some administrative agencies collect information which has by-product use as general-purpose statistics. The largest general-purpose statistical agency is the Bureau of the Census in the Department of Commerce. The other principal general-purpose statistical agencies are the Bureau of Labor Statistics in the Department of Labor, the Statistical Reporting Service in the Department of Agriculture, and the National Center for Health Statistics in the Public Health Service of the Department of Health, Education and Welfare. The Bureau of the Census, the largest statistical agency, is considered in depth in this chapter. The other agencies collect comparatively little data about individuals—and what they do collect is on small samples of people. It might be useful to note at this point that there are specific and general reviews of what information is collected. The specific reviews are the responsibility of the Bureau of the Budget.[2] More general reviews are carried out by Congressional committees, Presidential special review committees, and professional advisory committees.

The principal agencies with administrative missions that collect data about and from individuals are the Social Security Administration and the Internal Revenue Service. Many other agencies in each of the executive departments of the federal government collect some information about people as part of their tasks in administering their programs. Usually, these data are for only a relatively small group. The work of the Social Security Administration as it relates to the collection of individual data is discussed in some detail in this chapter. The work of the Internal Revenue Service affecting taxpayers is well known. Data collections concern matters affecting tax liabilities and arise through the informational reports of employers and other income payers, as well as the tax reports of the individual. Many of the elements of general procedure are common among administrative agencies, while differentiated in specifics by the needs for proper administration.

The collection of information about individuals in the statistical agencies is independent of that of the administrative agencies. None of the information collected by the Census Bureau is ever available to the Internal Revenue Service or other administrative agencies. As will be noted below, statute protects the confidentiality of the Bureau of the Census information. Similarly, statute and regulations define the confidentiality provisions

[2] Bureau of the Budget, Office of Statistical Standards, "Controlling Federal Government Questionnaires," *Statistical Reporter*, July, 1968, no. 69–1, pp. 1–7.

of information at administrative agencies, such as the Social Security Administration.

In general, information requests by governmental agencies are reviewed in detail by the Bureau of the Budget. The Federal Reports Act of 1942 provides that requests for information from the public by federal agencies subject to the act may be made only if the Director of the Bureau of the Budget does not disapprove the proposed collection of information.[3] In addition, under the Budget and Accounting Procedures Act of 1950, it is responsible for the development and coordination of the federal statistics program. The Bureau's responsibility under the Federal Reports Act extends to the obtaining of data for all uses—specific administrative uses as well as general-purpose statistical uses. The review ensures that:

1. The information sought is necessary and relevant to the program of the agency;
2. The information is not already available from reports collected by the same or any other agency;
3. The form is as comprehensible as possible;
4. The number of respondents is held to a minimum and the information is collected no more frequently than necessary.

The number of reports formally disapproved is small. The review has served mainly to discourage some requests and to impose an element of self-discipline on the part of government agencies. The Federal Reports Act specifically exempts from the provisions of the Act several units of the Department of the Treasury. The principal agency collecting data on individuals that is excluded is the Internal Revenue Service. Ultimate control of the tax return forms is through regulations that interpret the intent of the revenue laws. In the preparation of regulations, public hearings and participation occur in accordance with the Administrative Procedures Act prior to promulgation of the regulations in final form.

THE BUREAU OF THE CENSUS

The Bureau of the Census is the largest statistical agency of the federal government. It collects data about individuals at each of the decennial censuses and in periodic sample surveys. Special censuses and other sample surveys also provide additional data collections.

[3] Subcommittee on Economic Statistics of the Joint Economic Committee, Ninetieth Congress, First Session, Hearings: The Coordination and Integration of Government Statistical Programs, May 17–18; June 7–8, 1967.

Historical Review of the Federal Census

Official census-taking in the United States began in 1790.[4] The constitutional requirement under which the census is taken is contained in Article 1, Section 2. This article was included in the Constitution for political reasons, and with no thought of providing for any systematic collection of statistical data beyond the political necessities of the government. Under this constitutional requirement the United States was the first country to provide for a regular periodic enumeration of its inhabitants. The organic act providing for the first enumeration was passed at the second session of the First Congress and was approved March 1, 1790. U.S. marshals and assistants they appointed carried out the enumeration. The Secretary of State, presumably acting under the direction of the President, sent each marshal copies of the act prescribing the inquiries to be made. In addition to enumerating the population, and collecting information required to satisfy the constitutional provision, the act also required collection of data on sex and color of free persons and identification of free males sixteen years of age or over.

In each subsequent decade there has been an enumeration. The first six censuses taken (1790–1840) limited their inquiries to the numbers of the population by age, sex, color, and whether free or slave. The census of 1830 was the first to employ a printed schedule. Written instructions explaining the inquiries in detail were first provided in 1850. Information was obtained about each person instead of only the number of various classes of persons in each household. In 1880, the enumeration responsibility was vested in census supervisors appointed for each census district. This census is generally considered the first modern census of the United States. A census office was established in the Department of the Interior. The number of inquiries was increased. From time to time changes have continued to be made in the subject matter covered. In 1902, the Census Office was created as a permanent agency.[5] Sampling techniques were used for the first time in the 1940 census for collecting some items of information. The 1950 census saw the introduction of formal methods of evaluation of the quality of the coverage and content of the census. Sampling was more extensively used in the 1960 census. The basic census laws under which the Bureau of the Census now operates were codified in 1954 by the 83rd Congress under Title 13 of the United States Code.[6] Several

[4] Senate Committee on the Census, Fifty-sixth Congress, First Session: Wright, Carroll D., "The History and Growth of the United States Census, 1790–1890," February 24, 1900.

[5] U.S. Bureau of the Census, 1960 Censuses of Population and Housing: Procedural History, Washington, 1966.

[6] United States Code, Title 13.

amendments have since been enacted. Census proclamations relating to each census are signed by the President. After signing, they now appear in the *Federal Register.*

Information Gathered in the Decennial Census

The Bureau of the Census is now at the semifinal stage of its preparations for the nineteenth decennial census.[7] The information likely to be gathered by the 1970 census has been selected.[8] While the census queries are still subject to change, if unanticipated problems or changed conditions warrant, it is possible to examine the subject content. The proposed inquiries may be compared to the content of the previous census and also examined from the historical perspective of when the specific or similar inquiry was made. Since sampling is used so extensively, it is important to note which subjects are covered for every person or household, and which are collected only for a smaller sample. It is important to note that while name and address are recorded on the forms or questionnaires, these items of information are not used as identifiers in subsequent stages of processing or recording on the tapes to be used in the computers. Once the information is on computer tape there is no personal identifier of any kind on the tape that ties the information to the individual or the household.

Table 1 shows the planned subject content of the 1970 census and related matters of interest. Many questions were proposed that are not included. Some are not being included as too personal. Others are being excluded as too complex. As noted in a subsequent section, others have been ruled out as not in the public interest or not needed for small areas, and therefore more appropriate to a national sample survey.

Who Uses the Information?

The needs of the federal government for statistical data on a small-area basis is the primary purpose for most of each decennial census. The small number of new items added for the planned list in the 1970 census are primarily to meet program needs of federal agencies. Since the data, when published, are available to all, the needs of state and local governments, industry and business, and any individual researcher are also served by the millions of statistical results in the many census reports.

[7] Kaplan, David L., "Plans for the 1970 Census of Population and Housing," *Statistical Reporter*, November, 1967, pp. 73–79.

[8] U.S. Bureau of the Census, 1970 Census of Population and Housing, Dress Rehearsal, Informational Copy of Subject Content Planned for the 1970 Census, Form D–60(x), November 30, 1967.

TABLE 1 *Subject Items Planned for 1970 Census, Sample Size, and Date of First Census Collection*

	Sample Size		First
Population items	*1970*	*1960*	*collected*
Relationship to head of household	100%	100%	1880
Color or race	100	100	1790
Age (month and year of birth)	100	100	1790
Sex	100	100	1790
Marital status	100	100	1880
State or country of birth	25	25	1850
Years of school completed	25	25	1940
Number of children ever born	25	25	1890
Activity 5 years ago	25	—	New
Employment status	25	25	1880
Hours worked last week	25	25	1880
Weeks worked last year	25	25	1880
Last year in which worked	25	25	1880
Occupation, industry, and class of worker	25	25	1840
Income last year:			
Wage and salary income	25	25	1940
Self-employment income	25[a]	25	1940
Other income	25[b]	25	1940
Country of birth of parents	20	25	1850
Mother tongue	20	25	1910
Year moved into this house	20	25	1940
Place of residence 5 years ago	20	25	1940
School or college enrollment (public or private)	20	25	1850
Veteran status	20	25	1930
Place of work	20[c]	25	1960
Means of transportation to work	20	25	1960
Occupation-industry 5 years ago	5	—	New
Citizenship	5	—	1890
Year of immigration	5	—	1900
Marital history	5	25	1910
Vocational training completed	5	—	New
Presence and duration of disability	5	—	New
Housing items			
Number of units at this address	100[d]	—	New
Telephone	100[e]	25	1960
Access to unit	100	100	1960
Kitchen or cooking facilities	—	100	
Complete kitchen facilities	100	—	New
Rooms	100	100	1940
Water supply	100	100	1940
Flush toilet	100	100	1940
Bathtub or shower	100	100	1940
Basement	100	25	1960
Heating equipment	100	25	1940
Tenure	100	100	1890
Commercial establishment on property	100	100[f]	1940

TABLE 1 (*cont.*)

Population items	*Sample Size* 1970	*Sample Size* 1960	*First collected*
Value	100	100[f]	1930
Contract rent	100	100[f]	1930
Vacancy status	100	100	1940
Months vacant	100	25	1960
Components of gross rent	25	25	1940
Year structure built	25	25	1940
Number of units in structure	25	25	1940
Farm residence	25	25[g]	1890
Source of water	20	20[g]	1960
Sewage disposal	20	20[g]	1960
Bathrooms	20	20	1960
Air conditioning	20	5	1960
Automobiles	20	20[h]	1960
Stories, elevator in structure	5	20[i]	1960
Fuel—heating, cooking, water heating	5	5	1940
Bedrooms	5	5	1960
Second home	5	—	New
Clothes washing machine	5	5	1960
Clothes dryer	5	5	1960
Dishwasher	5	—	New
Home food freezer	5	5	1960
Television	5	5	1950
Radio	5	5	1930

[a] Single item in 1960; two-way separation in 1970 by farm and nonfarm income.
[b] Single item in 1960; three-way separation in 1970 by social security, public welfare, and all other receipts.
[c] Item will be expanded to include street address if the appropriations for the 1970 census include an allotment for this purpose.
[d] To be collected only for coverage check purposes; will not be tabulated.
[e] Required on 100 per cent basis for field follow-up purposes in areas where census is planned to be conducted by mail.
[f] 100 per cent in places of 50,000 or more, 25 per cent elsewhere.
[g] Omitted in places of 50,000 or more.
[h] 20 per cent in places of 50,000 or more, 5 per cent elsewhere.
[i] Collected only in places of 50,000 or more.

NOTE: The list of items planned for 1970 does not differ materially from the content of the 1960 census. The 1970 census focuses on greater use of the existing subjects by more intensive cross-tabulation and by providing additional data for small areas.

The Secretary of Commerce in a letter to all members of the House and Senate on April 17, 1969, advised that he had ordered a reduction in the sample size for the 1970 census. The basic sample questions would be asked of 20 per cent of households (previously planned as a 25 per cent sample). Another set of sample questions would be asked of 15 per cent (previously planned as 20 per cent).

SOURCE: Bureau of the Census; *Statistical Reporter,* November, 1967, pp. 73–79.

It may be useful to consider some of the subjects covered in the census and to see how the data needs of this country are served. At all times, the publication program is geared to preserve the confidentiality of individual information by the limitation of data to those areas of tabulation that would ensure this principle. Thus, it is only as processed results, not information on any one individual or family, that any of the collected data become available.

The educational level of the population is an important cross-classification variable with virtually all other data collected in the census. The social and economic status of an individual is strongly influenced by educational level.

The labor force activity questions are the only source of data for small areas. Manpower training, welfare, education, and other programs depend on these data. Labor market analysis depend on these data as well as on facts on occupational skills. Public and private economic development and planning are based on analysis of these data. Data on activity five years ago and on occupation and industry five years ago will provide measures of individual changes in contrast to data on net over-all changes. Job and occupational mobility analysis will allow deeper understanding of the dynamics of manpower utilization and assist in evaluation of changes in economic opportunity.

Income size distribution data for small geographic areas, cross-classified by a host of other available variables, are one of the best indicators of the general welfare. These data aid business and government in a wide variety of program-planning and analysis efforts. Since data are available by family groups as well as individuals, meaningful analysis in regard to basic units of measurement is possible. Current interest in regard to poverty, disadvantaged groups, state and regional areas with need for development are all assisted by these statistical data.

Significant government planning is facilitated by the results of data collected on veteran status. Since there is no direct contact with many veterans, these data represent the only broadly based means for studying their social and economic characteristics and for evaluating the benefits of programs for veterans.

The Bureau of the Census has announced that an item on religion would not be included in the 1970 census.[9] It did so after weighing the matter carefully, cognizant of needs and concerns, and possible effects on the whole census-taking activity. Legally, section 5 of Title 13 would have permitted inclusion of the item. Proponents pointed to the importance of religion in American life and to the fact that the census of the United States has never collected such information, though Canada and many other countries include it in their censuses. They stressed the need for informa-

[9] Subcommittee on Census and Statistics of the Committee on Post Office and Civil Service, House of Representatives, Ninetieth Congress, First Session, Hearings: 1970 Census Plans, May–June, 1967.

tion on the distribution, growth rates, educational levels, and occupational distribution of members of various religious groups. Because religious practices have consequences for marketing, business representatives are interested in such information. It was also argued that churches could use the information in planning their activities. Those who opposed the inclusion did so primarily on the grounds that it would be contrary to the traditional division of church and state and an improper invasion of privacy if required under the mandatory provisions of the census.

Another item recommended for inclusion, but not to be included, is social security number. Proponents argued that social security numbers are so widely used that there would be little hesitancy about providing the information. This number would make it possible for future censuses to report changes for identical groups of people over time, without asking them to report about the past. This information could be reported more accurately, and with less burden on the public, if matched through social security numbers. Information from other records could also be transferred to the Census Bureau to supplement the census records. The information thus transferred would be subject to the same guarantees of confidentiality as any information collected directly in the census. The opposition to inclusion of the social security number was based on the belief that this practice could contribute to significant invasions of privacy. It was felt that, should some official choose to disregard the statutes requiring confidential treatment of individual census records, the effects of his violation would have wide ramifications because of the availability of this identifying number. Because of the opposition and reservations about whether or not this was an attempt by the government to formulate a dossier on everybody in connection with the proposed question, the Census Bureau decided not to include social security number on the complete census or even on the 25 per cent sample.

How Data Are Used and Processed

By law, data collected by the Census Bureau are confidential[10]—they are processed only by employees of the Census Bureau who are under the legal constraint of Title 13 of the U.S. Code. Data on individuals may be used only for statistical tabulations. Violation of confidentiality of any information about any individual is punishable by fine and imprisonment. The legislative history of census confidentiality reveals the increasing concern of Congress over the past eighty-five years that census reports be

[10] Taeuber, Conrad, "Invasion of Privacy," *Eugenics Quarterly*, vol. 14, no. 3 (September, 1967), pp. 243–246.

safeguarded against disclosure and that the information be used for statistical purposes and not made available to other agencies of government for purposes of taxation, investigation, or regulation. There never was any challenge to this in connection with a record in possession of the Census Bureau. On December 11, 1961, the Supreme Court ruled in the case of the St. Regis Paper Company v. The United States, that copies of reports filed with the Bureau of the Census could be subpoenaed by the Federal Trade Commission and the information thus obtained used in legal proceedings against the reporting company.[11] The Federal Trade Commission, acting under section 6 of the FTC Act, had ordered the company to submit records, including its file copies of census reports. The company failed to furnish all the requested data and then was ordered to do so by a federal district court. The case was appealed. The Second Circuit Court of Appeals ruled that the company had to submit its file copies of census reports to the FTC. This ruling being contrary to the ruling of the Seventh Circuit Court in a similar case led to the Supreme Court consideration and then, decision. In 1962 Congress, in Public Law 87–813, then amended section 9 of Title 13 of the U.S. Code to extend confidentiality to company-retained copies of census reports. Thus, the law on confidentiality now covers both the records at the Census Bureau and any copy retained by the respondent.

To ensure confidentiality, reports of individuals may not be examined by other than sworn officers or employees of the Department of Commerce or the Census Bureau. Further, data which might reveal the identify of the source may not be published. Thus, tabulated data are analyzed to ensure that no information of detriment to an individual is released in any statistical compilation of sets of data. In practice, as well as in theory, the steps taken are designed to ensure this constraint. The only place where data and individual identifiers exist are the basis schedules used for the data collection.[12] Access to the original census schedules or their microfilm copies is limited to sworn employees. Any violation is subject to the penalties of the law. Thus, the maximum protection to these data is by law and procedure. Physical protection of confidentiality during use or destruction of schedules is accorded importance in the administrative procedures of Census and Archives. The later data files have only numeric identifiers to tie the information on these tapes or other data records back

[11] Corcoran, Thomas F., "On the Confidential Status of Census Reports," *The American Statistician,* June, 1963, pp. 33–40.

[12] Subcommittee on Administrative Practice and Procedure of the Committee on the Judiciary, United States Senate, Ninetieth Congress, First Session, Hearings: Computer Privacy, March 14–15, 1967.

to the basic schedules. These numeric identifiers are primarily geographic codes. Thus, each processed record shows region, state, county, city, and block if an urban dweller is involved. In rural areas, the basic units of geography that are identified are called enumeration districts. Since enumeration districts are subdivisions of the civil (or census) divisions of a county, larger entities are identifiable. In the 1970 census, each side of a city-type block will be identified (block face). The individual and his household are identified by the number assigned at the time of enumeration of a particular census. Thus, no data from two or more censuses are ever available for the same individual in the same place. Each census file is discrete.

After the data have been assigned numeric codes for those subjects requiring this process, the numeric entries or codes are then the only data on the magnetic tapes used in the computer tabulation process. In the 1960 census, and in the 1970 census, an intermediate part of the processing involves the use of the Fosdic machine. This machine, the Film Optical Sensing Device for Input to Computers, is capable of "reading" information from a microfilm copy of an appropriately designed and marked schedule. Much of the information collected is properly marked directly on the schedule. For those requiring coding the clerical staff marks the codes in the proper manner on the schedules. After the data are on magnetic tape all further processing of the data is through use of the tape. The many millions of facts that are tabulated and published are therefore taken from this impersonal source.

The Census Bureau does provide special tabulations as a special service.[13] These services, undertaken at cost, are under the same provisions of confidentiality as the general-purpose tabulations. The policy governing these special services is carefully spelled out and publicly available. A personal census records service is provided to individuals concerned, at cost. Personal data are sometimes available to an individual in no other place than in some past census record. Extracts from a prior census are often accepted as evidence of age and place of birth, for obtaining employment, social security benefits, old-age assistance, passports, naturalization papers, delayed birth certificates, and the like. Inasmuch as the personal information recorded at the census of 1900 and later censuses is confidential, it is furnished only if desired for a proper purpose, upon the written request of the person himself or his legal representative.

[13] U.S. Bureau of the Census, Data Access Descriptions, Policy and Administration Series, PA–1, "Policy Governing Access to Census Bureau Unpublished Data and Special Services," February, 1968.

In general, all data processing of census data is by census staff operating under the requirements to maintain confidentiality. In the 1960 census, a basic small sample of 1/1000 was identified and information for this sample was released for tabulation by social science researchers. The release of information in this form was carefully screened to comply with all the requirements of confidentiality. The records gave no information which would identify the area in which the person lived except by broad region and size of place. Other data were coded in categories so broad that it was impossible to identify even unusual individuals.

The Decision Process

By law, the basic responsibility for determining what is to be collected rests with the Secretary of Commerce. The legal basis in Title 13 provides that: "The Secretary shall prepare schedules, and shall determine the inquiries, and the number, form, and subdivisions thereof, for the statistics, surveys, and censuses provided for in this title." The Secretary may, and does, delegate these functions and duties to the Director of the Bureau of the Census.

One of the first aspects in planning for a forthcoming census is a detailed review of the experience with the types of questions in the preceding census. During the past two decennial censuses, extensive evaluation programs were part of the basic program of data collection. Intercensal research projects provide additional insight on concepts and measurements. Users, particularly of small-area data, obtain additional insight into the uses, values, and deficiencies in the data. Illustrative of the review is the research effort on measuring the quality of housing in a census. This research, part of a continuous program ever since the concept was first measured in the 1940 census, has apparently shown that data on direct measures are not sufficiently valid to justify their inclusion in the 1970 census.[14]

The fact that a decennial census is of a mandatory character plays a role in determining whether questions should be included. The Census Bureau has preferred to depend on the cooperation of the public in this regard, while using the courts to consider imposition of penalties required by law only in flagrant and extreme cases.

Part of the planning for a census also entails review of proposals for changes, additions, or deletions that come to the attention of the Director

[14] U.S. Bureau of the Census, Measuring the Quality of Housing, An Appraisal of Census Statistics and Methods, Working Paper No. 25, Washington, 1967.

and his staff.[15] Basically, the content of any census is in fair measure related to the content of the preceding census. Over a decade, changes of emphasis and of interest may appear in the light of new policy areas that require extensive data-based examination. In general, the demands for data from a census have as their essential core the need for small-area data. In carrying out the review the criteria for the decisions are as follows:

1. A question to be included must be of broad public interest. The burden of proof for inclusion is borne by the proponents.
2. The information must be needed for small areas, such as counties, municipalities, tracts, or blocks, for which only a census can provide data.
3. The question must be one to which the respondent can give accurate and unambiguous answers.
4. The question must be one which is generally accepted by the public as relevant to the census.
5. The questionnaire as a whole must not involve an undue burden on the respondents.
6. The entire census needs to be conducted within the appropriated funds made available for the purpose.

The review of inquiries to be included entails lengthy efforts. The Census Bureau establishes a number of advisory committees of knowledgeable users of census data. Professional and user groups establish Census Advisory Committees. For example, the principal advisory groups for the 1960 censuses were:

1. Technical Advisory Committee for the 1960 Population Census
2. Advisory Committee for the 1960 Housing Census
3. Technical Advisory Committee on Residential Finance
4. American Statistical Association, Census Advisory Committee
5. American Marketing Association, Census Advisory Committee
6. Council of Population and Housing Census Users
7. Federal Agency Population and Housing Census Council
8. Population Association of America, 1960 Census Committee
9. Panel of Statistical Consultants

[15] Miller, Herman P., "Considerations in Determining the Content of the 1970 Census," *Demography,* vol. 4, no. 2 (1967), pp. 744–758.

For the 1970 census similar efforts have taken place. The Census Bureau made direct efforts to obtain suggestions and comments through intensive discussions. A series of locally sponsored public meetings in 23 cities across the country were held, involving more than 2,000 persons.

The House of Representatives' Committee on Post Office and Civil Service has a Subcommittee on Census and Statistics. The full committee held hearings in August, 1966, to consider and give advice and counsel on questions to be asked in the 1970 Census of Population and Housing.[16] Ordinarily, such a matter would be considered by the subcommittee, but the subject was considered important enough for full committee hearings. Issues of possible violation of individual privacy because of the nature of the questions and the use of computers in the compilation of the information were raised in these hearings.

Similar issues were raised in a series of bills introduced to limit the number of questions asked in the 1970 Census of Population and Housing. Hearings on limiting the mandatory list of questions were held in October, 1967.[17] The matter continued to be a subject for discussion during the second session of the Ninetieth Congress in 1968 and continues in 1969.

The need for decisions reached at an early date derives from the complexities of the operation that must be performed properly if the census is to be carried out to produce useful timely results. The situation for the 1970 census is in some ways reminiscent of the one prior to the 1940 census. The discussions concerning inclusion of information on income for the first time, and the need for ensuring privacy led to use of a special form by those respondents who preferred to supply the information by mail directly to the Census Bureau in Washington instead of giving the information to an enumerator. However, the more extensive use of the mails for the 1970 census already planned has not seemed to satisfy the proponents of a reduced set of mandatory questions—supplemented by a voluntarily answered set of other (still reduced) questions.

Special Censuses and Sample Surveys

The Census Bureau collects data about individuals at other times than the decennial census.[18] One type of collection is the special census. A spe-

[16] Committee on Post Office and Civil Service, House of Representatives, Eighty-ninth Congress, Second Session, Hearings: 1970 Census Questions, August 23–25, 1966.

[17] Federal Statistics User's Conference, Proposals to Limit the Number of Questions Asked in the 1970 Census of Population and Housing. Special Newsletter, no. 10, December 21, 1967; Subcommittee on Census and Government Statistics of the Committee on Post Office and Civil Service, House of Representatives, Ninetieth Congress, Hearings: Limit Categories of Questions in Decennial Censuses. October 24, 1967.

[18] U.S. Bureau of the Census, Bureau of the Census Catalog. (Quarterly and Annual volume.)

cial census usually is requested and paid for by a given city or other area. It is usually taken to provide a more recent statistical official count of the population of the area. State or other laws sometimes provide that localities may receive a larger share of funds if they can demonstrate a larger population than recorded at the last decennial census. Data collected in smaller places are usually only on sex and color of each person. Age is collected and reported on for places of 50,000 or more. The same confidentiality provisions apply as in any census activity carried out under Title 13 of the U.S. Code. However, these are generally voluntary.

Other surveys are taken at more frequent intervals under either the provisions of Title 13 or for other agencies of the federal government under provisions of their laws. In the latter cases, the Census Bureau is involved primarily in collecting and compiling as a service. In general, replies to such surveys are voluntary even though one or another provision concerning confidentiality obtains. The same care is observed that no data of detriment to an individual is made public. Since these surveys are small-scale sample surveys (usually 1/1000 or smaller), the very fact of sampling provides a basic protection. However, all provisions of ensuring privacy in the collection, processing, and tabulation obtain equally for sample surveys as for the decennial census.

The content of these sample surveys is quite varied. There are, however, some repetitive survey operations whose content may be considered. The Current Population Survey is a monthly survey.[19] At present it includes about 50,000 households scattered in some 450 areas of the country. Under various titles this survey has been conducted monthly with changing samples of households since 1940. Its primary purpose is to provide the basis for the official statistics on employment and unemployment published monthly by the Bureau of Labor Statistics of the Department of Labor. The monthly data collection concerns employment status, hours worked last week, occupation, industry, and class of worker, duration of unemployment if unemployed, and the like. Basic demographic information is collected in the first interview. This includes the relationship to head of the household, color or race, date of birth, sex, marital status, veteran status, education, and some limited housing information. Thus, since sample households are included in the sample for eight months (in two separate periods of four months, one year apart), the monthly collected data on labor force status may be related for tabulation to the basic demographic variables.

[19] U.S. Bureau of the Census, The Current Population Survey—A Report on Methodology, Technical Paper No. 7, Washington, 1963.

At various times during the year, supplementary questions are added, usually to serve the statistical needs of other federal government agencies. These may be as varied as smoking habits and kinds of immunizations. Other questions are added by the Census Bureau on its own behalf. Once a year, there is a "miniature census" collection. Principally such questions as income last year or migration are added. The specific content may be noted in the public descriptions in the publications of the Census Bureau or the other agencies involved. The *Statistical Reporter*, published by the Office of Statistical Standards of the Bureau of the Budget, reports content of the new reporting forms or of publications as they occur. For example, in fiscal year 1967 the supplements to the Current Population Survey were as follows:[20]

July, 1966: Quarterly Survey of Intentions to secure information on consumer buying plans for houses, automobiles, and seven durable goods.

August, 1966: Survey of Incidence of TV Availability to secure information on the incidence of TV ownership and the proportion of households with the capability of receiving color and UHF-TV.

September, 1966: National Immunization Survey to obtain information on skin test for detection of TB, both oral and injection forms of polio protection, diphtheria-pertussis-tetanus protection, and measles incidence.

October, 1966: School enrollment supplement to collect school enrollment and related information on persons 5–34 years old, questions on school dropouts, nursery school attendance, and extent of enrollment at colleges, type of college housing, and major fields of study; also the Quarterly Survey of Intentions.

November, 1966: Survey of voting characteristics of the population to secure information about registration and voting in the November, 1966, election.

December, 1966: Hired Farm Work Survey to obtain information on the economic and social characteristics of migratory and other farm wage workers.

January, 1967: Quarterly Survey of Intentions

[20] Supplements to Current Population Survey, FY 1967, *Statistical Reporter*, September, 1967, pp. 48–49.

February, 1967:	Work Experience Supplement to establish the work experience of the population during the previous calendar year; and a Survey of Men 20–64 Not in the Labor Force to secure information on their past work experience and reasons for current nonparticipation.
March, 1967:	Annual Demographic Supplement covering migration during the past year, date of first marriage, and income from all sources the previous year.
April, 1967:	Work Experience Supplement (for a group first in sample in March); Survey of Men with College Degrees to collect information on the type of college attended, major field of study, and degrees earned.
May, 1967:	Survey of Persons Receiving Overtime and Premium Pay and a Survey of Factors Affecting Underemployment.
June, 1967:	Survey of Incidence of TV Availability (as in August, 1966).

Sources of Information and Users

The individual or a responsible household member is virtually always the source of information obtained by the Census Bureau. Sometimes, after repeated calls, it is quite apparent that no one in a given household is likely to be available to give the information to the census enumerator. The statistical needs are best met by information directly from a responsible respondent about his own household. However, to the extent that some limited information is better than none, and to get as complete a count of the population by a few basic characteristics as is possible, occasionally information is obtained from a proxy—usually a neighbor. However, the incidence is quite small. All the information is used solely for statistical purposes—tabulation of counts of the population with various characteristics. Thus, the use of information from proxy respondents serves to improve the statistical product, on the average. Users have access only to the statistical products. They range from those with simple informational needs to those with the most sophisticated analytic interests in the political and social science community.

Records Disposal and Retention

Title 13 does not protect census records prior to 1900 as confidential. The available census records for 1790–1870 are open to public inspection at the National Archives. Those for 1880 are unavailable because of the condition of the paper. The 1890 records were almost completely destroyed by fire.

Census schedules from 1900 to 1940 were destroyed in 1956. However, the microphotographic copies retained are available for census confidential use. The 1950 population census schedules were to be destroyed after the 1960 census was completed. A Records Retention Plan, developed in cooperation with the National Archives and Records Service, determines the length of time records are retained and their physical location. Microfilm copies are accorded census confidential treatment under custody of the National Archives as well as at the Census Bureau itself. Specific procedures adopted by the Census Bureau in collaboration with National Archives provides the basic protection of Title 13 to these data.[21]

THE SOCIAL SECURITY ADMINISTRATION

The Social Security Administration is one of the largest administrative agencies of the federal government whose mission involves knowledge and need for data about individuals.[22] Information collected is available through applications for social security numbers, reports of earnings, and administrative actions such as the filing of claims for cash benefits. The new service benefits in the health area have made available significant amounts of demographic data concerning aged persons not otherwise beneficiaries under the cash benefits program. For all persons aged sixty-five and over, data on utilization of hospital services, as well as information on providers of the services, are part of the ongoing information flow for administration. For persons enrolled for supplementary medical benefits, data on significant uses of doctors' services have become available.

Demographic and Economic Data for Individuals

The Social Security Act as amended is the generator of data needs. As Congress amends the Act, to achieve objectives relative to the scope or nature of the program, or to simplify or change its administrative aspects, data needs are identified or changed.[23]

Basic information about individuals is supplied by the individual on the application for a social security number. These applications call for information on name, date of birth, sex, race, place of birth, father's name,

[21] Goldfield, Edwin D., "Preservation of Confidential Source Records," presented at Conference on the National Archives and Statistical Research, Washington, May 27–28, 1968.

[22] Steinberg, Joseph, and Heyman C. Cooper, "Social Security Statistical Data, Social Science Research, and Confidentiality," *Social Security Bulletin*, October, 1967, pp. 3–15.

[23] Heller, Robert N., Harry Shulman, and Herbert R. Tacker, "Cash Benefits: From Inputs to Outputs," Second Annual Conference, New York Area Chapter, American Statistical Association, May, 1967.

and mother's maiden name. Form SS–5, Application for Social Security Number, is the primary paper form. For a short time, IRS Form 3227, Application for Account Number, was used in cooperation with the Internal Revenue Service in providing numbers for taxpayer identification. That form made no provision for recording race. Several other forms have been used for special groups—civil service employees, or persons applying for a health insurance claim number. The data on the application initiate the establishment of a machine-readable record for the individual.

As the individual works under covered employment, his employer uses the social security number as the numerical identifier for reporting quarterly wages. For agricultural workers, data are reported annually. These earnings reports are the primary source of data for accumulating information on the quarters of coverage and the annual summary on taxable wages in the machine-readable record of the specified employee. In a similar fashion, information on earnings for self-employed persons becomes available through information filed by the individual with his federal tax return as part of his Schedule C or Schedule F. Only the minimum information needed for proper and efficient administration is part of the machine-readable record for each account number.

A 1 per cent statistical probability sample, the Continuous Work History Sample, is the sole machine-readable record that compiles quarterly data, together with codes for county of employment and industry for the sample account numbers. The sample is selected on the basis of the social security number with constant selection pattern since the start. This sample is used solely for statistical purposes and is not part of the basic administrative record system. This sample design provides the basis for linkage of the more detailed information that is maintained for statistical purposes.

Neither paper records nor machine-readable records of the Social Security Administration show the home address at present or in the past for other than a small fraction of the social security number holders. Unless the individual is receiving a cash benefit at the time, the Social Security Administration does not systematically have a reasonably current residence address. The only purpose in having an address is to forward a benefit check or when it is necessary to obtain payments for supplementary medical insurance coverage. The records that provide the information on work under covered employment only identify the individual as having last worked for a given employer. The basic machine-readable record does not directly carry this type of information.

An individual's social security number does not convey any demographic or economic information.[24] It is strictly a numeric means for enabling the Social Security Administration to cumulate, in summary form, the earnings information while an individual works. It permits cumulation, when the individual or his survivors become beneficiaries, of those items of information needed to carry out the proper payment of benefits. Many do not realize that no information concerning the individual is contained in the account number, although this policy has been followed since the beginning of the social security program. Unlike some numbers used in this country or abroad, not even year of birth can be inferred directly or indirectly from the number.

Data about Claimants and Beneficiaries

Information needed to establish entitlement to a cash benefit is supplied by the claimant. The nature of the information depends on the type of benefit and the claimant. A general discussion of the social security programs and each of their aspects is provided by the *Social Security Handbook.*[25]

Each type of claim calls for information concerning the specific factors of entitlement involved in the claim. Ordinarily an application must be filed for a person to be entitled to cash benefits or to establish a period of disability. The application must be made on a special form provided by the Social Security Administration.

Each claimant must prove his identity and establish that he has met all the requirements to be entitled to the benefit that he is claiming. The general factors of entitlement and of evidence vary. The total set of factors include evidence on age, relationship—marriage, divorce, and, where needed, that of parent-child; dependency or support, school attendance, whether a child in her care, and death of the worker. Additional evidence may be required in some cases. In claims involving disability, evidence furnished must include medical evidence concerning the nature and extent of the impairment; evidence as to training and education, work experience, and daily activities both prior to and after the alleged onset of disability; evidence of any efforts to engage in gainful employment; and any other pertinent facts showing the effect of the impairment on ability to perform work-related functions.

The occurrence of specified events may lead to suspension or termination of cash benefits. Each newly entitled beneficiary is advised of the

[24] Steinberg, Joseph, "Some Aspects of Statistical Data Linkage for Individuals," Fourth Annual Conference of the Council of Social Science Data Archives, June, 1967.

[25] Social Security Administration, *Social Security Handbook,* 3rd ed., October, 1966.

events he must report because they may affect his benefits. These include earnings over specified amounts, marriage, adoption, death of the worker, cessation of disability, or attainment of specified age—in the case of children. All the reports required for the proper administration of the program under the law are associated through the account number of the worker on whose account the benefits are founded; other beneficiaries on the same account have the same account number—but a letter (s) suffix distinguishes one from another in the claim account number.

Health Service Utilization Data for Individuals

Administration of the health insurance program for the aged provides data on the utilization of health services for persons aged sixty-five and over.[26]

Records for the hospital insurance part of the program show the number of days of care received by each person in a hospital or extended-care facility and the number of home health visits received during specified periods that relate to the program concepts of "deductible" amounts and "spell of illness." Each episode of hospitalization provides data on length of stay, discharge status, charge and payment data, primary diagnosis, surgical procedures, and preoperative and postoperative lengths of stay. Diagnostic and surgical information is coded by the Social Security Administration for a 20 per cent sample of the hospital insurance beneficiaries. The diagnostic code is for the primary discharge diagnosis reported by the hospital, and the surgical procedure code relates to the primary discharge diagnosis. For outpatients, coding is, at present, for a 40 per cent sample; all home health bills and extended-care facilities bills are coded for diagnostic information.

Data available on utilization of physician and related medical services come from payment records and from a sample of bills. The data cover time and place of each service, the exact procedure or service provided, the condition treated, the physician's or supplier's charge for the specific service, and the charge allowed for the same procedure or service. For nonsurgical medical services, there are some descriptive data available on the type of services provided by the physician at each visit. For surgical cases, data on the surgical procedure, the diagnosis, and the over-all charge for the entire procedure are available. The data become available through the administrative requirements for submission of bills (at least $50 of services during the year is required, essentially). These data on

[26] West, Howard, "Health Insurance for the Aged: The Statistical Program," *Social Security Bulletin*, January, 1967, pp. 3–16.

services under the medical insurance program are centrally recorded for a 5 per cent sample of all enrolled persons (a subsample of the 20 per cent sample for the hospital insurance diagnostic coding).[27]

How Data are Used and Processed

The data available to the Social Security Administration serve their basic function, without too much oversimplification, as the basic ingredients in an administrative information system. The social security program pays cash benefits upon the retirement, disability, or death of a worker. Almost every cash benefit, as well as the taxes or contributions which finance the program, are based on workers' earnings. Thus, earnings data as well as the claims and benefits data are part of the cash benefit data system. The earnings records for over 170 million living or deceased account number holders[28] are summarized on magnetic tape files and backed up by details of the account number holders, their quarterly earnings, or annual reports on farm earnings or self-employment earnings on microfilm and paper. A tape record for each of the roughly 33 million individual beneficiaries, including those terminated in the last several years, is backed up by paper files.

The application for a social security account number results in the issuance of a number. Individuals, as necessary, also submit cards with a name change or a change in other pertinent data. All applications and cards are microfilmed to guard against possible loss or damage to the original record. The original records are filed in a numerical sequence by individual account numbers. This file now numbers more than 200 million items and grows by about 30,000 cards a day.[29] This file is referred to manually more than 6,000 times each day, when an application for benefits is filed, when identifying information contained on the original application or a change card is needed to verify an account, to reinstate earnings to an account, and for a variety of other administrative needs. The microfilmed records are maintained and filed at a different geographical location from that of the original data files.

A microfilm file containing over 225 million names classified according to a Soundex Code is a separate administrative record system derived

[27] Krute, Aaron, Newton Dikoff, and Jack Scharff, "Medicare, the Statistical Elements," Second Annual Conference, New York Area Chapter, American Statistical Association, May, 1967.

[28] Social Security Administration, Office of Research and Statistics. "Issuances of Social Security Account Numbers, 1966," Research and Statistics Note, No. 17, 1967.

[29] Social Security Administration, *Data Processing in the Social Security Administration,* Nine lectures by Joseph L. Fay, Washington, 1967.

from the account number applications.[30] These microfilm files are called the National Employee Index. The Soundex Code is a principle of indexing or grouping similar names together by means of a simple numerical code. The surnames are classified by the sound of their major consonants. Each surname is reduced to a three-digit code and the first letter of the last name. The file contains the Soundex codes, names, dates of birth, and social security account numbers of all account number holders, and an indication of any existing cross reference, i.e., a name change on file. If an individual is receiving benefits, this is also indicated on the microfilm. This file is a means of locating an account number when it is unknown. This national index is used for locating the account numbers of persons who apply for a duplicate number card. This file assists in crediting the accounts of individuals when information is reported without numbers or with incorrect ones, and for many other administrative uses.

Every employer of one or more workers whose earnings are covered under social security is required to obtain an employer identification number (E. I. Number). Each employer files an application for a number with the Internal Revenue Service. E. I. Numbers are generally issued by the Internal Revenue Service. This is a nine-digit number, with the first two digits generally identifying the Internal Revenue District which issued the number. The Social Security Administration receives a copy of this application from the IRS. Information of use in the SSA statistical system on the nature and location of the business is derived in major part from this application. Information from this source is maintained on tape as well as the paper files and their microfilms. The information is updated as changes occur.

Earnings are reported in a variety of ways. Most wage reports are submitted, through the IRS, on a form entitled "Employer's Quarterly Federal Tax Return." Computer tape is used by some large employers to report their wages directly to the SSA. Earnings of agricultural workers are reported annually on another form. Earnings of state and local government employees and household workers are reported on still other forms. The paper reports of earnings are microfilmed. One copy is sent to a security storage center, while another copy is used in some of the reference activities required. For the most part, the earnings information is processed by the preparation of a punch card for each earnings item. These punch cards are then converted to magnetic tape for computer processing. In addition, an optical scanner is now being used for process-

[30] Social Security Administration, "Recordkeeping in the Division of Accounting Operations," Baltimore, Md., June, 1962.

ing a substantial proportion of the quarterly earnings reports, with a magnetic tape being the result. The current earnings tapes, miscellaneous adjustments or additions tapes, and the previous summary records tapes are collated and processed through computers to result in updated summary records tapes. Earnings items which do not immediately match the summary records are written out onto separate tapes and are processed through a series of steps leading to reinstatement of the information to the proper account.

The claims process is initiated by filing of an appropriate application for benefits. A claims representative, in a district office, assists the claimant for a cash benefit in completing the application. Required proofs are also submitted by the claimant. An additional element in the claims process is the necessary information concerning earnings of the worker. The earnings record request is sent through a highly automated process into the central office computer system. This process involves paper tape in the district office, a wire transmission system, and then receipt on magnetic tape. The required earnings records found in the daily search are combined with data received from the district office. These data are processed through a series of computer operations and result in a printed-out form. This form includes the preliminary calculated benefit amount as well as the additional information from the claims form and the earnings record needed in subsequent steps. At the requesting district office, this completed claims record, the application, and the necessary proofs are reviewed and then forwarded to a payment center. The claims authorization process takes place in the payment center. There, all the entitlement information is reviewed by a claims authorizer. If he agrees with the district office's determination, the claim is then processed for the forwarding of the award notice. A magnetic tape record is used to notify the Treasury Department that the beneficiary should begin to receive stated benefits at a given mailing address. In disability claims, the disability determination is usually made by an appropriate state agency. The paper records involved in the claims process are a part of the file reference maintained for each case in the payment center. A variety of beneficiary initiated records becomes part of this file as changes of address, occasional work reports, and other events are reported.

The Master Benefit Record is a computer tape record which carries the needed cross-section benefit data for efficient administrative processing of the cash benefit system. This tape carries a substantial amount of information for every person entitled to benefits. The record is indexed by the account number of the worker on whose account number the benefits have become available. Thus, this is a primary record by a "benefit family." A cross-reference is also kept to each secondary beneficiary's own account number. The information on this record contains items relating to the worker, each individual beneficiary, the benefits, the name and address of the payee, and a five-year history of payments. The most important purpose of this record is in connection with the monthly benefit process. Checks are prepared and mailed by the Treasury Department on the basis of a certification by SSA as to the names, addresses, and benefit amounts. The tape involved is first prepared from the master beneficiary records and is updated by regular monthly action tapes. Part of the monthly update of the master beneficiary records consists of a variety of post-entitlement data. These data may arise as a result of changes of a beneficiary's payment status, a recomputation of the basic amount involved in the calculation of benefits, an adjustment to the monthly benefit amount because of some work during the year, or perhaps termination of benefits. This tape and other data generated from other tape records are the basis for a wide variety of statistical records and tabulations.

The health insurance program[31] entails record-keeping for proper administration of the provisions of the law. Hospital insurance, utilization of extended care facilities, home health care, and supplemental medical benefits each require a variety of informational inputs and outputs. Administration of the program involves intermediaries, such as Blue Cross or Blue Shield or insurance carriers. The record flow involves the intermediaries in the fiscal arrangements and approvals. The SSA is involved in the utilization considerations of the administration of the program. The basic record of the use of service is processed by the intermediary for all types of health insurance. The primary record of utilization of services is maintained by the Social Security Administration. In the case of hospital utilization, the record system is queried to establish whether a person is eligible and the number of days remaining for a given spell of hospitalization. This requires continuous entry into the computer system of information for each stay. For supplementary medical insurance, the record system enables outputs to be provided concerning the status of the individual in regard to the deductible, coinsurance, and other provisions of the law.

[31] Cohen, Wilbur, and Robert M. Ball, "Social Security Amendments of 1965: Summary and Legislative History," *Social Security Bulletin*, September, 1965.

Statute and regulations protect the confidentiality of records and information in the possession of the Social Security Administration.[32] The reasons derive from the considerations of public interest and efficient administration. Disclosure of information of a personal nature about individuals and their activities, which is in the possession of SSA, is prohibited unless required for social security or other purposes covered under the Social Security Act. The only exceptions are in cases involving national security. Disclosures may be authorized by an individual with respect to his own record, however.

Guardianship of the confidentiality of the vast set of records is a large and responsible undertaking. One of the first essentials involves setting up internal safeguards to prevent improper disclosures. Procedures have been established to make certain that the confidentiality provisions set forth in statute, agency regulations, and policy are carried out. The efficacy of the rules depends on the internal requirements regarding need to know the information relative to the administrative process as well as the degree to which the employees are well-informed on the policies and penalties and their individual obligations. The regulations governing the limits within which the disclosure policies operate are a matter of public record. Public knowledge serves as a deterrent for those who would seek improper access to social security information.

Substantial amounts of summary and analytic data are tabulated and published by the Social Security Administration.[33] The basic data are published regularly in the *Social Security Bulletin* and its *Annual Statistical Supplement*.[34] Special releases, such as *Health Insurance Statistics* and special reports, are additional publication media.

It has been recognized that the statistical records of the agency constitute a source of data of great potential for other research uses. The policy of the Administration is to make its data resources available, while ensuring the confidentiality of information on individuals and reporting units, subject to administrative feasibility while carrying forward its basic administrative mission. Appropriate rules and mechanisms have been developed for carrying out the general research policy. One approach that has been developed is a special tabulation program that permits cross-tabulation of social security earnings data with other data, subject to

[32] Social Security Administration, Regulation No. 1, as amended, Disclosure of Official Records and Information (Part 401, Chapter III, Title 20, Code of Federal Regulations), Washington, 1968.

[33] Social Security Administration, *Workers under Social Security*, 1960.

[34] Social Security Administration, *Social Security Bulletin, Annual Statistical Supplement*, 1965.

suitable tests of "nondisclosure."[35] Another approach makes data for a sample of individuals available on a tape record from which individual identifiers have been expunged. A set of case numbers on the records permit linkage with other data from the social security data base, over time, while preserving the confidentiality of the data. The sample files for which this procedure is available are those of the 1 per cent Continuous Work History Sample.[36]

The Decision Process

The Social Security Act, as amended, is the primary source of the decision process with respect to what information is to be collected and how it is to be used. The Secretary of Health, Education, and Welfare—and by delegation the Commissioner of Social Security—have the responsibility for the proper and efficient administration of the Act.

Each provision of the law entails requirements with respect to the nature of information, its sources, and methods that are needed for using the information. The development of an integrated system of information for use in the administrative mission involves a large number of persons with many different professional contributions. Lawyers, policy specialists, systems analysts, statisticians, computer specialists, actuaries, and many other types of professionals all contribute to determining the content of forms and the flow of information. Discussions are held with groups that are to be affected either in furnishing the information or in its processing. Proposed regulations, embodying the information requirements are approved for publication in the *Federal Register* by the Commissioner.[37] Then, the proposed regulations are forwarded to the Secretary with the recommendation that he approve them for publication in the *Federal Register*. After comments have been received and considered, the regulations are published in final form by the same decision mechanism. As required, the appropriate clearances and approvals under the Federal Reports Act are also involved.

The Individual and His Records

Information relating to an individual is always available for his appropriate checking and correction.[38] If a person wishes to change his name

[35] Social Security Administration, Office of Research and Statistics, "Some Statistical Research Resources Available at the Social Security Administration," Washington, 1967.

[36] Steinberg, Joseph, and Leon Pritzker, "Some Experiences with and Reflections on Data Linkage in the United States," International Statistical Institute, 36th Session, Sydney, Australia, 1967.

[37] *The Federal Register*, September 29, 1967.

[38] *The Federal Register*, October 27, 1967, and November 8, 1967.

or other identifying information previously submitted in establishing an account, a specific form and procedure is available. He may obtain information concerning earnings recorded in his account through a simple mail procedure. If he disagrees with a statement of earnings credited to his account, he may request a revision by a mail procedure, or other simple means. In all such cases, the Social Security Administration initiates an investigation. As required, employers and employees are contacted for the purpose of obtaining the information necessary to reconcile any discrepancy between the allegations of the individual and the records. The individual is notified of the determination made after the investigation and of his rights to a reconsideration if he is dissatisfied with the determination. In claiming benefits, it is the individual, or someone rightfully acting on his behalf, who files the application and establishes by satisfactory evidence the material allegations in his application. Reports concerning events that may suspend or terminate benefits originate with the beneficiary.

Many rights are built into the administration of the Social Security Act to protect the individual—rights with respect to the confidentiality of the information about the individual; and rights with respect to the decisions concerning entitlement to benefits. Anyone who is dissatisfied with an initial determination with respect to entitlement to benefits, payments, periods of disability, or his earnings record may request a reconsideration of the determination. If still dissatisfied, there are rights to a hearing. There are then rights to review by the Appeals Council and a court review.

GOVERNMENT STATISTICS—A COORDINATED SYSTEM

The current system of government records and statistics is a coordinated system, which resulted from the work of the Committee on Government Statistics and Information Services in 1933–1934. The statistical system is decentralized, and the basic statistical agencies are located in their respective departments. The dispersion of activities in the collection of data has advantages and disadvantages. Professionals in each substantive area can draw on their experiences in seeking answers to major problems, to develop the necessary elements in a data system. Parallelism in some areas reveals the strengths and also the weaknesses in each of the approaches used to develop answers. Dispersion usually leads to record collection from nonoverlapping elements in the universe. Where this occurs, comparisons may be made only at the aggregate level. When deliberate efforts are made to include individuals or households in an evaluative study, the analyst quite often finds that the coverage differences, and the differences in some or all of the content concepts, may indeed create a large set of difficult problems. Solutions to these problems entail substantial efforts.

Existence of a coordinated system creates dispersed record systems, each with their own statutory or regulatory confidentiality provisions. Each agency has its own mechanisms for data records and compilation.[39] Each agency has its own systems for maintaining records to serve the goals of its particular mission. Not only are systems designs sometimes such as to create problems of efficiency of integration within a single agency, but differences in identifiers and in coverage limit severely the possibilities of any integration among agencies. Small-scale efforts in many ways serve to demonstrate the nature of the problems and the complexities of even unsophisticated attempts at some solution. The legal difficulties and the regulations designed to protect the confidentiality of the dispersed record systems serve as effective protection of the privacy of the individual when he does provide information. The public knowledge of these protections, and of the few exceptions, helps to ensure that government records are reasonably accurate and worthy of the public trust.

The existence of the statutes and regulations concerning confidentiality has never been more important than in relation to recent discussions concerning a proposal for establishment of a National Statistical Data Center. Needs for greater centralization of the statistical activities of the federal government have been discussed for about thirty-five years. The American Statistical Association's Committee on Government Statistics and Information Services in 1933–1934 recommended a decentralized system. In 1949, a study of the statistical agencies of the federal government was made for the Hoover Commission. The computer has introduced a new dimension into the area. In March, 1965, a committee of the Social Science Research Council issued a Report on the Preservation and Use of Economic Data.[40] A Review of Proposals for a National Data Center was prepared for the Budget Bureau in November, 1965. Thereafter, a task force was appointed by the Budget Bureau to consider "measures which should be taken to improve the storage and access to U.S. Government statistics." Hearings of Congressional subcommittees have included discussions of the possibility of invasion of privacy potentially involved in these or similar efforts to centralize data. It is likely that the matter will

[39] Subcommittee on Administrative Practice and Procedure of the Committee on the Judiciary, U.S. Senate, Ninetieth Congress, First Session, Committee Print: Government Dossier (Survey of Information Contained in Government Files), November, 1967.

[40] Subcommittee of the Committee on Government Operations, House of Representatives, Eighty-ninth Congress, Second Session, Hearings: The Computer and Invasion of Privacy, July 26–28, 1966.

continue to be a matter of controversy and discussion for some time to come. The Freedom of Information Act, Public Law 90–23, which was passed in 1967, made many items and materials available for public use, but specifically exempted those items, such as individual data, which are by statute confidential. It seems logical to expect that statutory modifications in existing data collections of the federal government will provide the necessary protections against the possibility of detrimental use of collated data and through law and regulation under the law ensure that confidentiality will be preserved.

9 *The Dossier in Military Organization*

ROGER W. LITTLE

DOSSIERS IN MILITARY ORGANIZATION DIFFER FROM THOSE IN OTHER INSTITUTIONAL settings in at least three ways. First, the basis of legitimacy is a supreme societal goal—national defense and security. This overriding consideration justifies more extensive investigations and a more elaborate and costly investigatory apparatus. It allocates final responsibility for the dossier to intelligence agencies, which operate in a context of secrecy and autonomy and which interpret behavior in terms of latent or active vulnerability to relations with the "enemy." It greatly expands the scope of inquiry and documentation to which the individual may be legally compelled to submit.

Second, dossiers of some kind are compiled on all persons who come into contact with military organization, whether or not they are accepted for service. Thereafter they become public records with varying degrees of accessibility. Thus, every American male of military age must have either a draft card which identifies his mental or physical condition, or a discharge which provides an evaluative index of the quality of his service. Such records are permanent credentials by which military organization continues to influence the careers of individuals throughout their lives although they are not under organizational control.

Third, military organization—as an occupational community—provides unusually favorable conditions for compiling dossiers. Most of the individual's behavior occurs within the boundaries of the military community, rather than being distributed among many institutions of the larger society. Many members remain with the organization for extended periods of time and are under almost continuous surveillance in a wide variety of circumstances. More kinds of behavior, especially those which might be classified as "deviant," are defined as requiring a "report" of some kind, which must be distributed through channels to a central echelon. The military dossier thus has a quality of completeness that is missing from the segmental accounts of his behavior derived from specific institutional settings such as a school, hospital, or prison.

The increasing significance of the dossier in military organization is related to the development of the mass army. As military personnel are recruited from more diverse social origins, it has become more difficult to identify precisely their preservice affiliations and consequently to assume their loyalty. At the same time, organizational structures have become more complex, the number of communication devices and centers have increased, and correspondingly more personnel are involved in processing organizational secrets. A complex occupational structure with high turnover and continuous responsibilities requires that information about the potential competence of an individual be "on file" at the time a decision is made to assign him to a specific role. Rapid spatial and organizational mobility also diminishes the chances that a commander will have personal knowledge of the competence and character of any more than a small number of his subordinates.

FORMS OF MILITARY DOSSIERS

Records maintained on military personnel vary according to agency function, status group (officer or enlisted man), and final disposition. Seven general categories of records may be identified.

Entry Records

Entry records define the individual's eligibility for service, and if acceptable, his qualifications for specific positions within military organization. They are compiled by Local Boards of the Selective Service System and by the Armed Forces Examining and Entry Station (AFEES). Such records have been compiled on over 34 million men who registered between July, 1950, and September, 1966. Similar records exist on men who registered for the draft in World War II.[1]

All male youths at age eighteen must register with the Local Board of the Selective Service System in the area of their permanent domicile. Registration consists of filling out the "Classification Questionnaire" which constitutes the basic document of the "Registrant File." Other documents periodically added are records of the Local Board action in establishing his classification, correspondence related to his status, and—if he has been called for a pre-induction examination—a record of the medical and mental examination conducted at the Armed Forces Examining and Entry Station.

The custodian of the registrant file is the Clerk of the Local Board, a civil service employee of the Selective Service System. Registrants are permitted to examine their file at the Local Board office at any time. They are able to influence its contents only indirectly by the information provided in the Questionnaire, their correspondence with the Clerk, or by appeals to higher organizational levels of the Selective Service System. No persons outside the Selective Service System except officers of federal investigatory or judicial agencies are permitted to examine the registrant file.

Additional entry records are compiled at the Armed Forces Examining and Entry Stations. Such records were compiled on over 23 million men between July, 1950, and December, 1966. (See Table 1.) Similar records were compiled on an estimated 17,594,000 men between November, 1940, and August, 1945.[2]

All Selective Service registrants who are called for pre-induction or induction examinations, and all applicants for active duty in the armed forces are examined at these stations. A complete physical examination is conducted (including a psychiatric examination when indicated), intelligence tests are administered to registrants or applicants for enlistment (the Armed Forces Qualification Test, AFQT, and in some cases, aptitude tests as well). The record of the physical and mental examination is returned to the registrant's Local Board. If the examinee has been rejected

[1] *Review of the Administration and Operation of the Selective Service System.* Hearings before the Committee on Armed Services, House of Representatives, Eighty-ninth Congress, 2d Session. Committee Print No. 75, Government Printing Office, Washington, 1966, p. 10,004. There were 32,337,000 registrants in April, 1966. About 1.8 million new registrants were added in 1967. Since all male youths who attain age eighteen must register, the number of registrants will increase by predictable numbers of about 1.8 to 2.1 million each year through 1974.

[2] Foster, William B., *et al., Physical Standards in World War II,* Government Printing Office, Washington, 1967, p. 16.

TABLE 1 *Estimate of AFEES Entry Examinations*

July, 1950–December, 1966

Personnel type	*Number of examinees*
Pre-inductees[a] (Disqualified: 4,353,139)	11,019,216
First-term enlistees[b]	6,627,328
Reserve Active Duty Basic Training[c]	1,444,544
Senior ROTC[d]	4,791,510
Total	23,882,598

SOURCES:

[a] "Results of the Examination of Youths for Military Service, 1966," *Health of the Army*, Department of the Army, Washington, March, 1967, p. 14.

[b] *Selected Manpower Statistics*, Department of Defense, Washington, April 15, 1968, pp. 43–44.

[c] *Ibid.*, p. 93.

[d] *Ibid.*, pp. 95–96. Data are for period from October, 1950, through October, 1967. These data do not include active duty personnel who were subsequently enrolled to fulfill their reserve obligations.

for service, the records remain in his Registrant File at the Local Board. If he is accepted for service, the medical record is forwarded with the registrant when he is called for induction.

Thus, even if the registrant is rejected for service, a substantial record has been made of his brief contact with military organization. An intelligence test has been administered and the individual classified into a "mental group" which not only establishes his eligibility for service but also compares his performance with that of the total population. The medical examination may have elicited a claim of mental illness, sexual deviation, or drug usage, often alleged only for the purpose of avoiding service. Such information thus becomes a permanent element of the registrant's file only because he has been called for examination.

Other records are obtained at the induction station. A "Security Questionnaire" is filled out which requires the examinee to disclose a record of civil delinquency, his affiliation with civilian organizations, and to deny his affiliation with organizations which have been designated as "subversive" by the Attorney General. A fingerprint record is made of all examinees who are accepted for service (and pre-induction examinees who refuse to complete the security questionnaire or to be inducted). The fingerprint record exposes examinees to special vulnerability in crime detection since the record is available to any law enforcement agency. The Armed Forces constitute one of the major sources of fingerprint records of the Federal Bureau of Investigation. As of April 30, 1968, the FBI files included 187,777,997 fingerprint records representing about 81 million

TABLE 2 *Sources of Fingerprint Records from Armed Forces and Coast Guard*

Branch	*Number*
Army	26,030,977
Air Force	2,044,425
Navy	9,252,471
Marine Corps	2,229,865
Coast Guard	763,022
Total	40,320,760

SOURCE: Public Information Office, FBI, April 30, 1968.

persons. Over 40 million records were obtained from Armed Forces and Coast Guard entry examinations. (See Table 2.)

It is important to note that a selective bias exists in the acquisition of such records. Only persons called for induction examinations are fingerprinted.[3] Thus persons with claims to deferment after high school (such as college students or skilled workers) may never be called for examination. Negroes and lower-class whites (with low educational attainment) are more likely to be called than whites generally.[4] Consequently, social class biases in the Selective Service System are transformed into relative chances of being identified for criminal activity by means of the fingerprint record.

Records of contacts with both the Selective Service System and the AFEES culminate in the "classification" of the registrant in various degrees of availability and eligibility for military service. The classification is stated on the "Draft Card" which is issued to each registrant. Since the draft card is a public record which may be routinely requested for identification in transactions with government agencies, the classification status of the registrant becomes public information. If the registrant refuses to disclose his classification, it may be obtained from the Clerk of his Local Board without his consent. Since draft status is an important consideration in employment, the classification—especially when it signifies rejection—often requires an explanatory disclosure of the information on which it is based when a registrant applies for a job. This is especially important when the rejection has been based on "moral" grounds, or a past record of deviance which would not have been revealed if he had not been called for an induction examination.

[3] Fingerprint records are obtained in pre-induction examinations only from those registrants who refuse induction, or who refuse to complete the security questionnaire (which elicits information of past activities or affiliations).

[4] See "In Pursuit of Equality: Who Serves When Not All Serve," *Report of the National Advisory Commission on Selective Service*, Government Printing Office, Washington, 1967, p. 22.

Assignment Records

Assignment records document the individual's eligibility for various positions within military organization upon acceptance for service.[5] Compilation begins at the Reception Center, adding to the basic entry records obtained at the AFEES (record of physical examination, AFQT scores, and fingerprint record). A battery of aptitude tests are administered. A classification interview is then conducted by a personnel technician to elicit information about preservice occupational experience or training. Other information obtained at this time are family and religious status, educational attainment, hobbies and athletic skills. Racial indicators are not recorded. This information is then coded according to the Dictionary of Occupational Titles, and the individual is assigned a "DOT Code." The DOT Code and aptitude scores for each person are sent to a central personnel allocation echelon, where they are matched with existing position vacancies, service school quotas, and replacement needs.

Classification records thus have an "ascriptive" quality that endows them with special significance. Persons with scarce skills or training in the larger society are rapidly identified and subsequently assigned to service experiences which are continuous with their preservice social origins. Conversely, men without such skills or training upon entry, or with unmeasured aptitudes, are most likely to be assigned to residual tasks which require relatively brief training in a purely military occupation. Once assigned by a highly centralized personnel agency, opportunities for lateral mobility to other tasks because of individual achievement are very rare. Unlike the employment interviewer who exploits personal observations and informal contacts with previous employers, the classification technician is primarily concerned with identifying abstract indicators which will facilitate the allocation process. The classification process thus tends to make placement in military organization continuous with the entrant's prior social class affiliation in the larger society.

Assignment records are compiled and maintained by enlisted men who are usually members of the same organization as the individuals whose records they keep. Although there are no specific educational requirements for this position (personnel technician), the men are usually high school graduates or higher in educational attainment. They are trained in service schools and work under the nominal supervision of a personnel

[5] Throughout this chapter references will be made primarily to Army regulations. However, since they are based on statutory and service-wide directives, they exemplify similar rules and procedures in the other services. The basic regulation is "Records Management—Program Policies and Procedures," *Army Regulation 345–200,* Washington, Department of the Army, October, 1962.

officer. One technician usually has custody of the records of a company or similar unit (about 200 men).

Individuals are always authorized to examine their assignment records, but this may be difficult because the individual and his records are often separated by great distances. Any commander may inspect the records of men under his command. The records are routinely used for determining fitness for promotion, and eligibility for service schools or technical assignments (on the basis of aptitude scores, prior organizational affiliations, and work history). Chaplains may survey the records for identifying religious preferences. Intelligence and military police technicians may examine the records of persons under investigation. Thus assignment records are probably more accessible to outsiders than any other type of military dossier.

Entry and assignment dossiers (as well as medical records) are usually "hand carried" by the person to whom they refer when being transferred from one organization to another. Because of their crucial significance in determining the individual's fate in the organization, it is sometimes possible for the person to alter or insert significant items, such as aptitude test scores, or service school attendance, or to remove items of a prejudicial nature. Successful "doctoring" of the dossier, however, requires sophisticated knowledge of the records, the relevant items, and access to blank forms. Manipulation of the records thus usually requires collusion with a personnel specialist who has access to such scarce resources.[6]

Medical Records

The individual medical record[7] is a chronological account of a member's contacts with military medical agencies. It is maintained by enlisted and civilian clerks at the military medical facility where the individual receives his care. Compilation begins with the original induction or enlistment physical examination. The individual is not authorized to inspect his own medical record. However, when he has it in his possession (in clinic visits or while being transferred from one post to another) it is sealed only with staples and is often examined surreptitiously. By regulation, only medical personnel, military police, and intelligence agents have access to medical

[6] One of the latent functions of service schools for personnel specialists is to train them in an operational argot which will enable the organization to monopolize this knowledge. See Little, Roger W., "Headquarters Soldier," *Army*, vol. 7, no. 4 (November, 1956), pp. 58–65; and Schneider, David M., "The Culture of the Army Clerk," *Psychiatry*, vol. 9, no. 2 (May 1946), pp. 123–129.

[7] "Medical Service: Individual Medical Records," *Army Regulations No. 40–400*, Department of the Army, Washington, September 23, 1955. To simplify documentation, references will be made only to Army regulations in this chapter. However, comparable regulations exist for each of the other services.

records. In practice, however, they are often examined by commanders, personnel officers, and legal officers involved in courts-martial proceedings, and others authorized by the senior local medical officer.

The military medical record is unique because it is both a clinical and a legal record. Like comparable civilian records, it consists primarily of descriptions of transactions between doctor and patient. In addition, however, the military medical record constitutes the legal basis for the government's permanent responsibility for sickness or injury incurred "in the line of duty." When it can be established that such a condition was incurred through no fault of the individual, and that it is long-term in nature, the government is obligated to provide continuing care in Veterans Administration facilities, and/or monetary compensation for a disability.

The legal function of the medical record generates requirements of compulsion and completeness. Thus certain kinds of medical care are routinely demanded of all members such as periodic inoculations and physical examinations. Officers, for example, must be examined at least once a year, and in addition when nominated for promotion. Statements made to the physician during an examination (or entered on forms by the patient) which allege or deny the existence of a condition constitute official reports, subject to investigation and punishment or disqualification if found to be false.

Legal responsibility for physical condition also requires that all of the individual's medical care be with facilities under military control. Records of civilian medical care are usually spread among several practitioners and facilities. Military medical records, however, are centralized accounts of all treatments and examinations. Treatment by civilian practitioners is generally discouraged, and when incurred in emergencies must be verified by military medical agencies. This practice ensures that all significant medical events affecting the individual will be incorporated in his military records.

Entries in military medical records may also provoke further investigation by nonmedical agencies. Thus regulations require that a member who is injured in a vehicular accident, a fight, or whose condition may suggest the violation of a service regulation, must be reported to the military police or to his commanding officer. Such medical care situations may then become bases for derogatory interpretations in a nonclinical context, as well as expanding the number of persons who have access to the information.

Records of psychiatric examinations are especially vulnerable to misinterpretation when directed to nonclinical contexts. Many personnel actions (such as clearance for hazardous or sensitive duties, or evaluations prior to courts-martial or discharge board proceedings) routinely require such examinations. The initial contact with the psychiatric clinic requires that the examinee submit to an interview with an enlisted technician for a "social history" and psychological testing. After subsequent examination by a psychiatrist, a "Consultation Report" is prepared with extracts from the social history and psychological tests to support the diagnosis of the examiner. Background material from other sources is interpreted in clinical language to suggest dynamic and predictive relationships. Anxiety reactions, depressions, or bouts of alcoholism, although originally situational in nature, may obtain a persisting significance apart from the original causal situational factors. The Consultation Report then becomes an exhibit in the personnel action for which the subject was originally referred. Contents of the medical record are thus diffused beyond the clinical context in which it was compiled. Such information may be interpreted differently when evaluated in a nonclinical context such as a security investigation.

Military Police Records

Post military police detachments—under the supervision of the chief military police officer, the Provost-Marshal, maintain a "name file" which is compiled from blotter entries.[8] Thus, any person who is involved in or mentioned in connection with an accident reported to the military police will be included in the name file. Such incidents would include those for which the military police have primary responsibility (on-post incidents) as well as those which civilian police have reported to military authorities. On-post incidents could consist of traffic offenses, absences without official leave, or complaints from neighbors about domestic problems. Off-post incidents are those in which military police town patrols have made arrests or issued a "delinquency report" (which is sent to the offender's commanding officer through superior commanders), or civilian police reports or blotter entries on military personnel. Military medical facilities are also required to inform the military police of injuries incurred in vehicular accidents, assaults, evidence of drug usage, or other incidents which might not otherwise come to their attention.

The name file is used primarily for the investigation of military crimes. Although the offenses included range from trivial to serious, any person identified therein is vulnerable to subsequent investigation. It thus has

[8] "Military Police: Records and Forms: *Army Regulation No. 190–45,* Department of the Army, Washington, September 6, 1960.

particular significance as a basic source in security investigations by intelligence personnel. Incidents suggesting emotional instability, drunkenness, drug usage, sexual misconduct (including adultery), or marital instability would constitute a serious item requiring further investigation and probably a psychiatric report. Furthermore, the name file becomes a permanent record when deposited with the intelligence records repository of the service branch whose military police compiled the information.

Career Evaluation Files

Career evaluation files are cumulative accounts of an individual's routine and exceptional behavior in the organization. Combined with the entry and assignment records, they comprise the "Military Personnel Records Jacket" or "201 File" which is maintained by the personnel section of the organization to which the individual is assigned. Items such as the following would be included: peer ratings in training situations, class standings in service schools, exceptional performance reports (used as bases for decorations, commendations, or punishments), records of trial by courts-martial or of investigations by boards of officers, medical reports of fitness for service or promotion, and classification for access to secret information ("security clearance").[9]

Almost all the evaluation records pertaining to an enlisted man are included in the Records Jacket, and are as accessible to him as are the entry and assignment records. The contents of the file are known to the individual and he is required by regulation to inspect it annually. It is carried by the individual when he is transferred from one station to another. However, the record remains the property of the organization. The individual does not retain possession of it, and when he leaves the organization it becomes a permanent government record, the contents of which may be disclosed without his consent.[10]

In addition to the local file which is identical to that compiled on enlisted men, a centralized dossier is maintained on officers at the headquarters of the service branch in Washington. The central dossier contains copies of all the materials in the local file, and also copies of all the efficiency or fitness reports rendered on the individual at least annually by his superior officers.

Such reports usually have two sections. One section is a set of rating scales in which the rated officer is compared with his colleagues in terms

[9] "Military Personnel Records Jacket, United States Army," *Army Regulation No. 640–10*, Department of the Army, Washington, February 15, 1967.

[10] "Release of Information and Records from Army Files," *Army Regulation No. 345–20*, Department of the Army, Washington, June 30, 1967.

of such attributes as leadership ability, promotion potential, and prospective assignments (command, staff, civilian or service schools, etc.). The values from the scales are combined into various kinds of composite scores which are used as summary measures of comparison with all other officers of his rank and branch. A second section requires a narrative description of the officer's duties and "manner of performance." It might include comparative evaluations of technical competence, social skills, financial judgment (i.e., personal credit, management of organizational funds and property), marital stability, and physical condition. There are very few limits to what can be stated in this portion of the efficiency report. Generally, the space is used for (and is interpreted as) a detailed supporting argument for the numerical scores in the rating scales. The content depends as much on the literary ability of the rater as on the behavior of the rated officer. It may be a very articulate behavioral description, or a medium for the recording of organizational gossip about the individual officer.

The efficiency report is originally prepared as a draft by the officer's immediate superior. However, if the rated officer is senior to the rater, the report must be prepared at the first higher organizational level with an officer who is senior to the rated officer. It is processed ("typed up") in one copy by trusted civilian employees or enlisted clerks, and then sent to two successive levels of command, the first for "indorsement" (and a comparable rating), and the second for "review." Each level requires additional administrative processing by persons other than the senior officer to whom it is addressed. From the review level, it is sent directly to the service branch headquarters in Washington for further processing and is finally filed in the central dossier.

Whether or not the subject is permitted to view his efficiency report before it is filed depends on the policy of the service to which he belongs. The general rule is that officers are not permitted to inspect the report until it has been filed in the central dossier. Army policy now is that it must be inspected by the rated officer after preparation by the immediate superior and before indorsement and review. Other services permit inspection only when derogatory information is involved, or when the report is distinctly unfavorable and will probably result in subsequent personnel actions such as reassignment, limitation on promotion chances, or termination of service. In any case, the inspection is usually performed in the presence of the rating officer and there is no opportunity (or inclination) for the rated officer to modify the contents of the report at that time. Thereafter the individual is permitted to examine his reports only at the central repository in Washington.

If errors are discovered upon examination of the central dossier, there are limited opportunities for correction. Any request for change must be originated by the affected officer at his organizational level (which may involve the responsible rating officer), and must pass through all echelons to the headquarters of the service branch. Statements of judgment or opinion by raters cannot be changed. An efficiency report can be set aside only because it contains serious factual errors, or because the rating officer was unqualified as a rater by position or seniority.

The central dossier is the most important record in the process by which officers are selected for promotion. Generally, all eligible officers are periodically arranged in order of their composite index from the efficiency or fitness report. Within groups of relatively equivalent scores, the promotion board considers the information in the narrative sections of the efficiency reports on individuals. It may thus constitute "the last word" in the promotion process. It is also given heavy weight in the selection of officers for critical or sensitive positions, or for advanced education in civilian institutions.

Intelligence Files

The most complete dossier is that compiled in the course of an investigation for a security clearance.[11] The security investigation is the culmination of record-keeping in military organization, since all other records on the individual, before or during service, are used as information sources. The end product of such an investigation is the granting or denial of a security clearance. The granting of a clearance implies that there are no significant negative reputational items in the person's intelligence file and thus qualifies him to be entrusted with graded levels of organizational secrets.

Regulations stipulate that a security investigation will be conducted only when the individual is likely to be assigned to a strategic position in the flow of organizational secrets, or has an explicit "need to know." Actually, however, a security investigation of limited form is made on all military personnel as well as on some civilian employees of the military establishment (the "Entry Check"). Any commanding officer can request a security investigation on a member of his organization of a more detailed kind, although it is usually initiated as standing policy for specific

[11] "Clearance of Personnel for Access to Classified Defense Information and Material," *Army Regulation No. 604–5,* Department of the Army, Washington, January 28, 1966. For Navy, see: *OPNAVINST* 5510.1C CH1, April 1, 1966, chap. 15, "Personnel Security Investigations and Clearances for Access to Classified Information."

categories of personnel (i.e., all officers, all intelligence and cryptographic personnel, most types of communications specialists, etc.). The results of the examination are never shown to the individual. Personnel action taken on the basis of information in the intelligence file cannot refer to that file as the source.

Each of the services maintains a separate domestic intelligence agency which conducts the investigations through regional detachments of enlisted "agents" under the supervision of intelligence officers. An investigation obtains information from three sources. First, for personnel currently on active duty, all available local military records are inspected and significant remarks extracted. These include the materials in the Personnel Jacket (entry and assignment and career evaluation files), the name file of local intelligence and military police, and medical record (for evidence of emotional instability, drug usage, sexual deviation, or marital instability). If derogatory items are developed at this preliminary level, clearance is usually withheld and the investigation does not proceed.

A second source is a central repository of investigations for all military personnel at Fort Holabird, Maryland (The National Agency Check Center and the Defense Central Index of Investigations). A "National Agency Check" consists of inquiries to federal agencies for "pertinent facts that might have a bearing on the loyalty and trustworthiness of the individual." These agencies include the criminal, subversive, and technical fingerprint files of the Federal Bureau of Investigation, the Civil Service Commission, Immigration and Naturalization Service (when appropriate), and the House Un-American Activities Committee. The fact that such "Checks" can be made by telephone suggests that central "rosters" are maintained and that pertinent information is obtained from an integrated computer system.

The third source of information for the intelligence file is the "background investigation" which is concerned with the individual's relations with the larger society, past and current. It is conducted by an enlisted agent of the regional intelligence unit, and includes the following:

1. School record: examination of school record and interviews with persons who might have known the subject while he was in school;
2. Interviews with previous employers and fellow workers to ascertain "the loyalty, character and reputation of the individual";
3. Survey of the records of law enforcement agencies in vicinities where the individual has resided or been employed;

4. Check of credit agencies in the vicinity of residence;
5. Interviews with neighbors at the subject's place of residence;
6. Interviews with at least two persons whose relationship to the subject is developed in the course of the investigation.

The security investigation, when ultimately compiled and evaluated, remains in the custody of the intelligence service conducting the investigation at a national intelligence records repository.[12] If derogatory information is developed in the course of the investigation, the requesting officer may be permitted to examine the file. The file of a general officer may also be examined by a superior officer. It remains a "live record" throughout the individual's period of service and may be referred to when he is under consideration for promotion or assignment to especially critical positions involving contacts with the public or foreign governments.[13]

Although the security investigation and intelligence file are legitimated in terms of the loyalty of the individual, they clearly serve other purposes. They protect the organization from the embarrassment of exposure of derogatory information in the background of a member who has become publicly prominent as a representative of the organization. Since the areas of behavior under surveillance are known to members of the organization, intelligence files are also effective instruments of social control. The loss of a security clearance for officers or senior noncommissioned officers is the effective end of their careers. Hence, they (and their families) are constrained to adhere to behavior standards that will not generate derogatory items for the record. Because affiliations with nonmilitary associations are especially "suspect," they are induced to restrict their social activity to the military community.

Agents and other intelligence personnel are specially trained for their duties in service schools after completing their initial military training. Some are recruited directly from college specifically for such assignments. Thereafter they live apart from military organization with other intelligence personnel in the civilian community. They wear civilian clothing and identify themselves as "agents" rather than by military rank. This operational context minimizes the lateral accountability of intelligence units to other elements of military organization. There is no intermediate echelon at which intelligence information is validated before it is included in the dossier.

[12] "Access to and Use of U.S. Army Counterintelligence Records Facility (USCARF) (Dossiers) by Representatives of Non-Army Agencies," *Army Regulation No. 381–46*, Department of the Army, Washington, August 27, 1965.

[13] "Filing of Adverse Suitability Information in Individual Records and Review of Intelligence Files Consulted Prior to Taking Personnel Action," *Army Regulation No. 640–98*, Department of the Army, Washington, July 19, 1965.

Terminal Records

Terminal records summarize and identify by implication an evaluation of the individual's behavior during his term of service. Such records, more generally known as "discharge certificates," are unique because the individual to whom they apply is himself the custodian, although the documents which determine the "quality" of the certificate are recorded elsewhere. Because it also serves as the credential by which the individual re-establishes his relationship to the larger society, the nature of the record becomes widely known. Issuance of a certificate (other than honorable) is usually preceded by a report of findings of a board of officers or a court-martial which remains in the personnel records jacket as the legal basis for discharge from service.

Discharges are classified as administrative and punitive. The conventional certificate is the "Honorable Discharge," which is the only one that entitles the holder to all rights and benefits of service. It denotes the absence of significant derogatory information in all other individual records compiled during his period of service.

Two other types of administrative discharge involve various degrees of stigma and disqualification in civilian life, The "General Discharge under honorable conditions" is issued to persons who are separated prior to completion of a required term of service because of some medical conditions (usually psychiatric) or minor misconduct. It may also be issued upon completion of the required term because of a record of chronic delinquency so as to prevent re-enlistment. The "Undesirable Discharge, under conditions other than honorable" is issued to persons with a chronic record of offenses leading to courts-martial, or the belated discovery of conditions which would have disqualified him for service if they had been revealed prior to entry, such as homosexual behavior, drug usage, a prior criminal record, or a previously unsatisfactory term of service.[14]

There are two types of punitive discharges. The "Bad Conduct" discharge may be awarded by the sentence of a Special or General Court-Martial and is usually evaluated as equivalent to the Undesirable Discharge. The Dishonorable Discharge is awarded only by sentence of a General Court-Martial and is irrevocable (unless the conviction on which it is based is set aside on issues of law). It is interesting to note that both the "Dishonorable" and "Bad Conduct" discharge certificates are yellow in color, whereas the others are off-white.

[14] *Military Justice,* Joint Hearings before the Subcommittee on Constitutional Rights of the Committee on the Judiciary and a Special Sub-Committee of the Committee on Armed Services, United States Senate, Eighty-Ninth Congress, Second Session, January 18, 19, 25, and 26; March 1, 2, and 3, 1966, Government Printing Office, Washington.

TABLE 3 *Terminal Discharges (Army), and Percentage "Less Than Honorable," 1962–1965*

Year	*Total discharges*	*Total "Less Than Honorable"*	*Percentage*
1962	192,880	21,423	11
1963	280,606	21,375	8
1964	182,849	22,068	12
1965	204,855	23,544	11
Total	861,190	88,410	(average) 10.5

SOURCES: *Military Justice, op. cit.*, p. 1036, Table c., corrected by subtraction of immediate and other re-enlistments (which imply discharges from the preceding term) and retirements, as cited in *Selected Manpower Statistics*, Office of the Secretary of Defense, April 15, 1968, p. 44, "Summary of Enlisted Personnel Procurement," and *Military Justice, loc. cit.*, (retirements). Data refer to enlisted personnel only.

TABLE 4 *Discharges Less Than Honorable by Type and Service, 1962–1965*

Service	*Discharge type*		
	General	*Undesirable*	*Punitive*[a]
Army	69,020	45,626	5,138
Navy	37,366	27,477	6,817
Air Force	24,683	5,308	1,599
Marine Corps	11,720	6,429	3,991
Totals	142,789	84,840	17,545
Total, all types of discharges	245,174		

[a] Bad Conduct Discharge and Dishonorable Discharge.

SOURCE: *Military Justice, op. cit.*, Army, p. 1036; Navy, p. 1001, Air Force, p. 1045; Marine Corps, p. 1005.

The magnitude of these discharges is indicated in Table 3 for a limited period (1962–1965). However, their significance is cumulative, since few are ever modified or revoked. About 10 per cent of all discharges from the armed forces are "less than honorable." (See Table 4.) Some have much more stigma attached to them than others. For example, the Navy discharged over 1,000 men each year from 1961 (1,148) to 1965 (1,365) for homosexual behavior. Such men are permanently identified as homosexuals regardless of personality changes which might occur later in life.[15]

Any discharge less than honorable seriously affects the individual's life adjustment after service. It must be revealed in most employment applications, few of which distinguish between the various types. It also constitutes a bar to most forms of public service. It is recorded in the records of the Federal Bureau of Investigation and consequently routinely furnished

[15] For all services, homosexual behavior is the most common cause for discharge as "undesirable," although many men are also separated with a General Discharge if accused of only a single act which is attributed to curiosity or intoxication. The fact that the behavior occurred in the civilian community or with nonmilitary persons is no defense against such an accusation. Such discharges are issued on the basis of administrative board proceedings rather than judicial proceedings under the Uniform Code of Military Justice.

Table 5 *Actions by Navy Discharge Review Board, 1965*

Board action	Discharge type: Dishonorable	Bad conduct	Undesirable	General
(Issued)[a]	(8)	(947)	(2,854)	(5,425)
Reviewed[b]	37	187	92	47
Changed to Undesirable	0	0		
Changed to General	9	44	30	
Changed to Honorable	1	2	10	16

SOURCES:
[a] *Military Justice, op. cit.*, p. 955. The Discharge Review Board is not involved in the original issue of the discharge by subordinate commands.
[b] *Ibid.*, p. 1001. Review action does not always occur in the year of discharge, especially of dishonorable discharges. The number of Dishonorable Discharges issued by the Navy declined from 791 in 1950 to 5 in 1965. Thus the number of Dishonorable Discharges *reviewed* in 1965 probably reflects the larger number of such discharges issued in earlier periods.

Table 6 *Actions by Army Discharge Review Board, 1965*

Board action	Discharge type: Dishonorable and bad conduct	Undesirable	General
(Issued)[a]	(1,058)	(8,561)	(13,925)
Reviewed[b]	266	1,586	716
Changed to Undesirable	1		
Changed to General	8	348	
Changed to Honorable	5	26	159

SOURCES:
[a] *Military Justice, op. cit.*, p. 1036.
[b] *Ibid.*, p. 926. Data include changes by Army Board for Correction of Military Records.

in identification inquiries by law enforcement agencies. The Dishonorable Discharge is especially significant in this respect since it is more traditional and is mentioned in many States as a disqualification for public employment. Conviction for a single offense may thus discredit an entire career.

All services maintain Boards of Review for the correction or modification of administrative and punitive discharges. The review is not automatic, however, and thus depends on the knowledge and resources of the person. Usually petition for a review occurs after a prolonged period of unsuccessful attempts to find employment.[16] Even upon review, however, the modification is most likely to be a single step reduction, i.e., from "undesirable" to "general" rather than a revocation of the less-than-honorable discharge. (See Tables 5 and 6).

[16] *Military Justice, op. cit.*, Appendix A. Testimony of Robert E. Byrne and A. F. Zerbee on effects of discharge in employment, pp. 833–834.

DISPOSITION OF RECORDS

Records accumulated on military personnel are retained by the organization after their separation from active service, and thus constitute a permanent source of information about the individual to whom they apply.

Registrant files of the Selective Service System are retained by the Local Board until the registrant attains age thirty-five and is no longer liable for military service. The file is then transferred to warehouse storage at the state headquarters or to a Federal Records Depot. Because the Selective Service System reports the volume of records by linear feet rather than number of individuals, the magnitude of this information can only be estimated. In 1967, about 33 million registrant files had been accumulated since the reactivation of the draft in 1948. Most of the records of registrants during World War II have been destroyed or "donated" to state governments. However, a substantial number must still be available, since information based on such files is provided to about 18,000 persons annually to help establish eligibility for social security benefits. These files are the sole remaining source for such data in both state and federal records.[17]

Personnel and medical records of discharged active and reserve military personnel are filed at the National Personnel Records Center, St. Louis, Missouri, in the custody of the Administrator of General Services. Copies of medical records or information from them may be furnished to federal or state hospitals or penal institutions when the individual is a patient or inmate. They will also be given to authorized representatives of accredited research agencies when engaged in medical research with the approval of the Surgeon General. Personnel files may be examined for approved research projects, to members of Congress when authorized by the headquarters of the service branch, or by federal investigative agencies.[18]

The general policy is that maximum information will be made available from inactive service files, unless the request involves a category which is exempted from the requirement of disclosure by 5 U.S.C.522. Regulations clearly prohibit disclosure of "information in personnel or medical files, as well as information in similar files that, if disclosed to a member of the public, would result in a clearly unwarranted invasion of privacy." However, this prohibition is seriously compromised by an interpretation that makes such information available:

[17] *Annual Report of the Director of Selective Service, 1964,* Government Printing Office, Washington, 1965, pp. 30–31.

[18] "Release of Information and Records from Army Files," *op. cit.*

> Consideration should be given, in cases involving alleged misconduct, to the relationship of the alleged misconduct to the individual's official duties, the amount of time which has passed since the alleged misconduct, and the degree to which the individual's privacy has already been invaded by Army investigation or proceedings which have already taken place.[19]

This interpretation has been used to authorize the release of information on persons accused of notorious crimes.

Intelligence and military police files are maintained at repositories of the separate services. Individual case files are listed with the Defense Central Index of Investigation and Department of Defense National Agency Check Center, Fort Holabird, Maryland. Such files are generally accessible only to federal investigative agencies.

ISSUES AND IMPLICATIONS

The sheer number, completeness, and duration of existence of military dossiers pose special problems of the relationship of military organization to the larger society. For example, pre-induction examinations for the Selective Service System provide limited records on a major portion of American men. The results of these examinations have implications that transcend the simple organizational purpose for which they were conducted in their effect on the subsequent life adjustment of even those who are rejected. In the aggregate these data have provided strong evidence of the need for various social programs of occupational training and placement.[20] In individual cases, however, the effect may be less favorable. The record provides permanent documentary evidence of the unfitness of the individual for military service, and his draft classification may be interpreted by prospective employers as an index of his corresponding lack of qualifications for civilian employment. (An unexplored question is the extent to which the higher Negro rejection rate in the examinations now contributes to the disproportionate unemployment of Negroes in the same age group.) It is possible that the Selective Service classification process has fostered the development of a new dimension of stratification in our society, one to which the poor are especially vulnerable and which thus reinforces their lower class status.

The immediate issue, however, is the extent to which realistic boundaries may be established and maintained between the military dossier and the demands of other government agencies for the information that it contains. Access to the military dossier must be considered in terms of

[19] *Ibid.*

[20] *One-Third of A Nation,* Report of the President's Commission on Manpower, Government Printing Office, Washington, 1964.

the unusual setting in which it is compiled. The individual to whom it applies is subject to a rigid authority structure and normative system. He is exposed to more complete and coordinated surveillance of his behavior than would occur in the civilian community. The information is extracted from him under the legal compulsion of service, or based on observation of his behavior in strange and unusual circumstances. These factors militate against the validity of the information for predicting performance in other settings.

Even upon termination of service, the record of the soldier's performance is in effect published by the quality of the discharge certificate that he is issued, a personal record with lifetime significance for occupational success or civic status. An unsatisfactory discharge is often associated by the public with criminal activities and constitutes a serious impediment to a normal social life.

The prospect is that records compiled on individuals during their military service will be increasingly demanded by other institutions of the larger society for purposes other than organizational efficiency. Military organization has been moving into closer relations with the larger society so that it no longer exists as the traditional separate establishment. Occupational similarities, the high rate of personnel turnover, and greater exposure in the mass media have contributed to this trend. In addition, the military establishment is increasingly called upon to perform a variety of civic functions, including social welfare programs. The most notable of these are the current Projects 100,000 and Transition under which marginally disqualified youths are accepted for service, and others are trained in civilian skills prior to discharge.

The computer has already facilitated an almost complete centralization and automation of the intelligence dossier in the form of the National Agency Check Center and the Defense Central Index of Investigations. These agencies routinely exchange information from military personnel records with other government agencies, both federal and state. The substitution of the social security number for the traditional service "serial number" will facilitate the convergence of military and civilian records at the national level.

10 *Security Investigations*

JESSE ORLANSKY

A candidate for employment expects to fill out an application form, describe his education and experience, and provide professional and character references. He will probably be interviewed; he may be required to take psychological tests; and he may have to show samples of his accomplishments. If he passes these hurdles, he is eligible for employment. However, if the work requires access to classified information, he has to fill out another set of forms and wait until he receives security clearance before he can do classified work. For employees of industrial establishments, the security investigation can take place only after the individual has been employed; while for civil servants, it is part of the preemployment procedure. Whereas potential employers decide whether or not a person can work, the government decides whether or not he can work with classified information. Thus, two independent qualifications apply to all persons in private employment, in the federal civil service, and in the military services, that is, to private citizens, to civil servants and to men in uniform whose work requires access to classified information. In

The author is a member of the Institute for Defense Analyses, Arlington, Virginia. The views expressed in this chapter are those of the author and not necessarily of the Institute for Defense Analyses, of any of its clients, or of any agency of the Government of the United States.

this chapter, we are concerned only with the procedures used to grant access to classified information and not with whether an individual should be employed.

FEDERAL PERSONNEL CLEARANCE PROGRAMS

All governments seek protection against subversion and espionage and desire key personnel who are trustworthy and reliable. Since no single method can guarantee protection, a variety of means are employed to achieve this purpose. Generally, there will be an effort to identify important information and to control its dissemination. Considerable reliance will also be placed upon intelligence operations, counterespionage, safes, burglar alarms, and armed guards. Here we shall consider only how the trustworthiness of individuals permitted to handle classified information is established in the United States and not the other aspects of a comprehensive security program.

The rules and regulations used to administer the security programs of government departments and agencies may not be widely known, although they are publicly available in many Security Manuals and Directives[1] as well as in the excellent *Government Security and Loyalty,* a looseleaf manual which is brought up to date each month.[2] The present chapter is based largely on such sources, which are identified at appropriate places in the text. Our emphasis is to *describe* rather than to *evaluate* the effectiveness of the security program in the belief that information is a valuable commodity. In any case, so little is known about the security program that it would be impossible for an outsider to evaluate its effectiveness. One reason for the lack of knowledge is the traditional reticence of security organizations and another is that a lack of knowledge may make it more difficult to circumvent security measures. Of course, we know that the Federal Bureau of Investigation is responsible for protecting internal security; but beyond that, most of us do not know how security procedures really operate or how effective they may be.

The administration of the government's security program from 1950 to 1956, with a highpoint in the Oppenheimer hearings of 1954, has left a

[1] *U.S. Personnel Security Practices,* Hearings Before the Subcommittee to Investigate the Administration of the Internal Security Act and Other Internal Security Laws of the Committee on the Judiciary, U.S. Senate, 88th Congress, 1st Session, Appendix, vol. I and II, Government Printing Office, Washington, 1963.

[2] *Government Security and Loyalty,* A Manual of Laws, Regulations and Procedures, The Bureau of National Affairs, Inc., Washington.

memory of which few Americans can be proud.[3] The memory of that period need not be the basis for criticizing the current program. Whatever the reason, there has not been, in recent years, any marked controversy about personnel security procedures.

In the opinion of the author, the personnel security program is now being conducted in a fair and reasonable manner. Very few individuals are denied security clearance. Before a clearance may be denied, the individual receives a Statement of Reasons and may be represented by his own counsel at a hearing where he may present evidence in his own behalf and may cross-examine adverse witnesses. An unfavorable ruling may be appealed. Although one may deplore the continued existence of a security program, the excesses of the McCarthy period are no longer in existence and complaints against the basic fairness of the present system have little basis in fact.

Legal Basis for Security Programs

The fundamental basis for security programs is the inherent right of a country to protect itself. There has always been a security program in the United States. Until recently, however, it did not involve the systematic investigation of personnel before entrusting to them the security of the nation. The systematic screening of personnel was started in the years prior to World War II when the growth of Communist subversion in the United States introduced the concept of "loyalty" into the security program. Loyalty and security are concepts which should be differentiated.

"Security" relates to the protection of the nation and, in practical terms, requires a judgment that access of a particular individual to sensitive information may permit him to influence policy against the interests of his own country. An individual could be judged to be a security risk through no fault of his own; for example, if he has close relatives in a Communist country or suffers from a serious mental disturbance. In theory, at least, an adverse security judgment might be viewed as objective; and it need not carry a moral stigma or preclude employment in a nonsensitive position in the government or in industry.

[3] Bontecou, Eleanor, *The Federal Loyalty-Security Program,* Cornell University Press, Ithaca, 1953; Brown, Ralph S., Jr., *Loyalty and Security,* Yale University Press, New Haven, 1958; *Case Studies in Personnel Security,* Collected under the Direction of Adam Yarmolinsky, The Bureau of National Affairs, Inc., Washington, August, 1955; *Report of the Special Committee on the Federal Loyalty-Security Program of the Association of the Bar of the City of New York,* Dudley F. Bonsal, Chairman, Dodd, Mead & Co., New York, 1956; Shils, Edward, Special Editor, *Secrecy, Security and Loyalty,* Special Issue of *Bulletin of Atomic Scientists,* April, 1955.

"Loyalty," however, refers to a state of mind, namely, that a person judged disloyal has a greater allegiance to another government than to his own. It is difficult to assess another person's loyalty. In practice, the judgment concerns disloyalty, i.e., expressions which reject our form of government and would supplant it by violence, if necessary. An adverse judgment in a loyalty case stigmatizes the individual.

The Hatch Act of 1939, which forbids federal employees to belong to any organization that advocates the overthrow of our constitutional government, led to the loyalty investigations of World War II. (The Hatch Act also forbids federal employees to engage in political activity.) President Franklin D. Roosevelt's Executive Order 9300 of February, 1943, established an interdepartmental committee to consider cases of subversive activity on the part of federal employees in order to protect the interests of the government of the United States.

> Determinations adverse to the individual shall be determinations in terms of the national interest and shall in no sense be determinations as to the loyalty of the applicant.[4]

Despite the practical difficulties of distinguishing clearly between the concepts of loyalty and security, it should be clear that both programs exist in the government at the present time and both are generally included in proposed revisions to the statutes.[5]

The Secretary or Director of each Department and executive agency of the federal government is uniquely responsible for maintaining security within his organization. The authority to establish standards for employment, to conduct personnel security investigations, and to make the final determination on each individual is based on this responsibility. Also because each Secretary or Director is responsible for security within his own organization, there are many government security programs rather than one program for all agencies. No single agency conducts personnel security investigations for all agencies of the government. In practice there are five programs, excluding the FBI and CIA:

[4] Industrial Personnel Security Clearance Program, DoD Directive 5220.6, December 7, 1966, amended September 30, 1967.

[5] H.R. 14675, "A Bill to establish a Central Security Office to coordinate the administration of Federal personnel loyalty and security programs, to prescribe administrative procedures for the hearing and review of cases arising under such programs, and for other purposes," introduced in the House of Representatives on January 17, 1968; S.2988, "A Bill to strengthen the internal security of the United States," introduced in the Senate on February 19, 1968.

Program of personnel security	*Basic authorizations*
Employees of the U.S. government (except FBI and CIA)	PL. 733, 26 August 1950 EO 10450,[a] 27 April 1953 Atomic Energy Act, 1954
Employees of private organizations working for the government (primarily Department of Defense, Atomic Energy Commission, National Aeronautics and Space Administration and Federal Aviation Agency)	National Security Act of 1947 EO 10501,[b] 6 November 1953 EO 10865,[c] 20 February 1960
Military personnel	DoD Directive 5210.9, 19 June 1956 DoD Directive 5210.11, 5 June 1954 DoD Directive 5210.31, 16 Jan. 1957
U.S. employees of international agencies	EO 10422,[d] 9 January 1953 EO 10459, 2 June 1953 EO 10763, 23 April 1958
Employees on merchant vessels of the U.S. of 100 gross tons or over	Magnuson Act, 9 August 1950[e] EO 10173,[f] 18 October 1950 EO 10277, 1 August 1951 EO 10352, 9 May 1952

[a] Security requirements for government employment, Executive Order 10450, amended by EO 10491, 10531, 10548, 10550.

[b] Categories of classified information, Executive Order 10501.

[c] Safeguarding classified information within industry, Executive Order 10865, amended by EO 10909.

[d] Prescribing procedures for making available to the Secretary-General of the United Nations certain information concerning United States citizens employed or being considered for employment on the Secretariat of the United Nations, Executive Order 10422.

[e] Regulations relating to the safeguarding of vessels, harbors, ports, and waterfront facilities of the United States, Executive Order 10173.

[f] On January 16, 1968, the Supreme Court ruled that the Magnuson Act did not give the government authority to inquire into seamen's beliefs and associations before granting them seamen's licenses. There is no doubt, however, that the government does possess the authority, on other grounds, to act to prevent sabotage.

Although this chapter addresses itself generally to the personnel clearance programs of the federal government, it often refers specifically to the industrial security program of the Department of Defense. This is one of three security programs operated by the DoD, the others applying to civil servants and to military personnel. Even though similar rules apply to all personnel security programs, the reader is forewarned that our general observations about policies, procedures, and practices do not necessarily apply equally throughout the government.

Access to Classified Information

Information which requires protection in the interest of national security is called "classified information." There are three major categories, defined as follows:

Top Secret Information. Defense information and material, the defense aspect of which is paramount, and the unauthorized disclosure of which could result in exceptionally grave damage to the Nation.

Secret Information. Defense information and material, the unauthorized disclosure of which could result in serious damage to the Nation.

Confidential Information. Defense information and material, the unauthorized disclosure of which could be prejudicial to the defense interests of the Nation.[6]

Standard and Criteria for Employment in a Sensitive Position

Given a security program, it becomes necessary to identify the individuals who may be granted access to classified information. Thus, the Army describes *derogatory information* as:

Information of such nature as to constitute a possible basis for denial or revocation of security clearance, rejection for or separation from service or employment with the Department of the Army. It includes:

(1) *Adverse loyalty information.* Information which reflects unfavorably upon the loyalty of an individual to the United States.

(2) *Adverse suitability information.* Information which, though not reflecting on an individual's loyalty to the United States, casts doubt upon his good character, trustworthiness, or reliability and hence raises a doubt that access to classified information would be clearly consistent with national security or which might serve as a bar to any favorable personnel action.[7]

The standard for employment of any individual in a sensitive position is that his employment be clearly consistent with the interests of national security.[8] In effect, a series of activities and associations, called "criteria," have been identified which may be the basis for denying employment in a sensitive position. The criteria are of varying degrees of seriousness, so that the ultimate determination in a particular case must be made "on the basis of an over-all common-sense evaluation of all the information." The criteria follow:

Unreliability
Misrepresentation
Disgraceful conduct, intoxicants, drugs, perversion
Mental instability
Susceptibility to coercion
Sabotage, espionage, treason, sedition
Sympathetic association with secret agents

[6] Categories of classified information, Executive Order 10501, November 6, 1953.

[7] Personnel Security Clearance, Department of the Army Regulation AR 604–5, May 21, 1962, in *U.S. Personnel Security Practices, op. cit.*, Appendix, vol. I, "Departmental and Agency Rules and Regulations."

[8] See Appendix A for details.

Advocacy of force to overthrow the United States government
Membership in or sympathetic association with subversive organizations
Unauthorized disclosure of classified information
Serving the interest of another government
Sympathetic participation in front organizations
Sympathetic participation in infiltrated organizations
Knowing participation in subversive organization
Sympathetic interest in subversive movements
Sympathetic association with members of subversive organizations
Close, continuing association with subversives
Risk of renewing a previous close continuing association with subversives
Hostage risk: relatives in Communist-bloc countries
Willful violation of security regulations
Poor judgment and instability
Claim of privilege against self-incrimination on charges related to security
Excessive indebtedness, unexplained affluence
Refusal to complete required security forms or to answer in security hearings.

In general these criteria are used by all government agencies. The Atomic Energy Commission can apply some of them to the spouse of an individual being considered for clearance. The basis for this unusual procedure is that the Atomic Energy Act of 1954 (Section 145a) requires an investigation and report on an individual's character, association and loyalty.[9] It is the policy of the AEC to apply its "Category 'A' derogatory information" eligibility criteria "to the individual or his spouse."[10] This category includes acts of or attempts to commit espionage, knowing association with espionage agents of a foreign nation, membership in subversive organizations designated by the Attorney General, advocating the violent overthrow of the U.S. government, deliberate falsification of the Personnel Security Questionnaire, mental illness which in the opinion of competent authority may cause a significant defect in the judgment or reliability of the individual, conviction of crimes indicating habitual criminal tendencies, and habitual use of drugs without adequate evidence of rehabilitation.

[9] *Personnel Security Handbook*, Division of Security, U.S. Atomic Energy Commission, AEC Appendix 2301, Part V; also Criteria, Annex A.
[10] *U.S. Personnel Security Practices, op. cit.*, Appendix, vol. II, pp. 717, 733.

Scope of Security Investigations

An individual must be investigated before he can have access to classified information. The scope of this investigation is determined not only by the category of classified information to which he may be exposed but by certain other conditions, such as whether he has been investigated previously (within the past six months) and whether he is an alien. The extent of investigation required in various cases is shown in Table 1. Interim clearances are not considered in order to simplify the table. The two principal types of investigation are called "National Agency Check" (or "NAC") and "Background Investigation" (or "BI"). An "expanded NAC" signifies an additional investigation undertaken to verify unfavorable information disclosed by a routine NAC. The phrase "Full Field Investigation" is synonymous with "Background Investigation." As a matter of interest, there is also a procedure for determining that a facility is eligible, from a security viewpoint, to handle and to store classified information of various categories. This is called a "facility security clearance." Thus, cleared personnel can handle classified information only at an appropriately cleared facility.

Information Provided by the Applicant

Security clearance, it may be emphasized, is granted by the government and not by private organizations. The single exception to this statement is that industrial organizations, following certain rules specified by the government, can grant Confidential clearances to employees who are also citizens. A DoD contractor cannot request clearance for an individual unless he is actually employed. In fact, the employer cannot even require that the clearance forms be filled out until he decides to hire the applicant and informs him of that decision.[11] Before the investigation can start, an individual must provide certain personal information by filling out one or more of the following forms:

1. Application and authorization for access to confidential information
2. Personnel security questionnaire
3. Certificate of nonaffiliation with certain organizations
4. Personnel security questionnaire (updating)
5. Immigrant alien questionnaire
6. Applicant fingerprint card

[11] Industrial Security Manual for Safeguarding Classified Information, Department of Defense, DoD 5220.22–M, July 1, 1966, p. 60.

TABLE 1 *Scope of Investigation for Various Types of DoD Clearances*

Type of clearance	*Military personnel*[a]	*DoD employees*[a]	*Contractor personnel*[b]
Top secret			
U.S. Citizens	Background Investigation or National Agency Check plus[c]	Background Investigation	Background Investigation
Immigrant aliens	Background Investigation	Background Investigation	Background Investigation
Secret			
U.S. Citizens	National Agency Check; Background Investigation for employees in critical, sensitive positions	National Agency Check plus[d]	National Agency Check
Immigrant aliens	Background Investigation	Background Investigation	Background Investigation
Confidential			
U.S. Citizens	Check of the military field 201 file, local intelligence files, Provost Marshal files and medical records	National Agency Check plus[d]	National Agency Check (for certain personnel prescribed for facility security clearance purposes)
Contractor employees			Cleared by the contractor in accordance with rules established by ISM, par. 24b[e]
Immigrant aliens	Background Investigation	Background Investigation	Background Investigation

[a] Personnel security clearance, clearance of personnel for access to classified defense information and material, Hdqs. Department of the Army, AR 604–5, Cl, February 6, 1963, in *U.S. Personnel Security Practices,* Hearings before the Subcommittee to Investigate the Administration of the Internal Security Act and Other Internal Security Laws of the Committee of the Judiciary, United States Senate, Eighty-eighth Congress, First Session, Appendix, vol. I, "Departmental and Agency Rules and Regulations," Government Printing Office, Washington, 1963, pp. 123–125.

[b] *Industrial Security Regulation,* DoD 5220.22–R, July 1, 1966, Section II, Part 3.

[c] NAC Plus

1. Continuous honorable active duty as a member of the Armed Forces, or a combination of such active duty and civilian employment in the federal government service on a continuous basis; with no break greater than six months, for a minimum of fifteen consecutive years immediately preceding the date of the current investigation, or current need for clearance, plus
2. Check of the military field 201 file, local intelligence files, Provost Marshal files, and medical records.

[d] NAC plus written inquiries to appropriate local law enforcement agencies, former employers and supervisors, references and schools attended, except that the written inquiries portion of the investigation may be dispensed with for employees who have been continuously employed for a period of five years (with no break greater than six months) immediately preceding the date of the current investigation, or current need for clearance.

[e] *Industrial Security Manual for Safeguarding Classified Information,* Department of Defense, DoD 5220.22–M, July 1, 1966, p. 59.

The personnel security questionnaire requires the following information:

- Name
- Any other name by which known (alias, maiden, or former legal name)
- Date of birth
- Place of birth
- Social security number
- Marital status
- Sex
- Height
- Weight
- Color of eyes
- Color of hair
- Education (all civilian schools, by name, location, time period, and degree if any)
- Citizenship status; certificate numbers required if by naturalization or by derivation
- Military service (by country, branch, service number, and dates; type of discharge; local draft board; draft classification; service in a military reserve component, if any)
- Residence (by street address and dates of residence for the last fifteen years or since the eighteenth birthday, whichever is shorter)
- All organizational memberships (except labor unions and certain other organizations considered below; organizations are to be listed by type, office held if any, and dates of membership)
- Foreign countries visited or resided in (with date and reason for each visit)
- Relatives (parents, spouse, children, brothers and sisters, even though deceased; by address, place and date of birth, and present citizenship; includes living relatives and relatives of spouse known to be residing outside the United States, regardless of age)
- Employment (employers, location, immediate supervisor, positions held, and dates)
- Arrest record (except for traffic violations for which the only penalty imposed was a fine of $25.00 or less, or for arrests or charges before the age of 16; for each case, date, place, charge and disposition)
- Record of previous security clearances (including possible suspension, revocation or denial, or termination of employment while a request for clearance was pending)

References (five personal references, by name, address and years known; names of relatives, former employers or persons living outside the U.S. are not acceptable)

Foreign affiliations (government, firms, corporations or persons for whom the applicant acts as a representative, official or employee)

By his signature to the completed form, the employee certifies:

1. That he has read every sentence before signing.
2. That all entries are true, complete and correct to the best of his knowledge and that they are made in good faith.
3. That he is a citizen of the United States.
4. That he knows that any misrepresentation or false statement may subject him to prosecution under the U.S. Criminal Code, with penalties up to five years imprisonment and $10,000 fine.
5. That he has read and understood each sentence of the certificate.

The employee's signature must be verified by the signature of a witness.

The certificate of nonaffiliation with certain organizations requires the employee to certify whether or not he was ever a member of or associated with specified subversive groups, movements, or combinations of persons which advocate overthrow of our constitutional form of government. About 300 organizations are designated on this form, comprising a list prepared by the Attorney General in accordance with Executive Order 10450. The list includes many Communist, national socialist, Ku Klux Klan, and other extremist groups.

Contractors apply for clearance of their employees by submitting the forms to the Defense Industrial Security Clearance Office (DISCO) at Columbus, Ohio. For a Top Secret clearance, five signed copies of the questionnaire, two signed copies of the certificate of nonaffiliation and one signed set of fingerprints are required; only one set is required for a Secret or Confidential clearance. An investigation will not be started until all required forms are properly filled in.

National Agency Check

The National Agency Check[12] attempts to determine whether certain specialized government agencies contain any information, in their area of interest, concerning the individual being investigated. For example, the FBI criminal files are searched to see if they contain a record of any arrests for that person. A separate search is made of the FBI subversive

[12] See Appendix B for details.

files. The files of the military services are searched if the individual has ever had military service, and of the Civil Service Commission, if the individual has ever been employed by the U.S. government. These files are searched primarily on the basis of name, date, and place of birth of the individual. In most cases, the result is a negative one or, to paraphrase the reporting style of one agency: on the basis of the identifying information provided, no assurance can be given that derogatory information on the designated individual does not exist in the files of this agency. Conversely, the report of any derogatory information will probably lead to further inquiry, such as a Background Investigation to confirm and evaluate the information. Security clearance cannot be denied on the basis of a National Agency Check alone while a favorable NAC (i.e., "no report") is acceptable only for Confidential and Secret clearances.

Background Investigation

The purpose of a Background Investigation (BI) is to collect all of the "pertinent facts bearing on the trustworthiness, integrity, reputation and loyalty to the United States of the individual."[13] It is supposed to establish the identity of the candidate, to verify the continuity of his life records from birth to the present (although the emphasis is placed on the past fifteen years), to verify each item reported on the personnel security questionnaire and to determine his loyalty to the United States and suitability for trust by interviews with references, present and previous employers, neighbors and associates. Individuals not cited as references are also interviewed; these are called "developed" in contrast to "given" references. A National Agency Check is included routinely as part of each BI. The BI also includes a check of local police records and of credit agencies in locations where the individual has lived. Various records, such as school, employment, citizenship (for naturalized citizens) and military service records are examined for consistency and continuity. If a discrepancy is observed, the original records, such as birth, will be certified by direct inspection.

The required records and references are searched out wherever they may exist. Since the average American family moves about once every five years, the pertinent records on an adult generally exist in several local areas. Usually, several field offices participate and only in rare cases does a single investigator or team conduct an entire investigation.

[13] Industrial Security Regulations, Department of Defense Directive 5220.22–R, July 1, 1966, paragraph 2–317.
See Appendix C for details.

The accumulation of information and reports on each individual is put in an investigative file. This material can be evaluated only after replies have been received from all sources, e.g., the FBI, employers, schools and interviews. The office which controls the investigation often requests the branch offices for additional information or to verify information received from other sources during the investigation.

Most National Agency Checks are completed in about twenty days and most Background Investigations in about seventy-five days.[14] Several years ago, the BI might take from 60 to 270 days. At DISCO, about 12 per cent of security clearance forms are returned for correction, e.g., signature, to complete items that had been omitted, or for clean fingerprints. About 4 per cent of the requests for secret clearance require additional investigation and adjudication.[15]

In recent years, few individuals have been denied a security clearance. According to data released by the Atomic Energy Commission (discussed more fully below) about two applicants in each 1,000, i.e., 0.2 per cent, are denied clearance. When the outcome is favorable, the applicant's organization receives a Letter of Consent; in the case of industrial security this would come from DISCO. The Letter authorizes the organization to release classified information, no higher than the specified security category, to that employee identified by name. The Letter of Consent can not be given to the employee.

Interviewing the Candidate

The subject of an investigation is not interviewed, although he probably knows as much about himself and perhaps more than would any of his references. As a consequence, the field investigation tends to be a diffuse matter, whereas a more precise investigatory effort could be mounted if the subject had been interviewed. Arguments in favor of not interviewing the subject are that a clever subject could mislead an interviewer and that many more highly trained investigators than are currently available would be required to interview all subjects. An exception to these remarks is that a subject may be called in for an informal interview in an attempt to resolve serious derogatory information before proceeding to a formal security review.

[14] Roberts, Lt. Col. W. W., USAF, "DISCO's Third Anniversary," *Industrial Security*, vol. 12, no. 3 (June, 1968), p. 63.
[15] *Ibid.*

Reinvestigation

After he is cleared, an individual whose work requires continued access to classified information will be investigated again and again, as the following occasions arise:

1. If he requires access to information of a higher security classification, e.g., from Confidential to Secret, or from Secret to Top Secret.
2. If, when he changes employers, it is more than six months since his last clearance.
3. At any time when significant derogatory information develops which, if confirmed, could lead to the revocation of a clearance.

Eligibility for a clearance may be reconsidered at any time on the basis of investigative reports already in the file, without need for a reinvestigation. An individual who holds a Top Secret clearance must fill out a new Statement of Personal History every five years, in which case the report of new information, such as a serious arrest, can also lead to a reinvestigation.

The usual scope of a reinvestigation is to bring a previous investigation up-to-date, a procedure called a "bring-up." However, any earlier period can be re-examined if the investigative agency chooses to do so. The discovery of any significant new derogatory information about a previous period would almost certainly lead to re-examining that period. If revocation of clearance is recommended, the procedures for review and appeal to be described below would also apply.

Thus, the dossier on an individual increases in size and so too does the likelihood of derogatory information. There is no way for the individual to know about or to comment upon any report in his dossier. He simply does not know about it and is not supposed to be able to learn what his dossier may contain unless, of course, he receives a Statement of Reasons in connection with the possible denial or revocation of his clearance.

On the other hand, the investigative agencies of the government may have access to the dossiers collected in previous investigations on an individual. This includes official files collected by government agencies, such as the FBI, the House Un-American Activities Committee, and military service records. In fact, these files provide the basis for the National Agency Check. By statute, certain files, such as those of the Internal Revenue Service, the Social Security Administration, the Veterans Administration, and the Census Bureau are not available for investigative purposes.

A file remains available to government agencies long after the occasion for which it was originally collected. Even after employment ceases, some files are kept active until a person dies or reaches the age of eighty years, in either case, long after the need for a security clearance has passed. Unless an individual's eligibility for a clearance is challenged, he is not afforded an opportunity to provide supplementary information of significance to him (under affidavit if it were required) about the unfavorable reports.

Derogatory Information in a Dossier

The presence of unfavorable information in a dossier is not rare. In its unevaluated form, it is referred to as "raw data," "unevaluated information," or as "possibly derogatory information." Derogatory information, of course, can be trivial or serious, true or false. It is trivial if an individual has been arrested for speeding; it is serious if he associates with known subversives. Serious derogatory information is not necessarily true and, by itself, it does not permit a department or agency to deny a clearance. This type of information must be proved or disproved beyond a reasonable doubt. The investigative agency is responsible for establishing the facts but it cannot deny a personnel security clearance. When it finds and can verify serious derogatory information which meets one or more of the criteria described above, it sends the complete file for evaluation to an independent review agency. The investigative agency is no longer involved except possibly to collect any additional information which may be requested by the review agency. In the industrial security program, if the investigation turns up substantial derogatory information so that DISCO is unable to grant a clearance, the file is sent to the Director of the Industrial Security Clearance Review Office (ISCRO). In the AEC, it would be sent to the Division of Security and, ultimately to the Personnel Security Board.

When no serious derogatory information has been found, the investigative agency reports this to DISCO, which grants the clearance. The review agency takes over when the investigative agency provides confirmed serious derogatory information.

DENIAL OF CLEARANCE

All federal agencies have a clearly defined procedure for dealing with cases in which security clearance may be denied, suspended, or revoked.[16] The information which follows applies solely to the Department of De-

[16] *U.S. Personal Security Practices, op. cit.*, Appendix, vol. I, "Departmental and Agency Rules and Regulations."

fense industrial personnel security clearance program[17] although, by interdepartmental agreements, it applies also to industrial personnel security clearances of other agencies such as State, Treasury, Commerce, General Services Administration, Federal Aviation Agency, the National Aeronautics and Space Administration, the Small Business Administration, and the National Science Foundation.[18] Similar programs exist for government employees and military personnel, but they will not be discussed here.

The Assistant Secretary of Defense for Administration, who is responsible for the Industrial Personnel Security Clearance Program, has delegated this authority to two independent offices. The Directorate for Security Policy is located in the Pentagon and includes the Industrial Security Clearance Review Office (ISCRO) and subsidiary boards and offices: a Screening Board, Field Offices, and an Appeal Board. DISCO, the Defense Industrial Security Clearance Office which administers industrial security clearances and investigations, is located in Columbus, Ohio, and is part of the Defense Supply Agency.

Therefore, a recommendation for denial or revocation from DISCO is referred to the Screening Board, which may direct:

1. Further investigation, specifying the particular matters to be investigated;
2. Written interrogatories;
3. Interviews with the applicant or other persons;
4. A medical examination for the applicant; and
5. A recommendation for suspension of the applicant's clearance pending further proceedings.

Ordinarily, an existing clearance is not suspended before the Screening Board acts unless, as an interim measure, certain statutory authorities determine that continued access to classified information would constitute an immediate threat to the national interest or, as an emergency measure, that there is significant evidence of espionage or sabotage. The Screening Board makes its determinations by majority vote. If it determines that clearance is clearly consistent with the national interest, a written statement is issued, and the matter closed. In this event, a candidate may not know that his case was referred to the Screening Board or

[17] Industrial Personnel Security Clearance Program, DoD Directive No. 5220.6, December 7, 1966, amended September 30, 1967.

[18] *Gaps in Internal Security Laws*, Hearings before the Subcommittee to Investigate the Administration of the Internal Security Act and other Internal Security Laws of the Committee on the Judiciary, U.S. Senate, Part 7, May 10 and 24, 1967, p. 336.

that he was investigated for derogatory information or that the possibility of denying his clearance was considered.

Where a favorable determination is not warranted, the Screening Board prepares a Statement of Reasons informing the applicant of the grounds on which his clearance may be denied or revoked. The applicant also receives a letter of instructions clearly outlining subsequent actions required of him, and information on his right to counsel and on his right to appeal.

To be entitled to a hearing, the applicant must submit within twenty days a detailed written answer under oath specifically denying or admitting each allegation. The answer must be sufficiently responsive to permit the Department of Defense to determine the issues which are controverted. Clearance will be suspended and further proceedings discontinued if the applicant fails to respond at any stage in the prescribed sequence.

The applicant may be represented by counsel of his own choice at a hearing before an Examiner in several locations around the country. He may present evidence in his own behalf and he may cross-examine adverse witnesses either orally or in writing. The applicant receives without cost one copy of the transcript of the hearing.

If the Examiner makes an adverse finding, the applicant is advised in writing and he may request an appeal. The Department Counsel may also appeal a ruling that is favorable to the applicant. The Appeal Board makes its determination by majority vote, with findings for or against the applicant on each charge in the Statement of Reasons. In the adverse case, the findings with respect to each allegation are given to the applicant.

If a clearance is granted, an applicant may be reimbursed for a loss of earnings resulting directly from the suspension, revocation, or denial of clearance.

Thus, before a final adverse judgment may be rendered, the applicant is given an opportunity to refute the charges in a quasi-judicial, adversary type of proceeding. Before the hearing takes place, he is advised in writing of the reasons for which his clearance may be denied. He can be represented by counsel, he can present evidence on his own behalf, and he can cross-examine adverse witnesses. He can appeal an unfavorable decision. Many of these protections were not available in 1955 in the cases collected by Yarmolinsky.[19]

The procedure, nonetheless, is an administrative determination conducted under the authority of the Secretary of Defense who is charged

[19] Yarmolinsky, Adam, editor, *Case Studies in Personnel Security*, The Bureau of National Affairs, Inc., Washington, August, 1955.

with responsibility for security in his department.[20] It is not a judicial hearing. According to the DoD Director of Security Policy, the *Industrial Personnel Access Authorization Review Regulation*[21]

has been effectively designed to enforce the highest standard of procedural fairness in balancing the rights of individuals basic to freedom and for the government to protect itself against unauthorized disclosures of classified information relating to the national defense.

During the 6½-year period the directive was in effect, the program functioned in a highly satisfactory manner. The Government's interests were adequately safeguarded without denying due process to the applicants concerned. Satisfactory though the program proved to be during that 1960–66 period, our experience over the years reflected the desirability of certain fundamental changes within the context of the Executive Order. Primarily, we discerned the feasibility of providing applicants an even greater measure of due process without doing injury to the national security. Consequently, the directive of December 7, 1966, was issued.[22]

For the first time, under the new directive, the procedure referred to above is called a "hearing."

Data on Clearances and Denials

It is difficult to determine the total number of individuals who have security clearances at the present time, how many are investigated each year, or the proportion who are denied clearance. Such information is published rarely and, when it does appear, generally in Congressional Hearings, the data are incomplete and difficult to interpret. All the information we were able to find, starting with 1947, is shown in Table 2. There are gaps in the table. In certain cases, we do not know the total number of individuals who were investigated or the number who receive security clearance. Some of the data involve overlapping time periods. Several

[20] Safeguarding Classified Information Within Industry, Executive Order 10865, February 20, 1960. This Executive Order was promulgated to confer on the Secretary of Defense and certain other Department and Agency heads the express authority the Supreme Court found lacking in the case of Greene v. McElroy, U.S. Supreme Court No. 180, June 20, 1959. In U.S. v. Robel, U.S. Supreme Court No. 2, December 11, 1967, the Court declared unconstitutional the section of the Subversive Activities Control Act of 1950 that makes it a crime for a member of the Communist party to take a job in a defense facility. In his opinion, Chief Justice Earl Warren said that "nothing we hold today should be read to deny Congress the power under narrowly drawn legislation to keep from sensitive positions in defense facilities those who would use their positions to disrupt the nation's production facilities." It is too soon after the event to know the effect of the Court's decision on security procedures.

[21] Department of Defense Directive 5220.6, December 7, 1966, amended September 30, 1967. This Directive supersedes an earlier one, with the same title, dated July 28, 1960, to implement Executive Order 10865.

[22] *Gaps in Internal Security Laws, op. cit.*, pp. 330–331.

agencies do not report the number of individuals who resigned or terminated their employment while under security review. There are no data on the Central Intelligence Agency or the Federal Bureau of Investigation. The security programs of three Presidents—Truman, Eisenhower, and Kennedy—are involved, but it is not clear that the data have been compiled in the same way throughout this period. A notable exception to these remarks is that the Atomic Energy Commission has provided complete information on its security program on a yearly basis from 1948 to 1963, and these data will be considered separately below.

With these severe qualifications in mind, Table 2 shows that from 1947 to 1963, at least 7,000,000 people inside and outside government were investigated for security clearance; the true number is probably greater. Over 50,000 (0.7 per cent) were referred to evaluation boards. Note, for example, that according to a feature article in *The Washington Post* in 1966, the Department of Defense alone has a central index of 21,500,000 name cards and has compiled 14,000,000 life histories in the course of its security investigations.[23] The astounding statement that there is a total of 187,762,000 security or investigative reports in government files may be found in "Government Dossier," a report prepared for the U.S. Senate.[24] Apart from the many difficulties encountered in compiling an accurate figure, this total is grossly inflated and impossible to evaluate. It includes, for example, multiple entries for each individual on each investigation, whenever several departments are involved. For example, a background investigation on a veteran would involve at least the Department of Defense, FBI, and the Civil Service Commission.

In Table 3, we examine the number of individuals who have been denied clearance as distinct from those "referred to evaluation boards"; the data are selected from Table 2 where rates can be determined. From 1947 to 1963, clearance was denied to at least 5,251 individuals (0.07 per cent) among over 7,000,000 investigated. (Table 2 shows at least 8,463 denials, but the true number is difficult to determine because of possible overlap.)

The rates of denial vary from 0.01 to 0.49 per cent among the agencies, being highest for the Port Security Program. We do not know the extent to which these differences are due either to the "clearability" of the applicants or to the administrative standards of the several departments.

[23] Harwood, Richard, "There's a Dossier on You," *The Washington Post,* May 29, 1966, p. El.

[24] *Government Dossier* (Survey of Information Contained in Government Files). Subcommittee on Administrative Practice and Procedure to the Committee on the Judiciary of the U.S. Senate, November, 1967, Table 4–B, pp. 26–27.

Table 2 *Some Statistical Data on Number of Individuals Investigated, Referred to Security Boards and Final Determinations*

Time period	*Security program*	*Department*	*Investigated*	*Referred to board*[a]	*Cleared*	*Denied clearance*[b]	*Terminations while under security review*[c]	*References*
1947–1953	EO 9835	All	4,756,705	26,236	16,503	560	6,828	1
May 28, 1953–Sept. 30, 1954	EO 10450	All except CIA				3,002	5,006	2
July 1, 1953–June 30, 1955	EO 10450	All except CIA (N = 65)	727,158	1,016[d]		342[e]	3,241[e] 5,684[e]	1
Jan. 1, 1947–June 30, 1963		AEC	716,695			546	5,026	3
–Dec. 31, 1955	Port Security		427,182[f] 397,206[g]			1,848 1,935		1
–Feb. 16, 1956	International Organizations		5,469					1
May, 1953–April, 1955	Industrial Security	DoD		1,672[h] 579[i]	622[h] 298[j]	1,050[h]		1
April, 1955–Jan. 1956	Industrial Security	DoD		206[h] 42[i]	145[h] 8[j]	61[h] 7		1
1958–1961	Civilian Personnel	Army		774	648	126		4
Fiscal year 1959–Fiscal year 1962	Civilian Personnel	Navy		12,639	11,041	1,488[k]		4
July 1, 1958–June 30, 1962	Civilian Personnel	Air Force		1,255	977	1	272	4
Sept., 1948–June 30, 1962	Civilian Personnel	Air Force		263	174	64	25	4

TABLE 2 (*cont.*)

July 1, 1958–June 30, 1962	Civilian Personnel	Labor	866	758		35	4
July 1, 1958–June 30, 1962	Civilian Personnel	NASA	25,500		20	97	4
July 1, 1966–June 30, 1967	Industrial	DoD	28,017 BI's				5
July 1, 1966–June 30, 1967	Industrial		217,866 NAC's[l]				5
July 1, 1966–June 30, 1967	Civilian and Military	DoD	195,938 BI's				5
July 1, 1966–June 30, 1967	Civilian and Military		1,387,117 NAC's[l]				5

REFERENCES:

1. *Report of the Special Committee on the Federal Loyalty Security Program of the Association of the Bar of the City of New York*, New York, 1956, Appendix A, pp. 219–226.
2. *Commission on Government Security*, U.S. Senate, 84th Congress, Committee on Government Operations, 1955, pp. 532–533.
3. Harold P. Green, "Q Clearance: The Development of a Personnel Security Program," *Bulletin of The Atomic Scientists*, May, 1964, pp. 9–15.
4. *U.S. Personnel Security Practices*, Hearings before the Subcommittee to Investigate the Administration of the Internal Security Act and Other Internal Security Laws of the Committee on the Judiciary, United States Senate, Eighty-eighth Congress, First Session, 1963, vol. I and II.
5. *Proposed Internal Security Act of 1968*, Hearings before the subcommittee to investigate the administration of the internal security act and other internal security laws of the Committee on the Judiciary, United States Senate on S. 2988, Part 5, April 10 and 11, 1968, pp. 352–354.

NOTES:

[a] Includes "eligibility questioned," "suspended under EO 10450."

[b] Includes "removed," "denied employment."

[c] Includes "resignations," "terminated by Civil Service procedures but declared by department heads to be because of security questions," "resignations . . . where files contained adverse security information," though it is not clear how many persons were aware of this information, cases discontinued by persons "left service or withdrew application . . . after they had been sent interrogatories or charges."

[d] October 1, 1953–September 30, 1955.

[e] May 28, 1953–June 30, 1955.

[f] Seamen.

[g] Waterfront workers.

[h] Screening level.

[i] Hearing level; part of above number.

[j] Cleared at hearing level.

[k] Includes resignations.

[l] Probably includes BI's, above.

TABLE 3 *Individuals Denied Clearance or Terminated While Under Security Investigation, Related to Total Number of People Investigated*

			Denied clearance		*Terminated while under security review*		*Total denied and/or terminated*	
Department	*Period*	*Number of people investigated*	*Number*	*Percentage*	*Number*	*Percentage*	*Number*	*Percentage*
All[a]	1947–1953	4,756,705	560	0.01	6,828	0.14	7,388	0.16
All[b]	1953–1955	727,158	342	0.05	5,684	0.78	6,126	0.83
AEC	1947–1963	716,695	546	0.08	5,026	0.70	5,572	0.78
NASA	1958–1962	25,500	20	0.08	97	0.38	117	0.46
Port Security	1947–1955[c]	427,182	1,848	0.43				
Port Security	1947–1955[d]	397,206	1,935	0.49				
Total		*7,050,445*	*5,251*	*0.07*				
(Excluding Port Security)		(6,226,057)	(1,468)	(0.02)	(17,635)	(0.28)	(19,203)	(0.31)

[a] EO 9835.
[b] EO 10450.
[c] Seamen.
[d] Dock workers.

SOURCE: Data selected from Table 2.

Brown[25] estimates that there were about 9,300 security dismissals between 1947 and 1956:

Federal employees	3,150
Military personnel	750
Industrial personnel	5,400
	9,300

Excluding the Port Security Program, 0.02 per cent were denied clearance, and 0.28 per cent terminated while under security review, for a total of 0.31 per cent for both causes, i.e., about 3 per 1,000 applicants. About twelve times as many people terminated their employment while under security review as compared to those who were denied clearance, i.e., 17,635 compared to 1,468.

Table 4 shows what happened to individuals who were referred to boards for security review (data from Table 2). These data are not complete with respect to those terminated while under security review; "unknown determinations" refer either to errors in the data or to cases pending final determination. For 39,934 cases referred to review boards (of the 53,589 cited in Table 2), about 58 per cent were cleared, 6 per cent were denied clearance, and 30 per cent terminated while under security review; about 6 per cent of these cases are not accounted for.

During 1966, DISCO received 215,241 requests for new industrial clearances in 1966[26] and 245,883 in fiscal 1967.[27] Of these, 3.8 per cent required additional investigation and adjudication while 0.3 per cent (584 cases in 1966) were referred to the Industrial Security Clearance Review Office.[28] From 564 cases completed, the results were:

Cleared	47.9%
Denied	29.1
Closed for administrative reasons without final action	23.0
	100.0%

The most complete set of data on any personnel security program was provided by the Atomic Energy Commission for an article by Harold P.

[25] Brown, *Loyalty and Security, op. cit.*, pp. 487–488.
According to our data for the same period, there were 8,463 denials and 12,512 terminations, for a total of 20,975. In addition, Brown estimates that state and local government programs led to the dismissal of about 1,000 employees while private programs in industry accounted for another 1,200, e.g., teachers in private institutions dismissed for refusing to answer questions or to take loyalty oaths, and blacklists in radio, television, and movies.

[26] *Gaps in Internal Security Laws, op. cit.*, p. 333.

[27] Hearings before the Subcommittee to investigate the administration of the internal security act and other internal security laws of the Committee on the Judiciary, U.S. Senate on S.2988, Part 5, April 10 and 11, 1968, p. 354.

[28] Roberts, "DISCO's Third Anniversary," *loc. cit.*

TABLE 4 *Security Determinations in Cases Referred to Boards*

Department	*Period*	*Referred to boards*	*Cleared*	*Denied clearance*	*Terminated while under security review*	*Unknown determi-nations*
All[a]	1947–1953	26,236	16,503	560	6,828	2,345
AEC	1947–1963			546	5,026	
DoD, Industrial Security	1953–1955	1,672	622	1,050		
DoD, Industrial Security	1955–1956	206	145	61		
Army, Civilian Personnel	1958–1961	774	648	126		
Air Force, Civilian Personnel	1958–1962	1,255	977	1	272	5
Air Force, Civilian Personnel	1948–1962	263	174	64	25	
Totals		*39,934*	*23,027*	*2,408*	*12,151*	*2,350*
(Percentages)		(100)	(57.7)	(6.0)	(30.4)	(5.9)

[a] EO 9835.

SOURCE: Data selected from Table 2.

Green in the *Bulletin of the Atomic Scientists.*[29] (See Table 5.) The AEC program has had a relatively constant population of about 150,000 Q-cleared personnel (i.e., full field investigation, equivalent to a Top Secret clearance). About 717,000 people were investigated from 1947 to 1963; in recent years, about 20,000 people are investigated each year. During the fifteen years of the AEC security program, significant derogatory information was found at a relatively constant rate on an average of 1.3 per cent of those who were investigated; the annual rate ranges from 0.6 to 2.7 per cent. The following tabulation summarizes the results of action taken against cases involving significant derogatory information:

Type of action	*Number*	*Percentage*
Applications withdrawn prior to final decision	5,026	52.7
Cleared without hearing	3,628	38.1
Cleared with hearing	330	3.5
Clearance denied	546	5.7
	9,530[a]	100.0

[a] This total differs from 9,528 given by Green because of rounding-off errors.

An interesting aspect of these data is that over the past ten years, i.e., from 1954 to 1963, the percentage of cases identified as involving significant derogatory information has dropped from a high of 2.7 per cent in 1955 and to a level of about 1.5 per cent in recent years. The percentage of applications withdrawn prior to final decision has decreased from a high of 68.3 per cent in 1954 to a level of about 40 per cent in recent years. The percentage cleared without a hearing has increased from a low of 24.8 per cent in 1954 to a recent level of about 55 per cent. The percentage cleared with a hearing has dropped slightly from a high of over 6 per cent in 1955 and 1956 to about 2.5 per cent in recent years. Finally, the percentage of those denied clearance has dropped from a high of 3.5 per cent in 1954 to a recent level of about 1.0 per cent. Very obviously, the AEC program has been changing slowly and steadily toward clearing more individuals including, according to Green, some with initial substantial derogatory information in their file that has been resolved to nonsubstantially derogatory information.

Green explains this trend by saying that

> the AEC security program has acquired a greater degree of sophistication, understanding, compassion, and courage. Unlike the situation during the early Eisenhower years when hearings and formal adjudications were regarded as the

[29] Green, Harold P., "Q Clearance: The Development of a Personnel Security Program," *Bulletin of the Atomic Scientists,* May, 1964, pp. 9–15.

TABLE 5 *History of the AEC Clearance Program*

Fiscal year	Number of full investigations	Cases identified as involving substantially derogatory information		Of cases involving substantially derogatory information: Applications withdrawn prior to final decision		Cleared without hearing		Cleared with hearing		Denied	
		Number	Percentage	Number	Percentage	Number	Percentage	Number	Percentage	Number	Percentage
1947–49	147,047	1,955	1.3	1,024	52.4	569	29.1	16	0.8	346	17.7
1950	41,106	240	0.6	99	41.1	92	38.5	12	5.0	37	15.4
1951	79,925	488	0.6	358	73.4	68	13.9	17	3.5	45	9.2
1952	90,076	889	1.0	635	71.5	192	21.7	38	4.3	25	2.5
1953	71,888	779	1.1	523	67.1	196	25.1	44	5.7	16	2.1
1954	51,360	775	1.5	529	68.3	192	24.8	26	3.4	27	3.5
1955	38,026	1,039	2.7	521	50.1	438	42.2	63	6.1	17	1.6
1956	33,135	705	2.2	294	41.7	360	51.1	46	6.5	5	0.7
1957	37,129	573	1.5	221	38.5	329	57.4	21	3.6	3	0.5
1958	25,328	465	1.8	187	40.2	259	55.7	13	2.8	6	1.3
1959	21,630	356	1.6	142	39.8	198	55.5	9	2.5	8	2.2
1960	19,488	286	1.5	95	33.2	182	63.5	9	3.0	1	0.3
1961	18,503	270	1.5	120	44.6	146	54.2	2	0.8	1	0.4
1962	21,746	311	1.4	137	44.0	163	52.5	6	1.9	5	1.6
1963	20,308	397	2.0	141	35.6	244	61.5	8	2.0	4	0.9
Total	*716,695*	*9,528*	*1.3%*	*5,026*	*52.7%*	*3,628*	*38.1%*	*330*	*3.5%*	*546*	*5.7%*

NOTE: Based on information made available by the AEC. Cases may be identified as involving derogatory information in one year on the basis of an investigation conducted during a prior year. Therefore, the cases shown in the second column as involving substantially derogatory information are not necessarily cases from among those shown in the first column as the total number of full investigation conducted in that year. The remaining columns, however, show the disposition of the actual cases in the second column.

SOURCE: Green, Harold P., "Q Clearance: The Development of a Personnel Security Program," *Bulletin of the Atomic Scientists,* May, 1964, pp. 9–15. The number of cases appearing in Columns 4, 6, 8, relating to "of cases involving substantially derogatory information" do not appear in Green's article, but were computed on the basis of percentage data shown in his table.

sine qua non of the program, since 1957 the AEC has used the informal interview in almost every case that previously would have gone to hearing, and the security doubts are resolved in most of these cases on the basis of such interviews. No longer does the security mechanism merely measure an investigative report against printed criteria and weigh the derogatory information under pseudo-jurisprudential procedures. There has increasingly been an attempt to assess the actual degree of risk, taking all relevant data into account, and to use the hearing procedures only in cases of genuine doubt.

Green comments further that

. . . there can be little doubt that, despite the greater security sensitivity of the AEC program, the more comprehensive investigations required by its statute, and the demonstrated effectiveness of its security program, a person with substantially derogatory information in his background has a much greater chance of obtaining an AEC Q clearance than a "secret" clearance from almost any other government agency. (I am personally aware of several cases in which the AEC has granted clearance to persons unable to obtain clearance in other agencies or persons who were discharged on security grounds by other agencies; or cases in which grave security problems were found by other agencies in the backgrounds of persons previously cleared by the AEC with full knowledge of the deragatory information which so troubled the other agencies.[30]

The government spends a substantial amount of money each year on security investigations. According to *The Washington Post*[31] the annual expenses of several departments for this purpose are as follows:

Department of Defense	$45,000,000
Atomic Energy Commission	5,600,000
Civil Service Commission	17,000,000

The cost of a Background Investigation is given by the Civil Service Commission as $350 to $352 during 1962 and 1963,[32] and as $173 by the Department of Defense in 1967.[33] The National Agency Check is estimated to cost the Department of Defense $4.25 in 1967.[34]

Contribution versus Risk

It is curious that security clearance can be denied for any one of approximately twenty reasons, i.e., the security criteria, without considering the

[30] *Ibid.*, p. 14.

[31] Harwood, "There's a Dossier on You," *loc. cit.* This article also reports that the FBI budget included $145,000,000 for security and criminal investigations and that the Internal Revenue Service spends $10,300,000. These probably include the cost of other activities as well as those related to personnel security. The source for the annual expense of the Department of Defense as $45,565,000 in 1967 appears in footnote 33.

[32] *U.S. Personnel Security Practices, op. cit.*, Appendix, Vol. I, "Departmental and Agency Rules and Regulations." Cost accounting for full field investigations, pp. 1149–1173.

[33] Hearings before the subcommittee to investigate the administration of the Internal Security Act and other internal security laws of the Committee on the Judiciary, U.S. Senate on S.2988, Part 5, April 10 and 11, 1968, p. 353.

[34] *Ibid.*

positive technical or administrative contributions the same person might make to classified programs. The individual is judged as a possible risk to security in an over-all common-sense way, based on all the favorable and unfavorable information that is available. This judgment does not ordinarily balance the extent of his contribution against the degree of risk associated with his employment. Exceptions to the security criteria can be granted and undoubtedly the contribution that a man could make is considered in some cases. Green says that "the government has regarded human talent as readily replaceable" and that "only those who can be trusted are in positions in which they have opportunity for access."[35] Again, the AEC security program is unique in that the General Manager, who makes the final determination, balances "the 'cost to the program of losing the services of a person against any possible risks involved.' "[36]

Modification of Criteria for Denying Clearance

The criteria for denying clearance are constantly being modified or changed. The number of reasons for which clearance may be denied has increased with time and there is no evidence that a criterion, once established, has ever been withdrawn. It is true, however, that taken as a whole, these criteria have been applied in a more reasonable manner in recent years.

Thus, in 1966, the Department of Defense added two criteria to the standard for employees in sensitive positions and for the employment of civilian applicants: (1) excessive indebtedness, unexplained affluence, or repetitive absences without leave; and (2) refusal, on constitutional or other grounds, of a person under investigation to answer pertinent questions.[37] The directive also sets forth the rights of employees to a hearing and describes the hearing procedures in more detail than heretofore.

Other critieria, such as the risk of coercion due to relatives in Communist-bloc countries, (the "hostage" criterion), notoriously disgraceful conduct or sexual perversion, and mental illness which might cause a significant defect in judgment or reliability, were added in similar fashion in previous years. It may be surmised that the reason for adding each new criterion is related to newly discovered violations of security not already covered by existing criteria. Since the purpose of the security program is to reduce security risk, it is almost inevitable that the program would grow with each discovery of a new type of risk.

[35] Green, "Q Clearance" *op. cit.*, p. 9.
[36] *Ibid.*, p. 11.
[37] Department of Defense Civilian Applicant and Employee Security Program, DoD Directive 5210.7, September 2, 1966 (with changes through January 31, 1967).

We should address, therefore, the difficult question of whether the various criteria are valid, in the explicit sense that an individual, with behavior as specified in the list, is a risk to security. Although the conduct specified in these criteria may be the basis for denying or revoking a clearance, the criteria are not meant to be applied in an arbitrary manner.

> The conduct varies in implication, degree of seriousness, and significance depending upon all the factors in a particular case. Therefore, the ultimate determination must be an over-all common-sense one based upon all the information which may properly be considered under this Directive including, but not limited to, such factors as the following: the seriousness of the conduct, its implications, its recency, the motivations for it, the extent to which it was voluntary and undertaken with knowledge of the circumstances involved and, to the extent that it can be estimated and is appropriate in a particular case, the probability that it will continue in the future.[38]

Is an individual who has recovered from a serious mental illness a security risk? The issue must be decided by judging whether or not the disorder may recur.

Membership in Communist front organizations is not necessarily a reason for denying clearance, such as when there has not been a continuing, sympathetic association. For example, a child enrolled by a parent in a health plan sponsored by an organization designated as subversive on the Attorney General's List would not necessarily be denied clearance as an adult unless there was evidence of a continuing, sympathetic association. In one case, the DoD reinstated Secret clearance to an industrial employee whose clearance had been suspended for her failure to disclose membership ten years before in two organizations on the Attorney General's List. The Board did not announce the reasons for its decision in favor of the employee.[39] In another case, the DoD sustained clearance for a man who announced publicly that he joined the DuBois Club.[40] The Screening Board concluded that the employee, a research assistant at a university, was not a Communist and that he did not have a sympathetic interest in the Communist movement. Rather, his publicized joining of the DuBois Club was a protest against the Attorney General's action toward having the organization declared a Communist front by the Subversive Activities Control Board, an action he regarded as unwarranted interference with the activities of a political organization. In 1967, the

[38] Industrial Personnel Security Clearance Program, DoD Directive 5220.6, December 7, 1966, amended September 30, 1967, Section VE.

[39] "Government Security and Loyalty Newsletter," The Bureau of National Affairs, Inc., Washington, November 30, 1965.

[40] *Ibid.*, July 31, 1967.

Supreme Court decided that the New York State loyalty procedures (the Feinberg Law) were unconstitutional inasmuch as "mere knowing membership without a specific intent to further the unlawful aims of an organization is not a constitutionally adequate basis for exclusion from such positions as those held by appellants" as instructors at the University of Buffalo, part of the State University of New York.[41] While this case affects employment under a state law and does not involve federal security clearance, federal security procedures attempt to avoid challenges that could be brought to the Supreme Court.

According to the "hostage" criterion, clearance may be denied when:

> The presence of a close relative of the applicant or of the applicant's spouse in a nation whose interests may be inimical to the interests of the United States, or in satellites or occupied areas of such a nation, under circumstances permitting coercion or pressure to be brought on the individual through such relatives which may be likely to cause action contrary to the national interest. The term close relative includes parents, brothers, sisters, offspring and spouse.[42]

In applying the criterion recently, consideration is given to the ties that a citizen from a Communist-bloc country has built up in the U.S., called "counter pressures." These could include length of citizenship status, children born and living here, owning a home, and professional and civic involvements. An attempt is made to evaluate whether the record shows evidence of commitment to the U.S. which could offset an attempt at coercion based on relatives in Communist countries. On studying the actual records of deliberate and unauthorized security violations and of defections to Communist countries, one might well find that fewer men with relatives in the hostage category have been involved than those without such relatives.

The basis for the denial of clearance on account of homosexuality is that a homosexual may be subject to blackmail. Even though homosexuality may be regarded as an illness and not simply as immoral behavior, its practice is regarded as a risk to security. The criterion has been challenged by homosexuals who are prepared publicly to acknowledge their status, claiming thereby that the threat of blackmail does not exist. In an attempt to establish a precedent, the Mattachine Society of Washington, a group of homosexuals, is supporting the case of an industrial employee who faces the revocation of his clearance on account of possible coercion due

[41] Keyishian, et al. v. Board of Regents of the University of the State of New York, U.S. Supreme Court, No. 105, January 23, 1967.

[42] Industrial Personnel Clearance Programs, DoD Directive 5220.6, December 7, 1966, amended September 30, 1967, Section VI S.

to homosexuality.[43] The individual admits he is a homosexual. It is not known how many individuals have lost their clearance because it was claimed they were homosexuals.

In 1966, the Civil Service Commission set forth its policy with respect to the suitability of homosexuals for federal *employment* as distinct from *security clearance.* According to the Commission, the applicable considerations

> . . . encompass the types of deviate sexual behavior engaged in, whether isolated, intermittent, or continuing acts, the age of the particular participants, the extent of promiscuity, the aggressive or passive character of the individual's participation, the recency of the incidents, the presence of physical, mental, emotional, or nervous causes, the influence of drugs, alcohol or other contributing factors, the public or private character of the acts, the incidence of arrests, convictions, or of public offense, nuisance or breach of the peace related to the acts, the notoriety, if any, of the participants, the extent or effect of rehabilitative efforts, if any, and the admitted acceptance of, or preference for homosexual relations . . .

John W. Macy, Jr., Chairman of the Civil Service Commission at that time, stated:

> We know of no means, consistent with American notions of privacy and fairness, and limitations on governmental authority, which would ascertain the nature of individual private sexual behavior between consenting adults. As long as it remains truly private, that is, it remains undisclosed to all but the participants, it is not the subject of an inquiry. Each case is to be decided on its own individual merits, is . . . reviewed by a panel of three high level, mature, experienced employees . . . , and is subject to further administrative review within the Commission.[44]

As part of the President's national campaign against crime, the Civil Service Commission has established a new policy to accept employment applications from former criminals who are judged to be good risks.[45] In addition, the federal employment form was modified so that arrests no longer have to be reported; convictions or forfeit of collateral must still be reported. Traffic violations involving a fine of $30 or less and any offense committed before age twenty-one also need not be reported. Previously the exclusion had been at age sixteen. Note, again, that the change in criterion relates to employment rather than to security clearance. It is

[43] "Homosexual Fights Rule in Security Clearance," *The New York Times,* November 26, 1967, p. 70.

[44] "Government Security and Loyalty Newsletter," *op. cit.,* September 30, 1966.

[45] Policies and Procedures Relating to the Federal Employment of Persons with Criminal Records, FPM Letter No. 731–2, U.S. Civil Service Commission, Washington, August 15, 1966.

included to show that criteria dealing with personnel policies change in time.

PRIVACY OF INFORMATION IN DOSSIERS

The files of many private and local public agencies are readily available to personnel security investigators. Thus, information from police departments, courts, hospitals, schools, and credit bureaus finds its way into the federal dossiers. There is, in addition, the data from personal interviews and reference checks. It is a striking fact that so much private and personal information can flow into the hands of the government and that, on the whole, the confidentiality of this vast hoard of information has been maintained. There is little evidence that this information has been used in an unauthorized manner and few transgressions come to public attention.[46] The importance of protecting these records is probably due to standards established by the Federal Bureau of Investigation, whose procedures are generally followed by other investigative agencies. Even though it may be disingenuous to say so, there is little basis in fact to argue that the investigative agencies of the government have not properly protected the privacy of information in their files.

Although security investigations probe rather deeply into a candidate's life, there are certain limits beyond which they may not go. Investigators are instructed specifically not to inquire into an applicant's opinions about religious beliefs and affiliations, racial matters, political candidates or parties other than those of a subversive nature, and the constitutionality or wisdom of legislative policies.[47] These instructions provide some evidence of the changes which have taken place since the 1950's.

Where mental instability may be a factor, it has been found that some (but not all) physicians and mental institutions will not release their records without the written consent of the individual. In such circumstances, the investigative agency must request the subject to sign a form authorizing the release of his medical records, but it cannot force the subject to do so. Suppose, however, that the matter is so serious that the review agency recommends that clearance be denied and the Screening

[46] The unauthorized disclosure of private information appears to have occurred concerning District Attorney Jim Garrison of New Orleans in 1967 and George C. Wallace, ex-Governor of Alabama, during the Presidential campaign of 1968. In each case, newspaper reports said that medical records on these men contained evidence of mental disorder during their military service. The disclosure of such information is clearly improper even though it did not involve a security investigation.

[47] *Civil and Private Rights,* Memorandum for The Under Secretary of the Army, The Under Secretary of the Navy, and The Under Secretary of the Air Force, from the Deputy Assistant Secretary of Defense, Security Policy, November 26, 1962, in *Government Security and Loyalty, op. cit.,* pp. 25, 409–411. See also Industrial Personnel Security Clearance Program, DoD Directive 5220.6, December 7, 1966, Section VC.

Board issues a Statement of Reasons to the subject (as in the case of industrial security). At a hearing, "the examiner may require the applicant to respond to relevant questions, to undergo a medical examination, or to authorize the release of relevant information in the possession of other parties."[48] Any refusal to furnish or to authorize the furnishing of relevant information, on constitutional or other grounds, will lead to discontinuing the review procedure as well as the suspension of any clearance that may be held.[49]

In May, 1968, a change in the procedure of filling out the Personnel Security Questionnaire made it possible for an employee to provide certain private information to the government without making it available to his employer. Previously, this had not been possible. The private information includes:

Arrest records
Type of discharge from military service
Prior security clearance suspension, denial, or revocation
History of mental or nervous disorders
Drug addiction
Excessive use of alcohol
Membership in organizations cited by the Attorney General

The employer reviews the partially completed form and returns it to the employee who then answers the private questions (at the end of the form) and places it in an envelope which he seals and signs. Privacy is maintained, via sealed envelopes, if the form is returned for correction or for additional information. The new form (DD Form 49, January 1, 1968) is a triumph of the art of paper work. The packet is about 42 inches long, and actually contains three different forms as well as four long and five short carbon sheets. Thus, one typing produces five copies of the Personnel Security Questionnaire (Industrial) (Multiple Purpose) (DD Form 49), three copies of the National Agency Check Request (DD Form 1584) and two copies of the Personnel Security Questionnaire (Industrial) (DSA Form 705). No questions have been added or deleted from equivalent previous forms. The new procedure insures the right of privacy on privileged or personal matters not previously available.[50]

[48] Industrial Personnel Security Clearance Program, DoD Directive, No. 5220.6, December 7, 1966, amended September 30, 1967, Sec. VIII C 5.
[49] *Ibid.*, Section VB.
[50] An excellent discussion of the balance between the right of privacy and the need for public disclosure may be found in Westin, Alan F., *Privacy and Freedom*, New York, Atheneum, 1967.

Concluding Comment

Inevitably, the "ultimate" security determination, is made by a process which relies entirely on human judgment, which operates in a quasi-legal manner, and which is expressed finally as a majority vote. Recognizing the problem it is supposed to deal with, personnel security investigations appear to be a necessary, although perhaps burdensome, aspect of our national security program. Standards assuring fair and reasonable treatment of applicants for security clearance have long been a part of the administrative regulations. In recent years, these regulations have been respected reasonably well.

Except for the AEC, insufficient data have been published on which to base a reliable over-all judgment on the operation of personnel clearance programs. The AEC conducted 716,695 full field investigations during the period 1947 to 1963. In this total, 1.3 per cent (9,528) of these cases involved substantially derogatory information; about one-half (5,026) of the latter cases (or 0.7 per cent of the total) were withdrawn prior to final judgment; 546 cases (0.08 per cent of the total) were denied clearance while the remainder (3,958 or 42 per cent) of the cases with substantially derogatory information received clearance. Thus, this record shows that few applicants are denied clearance. Although the data on other security programs involving 7,000,000 investigations are incomplete, they lead to about the same conclusion.

However, the personnel security program does operate at a cost. Among the known costs are those of the investigations themselves, i.e., about $4 for a National Agency check and from $175 to $350 for a Background Investigation (the estimates vary). The unknown costs, which can not be measured easily, if at all, would include lost productive time of individuals waiting for a clearance, the lost services of individuals who avoid employment requiring a security clearance, and the denial of employment to individuals who should have been cleared. People may not wish to be investigated for various reasons, such as a belief that they would not be cleared (the belief may derive from ignorance or fact, and perhaps an inability to wait for the process to be completed) or simply an unwillingness, based on conscience, to accept the attendant invasion of privacy. No one knows what the total costs of the personnel security system may be, but they surely exist.

Finally, there are several issues raised by a security program. First, there is no absolute right to employment. All manner of qualifications for employment may be found in every daily newspaper and announcements of the Civil Service Commission. Second, employment in a sensitive position is not an absolute right independent of standards of suitability and security. Third, there is a need to restore the balance between the individual's right to privacy and the need for information to pursue the substantive tasks of government.[51] Surely, a similar balance should apply to personnel security.

[51] Westin, *Privacy and Freedom, op. cit.*

APPENDIX A

Department of Defense
Standard and Criteria For Employment in a Sensitive Position[1]

A. *Standard*
The standard for employment and retention in employment is that, based on all the available information, the employment or retention in employment of an individual is clearly consistent with the interests of national security.

B. *Criteria for the Application of Standard*
In the application of the above standard, consideration will be given to, but not limited to, the following activities and associations, whether current or past. As the following activities and associations are of varying degrees of seriousness, the ultimate determination must be made on the basis of an over-all common-sense evaluation of all the information in a particular case.

1. Depending on the relation of the employment to the national security:
    a. *Unreliability.*[2] Any behavior, activities, or associations which tend to show that the individual is not reliable or trustworthy.
    b. *Misrepresentation.* Any deliberate misrepresentations, falsifications, or omissions of material facts.
    c. *Disgraceful conduct, intoxicants, drugs, perversion.* Any criminal, infamous, dishonest, immoral, or notoriously disgraceful conduct, habitual use of intoxicants to excess, drug addiction, or sexual perversion.
    d. *Mental instability, disqualifying illness.* Any illness, including any mental condition, of a nature which in the opinion of competent medical authority may cause significant defect in the judgment or reliability of the employee, with due regard to the transient or continuing effect of the illness and the medical findings in such case.

[1] Department of Defense Civilian Applicant and Employee Security Program, Department of Defense Directive 5210.7, September 2, 1966, Section VIII; Industrial Personnel Security Clearance Program, Department of Defense Directive 5220.6, December 7, 1966, amended September 30, 1967.

[2] The italicized headings in paragraphs 1 to 20 inclusive do not appear in the original text and have been added for clarity of presentation.

e. *Susceptibility to coercion.* Any facts which furnish reason to believe that the individual may be subjected to coercion, influence, or pressure which may cause him to act contrary to the best interests of the national security.

2. *Sabotage, espionage, treason, sedition.* Commission of any act of sabotage, espionage, treason, or sedition, or conspiring, aiding, or abetting another to commit or attempt to commit any act of sabotage, espionage, treason, or sedition.
3. *Sympathetic association with secret agents.* Establishing or continuing a sympathetic association with a saboteur, spy, traitor, seditionist, anarchist, or with an espionage or other secret agent or representative of a foreign nation, or any representative of a foreign nation whose interests may be inimical to the interests of the United States, or with any person who advocates the use of force or violence to overthrow the Government of the United States or the alteration of the form of Government of the United States by unconstitutional means.
4. *Advocacy of force to overthrow the United States Government.* Advocacy of use of force or violence to overthrow the Government of the United States, or of the alteration of the form of Government of the United States by unconstitutional means.
5. *Membership in or sympathetic association with subversive organizations.* Membership in, affiliation or sympathetic association with, any foreign or domestic organization, association, movement, group or combination of persons which is totalitarian, Fascist, Communist, or subversive, or which had adopted, or shows a policy of advocating or approving the commission of acts of force or violence to deny other persons their rights under the Constitution of the United States, or which seeks to alter the form of Government of the United States by unconstitutional means. (These include, but are not limited to, those organizations, movements, or groups officially designated by the Attorney General of the United States pursuant to Executive Order 10450.)
6. *Unauthorized disclosure of classified information.* Intentional, unauthorized disclosure to any person of classified information, or of other information, disclosure of which is prohibited by law.
7. *Serving the interest of another government.* Performing or attempting to perform his duties, or otherwise acting, so as to serve the interests of another government in preference to the interests of the United States.
8. *Sympathetic participation in front organizations.* Participation in the activities of an organization established as a front for an organization referred to in paragraph VIII.B.5 above, when his personal views were sympathetic to the subversive purposes of such organization. (See Internal Security Act of 1950, as amended (50 U.S. Code 782), reference (f), for a definition of Communist-front organizations).
9. *Sympathetic participation in infiltrated organizations.* Participation in the activities of an organization with knowledge that it had been infiltrated by members of subversive groups under circumstances indi-

cating that the individual was part of, or sympathetic to, the infiltrating element or sympathetic to its purposes.

10. *Knowing participation in subversive organization.* Participating in the activities of an organization, referred to in paragraph VIII.B.5, above, in a capacity where he would reasonably have had knowledge of the subversive aims or purposes of the organization.
11. *Sympathetic interest in subversive movements.* Sympathetic interest in totalitarian, Fascist, Communist, or similar subversive movements.
12. *Sympathetic association with members of subversive organizations.* Sympathetic association with a member or members of an organization referred to in paragraph VIII.B.5 above. (Ordinarily, this will not include chance or occasional meetings, nor contacts limited to normal business or official relations.)
13. *Close, continuing association with subversives.* Currently maintaining a close, continuing association with a person who has engaged in activities or associations of the type referred to in paragraph VIII.B.2 through paragraph VIII.B.11 above. A close continuing association may be deemed to exist if the individual lives with, frequently visits, or frequently communicates with, such person.
14. *Risk of renewing a previous close continuing association with subversives.* Close continuing association of the type described in paragraph VIII.B.13 above, even though later separated by distance, if the circumstances indicate that renewal of the association is probable.
15. *Hostage risk: relatives in Communist-bloc countries.* The presence of a spouse, parent, brother, sister, offspring, or any person with whom a close bond of affection exists in a nation whose interests may be inimical to the interest of the United States or in satellites or occupied areas of such a nation, under circumstances permitting coercion or pressure to be brought on the individual through such persons.
16. *Willful violation of security regulations.* Willful violation or disregard of security regulations.
17. *Poor judgment and instability.* Acts of a reckless, irresponsible, or wanton nature which indicate such poor judgment and instability as to suggest that the individual might disclose classified defense information to unauthorized persons, or otherwise assist such persons, whether deliberately or inadvertently, in activities inimical to the security of the United States.
18. *Claim of privilege against self-incrimination on charges related to security.* Refusal by the individual, upon the ground of constitutional privilege against self-incrimination, to testify before a congressional committee or Federal or State Court, regarding charges of his alleged disloyalty or other misconduct relevant to his security eligibility.
19. *Excessive indebtedness, unexplained affluence.* Any excessive indebtedness, recurring financial difficulties, unexplained affluence, or repetitive absence without leave, which furnish reason to believe that the individual may act contrary to the best interests of national security.

20. *Refusal to complete required security forms or to answer in security hearings.* Refusal by the individual on constitutional or other grounds, or intentional failure to complete required security forms or personal history statements, or otherwise failing or refusing, in the course of investigation, interrogation, or hearing, to answer any pertinent question regarding the matters described in paragraph VIII.B.1 through paragraph VIII.B.19 above.

APPENDIX B

National Agency Check

The description of the National Agency Check (NAC) which appears below is taken from Hearings on *U.S. Personnel Security Practices.*[1] In addition to the NAC, some agencies also send written inquiries to law enforcement agencies, former employees and supervisors, references and schools. If the individual has traveled or lived in a foreign country, the State Department records will be checked. The NAC with written inquiries is called "NACI" or "NAC plus WI."

A. *Components of a National Agency Check.* A National Agency Check consists of a check with the following agencies, as indicated, for pertinent facts having a bearing on the loyalty and truthworthiness of the individual:
   1. *Federal Bureau of Investigation (FBI).* The FBI headquarters criminal and subversive files will be checked in every case. A properly completed non-criminal type fingerprint chart will be submitted with each request.
   2. *Assistant Chief of Staff, Intelligence, Department of the Army (ACSI).* Will be checked when the individual is or has been in the Army or a civilian employee of the Department of the Army.
   3. *Office of Naval Intelligence, Department of the Navy (ONI).* Will be checked when the individual is or has been in the Navy, Marine Corps, or Merchant Marine, or a civilian employee of such agencies. (In the case of Coast Guard personnel, or personnel with Merchant Marine background, the files of the U.S. Coast Guard will also be checked.)
   4. *Office of Special Investigations, The Inspector General, USAF, Department of the Air Force (OSI).* Will be checked when the individual is or has been in the Air Force or a civilian employee of the Department of the Air Force.
   5. *Civil Service Commission (CSC).* Will be checked in all cases where the individual is or has been an employee of the United States Government.

[1] *U.S. Personnel Security Practices,* Hearings Before the Subcommittee to Investigate the Administration of the Internal Security Act and other Internal Security Laws of the Committee of the Judiciary, United States Senate, Eighty-eighth Congress, First Session, Appendix, vol. I, "Departmental and Agency Rules and Regulations," Government Printing Office, Washington, 1963.

6. *Immigration and Naturalization Service (I&NS).* Will be checked in all cases in which the individual is an alien in the United States, an immigrant alien, or naturalized citizen.
7. *House Committee on Un-American Activities (HCUA).* Will be checked when pertinent to the inquiry.
8. *Central Index Personnel and Facility Security File (Operated by the Department of the Army).* Will be checked when the Personal History Statement or other available information concerning the individual indicates that he is, or has been, an officer, owner, or employee of a firm which has, or has had, a Department of Defense classified contract.
9. *Other Agencies.* Will be checked when pertinent to the purpose for which the investigation is being conducted. Investigative agencies concerned will determine when such other agencies should be checked.

B. *Extension of Inquiry.* In the event derogatory or questionable information concerning an individual is disclosed by a National Agency Check, the inquiry will be extended as necessary to obtain such additional information as may be required to substantiate or disprove the information.

APPENDIX C

Background Investigation

The description of a Background Investigation which follows appears in *U.S. Personnel Security Practices.*[1]

A. *Scope of a Background Investigation.* A Background Investigation which is conducted for clearance purposes is designed to develop information as to whether the access to classified material by the person being investigated is clearly consistent with the interests of national security. It shall make inquiry into the pertinent facts bearing on the loyalty and trustworthiness of the individual. It will normally cover the period of his life during the fifteen-year period immediately preceding the investigation or from the date of his eighteenth (18th) birthday, whichever is the shorter period, unless:
   1. Derogatory information is developed in the course of the investigation, in which event the investigation will be extended to any period of the individual's life necessary to substantiate or disprove the information or, unless
   2. Additional investigation is specifically required by competent authority.

B. *Referral to Federal Bureau of Investigation (FBI).* In the event that derogatory information is developed concerning civilians which relates to any of

[1] *U.S. Personnel Security Practices,* Hearings Before the Subcommittee to Investigate the Administration of the Internal Security Act and Other Internal Security Laws of the Committee of the Judiciary, United States Senate, Eighty-eighth Congress, First Session, Appendix, vol. I, "Departmental and Agency Rules and Regulations," Government Printing Office, Washington, 1963.

the activities described in Section V.A.1. through 15, it shall be referred immediately to the FBI.

C. *Components of a Background Investigation:*

1. *National Agency Check.*
2. *Birth Records.* The individual's date and place of birth will be verified through school, employment or other records examined during other investigations. Only if a discrepancy appears will it be necessary to examine vital statistics and other records to establish the individual's date and place of birth.
3. *Education.* Attendance at last secondary school, in the absence of college attendance, if within the last fifteen years will be verified. Results of attendance at Service schools will, as a rule, appear in the individual's service record and need not be confirmed. In addition to examining school records, persons in a position to know the individual's activities while in attendance should be interviewed, if available.
4. *Employment.* The records of present and former employers for the immediately preceding fifteen-year period or since the individual's eighteenth (18th) birthday, whichever involves the shorter period, will be examined to verify the period of employment and efficiency record. Former employers and co-workers will be interviewed, if available, to ascertain the loyalty, character, and reputation of the individual.
5. *References and Other Sources.* References will be interviewed. Interviews will also be had with persons (not relatives or former employers) who have knowledge of the individual's background and activities, but who are not given as references by the individual.
6. *Neighborhood Investigations.* These investigations will be conducted when deemed necessary or expedient in substantiating or disproving derogatory information.
7. *Criminal Record.* The records of police departments and other law enforcement agencies in the vicinities where the individual has resided or been employed for substantial periods of time will be checked whenever considered appropriate, or if information developed from a National Agency Check is not considered adequate. The records of local FBI offices need not be checked unless special circumstances warrant.
8. *Military Service.* The service of the individual in the armed forces and type of discharge will be verified.
9. *Foreign Connections.* Any connections the individual has had with foreigners or with foreign organizations in the United States or abroad will be reported. The extent and purpose of any such connections will be ascertained as well as the relationship of the individual to such persons or organizations.
10. *Citizenship Status.* In all cases the citizenship status of the individual will be established.
    a. *United States Citizens.* (See 2 above).
    b. *Immigrant Aliens.* The records of the Immigration and Naturalization Service will be searched to verify date and place of birth, legal entry into the United States, and to ascertain whether the

individual has indicated an intention to become a citizen of the United States.

c. *Naturalized Citizens.* The naturalization and date and place of birth will be verified through records of the appropriate U.S. District Court. If the place of naturalization cannot be determined, I&NS Records, Washington, D.C., will be examined.

11. *Foreign Travel.* If the individual has traveled outside the United States during the immediately preceding fifteen-year period, except in military or naval service, the Department of State records will be checked to determine reasons for such travel. If such travel occurred after 1 July 1946, records of the Central Intelligence Agency (CIA) will also be checked.

12. *Credit Record.* Whenever necessary, credit agencies and/or credit references will be contacted in those places where the individual has resided for substantial periods of time during the immediately preceding fifteen-year period or since the individual's eighteenth (18th) birthday, whichever is the shorter period.

13. *Organizations.* During the course of the investigation, as set forth above and by examination of personal history statements and other records examined, efforts will be made to determine if the individual had:

    "Membership in, or affiliation or sympathetic association with, any foreign or domestic organization, association, movement, group, or combination of persons which is totalitarian, Fascist, Communist, or subversive, or which has adopted, or shows, a policy of advocating or approving the commission of acts of force or violence to deny other persons their rights under the Constitution of the United States, or which seeks to alter the form of government of the United States by unconstitutional means." (Section 8(a) (5), Executive Order 10450).

V *Welfare Institutions*

11 Record-Keeping and the Intake Process in a Public Welfare Agency

DON H. ZIMMERMAN

WELFARE INSTITUTIONS EXIST TO PROVIDE ASSISTANCE TO THOSE IN NEED—the aged, the young, the ill, the disabled. But before any assistance can be given, especially where public money is involved, the need must be established. A case must be built to justify the decision of the agency, whether it is to provide the applicant with all the aid he requests, some portion of it, or to deny it to him. In short, the applicant must be shown to meet the eligibility requirements of the program in question.

This chapter examines the way in which one welfare agency is organized to accomplish this task. The Lakeside Office, as it will be called here, is one of several district offices of a Bureau of Public Assistance located in a metropolitan county of a large western state. The specific focus of this chapter is on the record-keeping practices of the Lakeside Office from the time of initial contact between the applicant for aid and the agency,

Certain of the materials presented here were drawn from the author's unpublished Ph.D. dissertation, "Paper Work and People Work: A Study of a Public Assistance Agency," University of California, Los Angeles, 1966. Research funds contributing to the present work were provided by the Committee on Research, University of California, Santa Barbara, and by the Russell Sage Foundation. A number of people supplied valuable suggestions and needed encouragement in generous amounts. The author wishes to thank, and absolve from any responsibility, Lindsey Churchill, Melvin Pollner, Stanton Wheeler, D. Lawrence Wieder, Thomas P. Wilson, and Siu Zimmerman.

through the process of documentation and investigation of the client, to the eligibility decision.

Description, if it is to be coherent, requires some guiding concern; if it is undertaken at all, it usually serves some general interest. Records and record-keeping processes are rarely the main focus of organizational research, though they have figured in accounts of the relationship between the formal plan of the organization and its implementation in day-to-day work activities.[1] Concern for the record-keeping process of organizations has emerged as an integral element of "labeling theory" in the study of deviance.[2] The impetus for the study of "rate-producing processes" as phenomena in their own right may be found in Garfinkel's work,[3] which provides the fundamental resources behind this inquiry. Social scientists have also been concerned with the records generated by bureaucratic organizations as potential data. This interest is best exemplified by the issue of the adequacy of criminal statistics.[4] More general concerns of this nature may be found in Bauer[5] and Webb *et al.*[6] The present volume, of course, testifies to interest in the topic of record-keeping extending beyond the areas mentioned above.

The descriptive effort in this chapter has a somewhat different general concern, pointed up by an incident reported by an intake caseworker at Lakeside to her fellow workers. An applicant told her that she could not find the citizenship papers that were to be used to verify age—an important issue in determining her eligibility for assistance. The applicant went on to say that at one time she had copied her birthdate on a piece of paper, and then handed the paper to the worker. The caseworkers greeted the story with laughter.

As this incident suggests, not any piece of paper will serve to establish objective and factual grounds for administrative action. What is it that confers upon a particular piece of paper its authority for the determina-

[1] See, for example, Blau, Peter M., *The Dynamics of Bureaucracy*, University of Chicago Press, Chicago, 1962, esp. chap. 3; Francis, Roy G., and Robert C. Stone, *Service and Procedure in Bureaucracy*, University of Minnesota Press, Minneapolis, 1956, esp. chap. 7; and Cohen, Harry, *The Demonics of Bureaucracy*, Iowa State University Press, Ames, 1965.

[2] See, for example, Kitsuse, John I., and Aaron V. Cicourel, "A Note on the Use of Official Statistics," *Social Problems*, vol. II (Fall, 1963), pp. 131–139; Sudnow, David, "Normal Crimes: Sociological Features of the Penal Code in a Public Defender Office," *Social Problems*, vol. 12 (Winter, 1965), pp. 255–276; and Cicourel, Aaron V., *The Social Organization of Juvenile Justice*, Wiley, New York, 1968.

[3] See Garfinkel, Harold, *Studies in Enthnomethodology*, Wiley, New York, 1967.

[4] Sellin, Thorstein, "The Significance of Records of Crime," *The Law Quarterly Review*, vol. 67 (Fall, 1951), pp. 489–504; Wheeler, Stanton, "Criminal Statistics: A Reformulation of the Problem," *The Journal of Criminal Law, Criminology, and Police Science*, vol. 58, no. 3 (1967), pp. 317–324.

[5] Bauer, Raymond A., editor, *Social Indicators*, The MIT Press, Cambridge, 1967.

[6] Webb, Eugene J. *et al.*, *Unobtrusive Measures: Nonreactive Research in the Social Sciences*, Rand McNally, Chicago, 1966.

tion of matters of fact? How do such records achieve the authority of objective and impersonal accounts of persons' lives? What features give them currency, i.e., permit their utilization in varied contexts distinct from the special purposes for which they were originated?

It is an interest in these questions that motivates this chapter. The detailed account of the intake process provided here is undertaken in the belief that these issues can be illuminated by close examination of the daily round of work in a bureaucratic setting. The descriptive materials developed below are addressed by putting aside any preconceptions concerning the nature of factual and objective reporting in order to learn how reports displaying such properties are generated. The setting is characterized, first, by the routine collection, production, and use of records; and second, by the way in which the factuality, objectivity, and impersonality of the information contained in those records is an everyday, practical concern, and an everyday, practical accomplishment.

This choice of a focal point of inquiry necessarily means that issues critically relevant to other types of inquiry into welfare records will be slighted. We have not detailed, for example, the problem of access to the records by other persons or agencies; nor do we comment upon the specific record-keeping problems surrounding the withdrawal of eligibility from those who have had it in the past. These matters and many others are appropriate topics for research on record-keeping. But whatever the use or misuse of records, they attain their significance largely because they are regarded as official, authoritative accounts. It is the purpose of this chapter to show how they achieve this status in the setting of their production and use.

THE SETTING AND ITS TASKS

As necessary background to an examination of the Lakeside Office, this section presents a brief description of the legislative foundation of public welfare institutions, certain details of eligibility criteria, a description of the organizational structure of the Bureau and the Lakeside Office, and a brief review of the way in which the study was conducted. Concluding this section is a sketch of the intake process, including an initial discussion of the function of record-keeping in the organization.

The Social Security Act and State Public Assistance Programs

The Social Security Act, enacted August 14, 1935, with subsequent amendments, is the legislative basis and chief impetus of the present public assistance programs operated by state, territorial, and commonwealth jurisdictions. Titles I, IV, X, XIV, and XVI define, in general terms, categories of "needy" individuals. These titles authorize federal grants-in-aid to the states to assist in and encourage provision of financial aid and social services to the categories of people thus defined. In program terms, these titles refer to Old-Age Assistance (OAA); Aid to Families with Dependent Children (AFDC); Aid to the Blind (AB); Aid to the Permanently and Totally Disabled (APTD); and Medical Assistance for the Aged (MAA). The term "categoric" distinguishes assistance programs under the various titles of the Act from a "residual" program operated and financed on the local level, variously called "General Relief," "General Assistance," or "Indigent Aid." This program, which makes provision for certain persons not eligible under the categoric aids, will be referred to henceforth as "General Relief" or GR.

Eligibility

The Social Security Act specifies certain general conditions for federal grants-in-aid to the states. The states determine definitions of need, eligibility, and amount of assistance, usually by means of a Welfare Code enacted by the legislature. As a consequence, the definition of these requirements and the method of verification vary considerably between states and between categories.

Verification of need and eligibility, in the language of public assistance, involves a "means test." What is "tested" is the applicant's status vis-à-vis a set of "eligibility factors" specified for the particular category of aid by the State Welfare Code. In general, these factors are: age, residence, real property, personal property, transfer of property, responsible relatives, employment, and deprivation. The investigation through which the "means test" is accomplished is the responsibility of the intake caseworker at Lakeside and the other district offices.

An example will be helpful here. The specification of these factors for the OAA program in Western State, and thus in Metropolitan County and Lakeside Office, are that eligible applicants be sixty-five years or older prior to the receipt of assistance, that they have lived a specified number of years in the state, that real property not being utilized as a home not exceed a set maximum assessed valuation, that they possess no more than a modest amount of personal property (cash, stocks, bonds, etc.), that they have not voluntarily transferred any property (real or personal) to another person in order to qualify for assistance, and that a financially able spouse or adult children residing within the state be required to contribute support.

The factor of employability does not bear upon eligibility for OAA. However, if the applicant is employed, income from employment may render her "non-needy" relative to the maximum cash grant allowable on this program. For the person applying on behalf of a needy child on the AFDC program, employability and demonstrated motivation to seek, accept, and sustain employment may be a factor under certain conditions. The factor of deprivation pertains to the AFDC program alone, and designates the set of circumstances (e.g., desertion or death of a parent) whereby minor children come to be deprived of "adequate support."

County and District Office Organization

The particular administrative structure adopted by the state may further increase local autonomy by delegating to the counties the administrative control over the actual operation of the assistance programs, under state supervision. In Western State, the actual day-to-day operation is delegated by the Welfare Code to the individual counties. This responsibility is vested in the County Board of Supervisors.

Although not specifically mandated by the Western State Welfare Code, the counties of the state have each established an agency (Bureau of Public Assistance) which administers the receipt, processing, and disposition of applications for assistance.

Persons seeking assistance come into or are referred to the district office responsible for the particular section of the county in which they reside. In the smaller counties, temporary suboffices may be located in fire stations and other public buildings. There were a relatively large number of permanent district offices in the county in which Lakeside was located, each under the charge of a District Director.

The Lakeside Office

The Lakeside Office was located in a three-story building of moderate size, which housed the 263 administrators, supervisors, social caseworkers, and clerks of the district office staff. Working on the first floor were the 75 personnel responsible for intake, reception, and related functions. Located on the second floor were the 119 personnel charged with the management of "approved" caseloads, i.e., cases approved by intake and receiving assistance. Housed on the third floor were 69 clerical personnel.

As indicated earlier, the major focus of the author's field work was the intake unit. The intake unit in Lakeside consisted of a supervisor and, usually, five social caseworkers and a unit clerk. At the time of the study, there were eight intake units consisting of eight supervisors, eight unit clerks, and 39 caseworkers, a total of 55 personnel. The author divided his effort equally between three units, and made detailed observations of the work routine of three supervisors, three clerks, and 14 workers. More casual observation and interaction took place with the remaining five supervisors and a portion of the remaining workers. In addition, the research focused on the operation of the reception function, which was intimately tied to the work of intake.

The Intake Caseworker's Task

In broad outline, the intake caseworker's task is to assemble and assess information pertaining to the set of eligibility factors specified for the particular program of assistance in question. The intake interview is usually the worker's first contact with a new applicant. Subsequently, she will call upon the applicant in her home and in some cases, see the applicant again in the office. In the initial interview, and over the course of the investigation, the applicant's "story" unfolds. The story presents, from the applicant's point of view, the relevant facts about herself and her circumstances which have led to her obvious and pressing need for assistance (given the facts as she has depicted them).

To be counted as doing an acceptable job by her supervisor, the worker must treat the applicant's story as no more than a loosely organized and unprocessed collection of *claims* lacking evidential value as such for the issue of eligibility. In short, the applicant's report of her standing vis-à-vis the factors of eligibility cannot, for the most part, be taken at face value. Nor, for that matter, can the worker's unsupported opinions serve as grounds for decision.

It should be noted that the information stated and sworn to by the applicant, while not sufficient for the most part to establish eligibility without corroborating evidence, is sufficient to establish *in*eligibility. It is critical for subsequent discussion to point out why this is so. As will be indicated later, the applicant is presumed to have an overriding interest in being found eligible for assistance. Therefore, anything the applicant reports about her circumstances is treated as though it is designed to maximize the chances of securing approval of the claim (including the making of fraudulent statements). Hence, any statement made which, on the face of it, demonstrates ineligibility is accepted without corroboration. The applicant is not assumed to be motivated to make false statements damaging to her own interests.

To approve an application for assistance, evidence must be marshaled showing that eligibility and need criteria have been satisfied. Documents such as birth certificates, bank statements, medical records, and similar "official reports" bearing upon age, financial resources, state of health, and other factors furnish such evidence.

The applicant's dossier—called a "case record" in the Bureau—is a collection of such documents and a case narrative dictated by the worker reporting relevant transactions with the applicant. The narrative also interprets the significance of the assembled documents for the issue of eligibility. For those who know how to read it, the case record provides the required bureaucratic transformation of the applicant's story into an objective and factual account in terms of which official action can be warranted.

This transformation involves two related tasks: (1) making the relevant details of the applicant's life-in-society available for reconstruction in terms of eligibility factors; and (2) making the course of investigation-in-the-organization whereby (1) is accomplished available for reconstruction in terms of legitimate organization procedures. The case record serves as a composite document providing the chief focus of such reconstructions, e.g., it is consulted on the matter of procedural adequacy, and it furnishes a statement of the grounds upon which the decision was reached to approve or deny the case. Workers look to it to fashion a history of the applicant's contact with the Bureau, descriptions of her circumstances, assessments of her character, motivation, problems, and so on. The question is how the reconstruction accomplished by use of the case record provides ways of "looking again" at a preceding course of action—the intake investigation—and at the object of that investigation—the applicant's life-in-the-society—whenever a question arises requiring an authoritative answer.

The process of assembling a case record proceeds over a series of steps, each one informing the preceding. For reception and casework personnel alike, these steps are features of ordinary work practice which they make happen as observable events over a variety of occasions of concerted work, mutual instruction, discussion, and dispute. The way they are made to happen as observable events is a feature of the work of reconstruction. In order to display that work, it is necessary that these steps be described in some detail.

RECEPTION

The applicant approaching the reception counter seeking public funds to assist in the management of her personal affairs is at the threshold of a process. This process makes of her affairs a "case," and of her, a "client." This section examines first, the initial steps of this process and the ways in which this process provides resources for the reconstruction of the organization's treatment of the applicant.[7]

The Steps in the Reception Process

First Contact. The names of persons coming to the reception counter, and the business bringing them into the office, are entered in a "control ledger" maintained by date and time of entry. The entries in this ledger are treated as accountable matters. For example, in the case of persons seeking employment, the time at which they were called for an employment interview is entered in the ledger. For applicants, the time at which they were assigned to an intake worker is recorded. The screening performed by receptionists[8] generates a record of the screening operation and the disposition of the person screened. The twin entries in this ledger mark the beginning and ending phases of reception responsibility in the preprocessing of cases.

The entries in this ledger are preserved by reception because, as receptionists see it, it might become important at some future time that a particular person was in the office on a certain date, at a certain time, and was dealt with in a particular way. They take it that they must be able to provide a basis for demonstrating—when demonstration is called for—that they have conducted organizational affairs in an impersonal, objective, and efficient manner. They may be requested to do so by some individual or by some agency entitled to make such a demand. For example, the Metropolitan County Bureau of Public Assistance is subject to review by the State Department of Welfare for its administration of the categoric aid programs because these are funded by the state and federal governments. Appeal procedures exist in which the Bureau may be called to account for the procedural adequacy of its treatment of an applicant. In the experience of personnel, the Bureau, as a public bureaucracy, is vulnerable to the criticisms leveled at welfare programs and their handling by the press and public officials. (Some in the setting suspected the author of being either a "trouble-shooter" from the State Welfare Department, or an undercover newsman preparing an exposé.) As a setting for research, personnel are called upon to answer the demands of re-

[7] The analysis of the reception function reported here has been guided by Garfinkel's discussion of the reflexivity of accounts. See Garfinkel, *op. cit.*, especially chaps. 1 and 6.

[8] At Lakeside, there were two "regular" receptionists, i.e., employees whose duty it is to staff the reception counter. In addition, there is a third person, a clerk, who was routinely called upon to help at times of peak work load. Two other personnel performed tasks related to the reception function, but did not deal directly with applicants.

searchers in social welfare, sociology, and other disciplines for an account of its practices. In short, the adequacy of the Bureau's operation is, most of the time at least, an issue for *someone*.

With respect to whatsoever issue might arise in the future, e.g., at some point in the processing of a current application, or on future occasions of an applicant's contact with the organization, the "traces" preserved by that ledger stand potentially as "facts" in some yet-to-be-undertaken inquiry. How does an entry in such a book come to be treated as a "fact" upon the occasion of a subsequent inquiry?

First of all, although it is deemed important that specified features of given transactions between applicants and personnel be recorded in standardized ways, this does not exhaust the matter. A particular date and time and disposition noted next to a particular name becomes an "objective" document of one phase of the applicant-agency relationship by reference to (or assumption of) the routine, repetitive, methodical way in which they and *other* names, dates, times, and dispositions are entered. The routine character of the process, in turn, is reflexively established by reference to standard operating procedures specifying such activities, and by virtue of the fact that a *list* of such entries is available for any given day, i.e., the tangible product of compliance with those procedures.

The appearance of an entry on such a list is, furthermore, routinely readable by personnel as the trace of an encounter between public and organization independent of the personal characteristics and particular situation of the parties to the encounter. Any receptionist would produce the same sort of list, i.e., the receptionist, as a species of bureaucratic actor, would presumably be motivated to enact routine recording procedures in the absence of contrary information. This "motivationally transparent" aspect of accounts of bureaucratic activities will be discussed below.

Application. For those persons wishing to apply for assistance, the next step for receptionists is deciding which category of assistance is appropriate to the person's circumstances and executing an application for aid under that program. Organizational action on the applicant's request for assistance formally commences upon the completion and signing of an application, i.e., personnel will feel entitled to direct a series of questions to issues involving many intimate details of the applicant's life, and to demand that they be answered fully and candidly as a condition of the further processing of the application.

The signed application is also the countable unit of "work" in statistical reporting procedures used to assess staffing needs for the district offices, a fact impressed upon caseworkers by their supervisors. While procedures exist for "cancelling" applications for a variety of reasons, recourse to such procedures is discouraged by supervisory personnel in order to ensure reports depicting maximum work loads, thereby providing grounds for requesting additional personnel.

The receptionist, in moving the applicant to this further stage of processing, has thus generated a further document, a critical one in a number of respects. As has been noted, it serves as the warrant for the processing of the applicant's claim, and the unit in terms of which that processing is "counted" and thereby credited. A list of signed applications prepared by the file number of the assigned intake worker is completed at the end of each day. This list, transmitted to the assistant director in charge of intake, permits control procedures to go into effect, thus monitoring the progress of each case. The length of time permitted to the organization to process cases is fixed by state "due diligence" regulations, enforced by loss of state and federal matching funds for a specified period of time on the "delinquent case."

The application is also the basis for the creation of a dossier or case record on the applicant. Should the applicant already have an established dossier,[9] the newly executed application serves as the formal means of reopening the case.

The execution of this document restricts the subsequent activities of both applicant and agency personnel. To begin with, in initiating the application, the receptionist is committed to a series of further steps which "must" be accomplished (i.e., made visible as competently executed procedures) in order to discharge her responsibilities for the case. They become visible by virtue of the fact that they themselves leave their documentary traces. For example, she must see to it that a complete, i.e., competent, application is executed. She must "clear" the case. She must assemble the various forms which together constitute the initial collection of documents to be executed in subsequent processing. She must assign a caseworker to handle the case (and note the time at which the worker summons the applicant to the intake interview in the control ledger).

The receptionists' interests in the accomplishment of these steps is

[9] All family aid cases (AFDC and GR) which have been denied or discontinued at Lakeside are maintained in a suspense file in the office for three months on the supposition that a family aid case is more likely to re-apply than is an adult aid case. Adult aid cases (OAA, APTD, MAA) denied or discontinued in the office are sent to Central Records where they are maintained for five years and then destroyed. Family aid cases are also sent to Central Records after three months.

worth noting. Reference was made earlier to the motivationally transparent character of tasks in the setting—and by implication, bureaucratic tasks in general—as a feature of accounts of the execution of those tasks. In more detail, such transparency derives in part from the fact that bureaucratic functions, such as reception, get formulated in the following way by bureaucrats. The demands placed upon personnel by successive cohorts of clients are seen to require appropriately placed execution of routines which might be characterized as multiple dealings with a set of clients, employing sequences of procedures paced in their application with respect to the ebb and flow of demand and managed with an eye to the troubles that routinely but often unpredictably arise in their use. For personnel, "doing a job" consists of coming to terms with such features of the task and of the situation in which it must be addressed.[10]

Hence, one feature of the order of documentary activities visible to those engaged in it consists in the "normal" interests of personnel in "getting through" their day's work in a fashion acceptable to their superiors. There are, of course, a number of ways such interests could be satisfied, not all of them satisfactory to superiors. The point is, however, that the requirements of the particular bureaucratic task provide, in conjunction with recognized work circumstances, a set of practical concerns to which bureaucratic personnel are assumed to be oriented and to which bureaucratic personnel claim to be attentive.

Relevant to this "motivational" component of accounts of bureaucratic activity is the fact that the documents produced by those activities are seen to display not only "what happened" but also "good work" or "bad work" (through readings concerned with the review of personnel performance). Documents depict not only that the event occurred, but also that it was made to happen by the actions taken by personnel, actions which are subject to review.

Review of performance is partially "built in" by virtue of the interdependence of the phases of the processing routine. That is, the documents assembled by the receptionist are elements of further steps in the processing of a case, which is dependent on the completeness of the set and the adequacy of the information conveyed. A missing record and an incomplete or inconsistent set of items are "errors" routinely detected in the course of using previous events of documentation to accomplish further tasks.

[10] See Zimmerman, Don H., "The Practicalities of Rule Use," in Garfinkel, Harold, and Harvey Sachs, editors, *Contributions to Ethnomethodology*, Indiana University Press, Bloomington, forthcoming, for a detailed discussion of task structure and work in the reception function.

This "built-in" review underscores the fact that organization personnel, as a fundamental resource for their work, employ the documents produced by prior phases of the task as means for reconstructing what is known to date about the applicant, and what has been done to date with her case. Such work can and often does result in the detection of error, of "faulty interpretation," and frequently results in the institution of corrective measures. That the process is seen to be self-correcting to some extent is an important feature of its "aggregate validity," i.e., the routine acceptance of its products by personnel.

Assignment. The final step in the preprocessing routine is the assignment of the applicant to an intake worker. This too leaves its documentary traces.

The assignment procedure is organized around the "intake book," a ring binder containing ordinary notebook paper. Each page, representing one day's assignment, is ruled into six vertical columns and a variable number of horizontal rows. The rows represent the cohort of caseworkers available for duty that day.

Personnel describe how the matrix is "filled in" by reference to a rule which specifies that assignments are to be made starting at the top left (first worker, first intake) proceeding down the columns left to right until the bottom right cell (last worker, last intake) is reached. The order in which the previous steps in the preprocessing routine are completed determines, in most cases, the order in which they are to be assigned.[11]

In the light of these brief considerations, then, the documents produced by the reception function are treated, from the perspective of organization personnel, as the appearances of a determinate order of bureaucratic activities. The way the steps in the process are geared to one another, the nature of the mundane motivations that sustain their execution and furnish guarantees of their adequacy, and the various controls exercised upon their enactment are available to personnel as organizationally *embedded* accounts of an authoritative, competent, document-producing activity. Such accounts, for personnel, depict that order of activity as against alternative possible orders, e.g., free invention, the exercise of personal prejudice, sloppy work, and so on. The work of using documents to reconstruct particular events consists of treating the document as a normal event *within* a determinate order of activities, characterizable in terms of typical motives (e.g., "getting the job done") typical sequences

[11] See *ibid.* for a discussion of the intake assignment procedure as put in practice.

of action (e.g., bureaucratic routines), and typical products (e.g., completed documents).

The task of reception, as outlined above, consists of managing the routine induction of persons into the agency process as an accountably *rational* activity.[12] That is, the process must be managed so that two ends are achieved: (1) the applicant is readied for the intake investigation; and (2) the steps by which she is readied are recognizable as "proper," i.e., as the accomplishments of an organizationally legitimate set of procedures. The task of intake, in similar terms, consists of managing the routine investigation of applicants as an accountably rational activity, i.e., arriving at warranted decisions concerning eligibility, the grounds for which are rooted in the skilled use of defensible procedures for gathering and interpreting information. The work of conducting "routine investigations" is examined next.

THE INTAKE INVESTIGATION

A prominent feature of the investigative process is what may be called the "investigative stance." From the point of view of experienced personnel, the "stance" consists of a thoroughgoing skepticism directed to the applicant's claim to be eligible for assistance. As a mode of conducting an investigation, it is encountered in the setting by the observer (and by new personnel) as characterizations of "good work," and as advice extended by supervisors and "old hands" to novices, i.e., to those whose competence as caseworkers is problematic. In relation to the intake worker's task of making the investigation of eligibility an accountably rational enterprise, "being skeptical" is a way of displaying a hard-headed commitment to establishing the "facts of the matter" (as against the applicant's mere *claims*) as well as being a method for locating the courses of documentation which will determine the relevant facts. The following incident illustrates the skepticism of the investigative stance.

Skepticism

On New Year's Eve, an APTD applicant appeared in the office seeking carfare. His assigned worker was in the field, and another worker in the unit was designated to handle the matter temporarily. His request for carfare was supposedly in order to keep a doctor's appointment (a quite ordinary and appropriate request for applicants in this category awaiting final determination of eligibility). The worker consulted with the super-

[12] See Garfinkel, *op. cit.*, chaps. 1 and 8.

visor on the request and was directed to defer issuance of the carfare pending a review of the case record. The supervisor noted that he could not meet his scheduled appointment on time at any event. She also told the worker to contact the doctor to verify the existence of the appointment.

The amount of money at issue would total at the most two dollars, and probably would be less. At the time, the caseworker involved could not comprehend the effort extended by the supervisor to monitor the expenditure of such a small amount. She was not "skeptical" of the request. (It should be added that the author was also puzzled by the insistence on checking out such an apparently routine request.)

As it turned out, the case record depicted the man as a "chronic alcoholic." Furthermore, it was also learned that the doctor with whom the man claimed to have had an appointment was on vacation. This information recast the situation as that of a drunk attempting to secure liquor on New Year's Eve. (It should be noted that the case record was the determining factor here.)

A worker honoring a hasty, last-minute appeal for carfare without checking the story would be seen to have disregarded the existence of readily available routine procedures which could verify the "facts," for example, reference to the case record, calling the doctor. The moral lesson for the worker is: to permit what would be defined in the setting as applicant "manipulation" of the agency (e.g., last-minute, urgent demands presumably intended to make advantageous use of a limited time for decisive action) would be to mark oneself the rankest novice. Not only is "skepticism" (i.e., reliance on methods of verification prior to commitment of belief or action) of this sort a characteristic *modus operandi* and scheme of interpretation of the "old hand," it is frequently justified, as in this case. If the "skeptical" hypothesis proves mistaken, it is of no consequence, since the case had to be "proven" in any event. Thus, the relevance of the "investigative stance" is established and reasserted in the daily routine.

The Investigative Stance. The investigative stance is often taught to novices by insisting that they undertake some routine inquiry or initiate some procedure to verify some matter of which they are already persuaded. In one case, a new worker was adamant about giving an emergency grocery order (EGO) to one of her AFDC applicants, even though much investigation remained. She was convinced that the applicant was in immediate need. Her supervisor acquiesced on the condition that she deliver it personally and "look the situation over." Of course, the supervisor yielded nothing. What she required was the usual procedure of making a home call before the issuance of aid.

The worker took the EGO to the applicant, and found, somewhat to her chagrin, that the house (as she later reported) was "full of men" and that one of them was called "daddy" by the woman's child (although "daddy" was supposedly not on the scene). She did not give the applicant the EGO.

The point is this: The intake function as an *investigative* process comes to be appreciated through the discovery that the routine procedures insisted upon by supervisors can and do produce information which may run counter to the applicant's account of her situation and the worker's initial assessment of the case. The incident cited is perhaps a dramatic illustration of this point since, in a manner of speaking, the worker set herself up to be surprised.

Perhaps more important is the appreciation that the conduct of a recognizably adequate investigation involves displaying the *active* assumption of the investigative stance. A case is assembled over a series of interactions involving workers and their supervisors. Supervisors were observed to be closely attentive to the ways in which their workers talked about their cases, and quick to point out where and how a worker failed to transform a feature of the applicant's story into a matter resolvable through some course of documentation. For example, talk of the applicant's dire need over and against her eligibility was, for supervisors, a sure sign of a faulty grasp of the actual task of the intake division. This lack of appreciation of the "real" character of the task signaled the need for close supervision, particularly in the context of caseload and processing time limitations.

Work Relevancies. The task of investigating a case is best understood within the governing work relevancies of the setting. In general terms, these relevancies are (1) the reduction of a worker's caseload; and (2) an emphasis on disposing of the case within a thirty-day period so that it does not become "delinquent." The consequences of such constraints appear to require an organization of work which will permit the worker to exercise a timely demand both on ancillary functions of the Bureau itself and on the applicant to expedite the collection of the requisite documents. Achievement of such work organization does not appear to consist merely in the disciplined control over a set of routines (although this is deemed important) but initially upon the achievement of an understanding by the novice of the technical, investigative character of the task, and how it may be competently conducted, as suggested above.

A crucial consideration in the investigative process is the role of the applicant. She is the primary source of the information needed to initiate the documentation that will warrant a decision in the case. Often the generation of some requisite documentation depends upon her taking certain actions, e.g., keeping appointments at medical examinations arranged for her, contacting the absent father (if she knows his whereabouts) and asking him to come in for an interview, pressuring a doctor to submit a medical report, making application for unemployment insurance, securing addresses and names of persons and places to be contacted, and so on. This reliance on the applicant is formulated by personnel as "applicant responsibility." For example, a worker was asked: "What about the case where you have a complex situation? The applicant has moved around a lot, he hasn't led his life so as to leave convenient traces."

The reply was:

> Then we have to say the burden of proof is up to him. In other words, this is the agency feeling. You are applying for public assistance and it seems to me that if you are applying for a job with the government where you had to have a security clearance, you will have to have those addresses and if you really want it, the job, you are going to come up with them one way or another.

The caseworker's problem is to grasp what will need to be verified through the assembly of particular documents, to ask the applicant for such documents, and if she does not possess them, to initiate the procedures required to secure them.

In terms of the preceding, the investigative stance may be taken to refer to the variety of practices personnel employ to locate and display the potential discrepancy between the applicant's subjective and "interested" claims and the factual and objective (i.e., rational) account that close observance of agency procedure is deemed to produce. Producing an account which is recognized as adequate in these terms involves procuring and interpreting documents within the constraints of the work relevancies discussed above.

DOCUMENTS AS OBJECTIVE AND FACTUAL ACCOUNTS

It will be useful to recall here the assumption that the applicant has a vital interest in the outcome of her claim. The "facts," therefore, must be established by appeal to authoritative sources of information that are in no way subject to the influence or control of the applicant. What is required is some means for "objectively" deciding, for all practical organizational purposes, the factual character of the applicant's story. This problem may be illustrated by the examination of an OAA case in which there was an issue of the legal possession of funds.

The applicant was found to possess a joint bank account with her daughter, a relatively common occurrence in the OAA category. If the amount in the joint account (in conjunction with the value of other personal property possessed by the applicant) exceeds the maximum allowable amount, the applicant is ineligible.

The applicant, however, claimed that half of the amount was her daughter's property, a fact which, if established, would reduce her total personal property holdings below the maximum, and hence render her eligible, other factors constant. The issue, of course, was *how* this division of property was to be established.

In terms of the banking regulations governing joint tenancy, the tenants have equal legal access to the *full* amount in the account. Hence, in the absence of further documentation which would indicate the ownership of the funds deposited in the account (e.g., bank records of withdrawals from each individual's account matching deposits in the joint account), the issue of division of property was resolved by appeal to banking regulations. The statements of the parties concerned are not sufficient. The records of the bank, understood *against the background of banking conventions,* supersedes the statements of the interested parties.

As suggested by the example, certain documents and the interpretations they afford permit the determination of the organizationally relevant "facts" of the case independently of the applicant's statements. Considered here are (1) the sources of documents routinely employed to independently assess the applicant's circumstances and motivations, and (2) how such documents, in the way in which they are used in the setting, achieve the authority of independent assessments.

Sources of Documentation

Primary Organizational Records. A basic resource in the documentation of a case are the records produced by a variety of organizations in the society. These include marriage certificates, birth certificates, divorce papers, property settlements, court orders, and so on. In the words of a caseworker:

. . . the sorts of things which are no problem if the client has them, which occasionally they do. Otherwise, we have to start sending away to document procurement, which takes time.

Certain records are secured by the direct action of the worker, e.g., she may contact banks within the geographic boundaries of the district. Property records are searched by a "property unit," and a report is returned to the worker summarizing the "property situation."

It should be recalled that, in the worker's words, these documents pose no problem if they are in the possession of the applicant. The case takes longer to process with every document that the worker must take steps to secure.[13]

The Applicant's Own Records. A second resource consists of the documents produced by the applicant, and for which he or she is accountable to some organization or, more generally, to some body of law. Such documents include tax returns, associated business records, and account ledgers.

This set of documents would appear to contradict the formulation proposed earlier, since they seem certainly open to manipulation by the applicant. Their serviceability seems to rest on two considerations. First, they represent a set of statements for the accuracy of which the applicant is legally responsible. The second, and perhaps most pressing, consideration has to do with the availability of means for economically gathering information.

The applicant's mere statement of her circumstances is taken as sufficient under certain practically motivated conditions, e.g., the prohibitive cost of certain information. For example, routine investigation of property holdings is not undertaken. The applicant is queried on a number of points, e.g., real and personal property, including stocks, bonds, and cash on hand or in a bank, and must swear to the accuracy of the statements under penalty of perjury.

The affirmation of these facts must be prepared in a certain manner, i.e., completely filled out, properly dated, and witnessed and signed by the worker, a deputized county clerk. The applicant in this case is made legally responsible for the "factual" status of her claim. In turn, the document is a document of that claim by virtue of its correct completion, i.e., under the control of a procedure—in the sense developed in the section

[13] See Zimmerman, Don H., "Tasks and Troubles: The Practical Bases of Work in a Public Assistance Agency," in Hansen, D. A., editor, *Explorations in Sociology and Counselling,* Houghton Mifflin, Boston, 1969, for an account of the temporal and other contingencies of caseload processing.

dealing with reception. (Subsequent action on suspected fraudulent statements may be blocked by discovery of omissions or other technical errors in the form.)

Another factor—one which the present study cannot attempt to assess—is the differences in the legislatively provided criteria of evidence. On AFDC, for example, residence must be proved by such documents as birth certificates, rent receipts, or landlord statements. On OAA, in contrast, statements of the applicant's friends (but not relatives) that she has resided in the state and county the appropriate length of time are acceptable.

Documents Produced by Transactions. A third source of recorded information consists of the documents produced by the transactions between individuals acting in specifiable "formal" role relationships, e.g., doctor-patient, landlord-tenant, creditor-debtor. These documents are not to be confused with affidavits executed by "interested parties" to the claim.

Affidavits are sworn relative to an issue affecting eligibility, and are thus generated in terms of that interest. The person making the affidavit is evaluated in terms of the nature of the interests involved and how they might affect the accuracy of the statement. Such documents have low evidential value, and are seldom honored in the absence of corroborating evidence and then usually only as a device for fixing legal responsibility for particular statements.

The burden of the separation of the motives implicated in the particular transaction from the motive of qualifying for assistance is placed on the fact that the "third parties" are presumed to be acting under the auspices of their respective, typified interests in the given relationship. It may be noted that securing documents from this source poses certain problems, since such individuals may not be oriented to or organized for the routine dissemination of information to such agencies as the Bureau. Typically, the responsibility for prompting the submission of such information, after the initial request by the worker, is placed upon the applicant.

The County's Determination of the Applicant's Condition. One prominent issue in the family aids is capacity to engage in work. Another issue is willingness to work. The former is resolved by sending the applicant to the "Work Test Clinic" at the County General Hospital. At this clinic, a county physician conducts an examination and passes an authoritative professional opinion on the employability of the applicant. The reports stand as the "fact" of the applicant's employability. It should be noted that workers may hold contrary—if unauthoritative—notions concerning these "facts." One worker remarked that unless the applicant arrived on a stretcher, she would be found "employable" by the Work Test Clinic. Another worker characterized Clinic physicians as producing two typical diagnoses: "Chronic Malingerer" in the case of men and "Menopausal Syndrome" in the case of women. She also referred, with considerable irony, to a report received on an applicant of hers which read: "Diagnosis: chronic and acute alcoholism. Fully employable."

In the case of the AFDC-U program, the unemployed parent (usually the father) is required to seek employment diligently. (The procedure for establishing the "diligence" of this search will be discussed later.) If unsuccessful in finding work, the applicant is required to accept assignment to what is called the Work Project for a number of hours at a standard rate of pay to work off the amount of the monthly assistance granted on various public works projects. The applicant's compliance with this requirement establishes his "proper motivation" for the record while at the same time offsetting part of the cost of the assistance provided.

The Authority of Documents

A discussion of the ways in which bureaucratic records come to arbitrate matters of fact is best launched by considering two related features of the use of documents in the setting. It may be observed, first of all, that in many situations, personnel simply treat a variety of documents as reports of "plain fact" for all practical organizational purposes. In other words, on many occasions the information found in official records is accepted without question. For example, the records generated by reception at Lakeside are ordinarily "plain facts" for intake workers. In yet other circumstances, personnel engage in the construction of accounts of *how* a document is to be honored as reporting "plain fact," i.e., they present grounds for accepting the testimony of the document over and against the testimony of the applicant. The latter work usually occurs in the context of worker-supervisor interaction over the details of a case, and over the course of instructing novice workers.

"Plain Fact." The "plain fact" character of documents-in-use in the setting is observable in the following ways. As suggested above, personnel regularly employ documents to decide issues of eligibility without comment, without question, and without challenge from superiors. The *de facto* authority thus achieved for documents by such routine decision-

making contrasts markedly with the thorough-going skepticism concerning the applicant's claim characteristic of the investigative stance. To oversimplify to some extent, the essentially problematic character of the applicant's claims is addressed and resolved by reliance on the essentially *un*problematic character of official documents. That is, the applicant's claims, as a general class, is *from the outset* open to doubt, just as the official document, as a general class, is *from the outset* seen as reliable. That personnel find an applicant's claims to be correct, or discover a record to be in error in a particular case, does not appear to alter their view of the essential character of either class.

It has already been indicated that the applicant, as a general rule, is not seen to be "trustworthy." The faith placed in official documents may be further exemplified by the following. The author posed the *global* doubt that records could be trusted as a matter of course, that indeed, they might be systematically falsified. The two workers queried in this fashion treated the suggestion as incredible. For them, the possibilities opened up by such a doubt, including the possibility of a conspiracy between the applicant and the document-producing organization, were not matters for idle speculation. The possibility of error was admitted, but only as a departure from ordinarily accurate reportage.[14]

The following are excerpts from an edited and annotated record of an OAA intake interview. From the point of view of the worker involved, the process of documentation proceeded in an ideal fashion, i.e., without encountering problems leading to an extended investigation. It will be worthwhile to examine this excerpt, for it illustrates the nonproblematic use of documents as "plain fact" reports on matters pertinent to eligibility as well as the relationship of the applicant to the processing of a "routine" application.

An Intake Interview. Emphases in the following selection have been supplied by the investigator. Materials in parentheses are the investigator's summary of what was said, a procedure employed when the pace of conversation became too rapid for verbatim notetaking.

The applicant was accompanied to the interview by her daughter. In the booth, the worker instructs the applicant in filling out the application, which is completed and signed prior to the "interrogation" to follow:
W: How long have you been supporting yourself until now?

[14] The application of this procedure to only two workers provides meagre evidence, to be sure, but its results fit closely with observations on the features of accounts of the authority of official records to be considered below.

A: (Her husband died ten months ago. She had been living on Social Security and VA pensions in the amount of $140 a month.)

The question about previous means of support is intended to produce an account of the amount and sources of income available to the applicant prior to the situation which occasions her presence in the office. The purpose is to provide a way of determining whether or not such means of support are still available and whether they could be considered to have produced accumulations—e.g., cash or property reserves which might be utilized in meeting the applicant's need. In this case, the previous means of support stemmed from easily verifiable sources, i.e., Social Security and Veterans Administration pensions.

The next question is motivated by the relatively high income currently received by the applicant.

W: Do you have a special need such as a diet?

A: No. (She shows a letter from her doctor to the effect that she needs a special medical treatment. She goes every two weeks at $7.50 per treatment.)

W: Do you take any medicine?

A: (She indicates that she has to wear a surgical corset.)

The worker is attempting to establish the existence of "special needs," the cost of which, taken together with the size of the grant computed according to her circumstances, might add up to a "need" in excess of the amount of income she has already claimed, and hence render her eligible.

W: Do you have your award letter from Social Security?

A: Yes. Here is the one from the VA. (W. copies onto the worksheet from the award letters.)

This nicely illustrates an episode of documentation. In her dictation of the case narrative, W. will record that she has seen award letters from these two agencies verifying the amount of income received by the applicant. W.'s narrative is an internally produced record generated in the course of asking routine questions, and accepted on the premise that in fact the worker saw these documents and recorded them accurately.

Thus, the applicant's income is "verified" by virtue of the worker's notation which becomes part of the case-record. The worker then secures "face sheet" information (e.g., date of marriage, names of children, etc.). She next asks for the applicant's social security number, which the applicant cannot find at the moment but produces a little later.

W: Now, are you living alone?

A: Yes.

W: What is your rent?
A: $75.
W: Do you pay your own utilities? (She does.) Do you have a rent receipt?
A: Yes, I have these. (W. copies information from the rent receipts onto the worksheet.)
W: Do you have a health plan?
A: Yes. (She hands policy to the worker.)
W: On some health plans, money can be put into the budget to cover them. Do you have anything to verify your age?
A: Yes. (Pulls out another document which the worker examines, and then records.)
W: How long have you lived in Western State?
A: Since 1936.
W: In Metropolitan County?
A: Yes.
W: Are there two people to whom we can send forms to verify that you have lived here for the past five years? (Applicant says yes and gives the names.)

(The worker then asks about real property, houses, etc.)

A: Oh no, not since 1938. I sold it in 1949.
W: Now, do you have any personal property; that is, savings accounts, checking account, stocks, bonds, automobiles, burial space?
A: Yes. (i.e., burial space.)
W: You are allowed personal property up to $1,200. We have to check and see that it does not go above. (Checks burial deed, records it.) Now, I will have you sign the affirmation. This is the form and then, I think, we will be through. (Instructs client to sign name and address.)

At the conclusion of the interview, the worker indicates to the applicant's daughter that "forms will be sent (to determine relative liability for the support of the mother) to her and the other children."

The "paper work" entailed in this case consisted largely of copying *from* documents in the possession of the applicant onto a worksheet for later dictation as a case narrative, that is, a record of the way in which the points of eligibility (age, income, property, etc.) were established. The only forms to initiate are the relative liability letters and the residence statement.

A review of the features of the case will indicate the sources of its apparent simplicity.

First, the applicant was "cooperative." That is, she had apparently taken care to find among documents in her possession those which would satisfy the agency's requirements.

Second, the worker was "experienced." She was familiar with what information was required, and exercised control over the interaction so that it was elicited in a relatively short time. A sense of what is considered by personnel in the agency to be a "skillful interviewing technique" may be gained by referring to another experienced worker's recommendations to new workers on this subject, the chief thrust of which was the importance of control over information.

> You say [to the applicant], "I noted on the application form that you say that you came in to apply for assistance because you are unemployed. When were you last employed? Do you owe a lot of debts? Could you tell me a little about the debts you owe? Why do you suppose you lost your last job? How long were you there? How long were you at your last job?" This way you are establishing residence, getting an idea of why they have been in, what happened to their job, how long they hold them, what their reason is. You are getting the names of their employers, also sometimes their addresses so you are actually taking care of a lot by this but if somebody wants to go into, "My mother comes over and we fight, and my husband, I think is going out with this person and I think that my child has this problem in school," they are not really pertinent to eligibility in intake. They are in approved but not in intake. Many workers will sit two and a half, three hours in an intake and just listen to this crap!

Third, given the above two features, the verification of eligibility proceeded in an almost "checklist" fashion, i.e., the worker requested corroborating documents in support of statements made by the applicant which she was able to provide on the spot in most instances. Indeed, the worker and the applicant joined together to produce and sustain a routine bureaucratic encounter in which the problematic character of the applicant's claim was resolved by reliance upon the definite character of official documents.

It should be noted that to treat the applicant's claims as essentially problematic does not necessarily entail overt suspiciousness or hostility on the part of the worker. In cases such as this, the routine "checkout" of documents quickly lays to rest each issue of eligibility raised.

Other cases and other applicants may be of altogether a different character. The issues in the case itself may prove complicated, e.g., an extensive history of property transactions, or the applicant unable or unwilling to provide the information required to document the "facts" of the case. (As indicated earlier, the applicant is to be assigned responsibility for the provision of this information.) Certain types of "complications" which challenge the authority of documents in the setting will be dealt with shortly.

The preceding seems to suggest that personnel automatically accept the testimony of official documents in most cases. However, over a range of cases *and* workers challenges to the authority of particular documents as decisive arbiters of eligibility do arise. For example, supervisors (and others in authority) view the display of the investigative stance by workers as a critical element of their competence as employees. Hence, as supervisors see it, there is a distribution of competence in the setting related in large part to the distribution of experience. It is *not* the case that inexperienced workers reject the authority of documents in principle; rather, they are seen to *miss the point* of documentary verification. That is, they are not properly skeptical of the applicant's claims; they do not display skill in relating the particulars of the applicant's story to the kinds of information made available by documents; they do not assign first priority to the collection of pertinent documents and perhaps most troublesome of all to their superiors, they tend to side with the applicant and attempt to "explain away" discrepancies between her story and the evidence of the record.[15]

Under such circumstances, supervisors usually provide *accounts* which display the ways in which the documentary evidence is visibly more reliable, more objective, more trustworthy than the applicant's word, and in the final analysis is required by the nature of the organization's mission. The general features of such accounts will be outlined shortly. It must be stressed, however, that accounts provided by supervisors deal with particulars, i.e., they attempt to show for the particulars of the case at hand the superiority of documentary evidence. They are "occasioned" accounts, fashioned in terms of available information on the case and those involved in it. As features of the occasions upon which they are constructed, they organize those occasions for further action and inference, e.g., for subsequent steps in the investigation and for the decision on eligibility.

Challenges arise in other ways. Documents are often found to be ambiguous or difficult to interpret; sometimes they produce marked incongruities for workers if they are taken as definite of some matter, e.g., age. Again, these challenges are not global, but are occasioned by problems encountered in particular cases, and resolved in terms leaving the essential character of records (and applicants) unchanged as organizationally actionable matters.

Below, certain general features of accounts of "plain fact" will be sketched. Of particular interest are the properties of documents and their mode of production which such accounts make observable as in-

[15] See Zimmerman, "Tasks and Troubles," *op. cit.*, for a discussion of these "troubles."

tendedly compelling grounds (for any competent member-of-society and, in particular, any competent member-of-the-organization) for accepting the authority of official records.

Accounting for "Plain Facts." Accounts of the "plain fact" character of documents are done by members of the organization for members of the organization; they are integral features of the situations they make observable and hence organize. By means of these accounts, the documents passing through the hands of agency personnel are seen as documents of the orderly processes of society, and as produced by them. (The Lakeside office is itself one such orderly process, a point made in the discussion of the reception function.)

Whether or not such accounts are accurate descriptions of document-producing enterprises is an issue here only insofar as it is an issue in the setting. How that issue is solved when it arises is how the "plain fact" character of documents is preserved in the face of a variety of contingencies and occasioned doubts encountered in the course of using documents to advance the work of the organization, i.e., the work of accountably rational investigation and decision-making.

First, accounts displaying the "plain fact" character of documents show them to depict such activities as buying and selling property, consulting doctors, getting married and divorced, paying taxes, and so on. Witnesses to these accounts are invited to see that such activities are everyday, matter-of-course pursuits, i.e., "natural" occurrences in the society. Further, the outcome of these pursuits, as accomplished-events-in-society, are to be seen as *produced* or *constituted* on the occasion in which the record is generated (e.g., the transfer of a title deed). The account *ties* the activity to a record-keeping enterprise.

Making observable the "necessary" link between an activity and the occasion in which it becomes a matter of record also makes visible the *transactional* character of the document-producing context. Apart from the person undertaking some ordinary activity, there are others involved whose task it is to monitor, facilitate, and record the course and outcome of that activity. In turn, the transaction between such persons is made accountable in terms of the *motivationally transparent*[16] character of their respective roles. That is, the person whose affairs a document reports is a person who, via the account, is seen to be pursuing some commonplace project (e.g., buying property) for understandable reasons appropriate to that project, and others are viewed as going about *their* commonplace

[16] Recall the discussion above of the reception process.

projects (e.g., selling property, recording titles, assessing taxes, etc.) for reasons appropriate to their occupational obligations. And that occupational obligations are viewed to be binding provides the way of seeing the transaction as under the control of some set of (usually unspecified) procedures.

In short, the authority of various documents is made accountable in terms of the routine, organized ways in which these unremarkable projects are geared to one another under the auspices of typified, generally known interests or motives, and with adumbrated reference to the more or less standardized procedures that presumably control the gearing.

The features discussed above are not offered as exhaustive. Nor can they be viewed as a set of criteria usable by the observer to decide the status of documents independently of their occurrence as features of an account delivered on some occasion of work in the setting. The adequacy of an account is not guaranteed by possessing these features. They represent a truncated view of how personnel accomplish the authority of a document when that authority is challenged. It remains to be seen, in particular cases, how these general features stand to the work actually done to make them observable and enforceable over the contingencies of interaction in the setting.

The balance of this chapter is focused on a detailed description of a portion of the investigation of one case. The process of investigation will show the investigative stance in practice, particularly on the part of the intake supervisor. It will also further illustrate the proposals set forth earlier about the nature of bureaucratic record-generation and interpretation, and in particular, the process of challenging and accounting for the authority of documents and documenting procedures. The worker on the case was relatively inexperienced, and prone to take the applicant's side. The supervisor was viewed by all workers in her unit (and many in other units as well) as being extremely rigorous in her standards of eligibility investigation.

Investigating a Case

The occasion for the AFDC-U application to be examined here was the default in payment due the applicant, Mr. A., for masonry work he performed as an "independent contractor."[17] The work was contracted by the owner of a manufacturing firm for improvements on his private resi-

[17] Unfortunately, the initial interview was not observed. The materials reported here are based on the account given by the worker, and the subsequent interactions (tape-recorded) with his supervisor and others in connection with the case. The interaction reported here took place several days after the initial interview.

dence. The applicant had been given a check for $300, which proved to be worthless. Mr. A. was persuaded to resume his work on the promise of an additional $350, which was never forthcoming, leaving him without funds and in debt. At the time of the application, Mr. A. presented a notice from the Labor Law Commission setting a date for a hearing over the dispute.

Verification. A major task for G. B., the worker on the case, was verifying a list submitted by the applicant of the places at which he had sought employment. One requirement of the AFDC-U program is that the unemployed parent actively seek work and give evidence of having done so. This policy is implemented by the use of a form on which is entered the name and address of the employers contacted, date and name of the person approached. The entries on the form are checked by phone to establish their "factual" character.[18] It is important to note that the results of such a procedure, recorded in the case narrative, have the status of a document.

G. B. secured the phone numbers of the firms listed from Information, and called each in turn. The first call produced the promise of a return call, since the person likely to have interviewed the applicant was not in, as was the case in the second call. G. B. was concerned to make what he called a "breakthrough" on the calls in order to produce more factual information on the case. He commented:

It will be easier to go through because we will have some more factual information to go by. You see theoretically, if worse should come to worse, if he were a complete fraud and just listed these places and Mr. D. (the debtor) is just a friend who will go along with his story—but the one bit of factual information is that letter I got this morning from the Labor Law Commission so if I were looking at it strictly from a fraud point of view, the only document I have concerning this whole dispute is that letter and the phone call and theoretically, that phone call could be arranged. He might have given me the number of a friend *but knowing the operation and having gone through a receptionist—through a general bureaucracy the way it is here—I can intuitively grasp that this is not a phony setup.*

These remarks merit comment. First, G. B. has raised the possibility, that the applicant's representations (and the evidence he has offered in their support) are fraudulent. Second, the character of the factual information G. B. is concerned to collect consists of information outside a "reasonable" possibility of collusion or manipulation. The one "bit of factual

[18] The entries on this list, if there are many, may be "sampled." The consideration here, as in other procedures, is the cost in time.

information" he possessed would seem to qualify as such for him. In discussing the matter of his contact with the debtor, Mr. D., he speculates that it could have been "arranged." But he discounts this as a likelihood because, in calling Mr. D. "at work," his call went through a switchboard —a "general bureaucracy the way it is here."

One may well ask the value of this fact. On the basis of earlier discussion, one aspect of the evidential force of documents produced by official agencies is formulated in terms of what it would entail to entertain the notion of a "conspiracy" with the applicant entered into by that agency. G. B. is evidently willing to consider that possibility with respect to a friend of the applicant, but not with respect to a person reached through a switchboard. The mechanism of the "general bureaucracy" by which such a person was reached permits him to "intuitively grasp that this is not a phony setup," i.e., to discount the likelihood of the applicant's manipulation of the situation. The information was delivered through organizational channels, hence it may be counted trustworthy by virtue of the occupational obligations implicitly assumed to be operating.

G. B. has yet to establish as factual the applicant's "diligent" search for employment.

Another call is placed revealing that the firm has no record of Mr. A.'s application. G. B. remarks, "I imagine he has gone there but the gentleman I spoke to didn't have the information." When asked why he concludes that, he replies:

> You generally ask what the procedure is. This one seemed to have records of other people. He (Mr. A.) may have just inquired to see if there were any openings, in which case, they wouldn't have a record. So we will just check some of the other places because it is not too likely that a client would say he went to a place and get the address and manufacture the results of the interview and put it down when he knows it is going to be subject to verification. That is very unlikely.

Given that a procedure for the production of such a record was in existence, G. B. invoked the conditions under which a record might nonetheless not be produced. By so doing, G. B. is apparently "taking into account" the conditions under which the applicant's contact with an organization might not routinely produce a record. By doing so, he is raising a challenge, the character of which will be seen shortly.

At this point, it should be made clear that such "contingencies" are often appreciated, particularly by workers. By proposing that the procedures of the agency rely on the "orderly processes of the society" it is not implied that the society is taken by such officials as simply a well-oiled, infallible machine. However, from the perspective of the task and its constraints, it may have to be treated *as if* it were for all practical organizational purposes. That is, should this resource fail to produce the requisite information, the matter may often be treated as indeterminate, however much the contingencies may be appreciated.

For instance, in an OAA case difficulties arose in the matter of age proof. The applicant in question had no birth certificate, as this record was purportedly destroyed in the Chicago Fire (the one attributed to Mrs. O'Leary's cow). At the age of 17 he had run away from home to become a boxer and adopted a new name, never legally changing his previous one. One document that might have established his age, an insurance policy taken out when he was quite young, was written in his "legal" name. An attempt to check military records (he had tried unsuccessfully to enlist in the Army under his new name in World War I) proved futile. His sister swore an affidavit that his name was as it appeared on the insurance policy, but this was not sufficient, because of her presumed interest in the outcome of the investigation. The applicant was unable to produce any third party who knew him under this name, and the application was denied on the grounds that age could not be established. The worker appreciated the contingencies of this matter and personally believed that the applicant was indeed 65, but had no recourse short of falsifying the case record.

Returning to the case under consideration, the worker placed another call, remarking that "this is one of the problems in these AFDC cases when there is an employable parent—*checking*—it takes an awful lot of time. In an OAA case, there are practically no phone calls." The phone call produced the same results as the preceding one—there would have been a record if he were there, but there was no record of his applying. G. B. commented:

Two places had no record. It may be that if they just weren't hiring anyone so that it would be pointless to make an application.

It is important to emphasize again that G. B.'s treatment of the results of the phone call rests upon at least two considerations: (1) the places contacted were found to routinely keep records of job applicants, and (2) the invocation of contingencies by G. B. which might intervene between an inquiry into employment and the production of a record of that inquiry, that is, the actual taking of an application.

G. B. then approaches his supervisor, A. B., to report on the outcome of the checking procedure.

I am trying to verify his search for employment, I've had no luck. (Referring to form:) No record . . . no record . . . will call back. This one they didn't know definitely, but the person said they had no record of it. But he might have gone down to another department or something.

Thus, G. B. repeats to the supervisor what he had already stated to the observer: The check has failed, but he is willing to grant a "reasonable" explanation of the failure.

To this, the supervisor proposes:

No record of him even being there even. Well, you see, a lot of these places . . . have you ever applied at one of these places? They have a record of you even if you go through the gate to apply.
I've walked the streets (looking for work) unfortunately, at a lot of firms in this area, and I'm well aware of it. They just don't let you in. For instance, if you go to Jordans, they won't let you in without taking your name. They have a record of some kind and they keep it for a certain length of time and then they destroy them.

She has apparently formulated for the purposes of the issue at hand the typical way in which job applicants are processed at the type of firm the applicant claimed to have sought employment. Her account does not detail the specific procedures, nor does it deal with the contingent factor of how, organizationally speaking, the request for information might be satisfied. But it does fashion from the particulars of the situation the vague but weighty procedured guarantees that if a certain event took place, a record of it would be available.

By so constructing the matter at this point, the efficacy of the verification procedure and of the document it produces is preserved. By readily admitting to the contingency posed by the worker that "he might have gone to another department or something" the procedure would have been rendered indeterminate. To allow such a supposition routinely would be consequential for the requirement of filing a case within thirty days. The consideration of what may be taken as evidence is never far removed from the costs of securing it.

The issue is the weight to be given to the "contingencies" of a process of recordkeeping (perhaps there were no job openings and the applicant did not bother to apply) compared to the force of the verification procedure to decide the issue. Taken in the context of the emphasis on caseload reduction and meeting time requirements, strong organizational reasons exist for protecting the determinateness of such procedures. Hence, the caseworker's attempt to provide a "reasonable" account of how it might be that the applicant had actually sought employment even though no record of it was available is set aside in favor of the organizationally more compelling interpretation that he had not, in fact, diligently sought employment.

In this case, however, the applicant was allowed a "second chance" on this issue. It seems likely that the worker's willingness to entertain "reasonable contingencies" may be a factor in such "second chances."[19] It is highly probable that had the failure to verify search for employment been taken at its face value, the worker could have denied the application and not been challenged, particularly by this supervisor.

G. B. remarked:

First of all, my supervisor: she's hard working. She doesn't like to be reprimanded for any of her cases. She will go out of her way to avoid any confrontations with the Assistant Director, and to make these confrontations not too devastating. I think the best way of doing this is not to have any delinquents. Since the vast majority of denials don't appeal cases, there's not too much of a problem here and you'll get into "high favor," as it's called, by having non-delinquent filings. The list of delinquent cases is very few. Then you are indeed in high favor and you can maintain your independence without being reprimanded too often. So there is then constant pressure to make quick decisions on cases.

How "far" a worker will go with an applicant in dealing with problems of verification appears to depend on how willing a worker (and, more crucially, a supervisor) is to accept the "risks" that accompany extended case processing.

The Applicant as a Course-of-Action

The conference proceeded (the matter of verification of the applicant's job seeking dropped for the moment) with the specification of further details of the applicant's situation. Observe what is made of the information about the applicant's occupation:

A. B.: A. is a contractor? An independent contractor? [Yes] Did you look at his income tax? [No] I'd like to see how he rates himself on an income tax declaration. I really would before I'd make a decision . . . Does he have a license, and all of this? What's his equipment valued at? You would need all of this. What kind of a contractor is he, cement?

G. B.: Masonry. He does landscaping type of stuff and gardening.

Note that from the single fact of occupation, the supervisor has now generated as pertinent facts for investigation, a number of features of his

[19] The author's presence should not be discounted as a factor in the granting of a "second chance." On several occasions, the author learned that administrative personnel had "adjusted" their conduct—presumably in accordance with their conception of his prejudices—only to change it later in his absence.

circumstances (and that she has specified the documents pertinent to them). A. B. continues:

I think the only thing you can do probably is one grocery order while you go on with your investigation and then check out everything as fast as you can, including the value of his personal, his business equipment. I would like to look at his income tax from last year, and why, if he's a landscape gardener, this just doesn't make sense, that he couldn't get a job this time of year. It doesn't make sense.

The notion of "what contractors do" has now generated a set of instructions for the worker which he will have to satisfy in order to act on the case. The features evoked are investigatable matters. That is, some document may be secured or produced which would, presumably, decide the matter. That he is also a gardener, given what is presumed to be the market of gardeners, also generates skepticism about the applicant, i.e., the remark, "it doesn't make sense" is roughly equivalent to "he isn't acting in the way he should," or, "his motivations are unclear given who he is." The worker attempts to make sense of his actions:[20]

G. B.: I think he sold his stuff, *and that makes sense of that.* On income tax you want to know if he considers himself self-employed or. . . .

The supervisor replies to this and raises further matters for investigation:

A. B.: I'd like to take a look at it if you don't mind. You take a look at it too, then I'll take a look at it. You make up your mind, then show it to me, and I'll make up mine and we'll talk about it, and you want to know, does he have a business phone, does he have a phone exchange, how does he get jobs? You see, these are the kind of things you're going to have to know. *How does he get a job?* You don't become . . . get contracts out of the Department of Employment, you bid on them. Just suppose you had a service to sell, put yourself in his place, as to how you were going to do it. You are not going to get it by going into the Department of Employment.

In turn, the worker provides other possible situations for the applicant by saying:

A. B.: I imagine he gets to a certain extent by word of mouth. He does small jobs, homes, and what not.[21]

[20] Yet another consequence of the matter of detailing the applicant's circumstances is assessing his motivation or at least, his good cause in applying through providing typical alternative courses of action a "person like him" would usually have available. That gardeners are assumed to be able to get jobs raises the question, why isn't he gardening?

Another aspect is to be noted: extensive detailing, which opens a number of avenues of investigation, heightens the saliency of the time-limited character of the process. Keeping in mind that there are numbers of cases to be processed by any one worker, the multiplication of aspects of the investigation multiplies the demands placed on both worker and client, multiplies the number of contacts between them, and makes the filing of the case "in time" a difficult matter.

[21] This counter-typification also has structural connections. Recall that the detailing of the applicant's life through the proposing of "the way it must be" in that kind of circumstance

She indicates a certain "suspicion" she entertains:

I have a feeling in my heart, I can't prove this you understand, that the only reason I can think of that he would come here is that it would sound real good at the [Labor Law Commission] hearing.

As indicated above, Mr. A. will be given a further opportunity to demonstrate his willingness to seek employment as required by the AFDC-U program. This "second chance" will be structured in such a way that subsequent failure of attempts to verify this search will be taken as definitive grounds upon which to deny the application. In the meantime, the investigation will proceed along the lines suggested by the supervisor, as witness the subsequent phone call to the applicant by the caseworker:

G. B.: (To the author) Well, we have about twelve things to check out . . . (He phones Mr. A.) Hello, Mr. A.? Yes, I've discussed your case with the supervisor and uh, we're going to issue a grocery order, but there's a little bit of information I'd like to get regarding your situation, and one is your garden tools. You have garden tools right now? Gardening tools, yeh, for landscaping and stuff. You have them huh, you have? Let me see . . . hedge clippers, electric hedge clippers? Manual. You have a lawn mower? You have what else? What else Mr. A.? You have a hose? Right, shovels? Okay, and you still have those, right? Now, your truck is broken, right? What kind of truck is that? 1947, what kind of truck, pickup? and where is that parked and what's wrong with it? Threw a rod? Well, how much will it take to be repaired? $45? Who told you that? What's the name? And when did the truck break down? What day in October? Around the middle . . . the last part of September. Yeah? It was the last part of September. Do you have your income tax statements . . .? I mean for you as a business owner? You don't keep business records? Okay, you started in business six months ago. Self-employed. When were you told about, eh, yeh, by the tax man what to do? When does he want you to file a business return, do you know? How do you secure your jobs, Mr. A.? Yes, word of mouth huh? Mr. G. saw you work at the doctor's. What was that doctor's name? Dr. R., I think I have it down someplace, and how did you get the job with the doctor? Through your house . . . at your house. Did you have jobs before that? Did you work for anybody else? Do you have a car? In other words, you have to rely on public transportation. . . .

---

is taken as the basis for a course of investigation. Each instance of such imputation, in the absence of information to substantiate the applicant's claim, reinforces the doubt that the applicant is a person worthy, as well as eligible, for assistance. Given merely the information that the applicant is a self-employed contractor who also does gardening, a typified pattern of action for a person of *that sort* is constructed, the verification of which would establish his claims to be a good person in a fix. Such constructions, taken as "probably the case" in the absence of further information, became an issue to be resolved by investigation. The worker's attempt to "make sense" of an apparent discrepancy in the instance of his "inability to secure" gardening work, and of the method by which he secures his work, may be the attempt to uncomplicate the case.

A review of the relevant features of this case is in order. First, both the worker and the supervisor were oriented to the essentially problematic character of the applicant's claim, albeit in different ways and in differing degrees. Similarly, both accepted the essentially unproblematic character of official documents, again with some differences. The essential differences between them lay in the extent to which the contingencies of action were treated as relevant considerations in assessing the authority of a particular verification procedure, and hence, of the document resulting from it. The supervisor's account made the sources of information pertinent to the applicant's search for employment visible as organized, procedure-bound enterprises that could be counted on to have a record of the applicant's inquiry if he in fact made one. The assertion of "contingencies" is a challenge, the response to which is an account which suppresses such contingencies as matters eligible for consideration.

The difference between the worker and the supervisor in the depth of skepticism concerning the applicant's story is worth comment. The supervisor employed the occasion (as they were often observed to do) to probe the case further and issue instructions for further investigation. These instructions made the applicant's circumstances accountable as courses-of-action which, if typically motivated and typically executed, could be expected to produce records serviceable for the task of deciding eligibility. Over the course of this exchange the worker introduced a variety of contingencies which could serve to rationalize departures from what the supervisor depicted as the ordinary course-of-action to be expected from someone like the applicant.

This case was eventually approved. The primary interest in it here, of course, has been in the process of investigation—particularly in the way the applicant's claims are rendered problematic and challenges to the "plain fact" of documentary procedures and their outcomes responded to. The end result is a "documented" case that both indicates the approved or disapproved status of the applicant, and provides a record of justification for the action taken, i.e., its accountably rational character.

CONCLUDING REMARKS

This volume is concerned with the impact of records on the lives of Americans. This chapter has been occupied with the problem of how records come to have an impact in the first place, at least the kind of impact they have in a public assistance organization. Such a problem is seldom posed; it seems an obvious matter. But the very obviousness of a phenomenon should motivate close inspection of it. Behind the familiar appearance is often a set of very complex matters in need of study.

It has been observed that for personnel in the agency studied, documents often had an obvious character. They were seen by personnel as obviously factual reports about a variety of circumstances relevant to the determination of eligibility, and equally important, as factual depictions of the organization's conduct of its affairs. Personnel trafficked in such facts—they collected them, generated them, and used them in consequential ways.

Yet, as noted at the beginning of the chapter, not any piece of paper with any set of entries would do. And although certain other pieces of paper did routinely "do" there are many occasions in which the authority of documents required demonstration. The persistent theme of the chapter, then, emerges as the continual interplay between the routine and the problematic, the taken-for-granted use of documents and the occasioned accounts which make their use observable as rational procedure.

The taken-for-granted use of documents, as analyzed by accounts given in the setting, is dependent on an ordered world—the ordered world of organizations, and the ordered world of the society-at-large. When simply taken for granted, the features of these ordered domains are matters of mere recognition for which no accounts are called for or given. Indeed, such routine recognition, and the action and inference proceeding from it, is the mark of the competent worker.

When a document is rendered problematic in a given case, the document-producing activities of which it is a part are made accountable as orders of necessary motives, necessary actions, and necessary procedures which may be used to analyze the features of the case and reach a determinate and warrantable decision. It is the artful accomplishment of personnel that they are able to provide such accounts which sustain the organizationally required use of documents over the manifold contingencies of everyday investigations. It is through that artful accomplishment, some features of which were examined in this chapter, that records achieve the impact they are ordinarily taken to have.

12 Records in the Juvenile Court

EDWIN M. LEMERT

PURPOSES OF JUVENILE COURT RECORDS

RECORDS IN THE AMERICAN JUVENILE COURTS REFLECT THEIR ANOMALOUS position in the court system as well as a synthetic combination of goals frequently working at cross-purposes.[1] The juvenile court in action variously seeks to raise and maintain standards of child care, punish children or their parents, facilitate enforcement of law, and act as an agency of conflict resolution within the community. Overshadowing these is the hard fact that juvenile courts are deficient in resources; since their inception most such courts have been substandard, lacking sufficient means to realize their goals, and suffering from "chronic overload."[2] One result is a large and persistent element of expedience in the decisions and actions of juvenile court judges and probation officers.

Juvenile court records have been criticized on several grounds: they are inadequate or incomplete as reports; they are uneven in their description and analysis of various aspects of the minor's problem and situation; and they fail to include the perspectives and feelings of the minor and par-

[1] There is a large literature on the confusion of goals in juvenile courts. See, for example, Tappan, Paul, "Confusion in the Court," in *Juvenile Delinquency*, McGraw-Hill, New York, 1949, ch. IX.

[2] Carr, Lowell, "Most Courts Have to be Substandard," *Federal Probation*, vol. XIII (1949), pp. 29–33; Vinter, Robert, "The Juvenile Court as an Institution," *Task Force Report: Juvenile Delinquency and Youth Crime*, President's Commission on Law Enforcement and the Administration of Justice, Washington, 1967, pp. 84–90.

ents.[3] Inadequacy of juvenile probation reports, long lamented by child welfare specialists, is an outgrowth of an older tendency in many juvenile courts to proceed in a highly informal, often *ex parte,* manner, deliberately done to preserve anonymity and protect youthful reputations. Countless thousands of juvenile court cases have been handled without leaving any legal or police record whatsoever. Much of this was a direct result of folk conceptions of juvenile justice in which police and sheriff's deputies as well as probation officers sought to "give kids a second chance" or "avoid giving a kid a record." A reinforcing factor was the dislike of early probation officers and police for "paper work." Finally, the original image of the juvenile court as a child welfare agency left it unclear whether it was a "court of record," which required a court reporter present during hearings.[4]

Growth of Record-Keeping

As social work and psychiatry became more professionalized, especially after 1920, and their philosophies took root and flowered into an "age of treatment," more and more attention was given to case study and record writing. Identifying facts, notes of action taken, description of client personalities, and running accounts of contacts between probation officers and their charges began to be recorded in greater and greater volume.[5] A kind of format for the juvenile probation report evolved, based upon the medical model advocated in Mary Richmond's pioneer treatise on social work; this stressed three phases in the process: case study (investigation), diagnosis, and treatment.[6]

Apart from the influence of a burgeoning treatment ideology, the sheer growth of caseloads in large juvenile courts coupled with bureaucratization of probation departments made written case records increasingly necessary. Today recording has become a major part of the probation officer's work, in large courts and departments consuming anywhere from 22 to 30 per cent of the officers' time.[7] Case records accumulate in number and grow in size, creating serious storage problems. Records may range from half an inch to six inches thick, and sometimes contain more words than a substantial novel or textbook. One selected at random by the author

[3] See Kahn, Alfred J., *A Court for Children,* Columbia University Press, New York, 1953, ch. VI.

[4] In California prior to 1961 court reporters were present at juvenile court hearings in only 26 of 58 counties. *Governor's Special Study Commission on Juvenile Justice Part II,* Sacramento, 1960, p. 15.

[5] Miles, Arthur P., "The Utility of Case Records in Probation and Parole," *Journal of Criminal Law, Criminology and Police Science,* vol. 56 (1963), pp. 285–293.

[6] Richmond, Mary, *Social Diagnosis,* Russell Sage Foundation, New York, 1917.

[7] Miles, *op. cit.*

in a California county probation department measured two and one-half inches thick, and contained 318 pieces of paper, 112 on the "legal side" of the folder, 206 on the social report side.

It is obvious even to an uninformed observer that certain kinds of facts, such as dated notices and summaries of actions taken, are minimally necessary for juvenile courts to carry on their daily or routine procedures. The mere mechanics of locating minors and relatives, acquiring and renewing jurisdiction, in addition to transfer of cases, requires names, addresses, and phone numbers, sometimes place of work. The recording of other data, such as age, sex, years of schooling of minors, and present status of the parental family and religion of parents is the consequence of various statutory requirements and the administrative responsibilities of probation officers. Still other record entries are necessary to provide particular services to court wards, such as medical care and school placements.

Specialization of function within larger probation departments leaves a direct imprint on records, reflected in such things as intake summaries, supervision summaries, and court hearing reports. Some materials find their way into records to justify decisions or actions of deputy officers to supervisors or administrative heads. Other data are included to compile annual reports, reports to county or state departments, or to meet research needs.

Discontinuity Between Decision-Making and Records

All the aspects of records described thus far are reasonably clear. What is less clear and in need of analysis is the relation of the contents of records to major decisions made in juvenile courts and probation departments. This includes placements on informal probation, taking jurisdiction, assigning minors to one of several jurisdictional categories (dependent, incorrigible, in moral danger, delinquent) and the choice of disposition of cases. Two points are relevant to the discussion of this problem: the first is the existence of a vast amount of information in juvenile court records, replete with numerous duplicates, which is seldom if ever used.[8] Second is the lack of discernible correspondence between the contents of records and recommendations made for disposition of cases.[9] This is striking to the "outsider" who reads probation reports, for he often finds it difficult or impossible to say how or why the investigator or a supervisor reached his conclusions.[10]

[8] Vinter, *op. cit.*
[9] Kahn, *op. cit.*
[10] Cicourel, Aaron, *The Social Organization of Juvenile Justice*, John Wiley & Sons, New York, 1967, pp. 27ff.

Some light is shed on this discontinuity by research showing little or no association between the amount of information available to welfare caseworkers and their clinical judgments. The studies point to a "locking in" process in which judgments are formed relatively soon after acquisition of limited amounts of data touching upon a small number of items. This remains unaffected by addition of the results of psychometric tests.[11] This is consistent with statements of probation officers, one of whom, for example, explained to the writer, "I can tell in twenty minutes what kind of a case it is."

If the idea that juvenile court work approximates procedures of clinical medicine is set aside, as well as the ideology that interests and welfare of the child are always its dominant values, then its activities become much more comprehensible. It is possible to examine operant values, "rules behind the rules," or implicit assumptions which guide the course of interaction within the court.[12] The juvenile court in effect can be seen to have institutionalized some simple ideas of mitigated justice in which family situation, demeanor of child and parents, and resources at hand, as well as the nature of the offense and the record of prior court contacts, become critical factors in sustaining jurisdiction and making dispositions of cases.

The record of previous contacts with the court hold a special *sui generis* significance because of an implicit notion that severity in dispositions should be linear or progressive; a corollary is the operating idea that a disposition once tried should not be tried again. The result is a kind of roughhewn justice derived from presuppositions that a delinquent is entitled to be given a chance on probation, placement in a foster home, then institutionalization in a nonpunitive setting such as a camp, approved school (England), before invoking a last resort of commitment to a training school or a correctional agency such as the California Youth Authority, under statewide planning, integration, and administration.

The working importance of the enumerated factors in court decisions—offense, family situation, demeanor, and prior record—is plain from entries and running accounts under some variant of these headings found in nearly all juvenile probation records. Their presence allows decisions and recommendations to be defended by demonstrating that all possible relevant factors have been considered. Their uneven and selective emphasis is a logical consequence of a need to give priority to facts and interpreta-

[11] Miller, Henry, and Tony Tripodi, "Information Accrual and Clinical Judgments," *Social Work*, vol. 12 (1967), pp. 63–69.

[12] Sociologists advocating ethnomethodology have given currency to the concept of "background expectancies" to describe the basis of routine activities of police and court people handling juvenile offenders. Cicourel, *op. cit.*, pp. 15–18.

tions which will justify a course of action to judges trained to look for rationales for their findings and orders.

Although it is common knowledge that lack of facilities or their cost to the county often enter as determining factors in making case dispositions, reporting and discussion of such facts is nearly always absent from juvenile court records, as well as from textbooks or manuals of instruction on investigation and case history writing for probation officers.[13] Indeed, one senses an unwritten taboo against publicly recognizing or reporting such deficiencies, for to do so is essentially an admission of failure on the part of the court to fulfill its high aims. A darker observation is that while lack of resources may lead to leniency or case dismissals, the reverse is sometimes true, for example, when a youth is sent to an institution for his first offense. This runs athwart the folk conception of progressive severity in punishments and may kindle a sense of injustice among minors and parents, as well as among those who take a legalistic view of the court.[14]

Another feature in the pattern of action in the juvenile court, but imperfectly reflected in its records, and making for discontinuity between their contents and recommended dispositions, is sensitivity and response to community pressures. Most notable in this respect are cases involving particularly serious or repugnant offenses, such as violence, sexual aggression, and drug use. Outraged victims who gain community sympathy, or threats to the interests of powerful groups, such as the press, police, county supervisors and business people, may magnify the issues in otherwise commonplace cases. Where strong indignation is aroused, or lines of battle drawn between community groups, the court may sacrifice interests of a child or parents in order to preserve a measure of public support and accommodation without which the court could not easily carry out its work.[15]

To grasp how decisions are made in such cases, one must "read between the lines" of records or solicit informal explanations from parties involved. Probation officers in such cases, seeking to protect the interests of the child, or at least temper the wind to the shorn lamb, face painful dilemmas in making their recommendations. They may resolve such impasses by simply holding to a recommendation more or less balancing the decision-

[13] Keves, Paul, *The Probation Officer Investigates,* University of Minnesota Press, Minneapolis, 1960.

[14] Voelcker, P. M. W., "Juvenile Courts: The Parents' Point of View," *British Journal of Criminology,* vol. 1 (1960), pp. 154–166.

[15] An illustrative California case was that of a fifteen-year-old boy who followed a rival into a drive-in theatre, beat him up in front of numerous witnesses, and slashed him repeatedly with a knife. Extensive press coverage and angry complaints led the judge to send the boy to the Youth Authority, even though he had no record, came from a "good" family, and was doing well in school.

making variables mentioned above, and let the judge make the uncomfortable choice of a disposition to please the community. More compliant officers may write their reports in a way to justify a draconic disposition order by the court, or file an amended petition in which "new facts" are brought to light more in keeping with harsh action. Thus the record is either ignored or adapted to the demands of the situation.

To summarize: thus far it has been concluded that records are made and cited in the juvenile court to satisfy a number of routine purposes, to comply with substantive and procedural law, and to validate or defend a particular recommendation or court order. But because cases sometimes lead to choice of a disposition not easily defensible in the light of the professed goals of the court there is much that is left unsaid in records. From this point of view the record is a residue of action, whose fuller implications are best inferred from the active processes by which records are made.

POLICE AND JUVENILE DELINQUENCY RECORDS

Minors often come to juvenile courts with prior records already established for them by police, school officials, and health and welfare agencies. Police records are the most significant because police have numerous direct ties with the juvenile court and because they account for the bulk of its referrals. Recording practices of law enforcement agencies and of individual peace officers vary tremendously in regard to juvenile offenders. Sheriffs' departments in sparsely populated areas characteristically pay small attention to keeping records of juveniles except in the most serious cases. In some localities this has been a part of the pattern in which sheriff's deputies passed on to probation officers the task of investigating cases.

Small-town police departments fall in between sheriffs' departments and large urban police organizations in the completeness and systematic employment of records, although here and there (for example, in Hamilton, Ontario) a small-town department or a sheriff's office is the exception.[16]

Much depends on the number and kinds of demands made upon law enforcement people and the ways in which their departments are organ-

[16] Lawrence, Leonard G., "Organization of a Crime Prevention and Juvenile Bureau," *Canadian Journal of Corrections*, vol. 4 (1962), pp. 212–215.

ized. Police departments which serve large urban populations and those which have broadened their function to embrace delinquency prevention, of necessity, depend heavily upon extensive record systems.

Juvenile as well as adult crime records are recognized necessities for several well-defined police operations.[17]

1. Informing investigating officers, juvenile court, other interested agencies in particular juvenile cases.
2. Planning for control or "prevention" of juvenile crime and related problems on a geographic basis.
3. Administrative control through the evaluation of policies, procedures, and individual officer performances.
4. In-service training programs with respect to juveniles.

In a rough way this list indicates common priorities in police functions. Whatever else may be said about the use of juvenile records, it is plain that dominant police values placed upon clearing cases by arrest and recovering stolen property determine how records are organized and what rules regulate their use. A little-appreciated fact is the extent to which detective bureaus connect with and overlap juvenile bureaus in departmental organization and how this affects their accumulation and use of information about juveniles. This relationship results from the high percentage of all car thefts and burglaries committed by underage youth.

Juvenile records in large metropolitan police departments consist of a diversity of files or jackets integrated by some form of index card system. Among these are files of complaint reports, field contact reports, investigation reports, family interview notes, taking into custody and arrest reports, and records of referrals either to juvenile court or other agencies, all pertaining to particular persons. Added to these is a variety of general information reports, on cars owned or operated by juvenile suspects, trouble-making gangs and their membership, nicknames of juvenile offenders or suspects, and their associates. An interesting and perhaps highly significant fact is that such records are more jealously guarded by police than individual record files.[18] Some police departments supplement their persons files with others on victims, on the assumption that they sometimes are or may become more than victims of criminal activity.[19]

[17] Kenney, John, and Dan Pursuit, *Police Work with Juveniles,* Charles C. Thomas, Springfield, Ill., 1965, ch. VII.

[18] *Ibid.,* p. 129.

[19] A girl repeatedly recorded as a rape victim may lead police to suspect her as being sexually promiscuous.

Fingerprint Records

Fingerprints in themselves scarcely are negative or damaging information about individuals. Nevertheless, when present in a police file, they have invidious implications because of police practice of taking fingerprints when serious crime is suspected. When minors are fingerprinted, intended or not, the procedure brackets them with a known and suspected adult criminal population. This practice seems manifestly at odds with traditional juvenile court ideals. Yet only seven states have special statutes to guard interests of juveniles in the matter. Such laws usually allow fingerprinting of minors only by court order. The juvenile court code of Illinois, revised in 1966, permits juvenile fingerprinting only by order of a judge or in criminal proceedings. It also specifically forbids transmission of juvenile fingerprints to either the Bureau of Public Safety or to the Federal Bureau of Investigation.[20] Chicago police in 1967 were following a departmental rule allowing fingerprints of juveniles to be taken only after authorization by a Divisional Area Commander or the Director of the Youth Division. After the needs of investigators in clearing cases were satisfied, the fingerprints were then destroyed.

Fingerprinting of minors in the great majority of states is governed by provisions of their general criminal codes, which in many states requires that prints of arrested persons be sent on to central identification or intelligence agencies. In the absence of specific references to minors in the law, local police usages dictate whether juveniles will be subject to fingerprinting and what is done with the files.[21] A considered conclusion is that in most jurisdictions fingerprinting is reserved for older minors suspected of more serious delinquencies or felonies. Hence, a decision to fingerprint a juvenile offender implies certain categorical judgments as well as routine practices.

Access to Juvenile Police Records

Ideally juvenile police records are segregated from adult criminal records, and access to them by other divisions than the Juvenile Bureau is controlled administratively. However, only fourteen states make this a statutory requirement.[22] It is also advocated that police files on neglected and dependent children be kept apart from those pertaining to delinquency, but it is impossible to say that any considerable number of police

[20] Juvenile Court Act, 74th G.A. (Illinois) 1965, Article 2, Section 2–8.

[21] Friker, E. Kenneth, "The Fingerprinting of Juveniles," *Chicago Kent Law Review*, vol. 43 (1966), pp. 144–152; Moenssens, R., "The Fingerprinting of Juveniles," *Fingerprint and Identification Magazine*, August, 1965.

[22] Kenney and Pursuit, *op. cit.*, p. 125.

departments comply. In fact, some separation does occur because sheriffs' departments are more likely to have investigated complaints about neglect or cruelty to children. In Denver, Colorado, the Welfare Department inquires into such cases. They are handled by a special attorney, who has a prosecutor's role in the courts, with the result that such cases only incidentally appear in police files.

There is a well-developed pattern of reciprocity between police departments for supplying each other with information about juveniles, efficiently implemented in most jurisdictions by telephone or wire services. The pattern asserts itself strongly even where legislative attempts have been made to restrict the flow of such information—in Colorado, for example.[23] Jurisdictional preserves, agreements between law enforcement officials, and sometimes statutes reinforce this pattern, as well as a need posed by migratory juveniles, runaways, probation and parole violators, and absentee parents. Police argue convincingly that they could not do their jobs without arrangements for the mutual exchange of information about problem juveniles.

Statutory provisions and the formal organization of juvenile justice require that police furnish facts from their records to the juvenile court. This usually is an offense report or an arrest report, or both. In the past and to some extent even now this has caused friction because police reports sometimes are sparse and ill-prepared to sustain findings, particularly in courts where rigorous legal standards prevail. With the growing influence of legal values and widespread insistence of a fuller measure of due process of law for juveniles, police reports are becoming much more precise and complete than in the past.

Apart from information given to other law enforcement agencies, juvenile courts, and to welfare agencies incorporated into a referral program, police departments tend to guard their records closely. Often the chief reserves to himself the right to decide what groups or persons will receive facts about juvenile offenders. It is doubtful if police are often motivated to impugn the reputations of run-of-the-mill juvenile misdoers; ingrained attitudes of suspicion toward unknown persons making inquiries also give a modicum of protection to minors. Exceptions to this general tendency usually apply to offenders in the older, marginal age categories, sixteen- and seventeen-year-old offenders charged with serious offenses or those who in police estimation have a record sufficiently bad to justify strong punitive measures. Police tend to believe more strongly than others

[23] *Proposed Colorado Children's Code,* Colorado Legislative Council, Research Publication No. 111, Denver, 1966, pp. 60ff.

in the deterrent value of publicizing facts in such cases, and on this basis, a chief may release information to newspapers.

How Police Use Juvenile Records

Large numbers of contacts between the police and juveniles concern no more than temporary dislocations of family care or minor misconduct and disorders, and are handled accordingly. These cases ordinarily will be "adjusted" within the department. For many lost and runaway children or those in need of care, records of the department are checked or other agencies consulted simply to discover an address to locate parents. If an offense is involved, more complex and substantive decisions must be made, i.e., whether to dismiss the case with a reprimand, refer it to a community agency, or send it to juvenile court. While criteria fundamentally similar to those which subsequently regulate decisions in juvenile court come into play, police tend to pay more attention to prior offense records of juveniles and their demeanor than do probation officers.[24] Normative flexibility operates most commonly with first offenders, where the offense is petty or can be interpreted as a "normal misdemeanor"; some police departments have internal rules that they will "never adjust a felony."

Givin a more than trivial but less than aggravated offense, police usually turn first to their records and those of police or probation departments in nearby towns or cities if so indicated. If there is no record or if the record has nothing very substantial, then the presence or absence of seemingly responsible parents may be decisive. If all factors more or less counterbalance, then the appearance of the minor and his demeanor during police interviews make the significant difference in outcome of his case. The weight of the several factors in police decisions and their place in a sequence of interaction is not always clear, but presumably at some point officers make moral assessments of the youth or his parents or both. This emerges in vernacular categories: a boy becomes "a good kid in the wrong crowd," "a punk," "brains of the bunch"; a girl is "a half-pint hustler," or one who "just likes to screw"; a parent is a "lush," or one who "gave the kid everything but what he needed," or a "mother who does her best."[25] Some youth get classed by police or acquire police reputations as "hard-core," "tough," "hood," "young con artist"; in other words, they become young criminals in the eyes of the police, deserving the same general kind of treatment given adult criminals.

[24] Pialavin, Irving, and Scott Briar, "Police Encounters with Juveniles," *American Journal of Sociology*, vol. LXX (1964), pp. 209–211.
[25] Cicourel, *op. cit.*, chap. 4.

The distinction between the "normal" delinquent who deserves another chance and the hard-core types can be inferred from action taken by police and the way records are processed. The latter, the "hard-core" delinquents, predictably are destined for juvenile court petitions, or even criminal charges in an adult court if it is feasible; thereafter they acquire folders in permanent files of the police department. In contrast, youth who avoid referrals to juvenile court stand a good chance that their police records will be destroyed when they reach the age of eighteen.

Rap Sheets

When police refer a minor to juvenile court, his offense usually is described in formal, literal, and legalistic terms calculated to support a court petition. A "rap" sheet listing all police contacts, interrogations, and arrests is sent to the probation department of the juvenile court. Rap sheets have been sharply criticized because they often record mere inquisitorial suspicion, error, contingencies, and happenstance, along with valid or provable law violations; as such they are likely to prejudice the interests of minors in juvenile court proceedings. One of the revisions sought in the California Juvenile Court Law in 1961 was to require that juvenile arrest information sent to California Intelligence and Identification Agency and to the FBI include a statement of the disposition of the case.[26]

The harmful effects of rap sheet information can be overemphasized, for probation officers are by no means mere tools of police, as shown by substantial numbers of minors whose cases are dismissed at probation intake after police referrals. Furthermore, many probation officers insist on handling referrals from police as first offenders if there is no court record, despite efforts of the police to represent them otherwise. While the current offense cannot be easily disregarded, the rap sheet contents count as only one of several kinds of information sought and used in juvenile court. In the last analysis the importance of the rap sheet varies with the values dominant in the court and in the kind of relationships holding between the court, police, and community agencies.

Delinquency Prevention Programs

Despite their laudable intent, delinquency prevention programs, insofar as they focus on specific youths or classes of youths, are likely to accentuate the importance of routine, or rap sheet information about

[26] *Governor's Special Study Commission on Juvenile Justice, Part I,* Sacramento, 1960, p. 47.

police contacts with juveniles. The same is true for facts recorded by community agencies seeking to discover "predelinquents," or youths "with problems." Organized referral programs, case conferences, coordinating councils, and Youth Bureaus which work through an exchange of information, such as a Central Juvenile Index, pose a special dilemma, because collective efforts to prevent delinquency raise the visibility of normal delinquencies, and help to build a systematic body of quasi-official records. The everpresent risk is that such programs will turn into surveillance systems, which police are tempted to bend to their own ends. To a degree this is inevitable, for police are not inclined to accept programs which shield or protect serious offenders against the law.

Police counseling, family visits, and referrals to community agencies may be unimportant as such; nevertheless, if these are systematically entered into records under some such heading as "community adjustment," they may have an adverse effect later when the case comes under jurisdiction of the juvenile court. They can spell the difference in the mind of a harassed judge between dismissal and probation, or between probation and commitment. In some jurisdictions where procedure is loose, and legal safeguards minimal, such records may help sustain allegations as well as affect dispositions.[27]

MAKING AND USING JUVENILE COURT RECORDS

In small probation departments serving the juvenile court the same person is likely to hold interviews, conduct investigations, make court appearances, and supervise cases. He also writes up the entire case history. In large departments, where specialization and division of labor exist, intake workers preside over the first phase of record-making, usually interviewing minors and parents with the police record in front of them. A preliminary check of department records is made for previous court contacts or to see if the case is currently under supervision. Intake workers seek to verify the formal factual allegations made by police, but also try to obtain admissions from minors, as well as to probe for confessions of other offenses and complicity in offenses of associates. In the past, this sometimes took the form of outright "conning" of minors by clever probation officers; today a changed legal climate makes this less likely.

Intake interviews are important sources of information because the

[27] For a research-based discussion of the larger aspects of delinquency prevention programs, see Toby, Jackson, "An Evaluation of Early Identification and Intensive Treatment Programs for Predelinquents," *Social Problems*, vol. 13 (1965), pp. 160–175.

"case is hot"; minors are more anxious and more willing to talk than they will be later. Parents, too, may be under great pressure to discuss their problems in initial contacts with interviewers. Some intake officers go beyond what is legally allowable and hear or seek information not admissible in court hearings because, as one put it, "the minor knows more about what happened than anyone else."

"Telling the truth" by the minor greatly simplifies the probation officer's task, and is welcomed as validating his "helping" role, likewise the purposes of the juvenile court. Finally, it may become an important criterion by which a first-hand judgment of the minor is made. In actuality, "telling the truth" often is more like a conversion of childlike or adolescent perspectives on events to an adult's view, or a redefinition of normal delinquency into the formal administrative terms consistent with anticipated departmental action. In the process the minor may become his own worst enemy without knowing it. Parents, too, contribute heavily to adverse records, for often it is very important to have their child admit the truth. More canny parents may see truthtelling in strategic terms, a possible way of securing a lenient disposition of the case.

Research has shown that records of clinical type interviews both omit and distort material. Omissions tend to be of highly emotional statements unbearable to the interviewer, feelings and attitudes which are unfamiliar or confusing, and of materials based on a conscious plan to leave out "useless" data. Distortion occurs when the worker compresses the unfamiliar into familiar logical categories:

> Another kind of omissiveness . . . fulfilling the worker's (interviewer's) needs is that in which a particular piece of pathological behavior is forgotten because it is new and unfamiliar and therefore confusing to the worker. He cannot quite understand the client's behavior or its meaning and in describing it in his recordings . . . he distorts it into behavior with which he is more familiar.[28]

The above excerpt reflects distortions more characteristic of interviews by social workers than by probation officers, who are less frequently disturbed by "pathological behavior." Their distortions are more consciously directed by the need to follow routine courses of action and lines they know are acceptable to supervisors and judges.

Intake interviewers at some point size up the total situation, they "configurate" and make a tentative decision as to what kind of a case it is, whether and what kind of jurisdiction will be assumed, and the probable

[28] Wilkie, Charlotte H., "A Study of Distortions in Recording Interviews," *Social Work*, vol. 8 (1963), pp. 31–36.

course of action. They then may review "facts," taking time to emphasize them to the minor or his parents before making notes for the record, which may be dictated on the spot. Following this, interrogators draw up a rough draft of the petition to go to the stenographic pool. Occasionally the intake officer leaves the definition of the case loose, and "bucks" the decision up to others, particularly if the minor is already under supervision and the gain from another petition is debatable. Meantime he has completed a variety of forms, such as Acceptance of Custody, a Central Index card, and made an entry in a booking log.

If a youth goes into a detention hall or center, his name and other information are entered there in a daily log. Counselors in the center also record observations on the minor's behavior during his stay, and even make their own estimations as to what kind of a person he is. These find their way into the compiled record for study by the investigating officer, sometimes the judge himself.

Intake officers and other probation workers, including juvenile hall staff, usually have free physical access to juvenile court files, although ordinarily a secretary is requested to pull files, which she does by first consulting a master index. Files of juveniles usually are separated into active and inactive cases, and those in which jurisdiction has passed to an institution or a Youth Authority. Individual case files are kept only briefly by intake officers, but in some departments supervising officers keep the case records in filing cabinets in their own offices. In lieu of this, field notebooks serve as working records for supervising deputies.

Probation department records on juveniles are separate and distinct from those of the juvenile court. The former are subject to administrative policy and rules, whereas the latter are more rigorously kept in accordance with law. In some jurisdictions they often duplicate each other; but in juvenile courts with large probation departments carrying a heavy load of cases, a court report takes the place of the more comprehensive dossier. This report is filed by the Clerk as part of the official legal record and in theory at least is a public document, although few Clerks actually so regard it. The availability of the court report to minors, parents, and their attorneys varies considerably; according to a 1966 survey, about one-half of respondents from 207 juvenile courts indicated that "sometimes" the report was seen by parties involved or their counsel; 81 said "always," and 16 replied "never."[29]

[29] "Survey of Juvenile Courts and Probation Services, 1966, in *Task Force Report: Juvenile Delinquency and Youth Crime, op. cit.*, p. 82.

The Court Report

The court report contains the allegations of offenses committed by minors, sustaining facts, and social information. The latter includes the results of investigation, interpretations of behavior, recommendations of the probation officer, school records, reports of clinical examinations and tests, and finally, the prior record of offenses and misconduct. In the early history of the juvenile court, the ideal practice was to carry out an investigation and write a social report prior to the court hearing; indeed, this was one of the more important innovations giving the juvenile court its distinctive cast. In recent years an issue has developed over the timing of the social report in relation to the court procedure. Some hold that no social investigation should be made before hearings on allegations or charges, or, if it is made, results should not be revealed to the judge until after he has made a finding and taken jurisdiction. The argument: the social report frequently contains hearsay evidence and impressionistic conclusions prejudicial to the interests of the minor at the "proof" stage of proceedings.

There is ample reason for concern over this problem inasmuch as probation officers make moral assessments much like police, in which prior records figure strongly. Granted that prior records may be discounted in favor of the minor, it also happens that a short or minor record can be interpreted as qualitatively bad, or evidence of the unfolding of a "pattern" of criminality, "hostility," or "antisocial" trends. Probation officers have few constraints about using second-hand or third-hand information or even rumors in reaching their judgments, at most observing a precaution of labeling hearsay evidence as such in their writeups.[30]

Some courts seek a solution to the dilemma by having two hearings, one to determine jurisdictional facts, the other to arrive at a disposition of the case. According to the survey cited, adjudication and disposition of cases were considered separately in 144 of the 207 juvenile courts. Yet 101 of the courts simply recognized adjudication and disposition as first and second phases of the same hearing. In 58 of the courts no attempt was made to differentiate hearings. Only 43 courts set two hearings at different times.[31]

The real issue here is not whether there should be two types of hearings but rather whether the social report should be read or received as evidence prior to adjudication. In California, for example, although hearings are bifurcated and called "jurisdictional" and "dispositional," approxi-

[30] Keves, *op. cit.*, p. 77.
[31] "Survey of Juvenile Courts and Probation Services, 1966," *op. cit.*, p. 81.

mately two-thirds of the judges in the juvenile courts of the state see the disposition (social) report before the jurisdictional hearing. About the same proportions of judges were found to proceed this way in New York juvenile courts, and likewise judges in the more recent survey cited.[32]

California judges generally have contended that they could not do their work in juvenile court without reading the disposition report beforehand, and their position is explicitly supported in the juvenile court law and in at least one appellate decision.[33] In contrast, however, a minority one-third of California and New York judges apparently manage somehow to carry out their adjudications of juvenile cases without previous study of the social report. Furthermore, English magistrates whose work the author observed in the inner London juvenile courts in the spring of 1967 were quite able to decide on charges in the absence of information customarily presented in the social report. Magistrates enter hearings and sit without any case files on hand; nothing beyond a charge and description of the offense is heard, and this from the barrister-clerk in a terse fashion. Only after police, witnesses, minors, and parents testify to the facts, and the magistrates make a finding, is the question asked, "What is known?" If education, welfare, and probation officers have information, it is presented.

Sometimes these workers have copies of records of prior court contacts which magistrates then study. Otherwise it is only by chance that a magistrate knows anything about the background or record of minors appearing before them. English juvenile courts follow the rule observed for adult criminal trials in both England and the United States, namely that a record of prior convictions or findings of crime shall not be allowable as evidence of probable guilt in a current charge. Only if the defendant or his counsel questions the character of a witness or complainant can the prosecution try to impeach the juvenile's testimony.[34]

All things considered, it must be conceded that there is no sure way to exclude all possible indications of a prior record when a minor's case is being adjudicated. For example, even though no prehearing investigation is made and no social report is present, a glance at the thickness of the

[32] Lemert, Edwin, "Legislating Change in the Juvenile Court," *Wisconsin Law Review*, Spring, 1967, pp. 437ff; Yehle, "Some Practices and Procedures in Children's Court," *Syracuse Law Review*, vol. 1 (1957), p. 9; "Survey of Juvenile Courts and Probation Services, 1966," *op. cit.*, p. 82; Krasnow, E., "Social Investigation Reports in Juvenile Court," *Crime and Delinquency*, vol. 12 (1965), pp. 150–159.

[33] Lemert, *op. cit.*

[34] See Wigmore, John H., *A Treatise on the Anglo-American System of Evidence in Trials at Common Law*, 3rd ed., Little, Brown, Boston, 1940, pp. 195–197; "Use of Prior Crimes to Affect Credibility and Penalty in Pennsylvania," *Pennsylvania Law Review*, vol. 113 (1964), pp. 382–414.

legal record may communicate the probable existence of a prior record. Again, the intensity or special manner in which a prosecutor or a probation officer presents allegations or proof offers strong clues that the minor is a recurrent offender. Finally, the judge himself may recognize names of minors or relatives and realize that it is an old case. In small communities and rural areas where a great deal of common knowledge circulates about individuals and families, the judge can easily infer facts about a case without need of a probation officer's report.

Utilization of Records in Juvenile Court

Probation or court reports are selected facts and interpretations presented in a way to influence judges' decision. Their influence, however, varies a good deal from one judge to another. Some judges do not read probation reports or if they do, pay little heed because they prefer to reach conclusions independently. In some instances judges rely upon questioning of probation officers during the hearing. On the other hand, in a busy court the judge may abdicate decisions to the probation department, intervening only where recommendations sharply diverge from his views.

The form and contents of probation reports reflect accommodations between probation people and judges they serve. The perspectives and biases held by a judge considerably affect the kinds of facts put into a report and the type of recommendations made. Probation officers are quick to deny any "slanting" of their reports to please judges; but in courts with only one or two relatively permanent judges, probation officers recognize the necessity of adapting to what some call the "pet peeves" of judges. For example, a probation officer may learn that it is pointless to recommend placement of a child with a couple living in a common-law relationship, no matter how stable, or that any references to drinking by minors should be played down to avoid arousing the special judicial ire.

Court reports also express conflicts, compromises, and accommodations within the probation department, detention center, or local placement facilities. Investigating officers consult with supervisors before recommending dispositions, or they "staff" cases with a placement officer and others before hearings to see if a recommendation is feasible or acceptable. Supervisors confer with court hearing officers, and sometimes top administrators enter the discussion to direct the plan of action. Now and then an anomalous case goes into court hearing without a recommendation, or a dismissal is recommended, but only after a full-fledged hearing to dramatize significant issues. The subtleties of these "behind the scenes" maneuvers and transactions account for the seeming opaqueness of many juvenile court records and their discontinuity between cited facts, interpretations, and final recommendations.

Degradation

Court reports and records are an integral part of the pressures and controls exerted during hearings. They may be openly reviewed to convince minors and their parents of the "reality" of the judge's views or to persuade them to cooperate with an order. A medical report is read aloud to impress on them the seriousness of physical injuries to a victim, or the costs of repairs to a stolen automobile are enumerated one by one to make restitution seem "only fair." A judge may leaf through a report, excerpting parts to read in conjunction with a running lecture, in some cases to reassure minors things are not so bad, especially if they follow the counsel of the court. In other cases the purpose clearly is to condemn or degrade. This pattern was very pronounced in English juvenile court hearings witnessed by the author. Invidious distinctions in the record and attendant denunciations seem more frequently directed at parents than at youths and in some sense are true "degradation ceremonies."[35] More aggressive and independent parents grow restive, indignant, or argumentative under such attacks, while others meekly or tearfully submit to their shame.

The Record as Organized Stigma

Shameful biographical facts known to others have long been recognized as personally degrading and also barriers to full participation in social life. This was memorialized in the writings of the French detective Vidocq, on which Victor Hugo is supposed to have based his famous novel *Les Miserables*.[36] The kind of folk ostracism of criminals depicted in these accounts changed markedly in the early nineteenth century as modern techniques of criminal investigation, identification, and record-keeping developed, giving place to what George H. Mead called the "modern elaborate development of the taboo."[37]

Criminal records today are more effective in protecting society than in the past, but at the same time their consequences are more damaging to their subjects and more difficult to escape or manage. Yet closer analysis

[35] Garfinkel, Harold, "Conditions of Successful Degradation Ceremonies," *American Journal of Sociology*, vol. 61 (1956), pp. 420–424.

[36] Vidocq, *Memoirs*, ed. and trans. Edwin Rich, Houghton Mifflin Co., Boston, 1935.

[37] Mead, George H., "The Psychology of Punitive Justice," *American Journal of Sociology*, vol. 23 (1928), p. 589.

of this generalization is needed to see how far it is true and under what conditions it holds. Among other things rules for access to criminal and delinquency records are highly important, but it is equally important to know something of the practical use organizations make of each other's records, and also the varieties of interpretations placed on them.

Among organizations which request and receive information on persons with juvenile court records are the police, correctional agencies, the armed services, civil service commissions or personnel boards, county, state, and federal government agencies, welfare agencies, schools, private business, and industries. The responsiveness of juvenile court officials to requests is conditioned by policy or common understandings; some, for example, require a signed waiver from wards or former wards, or from their parents before complying. Police inquiries about the disposition of cases they send to juvenile court are ordinarily honored without question, and reciprocity dictates that welfare agencies be given information on cases referred to them by the court, as well as school social workers in cases of truancy or incorrigibility. Adult probation and parole officers, and reception workers in correctional agencies to which juvenile and adult offenders go, freely tap sources of information from the juvenile court.

Probation officers and judges find themselves at a disadvantage when a private job or a government position is sought by a ward or former ward of the court, for to deny information sometimes has the unwanted effect of excluding the person in question from consideration. If the government position is important or needs security clearance, FBI or federal Civil Service investigators may go directly to neighbors, employers, and former teachers of the subject when court officials refuse facts. If there has been a record of delinquency, they usually discover it.

When court workers inform other organizations about a minor's record, it is usually confined to a statement of the offense and its disposition, an exception being made for welfare or clinical agencies, which receive a case summary, or even a copy of the probation report. The armed services currently send printed forms to probation departments, prompted by statements or admissions made during recruitment interviews or at an induction center. Draftees are known to exaggerate past delinquencies, as well as try to hide or minimize them. Replies to inquiries are usually brief, and most court representatives try to specify the offense or offenses in enough detail so that their seriousness can be gauged. Joy-riding is distinguished from grand theft auto, or petty housebreaking from burglaries accompanied by substantial property losses.

Mass Media and Juvenile Delinquency Records

The aim of protecting children from the stigma of public criminal proceedings, and the ethic of confidentiality taken from social work in its early years led partisans of the juvenile court to advocate closed hearings and denial of facts about cases to the newspapers. These values proved to be difficult to reconcile with the interests of journalists and their strong, almost sacred, commitment to the "freedom of the press." The incompatibility between the two sets of values left its mark in legislative compromises and conflicting appellate decisions on the issue in both England and the United States.[38]

The first English juvenile court law excluded from hearings the public but not bona fide representatives of newspapers or news agencies. In 1933, this was modified to forbid the publication of identifying facts about parties in juvenile court hearings. While London newspapers generally complied with this rule, it nevertheless aroused a share of criticism. Subsequent press acquiescence with the rule has been attributed to the fact that English youth as young as fourteen may be tried in adult criminal courts (assizes), where detailed publicity is permitted. A liberal attitude toward reception of visitors in the English juvenile courts also eases the situation. The large number of persons who come and go during hearings (the author counted twenty in one court) give it an open quality which contrasts sharply with American juvenile courts. The risk that the English court will turn into a secret tribunal is remote.

Both the U.S. Children's Bureau and the National Probation and Parole Association have taken stands against open juvenile court hearings and against the publication of names, pictures, or revealing facts about any child under the jurisdiction of the court. However, legislation from state to state, with few exceptions, seems to have left these matters largely to the discretion of court officials. An older survey disclosed that only seven states had laws excluding the public from juvenile court hearings, whereas twenty-four made it discretionary. Eight states forbid publication of the names of juvenile offenders without the court's consent.[39] By 1962 this figure had dropped to five.

In the 1950's, newspaper editors became alarmed at what they believed was a pronounced trend toward secrecy in government and arbitrary disregard by public officials of the "people's right to know." This coin-

[38] Geis, Gilbert, "Publicity and Juvenile Court Proceedings," *Rocky Mountain Law Review*, vol. 30 (1958), pp. 7–13, 16, 17.

[39] Cosulich, R., *Juvenile Court Laws in the United States*, National Probation Association, New York, 1939.

cided with a heavy swell of criticism of the juvenile court and contentions that rights of minors and parents were too often violated. One result was the demand for freer newspaper access to hearings and records of the court, and in some quarters the right to publish the names of juvenile offenders. A number of states have moved in these directions with new statutes: Virginia, New Mexico, Florida, and the District of Columbia among them. Montana has gone farthest, with a law which allows the publication of names of any youth proceeded against where he is charged with the commission of a felony.[40]

A broad conclusion from a review of the controversy is that discretionary action by judges and the policies of newspapers and new agencies are more significant than legislation in determining whether and what kind of publicity will be given juvenile court hearings. An underlying tendency is to reserve the right to publicize more serious juvenile crimes and to identify older, hard-core delinquents in news accounts, mainly because community interests and social protection are at issue in such cases. Complete secrecy in juvenile court proceedings is not in the public interest, nor consistent with justice under law. Finally, there is probably a greater need for public surveillance of the American juvenile court than is true for the English juvenile court.

CONSEQUENCES OF JUVENILE COURT RECORDS

For a majority of those who become wards a juvenile court record per se probably is not a major disadvantage so far as ordinary life opportunities are concerned. Such a record at most is no more damning than an adult record of arrests or convictions for misdemeanors. Yet social penalties do result from the record, however benign it may seem. Both welfare agencies and the armed services are known to reject youths who have been court wards. Social workers defend such action by insistence that youth exposed to the authoritarian controls of the juvenile court are unsuitable for their treatment. Rejection also may follow from strict adherence to agency policies which limit intake to dependent and neglected children. Tappan called attention to the undesirable consequences of the failure to refer minors with less serious problems to welfare agencies before bringing them under juvenile court jurisdiction. One result is to deny them opportunity to receive special help without acquiring the

[40] Geis, Gilbert, "Publication of the Names of Juvenile Felons, *Montana Law Review*, Spring, 1962, pp. 1–17; Woodson, "Newspaper Publication of Names of Juvenile Offenders," *Focus* (1954), cited by Geis, *loc. cit.*

stigma of wardship.[41] While the ultimate effects of this practice are uncertain, nevertheless it is a form of deprivation and an untimely imposition of legal stigma.

Rejection of youths by the armed services because of a juvenile court record fluctuates considerably. It depends on unclear and sometimes shifting judgments made by recruiting officers and military people at induction centers. Their decisions tend to change with the need to fill quotas and current experience with failures in training. Recruiting officers dare not risk too many such failures, lest their own assignment become endangered. Although being excluded from a soldier's life may be considered as a dubious loss by young men already in part alienated from society, the rejection nevertheless adds another invidious item to their records which may haunt them at a later date.

A "serious" juvenile court record usually means that a youth has been committed to a reform school or to a Youth Authority, with the usual implication of a past history of felony offenses. Such a record is a major stigma, stamping the youth as a "reform school grad" or a "CYA boy." At this point the record is reconstituted, for correctional agencies or institutions ordinarily compile their own dossiers, if for no other reason than because records furnished by the juvenile court are grossly inadequate or ill adapted to their needs. In California, for example, a new investigation and study are made at Reception Centers when committed youth are first processed. One result, by no means rare, is a conclusion that the local judge erred, and the youth is paroled back into his community directly from the Center. Despite this circumvention a major delinquency record is inscribed, which validates or documents a whole new set of differentiating reactions toward the subject.

Discharge or parole from a correctional institution means that a youth must return to his community under handicaps, in sum that, having been thrust out of his community, he is not now wanted back. This may apply to members of his own family, or it may apply to foster home placements, hard to find under any circumstances, especially for teen-age youths. Many schools accept such returnees only reluctantly, or set such stringent conditions for readmission that further problems and failures are inevitable.[42] Energetic and imaginative work by parole officers can overcome many of these problems, and cases which turn into out-and-out failures are not nu-

[41] Tappan, Paul, *Comparative Survey of Juvenile Delinquency, Part I: North America*, United Nations, New York, 1958.

[42] Costello, John B., "Institutions for Juvenile Delinquents," in Paul Tappan, editor, *Contemporary Correction*, McGraw-Hill, New York, 1951, p. 357.

merous. Usually the specific nature of the past offenses is the critical factor in failures. If a youth has a history of assault on a teacher, kidnap-rape, child molestation, arson, murder, or just generally being "a pain in the neck" to people, he can expect special difficulty in overcoming his past in old community settings.

The levels and points at which juvenile parolees seek to re-enter society, as well as their educational qualifications, set conditions of success or failure. On the whole, a juvenile court record, even when darkened by a correctional school record, is not an insurmountable barrier to employment in unskilled, skilled, and even clerical occupations. Systematic studies of the problems in the United States have yet to be made, but a survey in England showed that 80 per cent of large businesses and 21 per cent of small establishments knowingly employed persons with prior criminal records, mostly in manufacturing and service trade jobs. An impressive minority of the workers were engaged in the delivery of goods or collections, or served in clerical posts. Furthermore, when this class of employees became involved in further offenses, the tendency of the firms was to conceal their actions and protect them. One possible explanation for this was normalization of such thefts as a form of expected employee "pilfering."[43]

A study focused on juvenile parolees from the California Youth Authority revealed that 37 per cent of 1,020 males classed in the labor force were unemployed. This contrasts with an estimated 16 per cent of youths, age fourteen to twenty-four years, in the national labor force who were unemployed. Differences in percentages unemployed between the parolees were associated with ethnicity, region of origin, and years of schooling. A prior record of delinquency and the number of prior delinquencies did not seem to have much bearing on differences in the proportions who were unemployed, but significant differences did appear between those with first and later readmissions to CYA. The record in this sense seemed to operate more severely against older parolees, for reasons suggested in the following:

> Possibly older parole returnees were often recommitted by criminal courts, whereas first termers in the same age category were adjudicated during an earlier period by juvenile courts. A preponderance of felony convictions in criminal courts may have diminished employment opportunities for parole re-

[43] Martin, J. P., *Offenders as Employees*, St. Martin's Press, New York, 1962; also, Zeitoun, L., "Survey of Employers' Attitudes to Hiring of Ex-Inmates," *Canadian Journal of Corrections*, vol. 7 (1965), pp. 125–129.

turnees to a considerable degree. It is also possible that older returnees had accumulated long offense records, with the result that employers were more likely to learn about their violations and regard them as being poor risks.[44]

The stigma of a juvenile court record falls more heavily on youth or adults who seek upward mobility through education or job advancement than it does on less ambitious youth. While the record is seldom a bar to entering colleges or universities, nevertheless it makes admissions to professional schools uncertain. In the same way an application to enter officer's training school is jeopardized where there is a juvenile court record, and trade schools have at times refused enrollment to former delinquents. Detailed investigations usually are necessary for acceptance as an officer candidate, and, depending on the nature of the record, a negative decision is a distinct possibility. Admissions officials of professional schools must take care to avoid students whose character or integrity may be questioned by licensing boards at such time as they enter practice. Bureaus for licensed trades and occupations in a number of states reserve the right to decide independently whether delinquencies or crimes are evidence of moral turpitude and thus a bar to issuing a license.[45]

Adaptations of Juveniles to Court Records

When specifically queried on the question, probation officers minimize the effects of a juvenile court record on the job chances of youths. This is chiefly because the great majority of wards with whom they work have low socioeconomic status and low aspirations. Most seek unskilled or semiskilled positions in which employers are concerned with little beyond the worker's ability to perform on the job. Parole officers also play down the possible handicap of a correctional school record for juvenile parolees seeking employment. Lack of education and problems of personal adjustment are counted as far more important than prejudice or lack of opportunity.[46] The stress placed on these factors owes much to the social work philosophy shared by parole officers and their professional task of rehabilitating individuals rather than social action to make communities more receptive to parolees.

Motivation and the ability to present one's self in a favorable light remain central to establishment of a person in society. Successful rehabilitation is primarily self-rehabilitation—emphasized by the fact that parole

[44] Seckel, Joachim P., *Employment and Employability among California Youth Authority Wards: A Survey,* Research Report 30, Youth and Corrections Agency, Sacramento, 1962, pp. 12–14.

[45] See California Business and Professional Code S 1679 (1955); S 4358, 1965.

[46] Seckel, *op. cit.* p. 42.

officers and employment services obtain only a very small percentage of the jobs filled by juvenile parolees. Of those who remain unemployed, about one-half either are "unable to find work" or "just don't want to work."[47]

It is entirely possible that both lack of education and lack of motivation to find work among juveniles paroled from correctional institutions represent a complex internalized expression of the effects of a record or a form of "secondary deviance" on their part. The kinds of values, attitudes, and skills acquired by a youth who has a checkered career in and out of correctional schools poorly fit him for regular employment or competition for jobs.[48] However, it must be admitted that the way in which subjective awareness of a juvenile court and correctional school records influence motivation and social interaction to preclude or reduce chances of employment are not clear. Empirical observation by field workers are at least as enlightening at this stage of knowledge as more sophisticated sociological inferences. One parole officer offered the following crude typology of patterns as he saw them in the adaptations of youths on parole from the California Youth Authority:

1. Some kids use the record as an excuse for doing nothing.
2. Some become overconcerned about the possible adverse effects of their records.
3. Some boys rather doggedly keep trying without too much self-consciousness about the record—they "plow ahead."
4. In some cases the record is actually used to an advantage.

What may be inferred in sociological terms from these observations is that a certain portion of juveniles with records develop a kind of world view that the "game isn't worth the candle"; in other words, that the rewards of effort are too few or are greatly outweighed by the penalties associated with stigmatized status. Others may become ambivalent, or "try too hard," leading them to overstress routine frustrations and disappointments of everyday life. In either case, interaction with normals is likely to be strained and unproductive. More specifically, ex-delinquents must "play the guessing game," consider whether "others know," or if they don't "should I tell them." Experience alone may be a poor guide for answers to such questions. Persons in such positions more or less lead a precarious

[47] *Ibid.*, pp. 41, 35.
[48] See Lemert, Edwin M., "Human Deviance," *Social Problems and Social Control*, Prentice-Hall, Englewood Cliffs, N.J., 1967, ch. 3; Thrasher, Frederick, *The Gang*, University of Chicago Press, Chicago, 1927.

existence, on the brink of danger, and they tend to develop a set of anticipatory reactions to contingencies which mark them as different from others.

Surveillance

A class of special contingencies associated with a juvenile court or a correctional school record are those accruing from police surveillance. When a youth is placed on probation and this is known to the police, he may be singled out for special watchfulness and surveillance. Even more predictable is the police surveillance of youths who have been discharged from a correctional institution. In some cities police keep carefully updated lists of these youths, and clearly regard them as a suspect class. In one notorious instance in a small northern California town a list of CYA parolees and other police-identified "trouble-makers" was prominently posted in the main departmental office for all who entered to see.

A not uncommon police practice, which affects juvenile as well as adults, is "rousting," in which suspects are rounded up and questioned for possible leads in the solution of crimes. Rousting also may be employed to make a community uncomfortable for persons who are undesirables in the estimation of the police. Rousting is both humiliating and degrading for juveniles and adults; it keeps alive an unpleasant past and can engender a deep sense of injustice, mostly among victims who believe they have "paid their debt to society," and therefore should be left alone. Rousting and harassing by police can be disorganizing to an individual's family as well, and leave in its wake aggravating practical problems.

> Since 1964 I have been picked up several times and questioned by the police, but they have watched me even closer since last December (1966), when I came back from the City. My hair was long; I looked seedy and I had a chick with me. The police pulled me out of dances, saying I was drunk, even though I told them I don't drink. Finally one day they blocked the street in front of my house and pulled me out on a marijuana charge. They towed my car away and kept a hold on it even though no marijuana was found in it. There was a big storage bill and I had to scrounge the money to pay it. At different times I've had three cars towed away. Friends tell me that the police have showed them my picture; they try to make out that I'm part of a drug syndicate—imagine, here in Cowtown! The police play an ego game, but I try not to get pushed into playing their game because it would downgrade me.[49]

Ordinarily the police lose interest in a parolee or discharged youth after a period of time, but the problem of his record may recur after several years of trouble-free or even exemplary existence. In one such case in Cali-

[49] Interview with author.

fornia a young man, fully rehabilitated, was summarily arrested and charged with burglary, assault, kidnapping and forcible rape, solely because a victim of the actual rapist picked his picture out of a book of "mug shots" as that of her malefactor. He was held under heavy bail, grilled steadily by two detectives for eleven hours, and kept in custody for twenty days before a recurrence of rapes made it plain he was not guilty. Something of the depth of his feelings and his attitude toward his record are conveyed in the following.

> The strongest feelings I can remember through the early part of those twenty days were of being almost totally deserted. Only my immediate family and my sweetheart really seemed to think I was innocent. They were the only ones who offered me moral support during the roughest period before it became increasingly evident that I was innocent. . . .
>
> Most people probably assume that such an experience is little more than routine for anyone who already has a record, that is, has already been in jail and been through it all before . . . but regardless of whether a person has been through it before and already has a record, the experience is no less shattering. A person who has a record actually may be more affected than one who does not. He has usually experienced a long enough period of imprisonment to know what it is like, and is trying to "go straight," and avoid violating his parole agreement and being returned to an institution. He is probably going to be more upset than a person who has no past record to live down and has no well-developed dislike for prison.[50]

Expunging the Record

Laws in some states provide that a person who has successfully served out his legally prescribed period of probation can be deemed not to have committed the crime for which he was convicted, and after taking action to erase the record, can swear in a court of law that he has never been convicted of the crime in question. The idea is generally implicit and explicit in juvenile court philosophy; a number of the relevant statutes and also appellate decisions have held the proposition that proceedings in these courts are not to be deemed criminal and findings not convictions of crimes. Additional force was given these ideas by statutes which forbid subsequent use of the record of juvenile court proceedings for any other purpose, except in the same court on a later appearance of the same minor.[51] Later, the obvious came to be recognized, namely that juvenile court proceedings did indeed impart stigma, and that such stigma at most could be only partially diminished, if at all. This led to statutory relief specifying methods for expunging the juvenile court record.

[50] Interview with author.
[51] Wigmore, *op. cit.*

Expungement or sealing of juvenile court records usually prescribe a statutory waiting period of several years (five in California) after jurisdiction has been terminated by the court. Thereupon an order can be issued to seal the records of the court, assuming no subsequent criminal convictions have occurred. But such attempts to repair or restore the blemished reputation of former juvenile court wards are crude at best, and even when statutes are refined by amendments, they fail to accomplish their purpose.[52] Some writers have become sufficiently disillusioned to speak of the "expungement myth."[53] The weaknesses of expungement procedures are several:

1. Action must be initiated by the person involved, which means he must engage an attorney.
2. Courts lack the authority to order expungement in other jurisdictions or by public agencies, such as counties, states, the Federal Bureau of Investigation, armed services, Department of Motor Vehicles, and state licensing agencies.
3. Expungement orders fail to apply to police records of arrest or field contacts apart from those dealt with by the juvenile court, e.g., expungement orders may simply result in blacking out one or two items of a series on a police rap sheet.
4. The sheer magnitude of the task of searching out, erasing, sealing, or destroying all of the records makes the cost in time and money prohibitive.

The last point was impressively documented by a California legislative committee inquiring into the problem. It found, for example, that common documents on which a defendant's name may appear from the time of perpetration of a crime until its final disposition run over 100. The time and labor required to erase completely the public memory of crimes and offenders' identities from newspapers took on a staggering prospect. First, the newspapers which carried the stories would have to be determined from among 800 California newspapers; then a page-by-page search of these would have to be made, keeping in mind that some of these papers

[52] Baum, Terry, "Wiping Out a Criminal or Juvenile Record," *California State Bar Journal,* vol. 46 (1965), pp. 816–830.

[53] Booth, A., "The Expungement Myth," *Los Angeles Bar Bulletin,* vol. 38 (1963), pp. 63–66; Gough, Gidian R., "Sealing of Juvenile Court Records," *Santa Clara Lawyer,* vol. 3 (1963), pp. 119–124; Sprafkin, Benjamin, "A New Look at Confidentiality," *Social Casework,* vol. XL (1959), pp. 87–90; Report to Executive Committee, *Committee on Confidential Nature of Casework Information,* Family Welfare Association of America, New York, 1943; Perlman, *op. cit.* Probation officers currently are examining the problem of juvenile court records through a subcommittee of the National Committee on Crime and Delinquency.

carry several editions during the course of the day. But even if newspapers could successfully purge their own files or "morgues," there still would be the Herculean assignment of ensuring news erasures in other localities where more than 10,000,000 copies of California newspapers go—libraries, for one example. And finally, there would be left the need to locate and expunge copies of newspapers which have received crime, arrest and conviction reports via press services, in addition to all the items which have been disseminated by clipping services.[54]

In jobs where employers pay small attention to juvenile court records, expungement is gratuitous. Conversely, where a thorough investigation is made by a prospective employer, the existence of a sealed or expunged record may work to the subject's disadvantage. Employment forms or interview questions defeat the objective of sealed records with simple queries whether an applicant has even been arrested or "in trouble with the police," or indeed, if he has ever had a record expunged. Discovery that a sealed record exists may lend it more importance than if it were on file or its general nature routinely communicated. Expungement laws can confuse the record situation, as when a youth tells a recruiting officer he has a juvenile court history, but the probation officer on being queried, replies as required by law (in California) that there is no such record. The result may be rejection.

Some Interim Conclusions

Professional opinion on the unfair or unwanted consequences of criminal, juvenile court, or welfare records has moved through a cycle of strong protest on civil rights grounds to more realistic appraisal of what is admittedly a difficult problem.[55] Some tentative conclusions:

1. The belief that confidentiality of juvenile court records can be maintained is illusory or at best a naive assumption born of the idealism in early juvenile court philosophy. Diffusion of information from such records and access can be partially controlled but not precluded.
2. A record once created cannot in its entirety be erased. The costs of doing so would be excessive and in some cases it would create more problems than it would solve. Rules for the interpretation of records and their admissibility or probative value in making decisions are needed more than procedures for sealing or destroying them.

[54] Erasure of Arrest Records, Assembly Interim Committee on Criminal Procedure, 22, No. 8, Sacramento, 1962, pp. 11–38.

[55] Sprafkin, "A New Look at Confidentiality," *op. cit.*; *The Lawyer and the Social Worker*, Family Service Association of America, New York, 1959.

3. The most crucial questions are those which bear on decisions to initiate the record-making process, the particular subcultural contexts within which they are used, and the meanings which are given to them.

DOSSIERS AND THE "LAW EXPLOSION"

Despite the potential damage to reputation and livelihood inherent in the existence of juvenile court records and associated police records, certain protections more or less inhere in social and physical settings where they are used. Inefficiency of law enforcement officials, localism, rivalry among jurisdictions, and poor communication between the juvenile court and the police or community agencies frequently has meant that juvenile records remain unknown beyond a locality, or even outside a particular agency. Courts may distrust records of the police, or as pointed out, correctional institutions find juvenile court information ill suited to their needs, and so conduct their own investigations and compile their own dossiers. Finally, some research indicates that even within organizations there is far less consulting of available records than might be expected; indeed, certain features in the organization of police departments may actually discourage sharing or pooling of information by patrolmen and detectives or detectives in different divisions.[56]

Difficulties in physical access to records work in behalf of the person with a delinquent past on file; undoubtedly countless juvenile court records gather dust in courthouse basements scattered throughout the land, where they get "misplaced," "lost," or require so much work to find that requests for their information are ignored or unmet. Lack of storage space operates as constant impetus to destroy records. Some police departments destroy all juvenile records when subjects reach the age of eighteen, and probation departments in a number of areas follow a practice of burning their juvenile records five years after the cases have been closed.

Yet older, cruder record-keeping methods are rapidly being replaced with more efficient techniques, a process which is accelerated by professionalization of police, probation and correctional workers, and by bureaucratization of police departments and juvenile courts. The old pattern of purely informal handling of juvenile offenders by police and by the court without making any record of action is dying fast. Although youthful offenders continue to be dealt with by police intradepartmentally or handled informally by probation officers, nevertheless these actions be-

[56] See *Crime as a Profession,* L.E.A.A., President's Commission on Law Enforcement and the Administration of Justice, U.S. Department of Justice, Washington, D.C., n.d., mimeo.

come matters of record which substantiate the steady bureaucratization of juvenile police and court procedures.

Many signs point to a crisis in criminal record-keeping, brought on by volumes of cases coming to police and court attention and the proliferation of services in relation to these cases. This aspect of the "law explosion" of recent decades has outmoded manual methods for compiling and using records. Interagency exchange of information is an overwhelming problem in many areas due to the sheer accumulation of records, the fostering of a kind of "paper monster," whose storage and processing has outstripped capacity and clerical resources. Furthermore, "random access"[57] to records, one of the more valuable police tools, is seldom possible, and the interchange of reliable information at points in time when and where it is most needed often cannot be achieved. Large budget allocations must go to clerical personnel, money often poorly spent when measured in results.[58]

The Rationalization of Juvenile Justice

The records problem appears to be most acute and most visible in policing agencies. However, recent research has traced some of the basic problems of juvenile courts to inadequate record systems. According to these findings, the juvenile court is not an efficient organization. Ordinarily it does not have an adequate or efficient case-processing technology, sufficient to the volume and complexity of contemporary court operations. Moreover, it does not constrain decisions within the limits of uniform policy and decision criteria. These defects have been attributed to inadequate means of information storage and recovery, to the absence of techniques for the juvenile court to monitor its own operations, and to lack of methods for forecasting its own development.[59]

The records jam in law enforcement agencies and seeming inefficiency of juvenile court organization are best appreciated against the background of the startling new developments in electronic data processing and communications technology. The implied solution to these problems would seem to be greater rationalization of juvenile court procedures, presumably implemented by modern, computer-based methods for creating and processing records. It can be surmised that there will be growing pres-

[57] "Random access" is used here in the way police use it, i.e., crosschecking files in order to interrelate isolated facts about possible suspects.

[58] Comber, Edward V., *Activation of the California Criminal Justice Information Systems Design*, American Management Association, Los Angeles, 1967, pp. 2, 3.

[59] Vinter, *op. cit.*

sures for such innovations, coming from without the juvenile courts if not from within. If agencies in a network which includes the juvenile court introduce more efficient accounting and record-keeping procedures by automatic means, adaptations will have to be made. In other words, greater institutional accountability in juvenile courts to an extent inheres in such developments because court actions create more visible costs and consequences for these other agencies.

The uncertain nature of such developments is accentuated by the difficulty of ascertaining to what extent new, computer-style records will be adopted in various jurisdictions and which law enforcement and correctional agencies will find them suited to their purposes. Furthermore, even if juvenile courts, or, more likely, probation departments, join with centralized record systems to store and receive information about minors and parents, the consequences are not clear. It is uncertain whether code or machine languages can be devised sufficiently versatile or sensitive to communicate significant nuances of meaning which are involved in the understanding of childhood and adolescent problems. Whether computers will or can "make decisions" in matters of the control, treatment, and rehabilitation of delinquents is likewise an unsettled question.

Closer analysis of possibilities in the use of electronic information exchanges by juvenile courts reveals that much will depend on what forms of information are relinquished to the storage facility and what policy, rules, and practices develop to dictate its use. There is much to suggest that such use will reflect a good deal of resistance to the idea of rationalizing juvenile court procedures. One source of resistance may be the reluctance of welfare organizations or social workers to find themselves to a single, narrow or clearly stated set of purposes.[60] Perhaps more important than its welfare orientation is the multipurpose nature of the juvenile court and the contradictory rehabilitation-punishment goals of correctional institutions serving it, which together make clarification of over-all purposes and assessment of court functions difficult. Finally, it may be noted that juvenile courts have a peculiar local, or at most regional, character, often becoming arenas for resolution of community conflicts revolving around surcharged issues of parental responsibility, family-school relationships, and public order. In other words, the juvenile court in substantial part is inherently an irrational organization.

[60] Gouldner, Alvin, "The Secrets of Organizations," *National Conference of Social Work*, 1963, pp. 161–177.

Juvenile Justice and Accountability

The underlying issue in engineering more efficient means of keeping records about minors and parents is not only the numbers and kinds of actions for which they should be held accountable; there is also a question of reciprocal accountability of those who make the decisions on these matters. It is very likely that automated information systems if effective will produce constraints on those who use them.[61] They may, for example, abolish as uneconomic or unnecessary some of the actions of police toward juveniles which are public irritants, or peculiarly offensive to members of minority groups. Greater accountability of probation officers could mean that fewer juveniles become victims of whim, error, or incomplete information in the processing of cases in juvenile courts. If the juvenile court becomes more accountable as an institution, judicial caprice not only will become more conspicuous but will be measurable in terms of time and money costs, as well as the problems it makes for other agencies. Moreover, purposes of the juvenile court extraneous or contrary to child welfare will be difficult to sustain.

The whole question of securing greater efficiency in the administration of juvenile justice needs to be viewed in the light of the great emphasis which has been given to due process of law in juvenile courts, which has become part of the legal climate of the times, particularly since the U.S. Supreme Court decisions in the Kent and Gault cases.[62] Procedures instituted to protect the legal rights of minors and parents, particularly adversary hearings, often create purposes contrary to those of organizational efficiency. Due process of law for juveniles, made viable through representation by counsel, and exercise of various "rights of the accused" also introduces explicit accountability into juvenile courts, but accountability to its clients rather than to other agencies. The kinds of legal records required under due process of law are those which can reflect unfavorably on police, probation officers, and judges as well as on clients.

[61] Seaberg, James R., "Case Recording by Code," *Social Casework,* vol. 10 (1965), pp. 92–98.

[62] Kent v. United States, 383 U.S. App. DC. 541,568. U.S. Reports, Oct. Term 1965; In re Gault, 387 U.S. Supreme Court Oct. Term 1966, 1–81.

13 *Case Records in the Mental Hospital*

KAI T. ERIKSON AND DANIEL E. GILBERTSON

THE FILES MAINTAINED IN MENTAL HOSPITALS AND OTHER MENTAL HEALTH facilities are not just a passive record of the patient's dealings with the institution. They are an important part of the working machinery of that institution, and they affect, not merely reflect, the lives of the people who pass through it in many decisive ways. Indeed, if a stranger were to notice how many of the hospital's resources were devoted to the task of recording information about patients, he might very well conclude that the main objective of the institution was to generate information and keep systematic files rather than to treat illness. The stranger would not have captured a really accurate picture of the hospital, it is true, but he would have discovered a feature of its organizational landscape which is often underrated in the literature on the subject.

In some ways, of course, the dossiers found in psychiatric hospitals are like those found in other institutions. They contain the same general kinds of information: a summary of basic statistical data concerning the patient, a few selected facts about his past, a brief history of his relationship to the institution, a statement of his "condition" vis-à-vis the services performed by the institution, a word or two about his future potential. These files are not appreciably thicker than the ones found in other record rooms, and they are handled in much the same fashion.

In other respects, however, psychiatric records are quite different from their counterparts in most other institutional settings. For one thing, they include a far greater range of information about the client than one is likely to find anywhere outside the files of intelligence agencies, and they probe more deeply into areas of life that are ordinarily considered private. Most establishments that process people—schools, insurance companies, welfare agencies, military organizations, government bureaus—collect information relating to a special aspect of the client's life situation. We fully expect, for instance, that banks will keep records about our financial status, that schools will keep records about our academic performance, that doctors will keep records about our state of health, that employers will keep records on our occupational skills and liabilities. But we usually expect these records to be a limited and highly specific picture of our lives, a glance at one aspect of a deeper and more complex person.

The presumption in psychiatric facilities, however, is that there are no areas in the patient's life (and, for that matter, no areas in the lives of his associates) that lie beyond the legitimate interest of the institution. In this sense, the psychiatric dossier is not a brief inventory of selected information; it is a biography, a digest of one person's character and prospects, a portrait of him so sensitive in detail that he himself is not aware of all the privacies it reveals.

Erving Goffman writes:

> Current psychiatric doctrine defines mental illness as something that can have its roots in the patient's earliest years, show its signs throughout the course of his life, and invade almost every sector of his current activity. No segment of his past or present need be defined, then, as beyond the jurisdiction and mandate of psychiatric assessment. . . . The case record is an important expression of this mandate. . . . While many kinds of organizations maintain records of their members, in almost all of these some socially significant attributes can only be included indirectly, being officially irrelevant. But since mental hospitals have a legitimate claim to deal with the "whole" person, they need officially recognize no limits to what they consider relevant. . . .[1]

Perhaps the most critical difference between the psychiatric dossier and its counterpart in other establishments is that the information it contains presumably describes a change in the client's condition, and, to this extent, a change in his community status. Like a school, the mental hospital is organized to refashion those persons who move into its area of jurisdiction.

[1] Goffman, Erving, *Asylums,* Doubleday-Anchor, New York, pp. 155, 156 fn.

Unlike a school, however, no certificate can be issued to verify that the attempt was successful. Students are graduated, prisoners are released, soldiers are discharged, trainees are promoted; but mental patients usually leave the hospital with no indication on their discharge papers that anything very important has happened to them. The fact that someone has been allowed to leave does not necessarily mean that he is "cured"—not to him, not to potential employers, not to the physicians who signed his release. In a very real sense, patient records are kept on file in psychiatric institutions not only as a chronicle of past transactions but in recognition of the fact that the patient may very well return. The case is usually stamped "closed" only when the patient dies; the dossier is, at least potentially, the continuing record of a continuing relationship.

In this respect, patient records hide a certain paradox. Mental hospital administrators are aware that patients are exposed to a degree of stigmatization as a result of their hospitalization, and they know that the kinds of information filed away in the patient's dossier may add considerably to this source of discomfort. Thus, they usually go to considerable pains to protect that sensitive material; but in the process they also keep information from circulating that would otherwise support the patient's contention that he is getting "well" and is ready to resume a normal social life.

Because the information found in psychiatric dossiers is of such range and quality, it attracts a great deal of interest. Generally speaking, the files are kept for the convenience of the institution, but demands are continually placed on them by people and agencies who have something less than a clinical interest in the client but who nonetheless feel that they have some title to that information. Interested parties include employers who want to know more about an applicant's state of health, officers of financial institutions who want some indication of his credit rating, judges trying to draw a thin line between insanity and guilt, school administrators hoping to learn something about a candidate's fitness for academic study, police officials looking for investigative leads, and researchers of all descriptions and perspectives who are concerned with the broader contours of mental health and disorder. And this is only the beginning, for there are many other people in the community with a special interest in the content of those dossiers. Patients themselves, for example, have any number of reasons to be curious and concerned about the information recorded in them, and relatives are often aware that any privacies known to the patient may have found their way into the record room. Psychiatric dossiers touch sensitive nerves far out in the community.

These lines of interest reaching into the mental hospital meet in a great tangle at the record room and pose a number of very delicate problems for the administrator. On the one hand, of course, the establishment has a responsibility to the patient to keep his records confidential. The right to privacy is one of the strongest and most respected guarantees of the patient-doctor relationship, preserved by traditions of long standing. But the organization of the modern psychiatric hospital has blurred the character of that ancient privilege and has left a wide margin of ambiguity. The establishment itself has replaced the physician as the custodian of patient records, and it is no longer apparent from either a legal or an ethical point of view to whom these records properly belong. Should patients themselves be able to read what is written about them? Should employers or creditors have access to information of this sort? Should police have the power to consult hospital files in the search for criminal evidence? Should all other physicians, regardless of their training or their professional relationship to the patient, have access to those files? These issues are more complex than they may at first appear, for newer definitions of the patient's civil rights increasingly come into conflict with older definitions of the physician's obligations and privileges, and the curious employer or creditor is more often a representative of the state or federal government rather than a private party.

All these matters have an important effect on the way in which dossiers are assembled and managed in the mental hospital, and all of them touch upon the fate of those persons who become patients. In the following pages, then, we will discuss (1) the organization of record-processing in the psychiatric hospital; (2) the way in which these processes touch upon the patients who pass through the institution; and (3) issues of confidentiality raised by the presence of these records.

RECORD-PROCESSING

The psychiatric hospital is an information system. It draws in data from various sources out in the community, keeps careful track of the activities that take place within its walls, sorts out and processes this information in new ways, and sends certain portions of it back out into the community. What is easily overlooked is that virtually everything that happens in the hospital is a data-gathering procedure as well as a therapeutic or custodial one. Nurses patrol the wards, offer counsel, give medication, administer the day-by-day routines of the patients—and keep documentary accounts of their every activity. Physicians interview patients, give treatment, write orders, make decisions relating to intake and discharge—and these activities, too, become a source of written records. Hospital personnel are (quite literally) building a case as well as handling patients, and their contacts with inmates not only provide an atmosphere in which therapy can take place but a setting in which information can be generated and recorded. In this regard, the mental hospital is not just an asylum charged with the care of patients. It is a research institute trying to solve mysteries, a warehouse filled with great quantities of written material, a museum of clinical curiosities retained for the education of medical personnel. It is an establishment which means many things to many people, and all these purposes and visions are reflected in the material pressed between the covers of the dossier.

Building the Case Record

As far as the institution is concerned, patienthood officially begins when a file is opened in the patient's name and the first sheet of information is inserted into it. That file may grow to a thickness of several inches before it is retired into the archives and becomes part of that great pile of debris that modern bureaucracies leave in their wake. The information contained in those files, of course, is not a random scatter of data: it has been sifted and pruned according to rules that are only partly apparent to those who have the responsibilities of record-keeping, and these rules vary materially from one corner of the hospital world to another. In this sense, the dossier is a patchwork affair; yet by the time it is completed it contains an official institutional profile of the patient that has a profound effect on the entire establishment. Many persons in the hospital, including several who figure in decisions of grave importance, see the patient only through the oblique lens provided by the dossier, and to them the patient has a substance, a shape, a character, an identity, based almost exclusively on what is recorded in those files. Thus any sensible discussion of dossiers in the mental hospital must begin with an account of how they are put together.

To begin with, the various documents fed into the dossier are contributed by persons who not only have differing angles of vision on the patients they are describing but who approach the business of record-keeping with differing psychiatric ideologies and perspectives. Large numbers of people contribute to the files, beginning with doctors near the top of the status hierarchy and moving through a line of command that includes psychologists, social workers, nurses, occupational therapists, aides, clerks, and sometimes even work-crew foremen. Of the institutions discussed in this volume, probably none derives its record material from so many sources.

The actual process of record-keeping varies from hospital to hospital, but this variation has more to do with differentials in the ability of hospitals to maintain high standards of reporting than it does with real differentials in the standards themselves. Most hospital administrators would presumably agree that well-furnished files should include some variant of the following:

Ordinarily, the first piece of paper to find its way into the files is an application form filled out either by the prospective patient himself or by a close relative. The data on this form are primarily for the front office and do little more than identify the patient—name, address, date of admission, marital status, person to be notified in case of emergency, service to which patient is assigned, and so on. In one sense, the filing of this form serves only to place the patient on the hospital roster and declare officially that he is a responsibility of the institution.

The application form will be followed closely by a more complete "Patient Data" form which goes over much of the same ground but which usually performs a different service. This is the basic information sheet: state and federal hospitals that are required to report to a central office will normally send a copy of this form, as will university clinics that report to the offices of a larger hospital complex. Information on this form includes the usual identificatory material, but in addition it will briefly summarize the patient's status within the establishment—the legal basis of his stay, his diagnosis at admission, his record of previous hospitalizations, his mental level, and so on.

The filing of this form gives the patient a shorthand identity to which the rest of the institution can refer, and it may be repeated in the first sentence of a number of reports written about him: "Patient is a thirty-four-year-old white male, admitted with a diagnosis of acute depression, who functions at the borderline level of intelligence and has been hospitalized many times in the past." In teaching hospitals where staff conferences are called to discuss the disposition of a particular patient, for example, the reports submitted by nurses, social workers, psychologists, psychiatrists-in-training and everyone else, may all begin with some variant of the same sentence—as if it were a serial number.

The next form to reach the file is likely to be a medical evaluation. The patient is generally given a physical examination not long after his arrival, and the results of that examination are noted on standard charts and inserted into the record. The information stated here is of the usual sort, although from time to time a space is reserved on the chart for observations about the patient's general appearance, where one can find such important intelligence as "clean, well-nourished white female; no nits or vermin noted." Charts are also posted in the nursing station to keep track of any medication given the patient, any medical orders issued in his behalf, and periodic readings of his temperature, pulse, blood pressure, and other vital signs.

Soon the clinician who interviewed the patient upon admission will submit the results of his initial evaluation, an account which becomes a very important entry in the dossier. This Admission Note or Admission Summary includes a description of the patient's own complaints ("He has been drinking heavily since the death of his mother three months ago," or "He complains that people have been pushing him around") and a brief history of the events that lead to hospitalization:

Patient became involved in a political squabble Saturday, became very upset over feeling that people were trying to take a job away from his brother-in-law. On Wednesday patient had an altercation with a lady neighbor, calling her a lesbian. Thursday he went to work, broke down, was told to go home by boss. His wife made an appointment for him to come in on Friday . . .

or

Patient was discharged from Excelsior Hospital after treatment for similar episode sixteen months ago, and had done quite well. Was admitted there for hyperactivity, constant talking, sleeplessness, non-specific auditory hallucinations. Happily married nine years with a family of three children. Prior to his appearance here his father died and patient changed from an easy going, lethargic, hard-to-arouse guy to a hyper-alert, hard driving person who was alternately occupied with four or five things at once or relaxing completely from these tasks. . . . Has been on no drugs recently.

Ideally, of course, this section of the Admission Summary should include a lengthy history of the patient, sifting details out of his past life that help describe his present predicament, the cultural environment from which he came (and to which he will presumably return), the sources of support available to him at home, and so on. The case history would not seem complete, apparently, without careful notes on the patient's sexual activities, and case records can sound disappointed and skeptical if the patient does not have very much to report along those lines.

Some case histories are rich in detail on the patient and draw information not only from the psychiatrist's intake interview but from social work reports and other sources. Others, however, could be printed intact on the back of a postcard and offer very little in the way of relevant material. The following is a case record of a drug addict who has been hospitalized on five different occasions, quoted in full:

The infancy and childhood was normal. He began to have trouble during his adolescence. He was put out of school because he was fighting with the teacher.

At seventeen he went to jail for burglary and assault. He got two years in reform school. Six months later he got married. His wife was pregnant. He learned about sex from his friends, and he had his first sexual intercourse at age thirteen.

Following the personal history, a detailed admission summary will report on the patient's "mental status" at the time of evaluation, which normally means his appearance, mood, tractability, orientation, and coherence—that is, his general level of functioning. The most widely consulted part of the admission summary, finally, is the clinician's "formulation" of the problem, in which he tries to describe what is troubling the patient from a psychodynamic point of view, outlines a recommended course of treatment, and assigns a diagnostic title to the case—increasingly taken from the official nomenclature of the American Psychiatric Association or the Physicians' Auditing Service.

At this point, other materials are being added to the file in no particular order. Social workers may interview close relatives and provide a summary of the conversation for the files. Psychologists may perform various tests, and these results too will be inserted into the dossier. If the patient has been hospitalized elsewhere or has been treated by a private physician, records may be forwarded to the institution; and sometimes legal documents like commitment papers and court orders will also be included.

The thickest entries in the file, however, at least for those institutions with sufficient staff resources, are the periodic progress reports written by personnel who come into frequent contact with patients. These reports may be daily or even hourly observations on patient activity by nurses or attendants, or they may be monthly sketches of the patients' general progress. Most psychiatric hospitals rely primarily on the nursing staff for notes of this kind, and they sometimes represent an enormous investment of time. The presumption here, of course, is that busy physicians will consult these reports from time to time to learn what their patients are doing, but complaints are often heard that physicians are too busy (or too disinterested) to take advantage of even this economical source of information. Yet progress reports continue to pour into the dossiers. In wards where nurses have time to write occasional notes during a shift on duty, the records may read: "Patient complained of a headache upon awakening," "Annoying other patients with foul language," "Visited by husband," "At 10:30 P.M. the patient appeared to be sleeping soundly," and so on. In wards where nurses try to write capsule reports on the activities of a day or a week, the notes are more general: "Very depressed today," "He is still hearing voices," "Going to all planned activities," "Quiet, cooperative, depressed and crying at times," "Actively psychotic, conversation deals with sexual subjects, appears very fearful of male contact."

Here is a sample of notes covering forty-eight hours in the hospital life of a particular patient, taken from the files of an institution that stresses staff attention to patients. Each paragraph is a separate entry, identified by hour and by day:

Admitted to ward accompanied by mother and sister. Appeared quite depressed. Movements retarded. Answered questions in a somewhat negativistic manner.

Patient slept most of the night. Awakened around 5 A.M. by another patient. Seemed depressed.

Patient talks quite freely, cooperative, well-oriented, talks about her suicide attempt and her lonely life. States feels depressed since her parents divorced. Relationship between mother and daughter seems fair.

Patient attended movie with mother and sister-in-law. Discussion which followed revealed that mother is from a very strict family as is father whose parents were in their middle forties when he was born. Patient states that her husband was a diabetic and used that as a crutch refusing to do any work around the house.

Patient slept soundly all night.

After patient-staff meeting patient got upset, crying because Mrs. Jones was talking about her brother in Vietnam and how she blamed herself for it. Patient is very close to her brother. Says: "My brother cares for me." Seems more relieved when somebody listens to her.

Patient visited by mother, sister, boyfriend and boss. Spoke with me after she had spoken with boyfriend. Seems to realize that she is going to have to make a decision one way or another and that her boyfriend is still unable to see that attempted suicide is directed at him. Realizes suicide would not be a solution. States she is now also more confused as to her feelings and what she must do.

The final entry into the dossier, usually, is a case abstract or discharge summary which serves more or less as a digest of or index to the rest of the materials in the file. Most of the information on the Patient Data form will be repeated here in somewhat abbreviated fashion, and in addition there will be an account of the services rendered to the patient during his stay at the hospital and sometimes a final repetition of what has now become the official story or history of the patient. This abstract will note the kinds of treatment the patient has received, his condition upon discharge (check one of the following: marked improvement, moderate improvement, minimal improvement, no change, worse); the mode of termination (mutual agreement, decision of therapist, decision of patient, against medical advice); and a few words of advice about future treatment possibilities.

The discharge summary is important in several ways. For one thing, it is more likely than any other single item in the dossier to follow the patient outside the hospital; with his permission it is sometimes forwarded intact to interested parties in the community, and even when the rules of the hospital discourage distribution of this discharge summary outside the institution itself, other reports issued by the hospital will ordinarily be based on the information in it. Furthermore, the discharge summary is the nearest thing to graduation papers the patient will ever get, since it is the only document in the files which characterizes the condition of the patient upon termination of treatment. Finally, as we shall see later, the discharge summary is a document of considerable legal significance.

The information gathered together in a psychiatric dossier, then, reflects many diverse aspects of the patient's stay in the institution. The portrait of him that emerges from those files is a composite of many views, capturing him in a variety of postures and moods and peering into his life from several different vantage points. The contributions of the clinician to the file are based on interview material and are often supplemented by confidences and fantasies revealed in therapy; the contributions of the social worker are derived largely from contacts with persons from outside the hospital setting itself; the contributions of the nurses are limited for the most part to observations of the patient's everyday behavior on the ward; the contributions of psychologists or internists are usually the results of tests administered to the patient.

Moreover, these different glimpses of the patient have usually been gathered over a considerable span of time, and to this extent a number of histories converge in the file which have been chronicled in some detail—a history of the patient's life, a history of his illness, a history of his stay in the hospital, a history of the hospital's services to him. All these details together, then, should provide a rich and rounded profile of the patient; but often it does not turn out that way. Somehow all the data that touch in some way on the moving currents of the patient's life in the institution combine to produce a stiff and unchanging portrait of him, as if he were an object fixed in social space. There are several reasons. For one thing, of course, mental hospital dossiers seldom contain the highly textured material that textbooks recommend, if only because these institutions are faced by a serious shortage of staff. But even when dossiers are swollen with relevant information, they still appear static and flat; and it may well be that it is in the nature of dossiers to compress the data that are deposited in them into a one-dimensional caricature. We will discuss this matter more fully in a later section of the chapter. For the moment it is only important to note that the "case history" often looks more like a *case* than like a *history*.

Uses of the Case Record

The psychiatric dossier is a collection of bits and pieces drawn together from many different corners of the hospital, and it is put to a wide variety of uses. The most obvious service performed by the dossier, of course, is to keep clinicians informed about the activities and general disposition of the patients. Yet it seems that clinicians do not read them with any regularity. When the records are sketchy, there is scarcely any information in them worth knowing; when the records are stuffed with nursing reports and social work interviews, clinicians do not have sufficient time to review them. It is probably no exaggeration to say that most of the material placed in the file is never read by the people to whom it is addressed.

But the records have other uses—less visible in the official world of the hospital but quite important to its everyday operations. The dossier is not only a record of a particular patient; it is a record of the personnel who have contributed materials to it and a record of the institution. Among the most interested consumers of dossiers, then, are administrators trying to monitor the operations of the plant, teachers trying to measure the progress of students, attorneys trying to keep informed about legal difficulties, supervisors trying to evaluate the performance of the staff, researchers engaged in a variety of investigations, and so on. In addition, these are the institution's main accounts, and they are often consulted by interested parties from outside the hospital. They are examined when the hospital seeks accreditation from such organizations as the American Hospital Association and they are examined when applications are submitted for state and federal funds.

The mental hospital has a complex system of filters that governs the circulation of information up through the status hierarchy, across departmental lines, and in and out of the institution itself. Staff members of all ranks and descriptions may produce forms which eventually find their way into the patient files, but it does not always follow from this that the same persons have access to the information they have helped collect. In some hospitals, in fact, patient records are sorted into two different piles during the time the patient is on the grounds—with material like case histories and certain test results stored away in the central record room or in a locked closet off the ward, and the day-to-day operating files (medication records, nursing notes, doctor's orders) clipped in a metal folder on the ward where the patient is receiving treatment. Sometimes most of the patient's records are kept in the nursing station, sometimes not; but it is a reasonable rule of thumb that records leaving the ward and placed in storage are off-limits for almost everyone but attending physicians, while records maintained in the nursing station are open to almost everyone with a plausible claim to professional standing. The distribution of these records can be a delicate matter to administrators. On the one hand, the patient's privacy is best protected by keeping sensitive material off the ward, where students, aides, and even charwomen roam largely at will. On the other hand, the partitioning of records has the obvious effect of drawing status lines through the hospital staff in a manner that does not serve to improve tempers or the treatment offered the patient. There are hospitals, for example, where nurses do not have access to the more sensitive records of patients in their charge, and this can be a source of some irritation—particularly since it means that they are dependent on physicians for the most basic kind of information.

Upon discharge, the various records scattered throughout the institution are usually sent to a central record room, where they are assembled, collated, indexed, and stored in a records library. These records will stay available to the hospital for periods ranging from twenty-five to fifty years and even forever, although practice in this regard varies materially from institution to institution. State hospitals, for example, will often keep records for three or four years and then send them to a central storage facility kept by the state, where they are indexed for easy retrieval. Other institutions will simply keep all their old records on hand forever, and one can find mental hospitals with files reaching back a hundred years or more stacked to the ceiling in forgotten closets.

As far as the institution itself is concerned, however, the nerve center for managing and distributing records is the central record room, a facility normally presided over by a librarian with nominal responsibility for their maintenance and security. All requests for viewing patient charts and other forms are processed by the librarian, and it is she (usually) who must check the authorization of anyone desiring access to them. This can be a delicate matter, too, since the hospital world recognizes a wide status discrepancy between a records librarian and a doctor, and it is by no means the case that all persons of higher status than the librarian have permission to view the records. To this extent, "protection" of the files can be rather haphazard, depending as much on the ingenuity and fixity of the librarian as on the formal rules themselves. The relative status of the records librarian, of course, may be reflected in the amount of discretion she appears to exercise, and it is sometimes to her advantage to be a dispenser of privilege rather than an enforcer of rules.

One final note is in order about psychiatric dossiers. Looking in on the hospital from some distant vantage point, one might assume that these records serve as the main source of data about the patients. Yet the dossier contains only one of the several kinds of information that circulate through the hospital world. Although reports flow into the dossier from every staff level, they are addressed to the physician and written in the language he is presumed to like and understand, and thus the records attract only a limited portion of the information that is used and cited elsewhere in the institution. What does not filter up through the official communication channels is a more direct kind of usage, a sound and practical gossip, much of it in the form of unverbalized attitudes, which is communicated informally among the staff.

The records tell an official story about the patient, then, and provide a formal diagnosis of his complaints, but there are other stories and attitudes circulating around the hospital which are as accurate in their own way as the authorized version. To begin with, patients have their own accounts of the events that led to hospitalization and can sometimes supply a rather crisp summary of their own troubles and the people responsible for them. Fellow patients provide myths as well as acute observations to the growing fund of hospital lore. And members of the nursing staff, who see patients for hours every day, know a side of the story which is not portrayed anywhere in the dossier. The official story may stress something like "chronic schizophrenia," but the patient story is more likely to revolve around an ungrateful family, and the nursing story around the patient's manner on the ward. The stories are probably all true; each an abstraction, a kind of institutional folklore. But the official folklore is the one to reach the dossier and the one which in the long run will have the greatest effect on the career of the patient.

THE PATIENT

Thus far we have been primarily concerned with the formal mechanics of record-keeping in the psychiatric hospital. In concentrating on this aspect of the matter, however, the tone of the discussion has seemed to imply that persons with no particular stake in the record-keeping process have somehow drifted through the setting and paused long enough to leave a record of their passing in the files. Our spotlight has been aimed at a stationary spot; the patients appear to enter one side of this narrow stage and depart from the other as if their presence was but a transitory moment in the life of the hospital.

This is a perfectly feasible way to look at any social establishment, but it is important to appreciate that the hospital, in its turn, is sometimes no more than a transitory moment in the lives of those people who become its patients. The psychiatric hospital is a station through which persons pass on their way elsewhere, and in this section we will focus upon the patients themselves in an effort to see how the experience of moving through this station fits into the flow of their own lives.

Acts of deviation usually call upon us to re-assess the biographies of the people responsible for them, partly because we have a natural interest in understanding the causes involved and partly because we need to invent a plausible context in which to set what is otherwise a random and disturbing event. This process is at work throughout the social order. When we learn that someone of sound reputation has become involved in a criminal act or has been discovered in an embarrassing circumstance or has committed suicide or has distinguished himself by some other form of deviance, the rest of us will ordinarily try to compose a new history of the person in question—to search back in time for data filed away among older memories which may help make the event more explicable. If the person is prominent or his deviant act particularly newsworthy, then the various news media are likely to spend a good deal of time constructing a biography in which the new event makes some sense. One thinks, for example, of Ernest Hemingway, Lee Harvey Oswald, Charles Whitman, Ezra Pound, or, to cite a case from an earlier paper of one of the authors, Big Daddy Lipscomb.[2] Even if the person does not command notice in the news media, however, his neighborhood or circle of intimates is very likely to become engaged in a similar project—sifting through details of his past and rearranging them so that some are relegated to obscurity because they do not help explain the new "fact" and others are thrown into sharper focus because they seem to be important keys to the story. A friend threatens suicide and we remember episodes that now appear in retrospect to indicate that he has been in trouble for a long time. An associate is exposed as a homosexual and we recall mannerisms and passing conversations that make us wonder why we did not know all along. A neighbor is arrested for running numbers and we give new credit to old rumors, remember incidents that meant nothing at the time, and in general recon-

[2] Erikson, Kai T., "The Death of Big Daddy: A Note on the Writing of Case Histories," paper delivered at the annual meetings of the American Sociological Association, Miami, 1966.

struct our portrait of him in such a way that the arrest becomes a logical, consistent detail. It is usually the deviant event, of course, which gives the new biography its theme, as if this were the crowning achievement that the narrative now has to explain or make credible. In this sense, the history of a person whose latest and most visible exploit involves some form of deviation is very apt to become a history of his deviant leanings.

This is essentially what happens in mental hospitals, at any rate, when persons enter as patients. In the act of composing a case history about that patient, the hospital is in some ways inventing a biography that will explain his present circumstance and verify that he is a proper subject for clinical attention. In doing so, of course, the case record must concentrate on those moments in the past that seem to point logically to the present illness, as if to indicate that this outcome was almost inevitable. Erving Goffman puts the case with his usual perceptiveness:

> The dossier is apparently not regularly used, however, to record occasions when the patient showed capacity to cope honorably and effectively with difficult life situations. Nor is the case record typically used to provide a rough average or sampling of his past conduct. One of its purposes is to show the ways in which the patient is "sick" and the reasons why it was right to commit him and is right currently to keep him committed; and this is done by extracting from his whole life course a list of those incidents that have or might have had "symptomatic" significance.[3]

The following is a composite sketch of the kind of interview one is likely to encounter in a psychiatric hospital, and we cite it here to illustrate how a clinician reaches into the stream of information flowing by him to pick out those details that fit his conception of relevant evidence.

The interview involves a resident psychiatrist and a nineteen-year-old youth who has been referred by a local court for evaluation. The young man has been in trouble with police authorities for repeated acts of vandalism and his parents have complained on many occasions that they have lost whatever influence they once had on him and do not understand his behavior. In the course of the interview, the conversation touches on many passing moments of the boy's short career. He is asked why he seems to get into trouble so often, and he replies that he cannot think of anything better to do, that he has no close friends other than his delinquent comrades, that his mother is forever trying to keep him at home, and that he does not really do anything wrong in any case. He is asked about his childhood, and he recalls that he enjoyed immensely the neighborhood where he lived, that he used to cry from time to time for fear of the dark,

[3] Goffman, *op. cit.*, pp. 155–156.

that he always took pride in his reputation for eating well, that he once had an urge to hit his sister on the head with a hammer, that he enjoyed family picnics in the country, that he wet his bed repeatedly when his family moved away from the home in which he was born. He is asked about his school experiences, and he recounts his great fear of the fourth grade teacher, his exploits as a young athlete, the terrible dreams that haunted him for months at a time, the day he took the best marks in the class for spelling, his frequent truancy, the vicious arguments that used to take place at home, his close friendship with an unremarkable boy named Freddy, and the night he screamed for several hours in fear that some fierce creature meant him harm.

And so it goes. The interview ranges over a wide variety of subjects and deals in passing with many details of the young man's past, and as each item adds to the store of information flowing into the conversation the psychiatrist is noting those that seem particularly relevant to the case. It is entirely clear, of course, that he cannot record everything. He becomes very alert and attentive when the boy talks about his relationship to his mother, yet he relaxes when the boy talks about childhood friends; he notes the bedwetting and the incident with the hammer but not the pleasant memories of family picnics; he writes about the nightmares and the truancy but not about the high marks in spelling. The case history that emerges from this encounter is a highly selective abstract of the information relayed to the clinician, and the details reserved for the file all serve to make it a little more plausible that the young man is in real psychiatric trouble.

In short, then, case histories provide a number of useful services to the hospital. They supply a package of evidence to support the diagnosis made at admission; they offer background material of obvious relevance in choosing a course of treatment; and they furnish important information about the social environment from which the patient comes. But at the same time they have the effect of making it seem logical, reasonable, maybe even inevitable that the patient in question came to occupy the status in which he finds himself. In the mental hospital, the patient's illness provides the lens through which we look at his past or envision his future, and the life details we are able to see through that screen are very often ones which would seem irrelevant in other kinds of biography. Half-remembered dreams, moments of embarrassment or panic, periods of inactivity or loss of control—these are the materials of the case history. Again, Erving Goffman:

The case record . . . provides a means of systematically building up a picture of the patient's past that demonstrates that a disease process had been slowly infiltrating his conduct until this conduct, as a system, was entirely pathological. Seemingly normal conduct is seen to be merely a mask or shield for the essential sickness behind it. An over-all title is given to the pathology, such as schizophrenia, psychopathic personality, etc., and this provides a new view of the patient's "essential" character. When pressed, of course, some staff will allow that these syndrome titles are vague and doubtful, employed only to comply with hospital census regulations. But in practice these categories become magical ways of making a single unity out of the nature of the patient—an entity that is subject to psychiatric servicing.[4]

Thus the case history is the profile of a *patient* rather than a *person,* the difference being that the patient is someone whose status is derived from his special relationship to a therapeutic agency and whose self can be best characterized by his clinical condition. The psychiatric dossier plays a significant part here by giving the patient a past, a present, and a set of future prospects which define him as a suitable candidate for hospital care. The dossier, among other things, documents a change in status; and it is important not to overlook the fact that this transformation may be wholly necessary to the work of the institution.

Many people who work in mental hospitals are specialists. This means, for one thing, that they have mastered a special body of knowledge and have been exposed to a special kind of experience. But it also means that they approach clients in a very particular way. The specialist is surrounded by a thick tissue of obligations and privileges which help focus his concern and specify the nature of his relationship to those he sees as clients. As a responsible professional he must look at the social world through a highly disciplined screen, focusing his attention on a limited range of phenomena and ruthlessly keeping other less relevant details outside his line of vision. When a surgeon deals with someone he defines as a patient, for example, his job is *not* to look at the "total" person—if, indeed, such a creature exists at all—but to reach through the emotional scaffolding of that person and concentrate on the area of his expertise. In the process, he cannot afford to let other considerations intrude upon his judgment. He must filter out all irrelevant data, protect himself from human complications such as the affection he feels for the patient; he cannot indulge in the philosophical luxury, for example, of wondering whether the patient's family or the community or the world in general would be better off if he died on the operating table.

[4] Goffman, *op. cit.,* pp. 374–375.

Now *persons* are too complicated for this kind of specialization. They are contradictory when decisive action is called for; they are ugly at one moment and appealing at the next; they inspire affection here and disgust there; they have hopes and secrets, moods and fancies; no one, let alone a surgeon, can sort out this much data when he is trying to concentrate on the job at hand. The *patient*, however, is an appropriate subject for the specialist's attention because he is introduced into the setting on the basis of a limited portion of his total person. And this is as true in psychiatric settings as in surgical ones. In both situations, the patient is likely to be identified in the official records (as well as in ordinary conversations) by his disability and the information about him circulated among the staff will be largely confined to those life details which relate to his present illness. In these respects, the ability to view someone as a patient is often impaired if too much data about his civilian identity intrude upon the hospital world. This is one reason why physicians in general and perhaps even psychiatrists in particular are wary about treating members of their own family or other persons whom they know too well.

One of the most disturbing things that can happen in a mental hospital, for example, is the arrival of a patient who is known to the staff for his status or accomplishments on the outside. These troublesome people are usually known as VIP's and can be of several sorts: celebrities who bring their reputations into the hospital with them, doctors or other medical personnel who have such visible rank that they cannot be submerged conveniently into the anonymity of patienthood, and people who enter the hospital under the patronage of powerful figures in the community or in the hospital administration. VIP's are tricky management problems because the staff cannot easily forget who they are. The staff can be placed in the awkward position of responding to status details that are not relevant to patienthood. It is hard to relate to someone as a patient when his looks or manners or titles continually remind you that he is a person of very different stature elsewhere. In this sense, the case record serves as the patient's cover story; if too many facts betraying his "real" identity break through the cover, it is difficult to know how to deal with him.

Case histories of this sort are probably inevitable as long as we expose ill persons to the discipline of a hospital, but a critical question for the student of deviant careers would be: how do patients manage to revise their institutional biographies once they have resumed a normal social life? The problem here is that many other persons besides the staff of the institution itself have a stake in this characterization of the patient. The patient's friends and relatives, for example, have often contributed materially to the dossier and have revised their own portrait of him accordingly. Others who know nothing about the patient except that he has been hospitalized may draw conclusions about him on that basis alone. But most important, the patient often comes to define himself in the fashion peculiar to mental hospitals—indeed, this is one definition of successful treatment and sometimes even a condition of discharge. Thus the case history can have an effect which no one intends, of creating a past for the patient from which he cannot easily escape.

And more problems can arise in this regard when agencies elsewhere in the community petition the hospital for information about the ex-patient in the interests of writing their own biography of him. It is here that issues of confidentiality become particularly delicate. For all practical purposes, the mental hospital has taken the patient out of the normal currents of social life and has developed the most sensitive file on him available anywhere. The file itself is meant for the convenience of the institution; but increasingly, organizations of quite a different structure and purpose come to identify the people with whom they deal in the same terms that are current in the hospital. As a result, the institutional biography designed for local consumption in the hospital is in great demand elsewhere—and this is the question to which we will now turn.

ISSUES OF CONFIDENTIALITY

The dossiers collected and stored in mental hospitals are "confidential" —an expression that implies a great deal but is ambiguous almost to the point of meaninglessness in certain contexts. Medical confidence may be defined as a guarantee on the part of a professional person or agency not to disclose information offered by a patient in the course of consultation or treatment without that patient's informed permission. The moral contract involved here seems clear enough, but in actual practice confidentiality necessarily means that *some* of the information relayed by the patient will be protected from exposure and that *some* of the parties interested in that material will be denied access to it. Mental hospitals differ considerably in the way they define the scope of this principle.

Confidentiality depends not only on a certain measure of faith but also on a set of understandings shared by both partners to the contract as to what it means. Thus a physician may promise his patient not to disclose sensitive material but may instead do precisely that—not because he has broken faith but because he has misjudged what the patient is sensitive about. This can easily happen, for example, when a hospital releases its current roster and thereby divulges the simple fact that a certain person has become a patient—a fact which the new patient regards as private. Beyond that, however, most patients who have any sense at all of confidentiality assume that there is a personal contract between themselves and the physician with whom they are dealing, which is rarely the case in modern psychiatric institutions. The physician is an agent of some larger entity and circulates the information he obtains about the patient to many of those persons who belong to the structure he is representing. This larger entity may be a treatment team, a clinical service, or an entire institution; it may even be a state or federal bureaucracy. Confidentiality, then, becomes a responsibility shared among an expanding circle of people.

Although legal requirements are not standard throughout the country and policies differ from one institution to another, it is a generally accepted principle that confidential information (once defined as such) cannot be released by the hospital without a court order or a signed release from the patient concerned. This is true not only for information being sent to outside agencies but for information being forwarded to other hospitals and physicians. For a number of reasons, however, this guarantee of privacy does not always protect the patient very well. In the first place, the number of persons who have some access to patient records *within* the institution is usually large enough to constitute a leakage problem in and of itself. In the second place, the number of outside agencies which can legally inspect the records with or without the patient's permission is increasing along with the growth of the entire mental health apparatus. And in the third place, there are many ways in which a patient can be subtly coerced into signing a release whether he "really" wants to or not.

The number of persons within the mental hospital who have an opportunity to examine the files varies from place to place, but it is a fair estimate that this number is increasing—and with it the possibilities of leakage to outside sources. Some hospitals take elaborate precautions to avoid any problems of this sort. Highly sensitive records are stored separately from the rest and kept away from the traffic on the wards; names and other identifying data are removed from case records when they are passed to clerical personnel for typing; record librarians follow a strict policy of releasing files only to the attending physician or to others who have special authorization, and so on. In other hospitals, however, records are available to the entire professional staff, a category defined so broadly as to include almost everyone except the janitorial staff. In addition, the expanding use of clinical facilities for teaching purposes multiplies the number of persons who at one time or another come into contact with the records. Normally this does not pose a very serious problem for the institution or its patients because professional norms of long standing serve to protect the confidentiality of that information, but the sheer odds that someone will happen across private material on patients known to them in some other connection are inevitably increased. When VIP's are admitted to the hospital, however, the risks of disclosure are greater, partly because they become the subject of gossip and partly because hospital personnel are more frequently plied for information. To avoid this the hospital may provide a special "hot" file which is stored under special security.

The number of outside organizations with claims on psychiatric records or some portion of them is limited but important. Among these, agencies of the state or federal government are easily the most prominent. Those hospitals belonging to a larger state system not only send periodic reports to central offices on the patients in their care but are open to inspection at almost any time by officers of the state department of health. Federal hospitals like those operated by the Veterans Administration are subject to open-file inspection by a number of federal agencies, a prerogative which is not very often exercised but which must be taken into account by the personnel of the institution. In addition, agents of the Social Security Administration, the Immigration Service, the Census Bureau, and private health organizations such as Blue Cross are frequently found in record rooms checking claims or conducting research.

Police agencies are generally denied access to psychiatric dossiers without patient clearance or court order, but institutional policies in this regard sometimes allow a considerable margin of leakage. For one thing, many hospitals are required by law to submit the names of drug users to police authority, and in addition the Secret Service has recently requested mental hospitals and other psychiatric facilities to notify them of people who may endanger the lives of public officials—a tall if necessary order. As a general rule, hospitals follow a guarded policy of cooperation with the FBI and other police agencies, releasing certain information from the files in response to specific requests and generally retaining as many discretionary powers as they can. The police can resort to subpoenas when the information is important, and the contents of the records are scattered over enough offices that the police can often find what they want in one location if they are discouraged at another. For example, if police officials are denied access to the files of a state hospital, they may very well find the information they are searching for in the office of the state commissioner of mental health. In one medical center we observed in preparing this report, police officials were not allowed to inspect patient charts in the mental health clinic itself—but they could simply walk across the street to the offices of the general hospital and, by showing proper identification, gain access to files which often contained the same information.

Another category of outside organizations which have occasional access to patient records are those with a special interest in the condition of a particular person. Any number of institutions—military, welfare, business, educational—request psychiatric insight and evaluation of people within their own organization, and it is difficult to avoid these requests because the organizations have considerable leverage on the ex-patient and can easily persuade him to sign the necessary papers. Any former patient who admits, as he must, that he has received treatment in a mental hospital, runs the risk of losing insurance benefits or of being denied re-entry into a college or of losing chances for promotion or even of being drafted unless he agrees to sign over his papers. Such instances of semi-coerced releases are so common in this record-conscious society that mental health institutions have developed special strategies for dealing with them.

When a request for sensitive patient information is received by the institution it is often turned over to the clinician who had responsibility for the care of the patient when he was in treatment. He must then decide what materials are appropriate for the requesting agency and either write a special report or turn over certain portions of the available dossier to the organization concerned. This leaves a remarkable degree of discretion in the hands of the clinician, since he not only becomes the judge of the requesting agency's need but the judge of what serves the patient's interest best: and the proper use of this discretionary power depends on a high degree of sensitivity and shrewdness on the part of the clinician. When everything goes well, these reports can be models of restraint. When the hospital is understaffed and overburdened, which is often the case, then the clinician may write a poorly considered report or simply submit a portion of the discharge summary—a procedure that can be both unresponsive to the needs of the requesting agency and to the patient's needs for confidentiality.

Whether or not the institution should be obligated to release files in response to a written request from the patient is a controversial issue in many psychiatric quarters. Involved is the question of "ownership," both of the records themselves and of the information contained in them. Among psychiatric personnel the notion that "it's-your-life-but-our-records" has a strong appeal, not only because it is generally agreed that the patient should not see all the information collected about him but also because an open-file policy leaves the institution that much more vulnerable to legal claims of one sort or another. A similar situation prevails in those areas where "right to know" laws permit the patient to inspect his own files. A patient will ordinarily be discouraged from such a project, but if he wants to pursue the matter the institution has no legal recourse.

Thus the wall of confidentiality has many cracks. A patient's dossier may become public at any time, whether through a court order or some other means, and the hospital must always remain aware of this very severe possibility. A passing episode in a person's life, reported almost casually in the files, may have serious repercussions if it becomes public; diagnostic classifications may be misinterpreted by well-meaning but ill-informed persons; feelings and fantasies, important data to the clinician, are often not differentiated from actual behavior by untrained readers. Many clinical personnel, as a result, keep two separate files on their patients—one for the hospital dossier and another, more complete and detailed, for personal use. Others may make a special point of writing reports in ambiguous or highly technical terms, for example, talking about "psycho-sexual confusion" or "emotional problems of adolescent development" when they mean homosexual fears. A former patient in one of the hospitals we consulted was denied a judgeship because a comment was discovered in his files to the effect that he had "homosexual fears and fantasies." This kind of evasion can serve the patient well when outside organizations request an especially sensitive kind of information, but it has the disadvantage of making those files rather uninformative when they are transferred to another hospital or to a private physician.

In short, mental hospitals cannot always guarantee confidentiality. Pressures on them are great and the risks of unintentional disclosure grow with every expansion of the mental health apparatus in this country. And the problem is likely to grow more severe in the future.

In the first place, civil rights organizations are becoming more and more sensitive about the legal contours of patienthood and about the ownership of psychiatric records, and one consequence of this concern is quite apt to be some decrease in the physician's ability to control the flow of information about his patients. For example, the right of the patient to review his own records and learn what information is being circulated in them is likely to be recognized more widely, with a consequent risk to most current practices regarding record security. In the second place, patients now do a good deal more shopping around among available psychiatric facilities, which results in a heavy traffic of records from one institution to another. In the third place, pressures on mental hospitals for releasing psychiatric dossiers are increasing, not only from organizations with a special interest in the lives and fortunes of their employees but from organizations like the government with a strong legal claim to those records. Finally, the absence of simple legislation on most of these matters leaves remarkable discretionary powers in the hands of the hospital administration itself, and with the increasing trend toward standardization in the policies of mental health institutions, the possibilities of leakage will become greater as the conversion from one system of record-keeping to another takes place.

VI The Law

14 *Legal Control of the Dossier*

ABRAHAM S. GOLDSTEIN

OUR SOCIETY IS CAUGHT UP IN A CONFLICT BETWEEN RATIONALITY AND privacy. The man who lends money seeks information about the borrower, the employer about the employee, the motor vehicle bureau about the applicant for a license, the doctor about his patient, the Census Bureau and research agencies about all of us. Schools, insurance companies, the armed forces, hospitals and clinics acquire, at an expanding rate, information from clients or patients or applicants—in the belief that men's affairs should be guided by intelligence, and that a relatively free flow of information is most likely to produce a rational society. Yet as more information comes to be regarded as relevant to more issues—and as information is sought in settings in which it is not at all clear that the request can be denied—what starts as rational pursuit may become an invasion of privacy. The "file" may be transformed into the "dossier," with all the connotations that melodramatic word conveys about secrecy and the risk of overreaching.[1]

There can be little doubt that each institution which collects informa-

I should like to express my appreciation for the research assistance given me by Harold Rabner, formerly a student at the Yale Law School and now a member of the New Jersey Bar.

[1] The most useful discussions of the problem are Westin, Alan F., *Privacy and Freedom*, Atheneum, New York, 1967; Karst, The Files: Legal Controls Over The Accuracy and Accessibility of Stored Personal Data, 31 Law and Contemp. Prob. 342 (1966); Ruebhausen and Brim, Privacy and Behavioral Research, 65 Col. L. Rev. 1184 (1965).

tion about an individual is pressed by its circumstances to accumulate everything which may help it to make an intelligent decision about him. The same circumstances will also press for the exchange of information among them. It is reasonable to assume, therefore, that threats to privacy will increase unless countervailing pressures are introduced which speak for the individual and for the interest in privacy. In this chapter, I shall consider the role that law may play in minimizing the threats or in providing a means of organizing and rationalizing the competing interests.

The heart of the dossier problem is to be found in two interrelated areas: the first is in information obtained directly from the subject (*A*) by the inquiring person or institution (*B*). This, in turn, can be divided into issues of coercion or inappropriateness of inquiry. It may not be at all clear, for example, that the person who supplies information about himself does so freely—that the applicant for employment "freely" answers the questions put to him; or that the applicant for a loan "freely" divulges the state of his finances; or that either understands all the implications of the questions or the uses to which the answers may be put. More fundamentally, perhaps the questions should not be asked at all, because they are too intrusive or only marginally relevant to the needs of those making inquiry.

The second aspect of the problem is the distribution of information about *A* by *B* to others (*C et al.*). The distribution may occur without notice to *A*, so that he may have little or no idea at any given time who has what information about him, or the extent to which that information is circulating. The issues here are principally those of notice and consent, at least where the information was originally obtained from *A*. For example, did *A* contemplate that *B* might pass the information to *C*? Should *A*'s consent be required before *B* may do so or should *A*'s consent be presumed unless he restricts the disclosure? Once the consent issue is opened up, others quickly follow. When should consent be sought—at the time of the original disclosure or at the time of transmission to others? Should consent to one disclosure be consent to subsequent disclosure? If the information about *A* was obtained from others and did not originate with *A*, the consent issue is, of course, a subordinate one. However, the question of notice to *A* that information about him is circulating remains important, as does the larger question of what information may properly be sought and used.

Unfortunately, the courts have had relatively little occasion to address many of these problems, in part because the law on the subject is still rudimentary, in part because we rarely know when information we have disclosed has been passed on to others and used to our disadvantage. And the law that does exist derives from a period long before the alarm began to sound about data banks and computers, about "Big Brother" and "1984." Nevertheless, considerable material is clearly or potentially relevant to the dossier problem. The law of "privilege," for example, shields certain confidential communications from disclosure. The law of business torts shields others. The law of defamation provides some protection against false disclosures. An evolving law of privacy offers promise of new remedies. And recent legislation dealing with information in government records represents an effort to resolve some of the conflicts in more comprehensive fashion.

THE DIRECT INQUIRY: QUESTIONS TO *A* BY *B*

There is ordinarily no restriction on the questions which may be put to *A* by *B*.[2] On the other hand, there is ordinarily nothing which compels *A* to answer the questions. Indeed, the entire process of asking and answering is largely governed by the free market—with some people asking what they feel they must in order to conduct their affairs intelligently and others answering to the extent they feel they must in order to get whatever they want—a job or a loan or an automobile license. In general, employers and lenders and licensing agencies are regarded as having a legitimate interest in examining the reliability of employees or borrowers or applicants. This does not mean, however, that the issue is free of controversy. A dramatic illustration is the use of personality or polygraph tests. Initially the employer must decide how informative the tests are, how likely it is that potential employees will be unwilling to take them or will be willing but resentful, how probable it is that unions will find the tests objectionable. The applicant for employment, in turn, must decide whether to risk losing the job by refusing to take the test, or even by expressing distaste or reservation.[3] The courts do not ordinarily intrude unless there has been extreme coercion or misrepresentation. The parties are left to bargain and contract about the nature of the inquiries to be made and about the confidentiality and the disclosure to be accorded them. This "contract" rationale

[2] The same is true when *B* asks others about A. In general, it may be said that the latter situation is even less regulated by law than the inquiry made directly to A.

[3] See Hearings of Subcommittee on Constitutional Rights, Senate Committee on Judiciary, Psychological Tests and Constitutional Rights, 89th Cong., 1st Sess. (June, 1965); Creech, The Privacy of Government Employees, 31 Law and Contemp. Prob. 413, 419 (1966); Mirel, The Limits of Governmental Inquiry Into the Private Lives of Government Employees, 46 Bost. U.L. Rev. 1, 18–22 (1966); Note, Lie Detectors in Private Employment, 33 Geo. Wash. L. Rev. 932, 939–40 (1965) (referring to statutes in several states restricting or prohibiting the use of the lie detector in employment setting).

is, of course, somewhat strained because there is no genuine consent in many of the settings under consideration. The market is often not really free and there may be a good deal of undue pressure or inappropriate feelings of obligation to answer.[4]

Though legal limitations on what *B* may ask are rare, some do exist. Most important are the constitutional and statutory provisions which prohibit inquiry into race or religion or sex. Much less precise is the provision of a tentative draft of the American Law Institute that damages be awarded for invasion of privacy against "one who intentionally intrudes, physically or otherwise, upon the solitude or seclusion of another, or his private affairs or concerns, . . . if the intrusion would be highly offensive to a reasonable man."[5]

This language is so broad that it may well draw the direct inquiry within its scope. The asking of questions of a highly personal nature, for example, or the administration of personality or polygraph tests might be said to fall within the reach of the phrase "or otherwise" and to constitute intrusion "upon . . . private affairs" which might well be found by a jury to be "highly offensive to a reasonable man." The comments, however, say little or nothing about the direct inquiry. They refer either to physical intrusions, such as opening mail or searching a safe, or to intrusions involving violation of relatively confidential situations, such as examining a private bank account. Nevertheless, they also refer in open-ended fashion to "some other form of investigation or examination into his private concerns."[6] As public sensitivity increases, it is entirely possible that such a provision will be held to include objectionable direct inquiries.[7]

When the direct inquiry seeks to elicit information which is independently protected by law, as by the privilege against self-incrimination, the attorney-client privilege, or the physician-patient privilege, the interest in privacy is better protected, but still imperfectly.[8] The holder of the privilege may refuse to answer and no one can properly compel him to do

[4] See generally Prosser, Torts 102–10, 697 et seq. (1964); ALI, Restatement of Torts §§ 49 et seq. (1934); see also People v. Vaughn, 16 Cal. Rep. 711 (D. Ct. App. 1961) (discussing the criminal offense of falsely impersonating another in order to obtain a benefit).

[5] ALI, Restatement of Law of Torts, Second, Tent. Draft No. 13, § 652 B (1967).

[6] *Id.* at 103 et seq. The provision appears to be based in substantial part upon Prosser, Privacy, 48 Calif. L. Rev. 383, 389–92 (1960). See also Bloustein, Privacy As An Aspect of Human Dignity, 39 N.Y.U. L. Rev. 962, 972–77 (1964).

[7] There remains the problem of fixing a measure of damage.

[8] For a general introduction to the law of privileged communications, see 8 Wigmore, Evidence, § 2190 et seq. (McNaughton ed. 1961); McCormick, Evidence, chs. 8 to 15 (1954).

so, unless he has waived his protection or lost it in some way. Nevertheless, in the extra-judicial setting, which produces most of the contents of the dossiers under discussion, he is as much subject to the pressure of economic or social circumstance as one who enjoys no privileged status and almost as likely to "waive" his protection. Virtually nowhere is any effort made to assure that the "waiver" in these settings is genuinely voluntary or that it is preceded by adequate advice as to rights or that it is accompanied by advice of counsel.

It would be a mistake to conclude from past judicial reluctance to limit the direct inquiry that there is no prospect that such limitations will be developed. In recent years, the courts have given extensive recognition to rights of privacy. Severe restrictions have been placed on eavesdropping, wiretapping, search, and police interrogation. Outside the law-enforcement area, the right to practice birth control has been said to derive from a right to privacy.[9] Though the context has almost invariably been one of governmental intrusion, the cases sound the themes of privacy and the integrity of the human personality, with each individual to be given as much choice as possible to determine what he will say or do, or what uses will be made of what he says or does. This is not to suggest, however, that these "rights" will not yield to overriding public purpose, as when the interest in free discussion in the public forum is involved. Rather, the privacy interest is being taken more explicitly into account, and courts are more likely to be sympathetic to claims of invasion of privacy than in the past. Nevertheless, it is probable that the legislatures will become the principal forum for the privacy issue. As already noted, restrictions on questions about race, religion, and sex are now widespread. In several states, statutes have been enacted which prohibit the utilization of the polygraph as a condition of employment. And legislation has been proposed for the federal government which would drastically limit the authority to utilize either the polygraph or personality tests in administering the civil service.[10]

[9] The leading cases are Griswold v. Connecticut, 381 U.S. 479 (1965) (birth control); Mapp v. Ohio, 367 U.S. 643 (1961) (search); Miranda v. Arizona, 384 U.S. 436 (1966) (interrogation); Berger v. New York, 388 U.S. 41 (1967) (wiretapping); Katz v. United States, 389 U.S. 347 (1967) (eavesdropping).

[10] In addition to the references in footnote 3, see N.J. Stat. Ann. 2A: 170–90, (1966) (making it an offense for employers to "influence, request or require an employee to take or submit to a lie detector test as a condition of employment . . ."); Calif. Labor Code § 432.2 (1967 Supp.) (to similar effect but inapplicable to government employees); Ore. Rev. Stat. § 659.225; Hearings of Subcommittee of House Committee on Government Operations, Use of Polygraphs as "Lie Detectors" By Federal Government, 88th Cong., 2nd Sess. (1964).

THE INDIRECT INQUIRY: GETTING INFORMATION FROM *B* ABOUT *A*

The processes of direct inquiry lead to the accumulation in *B*'s files of information about *A*. In addition, *B* may have information about *A* which he acquired from third persons. Are there any limits on *B*'s freedom to pass such information to others (*C et al.*)? The answer to that question is divided into two parts: the first assumes that *B* does not wish to supply the information; the second that he does.

Compelling *B* to Make Disclosure

If *B* should wish to resist the request for information, *C* cannot compel him to respond except through the use of the subpoena power. If, therefore, *C* is himself a body which has the power to subpoena records or to compel testimony about the contents of records—such as a court or a grand jury or, on occasion, a legislative committee or an administrative agency —or is acting on behalf of such a body, he may compel the production of records relevant to the inquiry being conducted. Even here, however, there may be restrictions derived from the Constitution or statute or common law. The most usual is that coming from the law of privilege. A client's communications to his attorney may not be obtained or those of a penitent to his priest or of husband and wife to each other. In about two-thirds of the states, communications from patient to physician are shielded from view. In others, far fewer in number, protection may be given to communications in a variety of professional relationships in which confidentiality is regarded as important, such as client to social worker, informant to newspaperman, client to accountant, patient to psychiatrist or psychologist.

Finally, there is a broad and amorphous category known as "government privilege" which may shield from disclosure a wide variety of communications to, and within, governmental agencies. If, therefore, *B* received his information from *A* in the course of one of these protected relationships, he cannot be compelled to give it up. Of course, questions of interpretation of the various "privileges" remain, and there is always the possibility of new constitutional developments; but at least in the subpoena context, the issues are relatively clear-cut.[11]

[11] In addition to the references in footnote 8, see, for illustrative discussions of particular categories of privileged communications and the problems they raise, De Witt, Clinton, *Privileged Communications Between Physician and Patient,* C. C. Thomas, Springfield, Ill., 1958; Slovenko, Ralph, and G. L. Usdin, *Psychotherapy, Confidentiality and Privileged Communication,* C. C. Thomas, Springfield, Ill., 1966; Goldstein and Katz, Psychiatrist-Patient Privilege: The GAP Proposal and the Connecticut Statute, 36 Conn. B.J. 175 (1962) (also appears in 118 Am. J. Psychiatry 733).

Voluntary Disclosure by *B*

The more troublesome questions arise when *B* does not resist the request but instead is willing to turn over the information, or is willing to do so if certain conditions are met—e.g., that *A*'s consent first be obtained or that *C et al.* agree to limit the uses to which the information will be put or the extent of its dissemination. Typical of the situations likely to present these questions are the police investigator asking a psychiatric clinic whether *A* has a history of sexual pathology; a civil service investigator or a professional licensing agency asking a school or college whether *A* has done anything reflecting adversely on his moral character; a potential employer asking a bank about the state of finances of a man applying for employment; or a welfare inspector asking the motor vehicle bureau whether a welfare applicant owns a car.

If the record-keeper should disclose information in these settings, *A*'s only recourse is likely to be a suit for damages—based on a defamation theory, if the information is untrue, or on a claim of invasion of privacy or breach of trust. The remedies for defamation and invasion of privacy do not turn at all on whether *A* was the original source. The breach of trust remedy and those related to it may. In the remainder of this section, I shall outline briefly the scope of these remedies.

Defamation. Like all men, *B* is obligated to speak the truth. If he does not, then he may be held liable in an action for libel or slander, provided the matter disclosed by *B* tends to harm *A*'s reputation so "as to lower him in the estimation of the community or to deter third persons from associating or dealing with him." *A* will not have a remedy, however, if what *B* has disclosed is protected by a qualified (or conditional) privilege. That doctrine shields persons who make reasonable disclosure to others of their evaluative opinions and of facts relevant thereto, even if those disclosures prove harmful to the subject of the disclosure (*A*). The information must, however, be supplied without knowledge of its falsity and must bear some reasonable relation to a substantial interest of *B* or of the person to whom he supplies the information (*C*). The reports of credit agencies to their subscribers have been held to be protected by a qualified privilege, as have the reports of physicians to the families of their patients or to a variety of institutions, and reports of previous employers to prospective employers.[12]

[12] 3 ALI, Restatement of Torts, § 559 (1938). As to defamation and conditional privilege, see 1 Harper and James, Law of Torts, ch. 5 (1956); Prosser, Torts, ch. 21 (1964). For more detailed discussions of conditional privilege, see Anno., Defamation of employee, 6 A.L.R. 2d 1008 (1949); Anno., Report of mercantile agency as privileged, 30 A.L.R. 2d

The effect of these doctrines is to insulate from civil liability not only the persons who pass the false information along but also those who use the information in ways seriously damaging to *A*, as by denying credit or employment or admission to a school. Protecting such uses is particularly troublesome because material which *B* may regard as usefully evaluative may eventually be used by *C*, *D*, and others for purposes which have only marginal relevance to the underlying purpose of the privilege. Moreover, the injury to *A* which may result is peculiarly difficult for him to repair because he may have no idea that the untruth is circulating. He will ordinarily have had no access to his file (whether in the hands of *B* or *C* or *D*) so that he can correct the untruth or minimize its impact.

Suits for Invasion of Privacy. One of the bases of a cause of action for unauthorized disclosure by *B* to *C* is the invasion of *A*'s privacy which may be involved. Such an action does not depend on a showing of falsehood. Instead, its roots would be in what Warren and Brandeis first termed a "right to privacy." Drawing on a number of slender strands, not all of which supported their conclusions, they wrote in 1890 that:

> The common law secures to each individual the right of determining, ordinarily, to what extent his thoughts, sentiments, and emotion shall be communicated to others . . . and even if he has chosen to give them expression, he generally retains the power to fix the limits of the publicity which shall be given them.[13]

Though they had in mind principally invasions of privacy through publicity by newspaper gossip columnists, the concept they described was broad enough to encompass much more. For a long time, the "right to privacy" was more celebrated by commentators than by courts. But it was ultimately included in the American Law Institute's Restatement of the Law of Torts and has enjoyed considerable vitality in recent years.

The first Restatement described the action as one which may be brought against

> A person who unreasonably and seriously interferes with another's interest in not having his affairs known to others . . .[14]

The proposed revision currently under consideration is more specific. It provides that

---

776 (1953); Anno., Privilege of statements by physician, surgeon or nurse concerning patient, 73 A.L.R. 2d 325 (1960); Anno., Imputing credit unworthiness to non-trader, 99 A.L.R. 2d 700 (1965).

[13] Warren and Brandeis, The Right to Privacy, 4 Harv. L. Rev. 193, 196 (1890).

[14] 4 ALI, Restatement of Torts § 867 (1938).

The right of privacy is invaded when there is

(a) Unreasonable intrusion upon the seclusion of another . . . ; or

(b) Appropriation of the other's name or likeness . . . ; or

(c) Unreasonable publicity given to the other's life . . . ; or

(d) Publicity which unreasonably places the other in a false light before the public. . . .[15]

The second of the new categories has little or no application to the dossier problem. The first, which does, has already been discussed in the context of the direct inquiry. If it were given a broad construction, however, it would be the most significant of the provisions—because it "does not depend upon any publicity given to the person whose interest is invaded. . . ."[16] In contrast, the remaining two sections turn on the existence of "publicity," similar to that which led to the article by Warren and Brandeis. The comments distinguish explicitly between such "publicity" and the "publication" required by the law of defamation:

"Publication," in that sense, is a word of art, which includes any communication by the defendant to a third person. "Publicity," on the other hand, means that the matter is made public, by communicating it to the public at large, or to so many persons that the matter must be regarded as substantially certain to become one of public knowledge. The difference is not one of the means of communication, which may be oral, written, or by any other means. It is one of a communication which reaches, or is sure to reach, the public.

Thus it is not an invasion of the right of privacy, within the rule stated in this Section, to communicate a fact concerning the plaintiff's private life to a single person, or even to a small group of persons. On the other hand, any publication in a newspaper or a magazine, even of small circulation, or in a handbill distributed to a large number of persons, or any broadcast over the radio, or statement made in an address to a large audience, is sufficient to give publicity within the meaning of the term as it is used in this Section. The distinction, in other words, is one between private and public communication.[17]

It would be a mistake, however, to exaggerate the potential range of the privacy action. The qualified privileges generally available as defenses to defamation will probably also be available when the action is for invasion of privacy. An extreme illustration of this is *Voneye* v. *Turner,* which holds that no right of privacy is violated when a creditor communicates with the debtor's employer in order to enforce payment of a debt. The

[15] ALI, Restatement of Torts, Second, Tent. Draft 13, § 652 (1967).
[16] *Id.* at p. 103.
[17] *Id.* at pp. 113, 121.

reason advanced, though begging some of the questions underlying a right to privacy, illustrates the rationale:

Ordinarily, an employer is interested in the ability and reputation of his employees as to payment of debts, which makes for efficiency in work and saves the employer the annoyance and expense of answering garnishments. . . . A debtor when he creates an obligation must know that his creditor expects to collect it, and the ordinary man realizes that most employers expect their employees to meet their obligations and that when they fall behind in so doing the employer may be asked to take the matter up with them.[18]

That is not to say, of course, that the defense of qualified privilege will always prevail. Many of the cases raise the question whether persons who have an undoubted interest in disclosing "private facts" about the plaintiff may have crossed the line from reasonable disclosure to "undue harassment," as when a creditor decides "to publish in a newspaper that the plaintiff does not pay his debts, or to post a notice to that effect in a window on the public street, or to cry it aloud in the highway. . . ."[19]

The really critical question about the privacy action is whether it should be restricted, in any of its parts, solely to widely publicized facts. It is not at all apparent why the interest in privacy should be held to be violated only when a great deal of publicity has been given, any more than is the case in defamation where an action can be maintained if there has been "publication" to one person. In both instances, the law's concern is with protecting privacy unless there is a compelling social purpose for not doing so. Clearly, privacy can be invaded as arbitrarily in relatively unpublicized settings as in the mass media. However discreetly information about *A* is passed along to employers, schools, and banks, for example, devastating damage may be done to his sensitivities as well as to his pocket. The issue of publicity would seem to bear only on the latter, on the question of damages, as in defamation.[20]

The reason for the publicity requirement is probably the fear that too much litigation would ensue if it were abandoned. It is doubtful, however, that the fear is well-founded or that it should be taken so much into account. For one thing, even if there were no publicity requirement, many

[18] 240 S.W. 2d 588, 590–1 (Ky. 1951); see also Lewis v. Physicians and Dentists Credit Bureau, 177 P.2d 896, 899 (Wash. 1947); Neaton v. Lewis Apparel Stores, 48 N.Y.S. 2d 492 (App. Div. 1944).

[19] Prosser, Privacy, 48 Calif. L. Rev. 383, 393 (1960); see Santiesteban v. Goodyear Tire & Rubber Rubber Co., 306 F.2d 9 (5 Cir. 1962).

[20] With Prosser, Privacy, 48 Calif. L. Rev. 383, 392–98 (1960) (which supports the proposals of the ALI tentative draft), compare Wade, Defamation and the Right to Privacy, 15 Vand. L. Rev. 1093, 1109–10 (1962) ("There is little difference in the two torts in the requirement of publication"); and see Karst, The Files, 31 Law & Contemp. Prob. 342, 346–47 (1966).

persons would be found to have a qualified privilege to pass the information along. For another, an action for invasion of privacy is not likely to be brought casually because bringing it may sacrifice the privacy sought to be protected. Only in cases where the injury is great (without large-scale publicity) or where the defendant had acted with some special animus is a plaintiff likely to institute action. Finally, generous recognition of the privacy action may reduce the occasions when *B* and others will make objectionable disclosures.

Breach of Contracts Implied in Law or Fiduciary or Confidential Relationships. There are circumstances under which obligations may be imposed upon *B* to keep to himself the information he obtained from *A* or about him—obligations which are breached even by truthful disclosures or by disclosures which do not constitute the tort of invasion of privacy. For the most part, these obligations are found where there was a previous relationship of trust or confidence and where the parties have made no express provision for shielding their communications. The relationship of principal and agent has presented the issue most often. In a wide variety of settings, the unauthorized disclosure by an agent of information given him in confidence has been held to violate a duty of confidentiality. Using the language of contract or trust, speaking of confidential relationships and fiduciary obligations, courts have held employees liable for disclosure of trade secrets obtained in the course of their employment, banks for disclosing the state of account of their depositors, lawyers for revealing the affairs of their clients, and physicians for disclosures regarding their patients.[21] Arguably, these rationales are broad enough to permit the imposition of tort liability whenever it can be shown that an agreement of confidence or trust has been breached. Yet courts have been reluctant to push these doctrines very far.

This reluctance is all the more conspicuous when tort liability is held not to arise in settings in which the existence of a confidential relationship is clearly recognized, such as those giving rise to "privileged communications." The best known of these are attorney and client, husband and wife, priest and penitent, physician and patient. Yet in these settings the law does not necessarily provide a remedy for *B*'s disclosures in an extra-judicial setting. Stated somewhat differently, though *B* cannot be com-

[21] In addition to cases discussed *infra*, see 2 ALI, Restatement of Agency, Second, §§ 395, 396 (1958); 4 ALI, Restatement of Torts, § 757 (1938); Anno., Implied obligation of employee not to use trade secrets or confidential information . . . , 165 ALR 1453 (1946); Prosser, Torts § 123 (1964); Peterson v. Idaho First Nat'l Bank, 367 P.2d 284, 290 (Idaho, 1961) (information "concerning the customer's or depositor's [bank] account").

pelled to speak in court unless *A* consents, if he speaks outside of court to an employer or an investigator, *A* may be without a remedy.[22]

It would be a mistake, however, to treat the matter as settled. There have been too few cases speaking directly to the issue to warrant generalizing from them. *Hammond* v. *Ætna Casualty* & *Surety Co.* seems most nearly in point because it arose in a state which had a physician-patient privilege statute. The defendant insurance company was charged with inducing a physician to divulge information he had sent to the plaintiff, who was his patient and who was suing a hospital insured by the defendant. The court held that the relationship of physician and patient was fiduciary in nature and that one who induced a breach of trust was liable in damages. Though there was an underlying physician-patient privilege, the court's opinion suggests that the critical element was the existence of the confidential relationship, an implicit part of which is the promise that *A*'s communications would not be disclosed without his consent. The implication was that the relationship would have been protected even if there had been no privilege.[23]

Simonsen v. *Swenson* was a case in which there was no physician-patient privilege statute. Plaintiff brought suit against a physician for breach of what plaintiff described as a confidential relationship. The plaintiff, a stranger staying at a small hotel, had been diagnosed by the defendant physician (Swenson) as having syphillis. Swenson warned that the disease was contagious and requested that the plaintiff leave. Sometime afterwards, Swenson returned to the hotel and found that the plaintiff had not moved. He then informed the hotel owner of his diagnosis and the owner forced the defendant to leave. In the suit for damages which followed, the court found that professional ethics and the licensing statute imposed upon the physician a positive duty of nondisclosure. But the duty carried with it an implied exception to protect the public when necessary. And the exception was held to be applicable to the case before the Court. In the Court's words,

> No patient can expect that if his malady is found to be of a dangerously contagious nature he can require it to be kept secret from those to whom, if there was no disclosure, such disease would be transmitted. . . .

[22] See generally Note, Action for Breach of Medical Secrecy Outside the Courtroom, 36 U. Cinc. L. Rev. 103 (1967).

[23] 237 F. Supp. 96, 101–2 (N.D. Ohio, 1965) (opinion denying motion to dismiss complaint); *id.* 243 F. Supp. 793, 795 et seq. (N.D. Ohio, 1965) (opinion denying motion for reconsideration of foregoing denial).

In making such a disclosure a physician must also be governed by the rules as to qualifiedly privileged communications in slander and libel cases. He must prove that a disclosure was necessary to prevent spread of disease, that the communication was to one who, it was reasonable to suppose, might otherwise be exposed, and that he himself acted in entire good faith. The court held that under the circumstances the disclosure was justified.[24]

In *Hague* v. *Williams,* the court confronted the question whether a common law cause of action should be recognized for breach of confidence where there was no legislative declaration of policy at all—neither a licensing statute nor a testimonial privilege statute. The facts were these: the parents of a deceased infant brought an action against the defendant physician who had disclosed to an insurance company that, at the time of the application for insurance on the child's life, the infant had a pathological heart condition. The insurance company had made inquiry of the physician after the parents had filed a claim on the policy. The disclosure, of course, defeated the claim. The court held that the filing of a claim that was based upon the health of the child constituted a waiver of any right the parents might have had (derivative from the child) to prevent disclosure. "At this point, the public interest in an honest and just result assumes dominance over the individual's right of nondisclosure." The physician "was under a general duty not to disclose frivolously the information received from them, or from an examination of the patient. . . . Ordinarily a physician receives information relating to a patient's health in a confidential capacity and should not disclose such information without the patient's consent, except where the public interest or private interest of the patient so demands."[25]

The import of *Simonson* and *Hague* is that the courts are sufficiently uneasy about the breach of confidence to speak of it as a wrong but that, lacking a statute clearly addressed to the confidential relationship, they have conferred upon the physician a qualified privilege broad enough to eliminate any effective remedy. In *Hammond* the court built upon the

[24] 177 N.W. 831, 832 (Neb. 1920); cf. Furniss v. Fitchett, [1958] N.Z.L.R. 396, 403–4; Ohio Rev. Code Ann. § 3701.26.1 (Payne, 1966 Supp.). But cf. Quarles v. Sutherland, 389 S.W. 2d 249, 251 (Tenn. 1965). As to qualified privilege, see Iverson v. Frandsen, 237 F.2d 898 (10 Cir. 1956) (recognizing such a privilege in a libel action against the staff psychologist of a mental hospital who provided a school guidance director with a report about a child); Note, Medical Practice and the Right to Privacy, 43 Minn. L. Rev. 943 (1959). It should be noted that many states require medical people to report information regarding certain diseases to designated agencies and some provide that such reports shall not be actionable, either in damages or in disciplinary proceedings.

[25] 181 A.2d 345, 349 (N.J. 1962).

privilege statute to construct a remedy in damages. In all three cases, however, the courts have opened the door and have invited further litigation to test the limits of the remedy, not only in the physician-patient context but in all relationships which involve confidential communicaions, whether or not independently protected by law.

Injunction Against Disclosure; Correction of Records. All of the remedies discussed above refer to situations where the injury to *A* has already occurred and he seeks damages either to compensate him for any loss he may have suffered or to punish *B* or *C*. In most instances it would be preferable if *A* could prevent the disclosure from being made at all. This will rarely be possible because *A* is not likely to know what dissemination *B* is making. And there is ordinarily no obligation on *B*'s part that he put *A* on notice of such dissemination, so that *A* may participate in decisions about it. As a result, the remedy in damages, after the fact, is likely to be *A*'s only recourse. There may, however be instances in which *A* learns that *B* plans to transmit to others information which is defamatory, or violates a confidential relationship, or invades privacy. He may then wish to consider enjoining the objectionable transmission or compelling correction of an inaccurate record, or demanding the return or destruction of the record.

Unfortunately, there is very little law, statutory or judicial, on these matters. In principle, there would seem to be at least as much reason for issuance of an injunction before the fact as damages after the fact. Yet the courts have been reluctant to engage in prior censorship of speech or writing. Though it is doubtful that this reluctance would extend to the sorts of settings considered here, because they involve limited dissemination for economic or business or governmental purpose rather than for education of the public forum, the issue is by no means settled.[26]

So far as correction of records is concerned, there is even less guidance in the cases. This too has been left to the operation of the free market or to processes of persuasion. There is, however, one conspicuous exception. In recent years, there has been a steady increase in the number of states which make provision for expunging records of arrest or conviction, fingerprints and police photographers. But nowhere is provision made for tracing these records to the noncriminal files to which they may have been transmitted. Less conspicuous but pointing perhaps to a more significant development is a bill introduced in California in 1965 which

[26] See discussion in Karst, The Files: Legal Controls Over the Accuracy and Accessibility of Stored Personal Data, 31 Law and Contemp. Prob. 342, 350–53 (1966).

would have required credit bureaus to correct any false report, under threat of losing their qualified privilege for subsequent reports.[27]

Extra-Judicial Remedies. In the preceding sections, I have discussed only the remedies which might be available to the offended party in the civil courts, principally by suing for damages. There is, in addition, the possibility of recourse through administrative agencies or private regulatory groups. For example, the lawyer who transmits information about a client might be complained against in the grievance procedures of his local bar, not only because he may have violated the law but because he may have breached standards of legal ethics, which are possibly stricter.

The same is true of the physician who swears the Hippocratic Oath as to confidentiality and is subject to other principles of medical ethics requiring secrecy. Indeed, some states have statutes which provide that disclosure of a professional secret is ground for revoking a medical license. These statutes and procedures may, of course, bring their own problems of scope and interpretation. The standards are sometimes so broad that a physician is given the discretion to decide when it "becomes necessary to make disclosure in order to protect the welfare of the individual or of the community." Nevertheless, they provide a forum comparable to the courts and one which might well prove more effective because the sanctions of suspension and revocation may be regarded by the offender as more serious than an award of damages.[28]

The accountant, the social worker, the psychologist, and many others who hold information may be subject to comparable ethical obligations and/or professional or administrative controls. It is probable, however, that these extra-judicial remedies will play a minor role because there is likely to be more ambiguity about rights and obligations in the nonjudicial setting than in the judicial one and more pressure from those who want to maximize the flow of information—to serve business or educational interests or research purposes. The burden is likely, therefore, to be on the courts to use the tort suit, under the various theories descibed above, as the occasion for clarifying the norms of privacy and on the legislatures to include such norms among the factors to be considered by licensing and regulatory bodies.

[27] *Id.* at 358, 365 et seq. The California bill is described at p. 375 n. 152. See also United States v. Kalish, 271 F. Supp. 968 (D.P.R. 1967); N.Y. Civil Rights Law § 79–e (1967 Supp.); Baum, Wiping Out a Criminal or Juvenile Record, 40 Calif. St. B.J. 816 (1965).

[28] See American Medical Ass'n., Principles of Medical Ethics, § 9 (1957), quoted in Hague v. Williams, 181 A.2d 345, 347 (N.J. 1962); Tooley v. Prudential Life and Accident Insurance Co., 154 F.2d 619 (1st Cir. 1963); Note, Action for Breach of Medical Secrecy Outside the Courtroom, 36 U. Cinc. L. Rev. 103, 112–13 (1967).

GETTING INFORMATION ABOUT *A* FROM THE GOVERNMENT

When information about *A* finds its way into government records, it assumes a status somewhat different from that described for private records. For one thing, *B*-as-government-official may have an absolute privilege to make disclosures about *A*, provided that the disclosures are somehow connected with his official duties. If *B* should defame *A* in such a context, *A* will have no remedy. Even if *B* is not protected by an absolute privilege, *A* may be unable to recover against him for any of the causes of action referred to earlier because government officials are immune from suit unless the sovereign has consented. And most governmental entities have not given their consent to suits of the sort involved here. There are circumstances, of course, when the disclosure of information by a government official is so patently improper as to make his action fall outside the scope of his authority and thus make the action his own, and not the government's. *B* may then, at least in theory, become liable for damages because he no longer shares the sovereign's immunity. But these eventualities are relatively remote and the courts are clearly inclined not to reach them.[29]

With government files, therefore, the threat of a suit for damages by *A* is even less of a deterrent to disclosure than it is in the private sector. What serves instead are restrictions imposed by statutes and regulations as to the uses which may be made of government records by persons in the government and the extent to which persons outside government may have access to those records. Whether or not these restrictions are observed will depend, of course, upon the extent to which they produce feelings of constraint on the part of government employees who are asked for information in informal settings; and that may turn on whether they risk disciplinary action if they should breach their obligations.

Prohibitions Against Disclosure

The strongest protection of *A*'s file comes from statutes or regulations prohibiting disclosure of the contents to anyone other than the office which collected the information. Such provisions exist in a wide variety of areas

[29] See generally Barr v. Mateo, 360 U.S. 564 (1959); Gregoire v. Biddle, 177 F.2d 579 (2 Cir., 1949); but cf. Carr v. Watkins, 177 A.2d 841 (Md. 1962) (holding that county police officers have only a qualified privilege to publish defamatory matter). See generally Comment, Spying and Slandering: Absolute Privilege for the CIA Agent?, 67 Col. L. Rev. 752 (1967); Handler and Klein, The Defense of Privilege in Defamation Suits Against Executive Officers, 74 Harv. L. Rev. 44 (1960); Note, Remedies Against the United States and its Officials, 70 Harv. L. Rev. 827 (1957); 3 Davis, Administrative Law, ch. 25 (1958).

in both federal and state government, where secrecy is promised in order to assure maximum disclosure. For example, reports to the Census Bureau are to be used only for statistical purposes. Examination by other executive departments is prohibited, as is any use by which an identification can be made of the person supplying the information. Tax records are open to examination only by order of the President. Social security records may not be disclosed and state plans pursuant thereto must provide for confidentiality of records. Similar provisions exist with regard to selective service records, trade secrets and processes, and others. Although damages are not likely to be available for violation of these statutes, criminal penalties are usually provided.[30] They may also become the basis for disciplinary action against employees, as may the more general Executive Order which provides that "An employee shall not . . . make use of, for the purpose of furthering a private interest, official information not available to the general public."[31]

These specific prohibitions are important not only for the restrictions they impose upon the officials themselves but also for the protection they give when information is sought by subpoena or by persons pursuing their economic or other interests. Indeed, pressures of the latter sort have increased greatly in recent years with the enactment of "right to know" laws. These may pit the interest of members of the public in finding out how well the government is doing its job against the interest in privacy of those who are required to disclose information to the government.[32] Though legislatures have on occasion sought to strike a balance among the competing interests, the more common situation is one in which there are no statutes specifically addressed to the problem. Then the courts and agencies must make their own decision in the matter, often using as their organizing principle the concept of "government privilege."

[30] See, e.g., Census: 13 U.S.C. §§ 9(a), 214 (1967 Supp.); Internal Revenue: 26 U.S.C. §§ 6103, 7213 (1967); Social Security: 42 U.S.C. §§ 602 (a)(8), 1306 (1967 Supp.); 32 CFR § 9551 (1967); 18 U.S.C. §§ 1905 to 1907 (1951). See discussion of exemptions from Federal Freedom of Information Act, *infra* at fn. 39. But see State v. Smythe, 169 P.2d 706 (Wash. 1946) (holding that juvenile court was entitled to summon county welfare records, despite provision of Federal Social Security Act restricting use of public assistance information).

[31] § 205 of Executive Order 11222, set out in Hearings of Subcommittee on Constitutional Rights, Senate Committee on Judiciary, Privacy and the Rights of Federal Employees, 89th Cong. 2nd Sess., p. 620 (September–October, 1965).

[32] For cases describing the public interest that "debate on public issues should be uninhibited, robust, and wide-open," see N.Y. Times v. Sullivan, 376 U.S. 254, 270 (1964); Time, Inc. v. Hill, 385 U.S. 374, 388 (1967). On the problem of public access to information, see Cross, Harold L., *The People's Right to Know*, AMS Press, New York, 1953; Note, Access to Official Information, 27 Ind. L.J. 209 (1952); Providence Journal Co. v. McCoy, 94 F. Supp. 186, 195–6 (D.R.I. 1950), aff'd. 190 F.2d 760 (1st Cir. 1951), cert. den. 342 U.S. 894 (1951).

"Government Privilege"

The President and the federal executive have long laid claim to an inherent power, deriving from the separation of powers, to determine the extent to which they will reveal information in their possession to anyone else. Neither the judiciary nor the legislature, however, have acceded to this claim. *Marbury* v. *Madison* is the principal case. In it, the Supreme Court conceded that the President has "certain political powers, in the exercise of which he is to use his own discretion, and is accountable only to his country. . . ." As to these "political" matters, his decision is "conclusive." Where "individual rights" are concerned, however, the Court suggested that the President might be compelled to act.[33]

Despite the length of time since *Marbury*, the Supreme Court has never ruled specifically on the constitutional power of the Executive to refuse to disclose "official information" or the right to compel disclosure of information bearing on "individual rights." The few cases which have touched on the issue have usually involved distinctions between the government as a litigant and the government as the source of information in private litigation. In the latter situation, the courts have fairly consistently accepted the claim of government privilege and refused to compel disclosure of materials in government files unless there were statutes authorizing the disclosure. In the former, however, the courts have been reluctant to refuse disclosure because advantage might redound to the government in the very litigation in which the information was sought.[34]

The leading Supreme Court case, *United States* v. *Reynolds*, involved the government as a party under the Federal Tort Claims Act. Suit had been brought for damages arising out of the crash of a military airplane which was testing secret electronic equipment. Plaintiffs moved before trial for production of the official accident report and other documents containing statements taken in connection with the investigation. The Secretary of the Air Force made a formal claim of privilege, asserting that disclosure would not be in the public interest. The Supreme Court upheld his claim, but only after noting that "Judicial control over the evidence in a case can not be abdicated to the caprice of executive officers," and stating the conditions for an effective claim:

There must be a formal claim of privilege, lodged by the head of the department which has control over the matter, after actual personal consideration by

[33] 1 Cranch 137, 166, 2 L. Ed. 60, 70 (1803).

[34] See generally Bishop, The Executive's Right of Privacy, 66 Yale L.J. 477 (1957); Pickrell, Secrecy and the Access to Administrative Records, 44 Calif. L. Rev. 305 (1956); Cross, *The People's Right to Know*, ch. XIV (1953); 4 Moore, Federal Practice § 26.25 (1966).

that officer. The Court itself must determine whether the circumstances are appropriate for the claim of privilege, and yet do so without forcing a disclosure of the very thing the privilege is bound to protect.[35]

It then concluded that the claim of privilege was warranted in the case before it. It did not reach the question of a claim which had to be rejected. Indeed, the Supreme Court has never met that issue head-on. There are, however, lower court decisions which have required the government to elect, under such circumstances, whether it wished to forfeit its case or withhold the information. Though disclosure has not been compelled, the executive branch has often been required to pay a price for its failure.[36]

The executive branch of both federal and state governments has a powerful weapon, in the law of "government privilege," with which to deny requests or subpoenas for information from private parties. The weapon is less powerful when coordinate branches of government seek the information but even then they have considerable potency. If, therefore, the government chooses to invoke privilege, the interest in privacy may be served. But if the government does not, the individuals affected are left in the situation outlined earlier—one in which there is no real likelihood of a civil remedy and which requires that they look either to criminal penalties, where they exist, or to disciplinary action against the officials making disclosure.

General Legislation Dealing with Disclosure

Except for statutes dealing with disclosure in particular areas, there has been no specification as to what may or may not be disclosed and to whom. As a result, the doctrine of government privilege has tended to dominate the scene. For a long time, it was strongly aided in the federal government by a statute which provided that

The head of an Executive department or military department may prescribe regulations for the government of his department, the conduct of its employees, the distribution and performance of its business, and the custody, use, and preservation of its records, papers, and property.[37]

This statute was used by government officials as if it made the concept of government privilege applicable to all records within their charge. In regulations promulgated by the various departments and agencies, procedures were sometimes specified as to when access to records might be

[35] United States v. Reynolds, 345 U.S. 1, 7–8, 9–10 (1953).
[36] *Id* at 12; United States v. Andolschek, 142 F.2d 503, 506 (2 Cir. 1944); Bishop, *supra* footnote 34.
[37] Formerly 5 U.S.C. § 22, quoted in United States v. Reynolds, 345 U.S. 1, 4 n. 4 (1953). The substance of this provision is now found in 5 U.S.C. § 301 (1966).

had and under what conditions. But the over-all posture was one of restricting access and limiting disclosure, at least when requests came from outside government. It was not at all clear, however, that comparable caution was exercised when the information was sought by other governmental agencies. The pressures for access increased over the years, particularly in litigation in which it was felt that the government was gaining advantage from withholding information in its files or was acting capriciously in treating information as confidential. The result was an amendment to the federal statute which provided:

> This section does not authorize withholding information from the public or limiting the availability of records to the public.[38]

This language did not, of course, require disclosure. It merely deprived agency officials of reliance on what had come to be known as the "housekeeping" statute. Nondisclosure practices and regulations had to be based instead on the inherent power of the executive branch or on the general provisions of the Administrative Procedure Act.

The need for further clarification of the subject of privacy and disclosure in the context of government files led to enactment in 1966 of the Freedom of Information Act. The avowed purpose of the act was to make "information maintained by the executive branch more available to the public." Information available to one is to be made available to all; the public is to be told when and where information can be obtained and the kinds of materials which can be disclosed—among them agency statements of policy instructions to staff, etc.—subject to the condition that identifying details are to be deleted "to the extent required to prevent a clearly unwarranted invasion of personal privacy. . . ." The act then sets out a series of exemptions and provides for judicial review of an agency decision to withhold records. In short, access and disclosure is to be the general rule and denial of access the exception, with the judicial review provision placing upon the agencies the obligation to clarify their standards for nondisclosure so that they can meet the judicial challenge when it comes.[39]

On first inspection, the act seems so sweeping as to represent an abandonment of privacy in the interest of full disclosure, the "right to know" having won out over the "right to privacy." Closer inspection reveals, however, that there are a great many exceptions to the disclosure require-

[38] 5 U.S.C. § 301 (1966).

[39] 5 U.S.C. § 552 (1967). The reference to invasion of privacy is in section (a)(2). See generally Attorney General's Memorandum on the Public Information Section of the Administrative Procedure Act (June, 1967); Davis, The Information Act, 34 U. Chi. L. Rev. 761 (1967); Uretz, Freedom of Information and the IRS, 20 Ark. L. Rev. 283 (1967).

ment. In particular, the statute is to have no effect on matters that are "specifically exempted from disclosure" by the many statutes referred to earlier. It is not applicable to "trade secrets and commercial or financial information obtained from any person and privileged or confidential," which seems to bar disclosure if the described information is made privileged by law *or* if it was given in confidence. It is not to apply to "personnel and medical files and similar files the disclosure of which would constitute a clearly unwarranted invasion of personal privacy." And "investigatory files compiled for law enforcement purposes" are not ordinarily to be subject to disclosure.[40]

The exemptions appear to be sufficiently broad to authorize fairly extensive protection of the interest in privacy and confidentiality. But they do so in substantial part through leaving to agency heads the responsibility for deciding when disclosure is to be made, and when not. The statute does not address itself at all to the occasions when agency heads decide in favor of disclosure. The judicial review provision, for example, is available only when disclosure is withheld. No means of enforcing the interest in nondisclosure is provided. The individual affected, therefore, is thrown back on his "rights" under the general body of law, "rights" which do not define the parties who may have access to files and which leave him few effective remedies.

Some of these problems may in time be dealt with through regulations promulgated by the agencies. The Civil Service Commission, for example, has adopted regulations which ordinarily make available medical information about an applicant, employee, or annuitant only to the individual

[40] The complete text of the exemptions, 5 U.S.C. § 552(b) (1967), follows:

"(b) This section does not apply to matters that are—

(1) specifically required by Executive order to be kept secret in the interest of the national defense or foreign policy;

(2) related solely to the internal personnel rules and practices of an agency;

(3) specifically exempted from disclosure by statute;

(4) trade secrets and commercial or financial information obtained from a person and privileged or confidential;

(5) inter-agency or intra-agency memorandums or letters which would not be available by law to a party other than an agency in litigation with the agency;

(6) personnel and medical files and similar files the disclosure of which would constitute a clearly unwarranted invasion of personal privacy;

(7) investigatory files compiled for law enforcement purposes except to the extent available by law to a party other than an agency;

(8) contained in or related to examination, operating, or condition reports prepared by, on behalf of, or for the use of an agency responsible for the regulation or supervision of financial institutions; or

(9) geological and geophysical information and data, including maps, concerning wells."

For discussion thereof, see Attorney General's Memorandum on the Public Information Section of the Administrative Procedure Act 29 et seq. (June, 1967); Davis, supra footnote 39, p. 783 et seq.

or his representative.[41] Personnel records are less inviolable. The name, position, title, grade, and salary of a government employee are available to anyone. Prospective employers may obtain his term of employment, his civil service status, the length of service in the agency and, when separated, the date and reason for separation. The entire personnel folder, however, is available to officials of the executive branch who have "a need for the information within . . . [their] official duties." It is also available to members of Congress, except for matters relating to loyalty or security. But the employee now has access to his Official Personnel Folder and may presumably take issue with its contents. It is open to each of the agencies to make a similar effort to identify which of their records should be made available, and to whom, within the outlines provided by the new act. And it is to be hoped that they will not race headlong in the direction of disclosure, unmindful of the need to balance the "right to know" against the equally important "right to privacy."

Of great potential importance in striking the balance is the little-known but extraordinarily broad authority of the Budget Bureau Director to regulate both the collection of information by government agencies and the exchange of such information among them. The statute provides:

> Upon the request of any party having a substantial interest, or upon his own motion, the Director is authorized within his discretion to make a determination as to whether or not the collection of any information by any federal agency is necessary for the proper performance of the function of such agency or for any other purpose. Before making any such determination, the Director may, within his discretion, give to such agency and to other interested persons an adequate opportunity to be heard or to submit statements in writing. To the extent, if any, that the Director determines the collection of such information by such agency is unnecessary, either because it is not needed for the proper performance of the functions of such agency or because it can be obtained from another Federal agency, or for any other reason, such agency shall not thereafter engage in the collection of such information.[42]

With respect to interdepartmental or interagency exchanges, the statute goes on to provide that the Director may require any federal agency to make information available to another federal agency provided: (1) the information can be revealed in the form of statistical totals or summaries; (2) the information was not, at the time of collection, declared to be confidential; (3) in case of (2), the persons supplying the information consent to its release to the second agency; (4) the agency to which it is to be

[41] Civil Service Commission Regulations, §§ 294.401, 294.702, 294.703, 32 Fed. Reg. 9493, 9495–96 (July 1, 1967).

[42] 44 U.S.C. §§ 422, 423.

released has authority to collect the information, supported by criminal penalties for failure to supply it. In the event that confidential information is released in violation of these rules, the provisions of law applicable to unlawful disclosure are made applicable not only to those who release but also to those who receive the unauthorized information.

This statute creates a framework for resolving any disputes which may arise within the federal government about the collection and distribution of information. Under it, virtually "any party" may petition the Director to examine the necessity for collecting information. And the distribution of such information to others is to be carefully monitored by the Director in accordance with statutory standards emphasizing the importance of anonymity or consent to release.

STRIKING THE BALANCE

The law now deals in piecemeal fashion with the problems of files. This is, of course, inevitable since the contents of files are as varied as man's activities. Nevertheless, it may be possible to identify some of the dominant currents and concerns and to devise ways of ordering which are better than the patchwork pattern of the past. Any such effort will require recognition that the future will bring an ever-increasing search for information, public and private, and that this search will be reflected in pressures for more systematic acquisition and exchange of information, for the creation of data banks, and for the harnessing of computer technology.

These developments present us with the question whether the pressures should be resisted, by trying to reduce the flow of information, or whether the uses to which the product is put should be controlled. Should we destroy the monster or tame it? Existing law is not responsive to either conception. At the present time, there is ordinarily no right to have file information about oneself shielded from view. Instead, the person who has the file usually has the right to disclose whatever he likes as long as he makes the disclosure truthfully and he does not give it undue publicity. Even where the disclosure is not truthful, or is given too much publicity, there may be a qualified privilege which will protect the offender from liability. Moreover, disclosure of material which must be held confidential in judicial proceedings will not result in tort liability if it is disclosed in an extra-judicial setting. All these conditions are even more applicable to government records. The defense of sovereign immunity as well as the extensive privileges and other protections surrounding disclosures by public officials make it improbable that release of information will be much deterred by potential liability for damages.

It is quite clear, therefore, that the existing legal controls will give very little pause to pressures for more extensive distribution of information. If any significant halt is to be called to the current pattern, it will have to be through bold expansion of common law concepts or through new patterns of legislative and administrative control. Even in advance of such reform, however, certain changes are clearly indicated:

1. The publicity requirement for privacy actions should be no greater than for defamation.
2. The law of qualified privilege should be reassessed so that economic justification is not entirely determinative. At a minimum, the interest in privacy should be weighed against the economic interest, with the ultimate balance to be struck by a jury.
3. The doctrine of absolute privilege probably needs reconsideration, as does the doctrine of sovereign immunity, particularly in an age where government is extending its reach in every segment of life.
4. Consideration should be given to the development of procedures for the correction of records and for some notice that they exist and are available for inspection.
5. Statutory provision for liquidated damages may be necessary incentives to the use of the tort theories, because substantial compensatory and punitive damages are not likely to be recovered very often in the sorts of situations under discussion.
6. Persons bringing privacy actions should be permitted to petition the court for proceedings which would not be open to the public and which would not be fully reported in the mass media.

Limiting the Direct Inquiry

Though many changes in existing law may be suggested, the most fundamental way to deal with the problem is to limit the kinds of inquiries which may be made. If, for example, we could define the areas which should not be the subject of inquiry, and if such limitations could be enforced, we would cut off at the source much of the contents of files. Illustrative of this approach is the frequent prohibition of inquiry into matters of race, religion, and sex and the more recent prohibition of the use of personality and polygraph tests. Unfortunately, however, it is difficult to identify very many areas which should be immune from inquiry in all circumstances, or even to identify the particular circumstances in which inquiry should not be made.

A vehicle for beginning consideration of the problem is the American

Law Institute's provision authorizing recovery against someone who "intentionally intrudes . . . upon the . . . private affairs or concerns" of another in a manner "highly offensive to a reasonable man." This language is broad enough to permit case-by-case consideration of the limits of direct inquiry. Indeed, it may be too broad, leaving open for too long the question of what is a "private" affair or concern and what is not, what would be regarded as "highly offensive" and whether the mere asking of the proscribed questions would qualify as an intrusion. The result might be to inhibit inquiry too much, for fear of tort liability which might be imposed under a statute giving too little notice of what may be asked. Yet unless the law is framed in such open-ended fashion, looking to litigation and judicial decision as a means of developing more specific standards, there is a risk that inquiry will be circumscribed too soon and too much.

The risk would be minimized if we were to identify the principal areas in which objectionable inquiries are made and define the permissible scope of inquiry for each area. This is, of course, the approach of the law of testimonial privilege. It affirms a public interest in particular relationships, and classes of communications which require confidentiality. If we were to follow that pattern with regard to the acquisition of information for admission to schools, for loans, for credit, for research, and so on, and for each area, if we were to permit only inquiries *relevant* to the particular issue (admission, loan, credit, etc.) it might be possible to develop reasonably clear standards of direct inquiry. If, in addition, inquiries going beyond the purpose announced were specifically prohibited and if unauthorized inquiries were made the basis of tort liability or professional disciplinary proceedings, where appropriate, this standard might even be made enforceable.

Such a course of standard-setting would undoubtedly be fruitful. But it would also precipitate considerable controversy. Should a bank, for example, be prohibited from inquiring into a man's psychiatric history? Or a school from inquiring into an applicant's family situation? In each instance, the information requested may be relevant to a decision to lend money or to admit to a school but how much predictive power does it really have? And how should that predictive power be weighed against what would be intrusive and, in some instances, offensively so? Until now, there has been little or no need to resolve controversies of this sort because the judicial remedies have been largely illusory. But, if, as I have suggested, the judiciary should enter more energetically into the privacy protection area, it will soon become apparent that the judicial power moves very slowly responding only to the suits which are brought before it. Yet the absence of any basis for detailed standards makes legislation premature. What is called for under the circumstances is a serious effort to develop standards of inquiry and privacy for each of the major areas of concern, perhaps under the aegis of an organization like the American Law Institute. These standards would eventually become the bases for judicial decision and perhaps for legislation in the several states.

To develop these standards, it would of course be desirable to build upon a substantial empirical base, ascertaining for each area—schools, credit, the military, research—what kinds of questions are currently being asked, by whom they are being asked, the reasons for asking them, whether they are central to the need or marginal, and how intrusive and offensive the questions are regarded by the persons to whom they are put.

Regulating Waiver and Consent

Despite the undoubted centrality of the direct inquiry in the law of dossiers, it is probably less susceptible to generalized controls than is the indirect inquiry. Where the former raises the largest questions of power and privacy, the latter may be approached through intermediate concepts such as consent and coercion and waiver. Yet as we have seen, the law has injected itself hardly at all to the transmission of information from one file to another. Under present circumstances, the custodian of information acquired from *A* is ordinarily free to pass it along. This would be changed dramatically if the courts were to introduce a relatively simple requirement that information acquired from *A* could be transmitted to others only if *A* consented to the transmission. Such an extension would be entirely consistent with the freedom of choice which the law encourages in so many areas. It would place the burden upon each individual to decide how much of his privacy he would like to sacrifice, how many details of his life he would like to have circulating and to whom.

Introduction of a "consent" requirement would also help to solve another important problem, that of informing the potential plaintiff that his privacy has been invaded. "Private facts" are likely to be circulated quietly and to become the bases for decisions about him without his knowledge. This problem will begin to be solved when *B* will invariably request the consent of *A* before making disclosure to *C*. Unfortunately, however, consent will often be unobtainable, for reasons having little to do with protecting privacy. When *C* seeks the information, *B* may no longer be in touch with *A*, or it may be disproportionately difficult for him to locate *A*. As a result, he may refuse to release information which would benefit *C* and which would do no important damage to *A*. Or, responding to pressure from *C*, he may release too much and *A* may first learn from *C* that the disclosure has been made. Such situations will probably lead *B* to solicit from *A*, at the outset, the waiver of any objection he might have to *B*'s circulating information about him. And that, in turn, will present questions of the adequacy of the notice to *A* about the extent of circulation and the uses to which it may be put. These questions are likely to prove so troublesome that they will lead to a more fundamental one—whether one should permit *A*'s consent to be obtained at the time of the direct inquiry or whether it should have to be obtained at the time the information is sought by *C*.

The problem with the blanket advance waiver is that it raises once again the questions about the coercive setting in which the direct inquiry is so often made. The man for whom the award of a loan or the extension of credit or admission to college is currently important is likely to agree to subsequent disclosure, not because he genuinely wishes to do so but because he fears the loss of a current benefit. The question, therefore, becomes part of the much larger issue of what should be left to bargaining and what should be taken outside the scope of the bargain. It is so difficult to provide a general answer that some mediating approach should be sought—one which minimizes the risk of coercion while at the same time giving effective notice. One such approach would be to permit waiver only for those transmissions which serve purposes similar to the original disclosure. For example, if *A* makes disclosure because he wants a credit card, then it should be open to the person extending the credit to solicit his consent in advance for subsequent disclosures to others seeking credit information about him. If he should apply to a school, it should be open to the school to solicit his consent in advance to transmission of the information to other schools. The virtue of this suggestion is that it would focus the attention of *A* on what he is being asked to give up when he responds to the direct inquiry. At the same time, it would restrict *B* to inviting waiver only in areas functionally related to the setting in which he and *A* meet, so that each of them can direct their attention to whether the waiver is really needed and whether *A* should execute it.

The problem of consent, and transmission of information, takes on a special cast in a governmental context because there are so many agencies with information which may be sought by other agencies. For example, should the parole authorities be permitted to pass information obtained from *A* to the police? Should the mental health department be permitted to pass information on to welfare? Myriad problems of this sort could be raised but all point to the question whether government—

city, state, or federal—should be regarded as a single entity which may use in any of its parts information obtained from any of the parts, or whether each entity should be regarded as a separate body for information acquisition and transmission purposes. Here, the distinction between information obtained *from* A and information *about* A may be central. The concepts of consent and waiver should be as applicable to the governmental setting as to the private when A is the source of the information. But where he is not, there would seem to be no important reason why governmental (or private) agencies should not share what they know about him. No implied limited use, no aura of confidentiality, can be said to be involved in such situations.

Finally, it would be desirable to authorize A to bring an action against C as well as against B if C should obtain information from B about A which goes beyond what A has agreed to. This is particularly important because C should not request information too casually. He should somehow be required to ask himself whether he really needs the information, whether he should not try to get it from A directly, and whether B is authorized to pass it along. This should be as true of the governmental context as the private, perhaps more so because the opportunity is even greater to use what others have accumulated, some of which may be relevant to C's purpose but much of which may have little or no bearing.

If the issues of coercion and consent and waiver should become central to the dossier question, it would be immensely helpful, in fashioning doctrine appropriate to the need, to know what sorts of information are being transmitted, how much of it extends beyond settings functionally related to the original disclosure, whether A is likely to know what he is authorizing when he agrees in advance to disclosures of even the limited sort, how pressed A feels in each of the settings to agree to the request for waiver, and how important is transmission of information in each of the areas in which we assume it to be indispensable.

Data Banks and Computers

Much of the current concern about the dossier may be traced to fear of the consequences of the new technology of data gathering and processing. As the instruments for sorting and classifying data improve, the economic pressures to use them intensify. This adds to all the problems already discussed the issue of increasing centralization of data storage, greater distance of the storehouse from the individual who provides the data, and the correspondingly lesser likelihood that the data will be corrected or explained.

It has been suggested that the law should play a role in regulating not only the acquisition and dissemination of information but also in superintending the central data banks and those who administer them. This might be done by establishing licensing standards for persons who maintain such data collection systems to assure that they satisfy standards of good character and technical proficiency, by introducing procedures for notifying persons that they are "on file" and by giving them an opportunity to inspect their file and to correct or explain entries in it if they choose. Despite the foreboding, the coming of the data bank and the computer may prove a blessing because it may provide collection units which are susceptible to regulation in the interest of accuracy and privacy, in a way which the present decentralized situation makes virtually impossible.[43]

It should be apparent that "the law" provides no magic formula for controlling data banks or computers, the contents of dossiers or their dissemination. At best, it provides the outline of an inquiry which must be conducted in a wide variety of settings, weighing the interest in privacy against the interest in information with no clear guide as to how the balance should be struck. Nevertheless, through this search for standards of inquiry and dissemination and content and for the proper mix of legislative and judicial roles in resolving disputes about those standards, the legal process can play an important part in reinforcing the theme of privacy in a society moving far too casually to obliterate it.

[43] In addition to the references in footnote 1, see Michael, Speculations on the Relation of the Computer to Individual Freedom and the Right of Privacy, 33 Geo. Wash. L. Rev. 270 (1964), Kaysen, Data Banks and Dossiers, The Public Interest, p. 52, Spring, 1967; Note, Privacy and Efficient Government: Proposals for a National Data Center, 82 Harv. L. Rev. 400 (1968); Hearings Before Subcommittee of House Government Operations Committee, The Computer and Invasion of Privacy, 89th Cong., 2nd Sess. (1966).

INDEX